Karen Middleton is Chief Political Correspondent at the *Saturday Paper*. Canberra-based, she is a journalist, writer and broadcaster who has covered national and international affairs for almost 30 years. Her first book, *An Unwinnable War – Australia in Afghanistan*, was published in 2011 and tells the political back story to our longest military conflict – how John Howard's presence in Washington DC on September 11, 2001, led to Australia spending the next decade at war.

ALBANESE

TELLING IT STRAIGHT

KAREN MIDDLETON

VINTAGE BOOKS
Australia

A Vintage book
Published by Penguin Random House Australia Pty Ltd
Level 3, 100 Pacific Highway, North Sydney NSW 2060
www.penguin.com.au

First published by Vintage in 2016
This edition published in 2017

Addresses for the Penguin Random House group of companies can be found at global.penguinrandomhouse.com/offices.

National Library of Australia
Cataloguing-in-Publication entry

Middleton, Karen, author.
Albanese / Karen Middleton.

ISBN: 9781925324723 (paperback)

Albanese, Anthony, 1963–
Childhood and youth.
Politicians – Australia – Biography.
Mothers and sons – Australia – Biography.
Australia – Politics and government – 21st century.

Cover design by Luke Causby/Blue Cork
Cover image: AP Photo/Tertius Pickard
Typeset in 12/15 pt Goudy Old Style by Midland Typesetters, Australia
Printed in Australia by Griffin Press, an accredited ISO AS/NZS 14001:2004 Environmental Management System printer

Penguin Random House Australia uses papers that are natural, renewable and recyclable products and made from wood grown in sustainable forests. The logging and manufacturing processes are expected to conform to the environmental regulations of the country of origin.

For Maryanne
and all the parents
bringing up children alone

PROLOGUE

This was not how Anthony Albanese was used to being introduced. Kevin Rudd was back in charge, almost three years to the day since being removed as Prime Minister in mid-2010 and now Anthony was there alongside him in Parliament's Blue Room, wearing a new title.

'Let me make some remarks before I turn to the Deputy Prime Minister,' Rudd said, gesturing to his newly minted number two. The returning Rudd promised his second go at being the nation's leader would be accompanied not by vengeance but humility, honour, energy and purpose.

His pledge was in stark contrast to the many months of savagery and rancour that had delivered the Labor Party to this moment. Its parliamentarians had just ousted their second leader by the sword in the time it normally takes to serve a single term.

Having seized power from Rudd in June 2010, Julia Gillard had herself been overthrown in a razor-sharp return of serve. Although Rudd's revenge had been in train since the day he was dumped, it seemed strangely swift in its final descent. Swift and bloody.

This time, Anthony had played Brutus. Now he was being rewarded.

Some in the Labor Party were convinced reinstating Rudd gave them a tiny chance at stealing an actual victory from the wide-open jaws of looming electoral defeat. But others – in fact, most – believed they would still lose as expected, just not by quite as much. Rudd, they hoped, would at least 'save the furniture'. By the conventional wisdom of that second scenario, neither of these two men was going to be in his new job for long.

As things turned out, Anthony was Deputy Prime Minister for just 83 days, the shortest serving since the position was designated officially in 1968. He took that mantle from Frank Crean, who served 132 days back in 1975 and whose son, Simon, was Anthony's unsuccessful opponent in the ballot.

But as he stood beside the triumphal Rudd, lights and cameras trained on them both, Anthony was not focused on how long he might stay but how he'd got there.

These past weeks and months had been some ride. Gillard knew he had never supported removing Rudd in the first place. He had said so, publicly, in a now-famously tearful declaration on the eve of Rudd's first (and unsuccessful) return challenge in 2012. He was, he said, in politics because he liked 'fighting Tories', not other members of his own party.

Despite backing Rudd then, he had continued to serve as one of Gillard's strategic inner circle and had been loyal to her – right up until the point when he wasn't.

Standing there at the podium, he was thinking about a journey that had begun a lot further back.

Rudd spoke to the gathered journalists first, briefly and off the cuff. He hadn't written any speech notes, still not quite believing he was going to get there, despite having spent three years planning this very victory. Anthony also didn't have a formal statement prepared. But when it was his turn, he found he had something to say.

'It says a great thing about our nation that the son of a [single] parent who grew up in a council house in Sydney could be Deputy Prime Minister of Australia,' he said.

As they often are, his emotions were close to the surface, curling at the edges of his words.

'I didn't know I was going to say it,' he says, looking back. 'It was the ultimate gut instinct.'

Beyond those friends and colleagues who knew his real, whole story, few listening might have understood exactly what this moment represented for the boy from Sydney's industrial inner west, whose late mum had lived in that same council house for the whole of her life.

Some who *did* know still wished he wouldn't show his heart quite so readily. They feared it might seem indulgent when his tenure was likely to be so short or that he might seem like he'd somehow got there by accident, not through years of relentless political slog.

Standing before the nation with his South Sydney football team membership badge pinned to his suit lapel, acknowledging the third tribe in the triumvirate that had shaped him along with the Catholic Church and the Australian Labor Party, he promised to bring enthusiasm, passion and commitment to the job.

'I'll give my all for Labor,' he said. His mother had given much the same for him. He wished above everything that she could have been there for this momentous day.

After all they'd been through – her sacrifice, their struggle and a personal search he never thought he'd embark on – here he was on this podium, a heartbeat from the highest political office in the land.

CHAPTER 1

The News

Anthony Albanese never knew his father growing up. For his success in politics and in life, he credits his mother, Maryanne, most.

Bad health since childhood had made life a battle for Maryanne Therese Albanese – born Mary Anne Therese Ellery – and her schooling had suffered. She was determined her son would have the best sort of life she could make for him, starting with a good education.

She also encouraged his interest in politics. Her devotion to the Labor Party, and her parents' before her, meant he had little hope of escaping it.

From before she had even given birth, Maryanne had set her own direction by putting her son first in everything.

'She made a decision at that point in time that her life would be lived through me – through a child,' Anthony Albanese says of his mother. 'Lots of parents do that but the truth is, it's particularly women who do that, much more so than blokes. It's very selfless.'

When his mother died in May 2002, Anthony told those

gathered at her funeral service that she was the finest person he had ever known.

'A two-person family is *different*,' he said, standing before the congregation at St Joseph's Catholic Church, Camperdown, next door to his primary school, up the road from home and where most of his family's religious rituals had been performed since before he was born.

Six years into his parliamentary career, this address from such a familiar pulpit was easily the hardest speech of his life.

'Mum had to not only be a mother but also a father figure, brother, sister and best friend. She was my soul mate. I am so proud to be her son and so fortunate. Mum gave me strength – inspiration – and believed that I could be anything I wanted to be.'

As her coffin left the church, he crumbled with the wail of someone losing a part of himself.

While Anthony was not one of those who claimed lofty political ambition from an early age, Maryanne claimed it for him as mothers often do. She believed he could go far – as far as a person can go in the Australian political system – and she told her close family the same. Anthony's cousin Norm Howett recalls that his aunt, known by family and some friends as Mary, routinely declared an unfaltering belief in her son's capabilities.

'Mary said to me that he would be Prime Minister one day,' Norm says. She said it more than once – and to others more than to her son himself.

'Oh, you're bright enough,' she would tell him. She was, as Norm puts it, 'ultra proud'.

In contrast to the close relationship he had with his mum, Anthony knew nothing much of his father at all – just a romantic, tragic story of how he had come to exist.

He knew his father's name was Carlo Albanese and that he was Italian. Maryanne Ellery had met him on her greatest adventure, a trip to Britain and Europe when she was 25.

The younger Albanese doesn't remember specifically being told his parents' story in detail. He just recalls that from when he was young, he'd heard that Maryanne and Carlo had married after a short courtship during her eight months abroad, but that his father had then died in a terrible car accident, leaving his mother a widow with an unborn son.

The story was accepted without question among those who knew it, both within the family and around the neighbourhood – there was no reason to doubt it. And on the subject of young Anthony's father, that was the extent of any real discussion. Nobody talked about the issue much at all.

But one night when her son was 14, Maryanne sat Anthony down at the kitchen table and said, 'We need to talk.' And then she told him the truth.

It was a startling rewrite of his life's story.

Maryanne Ellery had, indeed, met Carlo Albanese on her trip to Europe – a four-week ocean voyage she and her older brother, George Ellery junior, had taken from Sydney to Southampton, in early March 1962.

George was an entertainer – a comedian who specialised in impersonations – and he was booked to perform on the ship, along with an American mate, Mel Young. Seeing the chance to travel but not go alone, Maryanne decided to join them.

They travelled on the *Fairsky*, a cruise ship of the Sitmar Line which was among those bringing out English immigrants under Australia's assisted migration program. Sitmar was offering cheap fares for the return voyage, to avoid sailing its vessel back empty.

Maryanne saved as much as she could from what she earned as an usherette at a city theatre and headed off to see the world.

They sailed up around the north of Australia to Asia, along the Suez Canal to Europe and on to Britain. Carlo Albanese had been a steward on board. He and Maryanne had begun a romance.

Although Maryanne skated over the finer details in the telling, on the raw mathematics of her son's birthdate almost exactly a year later, it was clear that her association with the dark-haired Carlo had not ended when the Ellerys disembarked into the British spring that April. For Maryanne, it would be a five-month stay.

The ship sailed between Britain and Australia in a continuous loop, four weeks over, four weeks back, so Carlo Albanese was off again almost immediately, then back in Southampton again two months later. After that next visit, the good Catholic girl discovered she was pregnant.

According to this new version of his origins tumbling out onto the kitchen table, the teenage Anthony heard how Maryanne had told Carlo of her situation. The response was not what she might have hoped.

He had explained that he could not marry her. He was engaged to wed a girl from his town in southern Italy and that was what he was duty-bound to do.

So, contrary to the story upon which he'd built his life to date, Anthony learned that his parents had never actually married at all. There had been no accident and probably no death.

Still a single woman, Maryanne had arrived back in Sydney in October of 1962, seven months overseas and now nearly four months gone.

She moved back in with her parents and acquired and wore wedding and engagement rings – to this day her son doesn't know where they came from – and took her lover's surname as her own, not bothering with the deed poll.

When her son arrived on 2 March 1963, he became Albanese too – pronounced in a plain, Australian way without any Italian flourish: Alban-eez.

She named him Anthony, after his late cousin, Anthony Howett, who had died in a car accident, killed by a distracted driver on the Pacific Highway in northern New South Wales, four years before. The first Anthony was the son of Maryanne's beloved eldest sister, Veronica, known as Ronnie.

In 1959, Ronnie and husband Arthur Howett bought land on the highway at Halfway Creek in northern New South Wales. They built a service station and were adding motel units to the complex when the accident happened.

An impressive semi-trailer rig had pulled up on the other side of the highway and Arthur decided to cross the road with his three youngest children to have a look. As he hoisted baby Shirley into his arms and six-year-old Helen took the hand of her four-year-old brother Anthony, a car rounded the bend, swerved and hit the little boy. Through the service-station window, his mother saw her son tossed into the air and then run over.

The family's eldest child, Norman, was away at boarding school in Yamba but can describe it as if he was there. 'Mum watched the whole thing,' he says.

Their accommodation units became known as Anthony's Motel.

Maryanne did her best to comfort her grief-stricken sister and when her own boy was born four years later, she named him for his departed cousin, choosing Norman as his middle name.

The death of the little boy would haunt the family. Many years later, the imprint of it would make his namesake, by then the federal Transport Minister, extra passionate about duplicating that deadly stretch of road.

After her own Anthony was born, Maryanne had gone about her life in an elaborate, well-intentioned ruse.

Seeking to avoid the innuendo she feared might come from being an unmarried mother in a tight-knit working-class Catholic community in 1960s Sydney, she presented herself to the world as a young widow, to protect her son from scorn and maintain their family's public reputation.

*

Sitting there in the kitchen with her teenage son that night, Maryanne was concerned about how Anthony would react to the extraordinary secret she had just revealed.

It was a lot for the 14-year-old to take in and although he doesn't know why she chose that particular time to tell him, she had clearly waited until she thought he was old enough to absorb it.

She feared he might be angry or worse.

'She, I think, was petrified somehow that I'd . . .' he pauses, searching for the right word. 'Not *reject* her . . . but that it would change our relationship.'

He told her it wouldn't and that he was neither embarrassed nor upset by her revelation. But it was clear that finally revealing what she had kept from him for so long was emotionally difficult for his mum.

She asked if he felt he was suffering by being in a single-parent family. And she wondered aloud if he would like to try to find the father who, suddenly, strangely, might have come back to life.

But the hard-edged teenager wouldn't hear of it. He felt his father hadn't cared for him enough to even contact him, so why would he want to go looking?

'I do remember at the time saying "I'm not interested",' he says. 'And I do know that that's what she wanted to hear. What she needed was for me to say, "You're all I needed."'

And he insists she was, so it wasn't hard to say it. He was her son; he loved her and she him. And that was enough.

That was pretty much where they left it. It meant that was also where he left it for more than 30 years.

Although Anthony tried to steer her back to the issue a few times when he was much older, Maryanne didn't add a lot to the sum total of his knowledge of his father or where he might be. Naples featured in her responses now and then, but, frustratingly, details were scarce.

As he grew up, he listened carefully as she dropped snippets into conversations with his closest friends about life and the world. But they were contradictory and confusing.

She wasn't deliberately being unclear, he knew that. By then, the many years of pain from chronic rheumatoid arthritis and its associated pharmaceutical treatments had simply taken the edge off her memory. But he couldn't be sure anymore what was true and what was embellished for the sake of the storytelling.

He didn't blame her for that but it bothered him a bit because in trying to sort out what was real and what wasn't, it didn't help.

Except for those occasional mentions, the brief and intensely personal talk at the kitchen table was the only time in his life that Anthony Albanese and his mother ever discussed the truth about his parentage directly, in any detail.

Anthony's lack of desire to find his father would remain largely unchanged for as long as his mother lived. Though he would sometimes wonder about Carlo and try to draw together in his head the fragments of things Maryanne said, he never did anything about it.

He insists he didn't suffer for the absence of a dad.

'It's the opposite of Joni Mitchell,' he says, referencing the Canadian singer's hit 'Big Yellow Taxi' and its famous line about not knowing what you've got till it's gone. 'You don't know what you've lost if you've never had it.'

Any curiosity he might have had about his father was always countered by the feeling that, somehow, he would be doing wrong by his mum to pursue it. It wasn't quite a sense of betrayal – it was something else.

'Discomfort,' he says. 'I didn't want anything to cause her discomfort.'

So for decades, he left his family history right where it lay.

His friends believe it had to have weighed heavily on him. He insists it didn't. But gradually, after Maryanne died, he started contemplating finding out more about Carlo and his own lineage.

In the final years of his mother's life, when Anthony had married his long-time partner, Carmel Tebbutt, and they had had a son of their own, his perception of family changed. He became more curious about the other half of his heritage. Then one day in the Catholic section of Sydney's Rookwood Cemetery, he was confronted by a question he couldn't answer.

He would go regularly to Rookwood – at least once every calendar month – to make sure Maryanne's grave was appropriately clean and tidy. She had paid $150 to reserve the plot 31 years before she died (and kept the receipt).

Visiting the cemetery, Anthony would sometimes take fresh flowers. Now and then, his young son, Nathan, would go with him.

The visits were – are – important to him, as much in honour of his mother's character as her memory. Maryanne had always kept an immaculate home, regularly sprucing it with fresh paint or new tiles, despite periods when neither her bank balance nor her body were really up to renovating. She loved plants and especially flowers.

In his youth, Anthony would tell would-be visitors faced with navigating the block of identical two-storey houses on Pyrmont Bridge Road that his was the one with flowers – often red geraniums – in the window box.

On this particular trip to Rookwood, the still-very-little boy Nathan asked his dad a direct question. Where was *his* father?

'It was just us,' Anthony recalls. 'And him asking where my father was – I remember that being an "oh dear" [moment]. What do I say to him?'

He fobbed off the question. It wasn't too difficult.

'You don't have to respond to a three or four-year-old. You know? "Oh, look at the tree over there."'

The moment faded. But the question didn't.

Anthony decided he needed to know something about the man whose Italian name they had both inherited – and whatever else he could find out about how they came to have it.

With his mother gone, the reluctance he'd felt about looking for his father started to subside because, as he says, 'Then it wasn't a matter of creating a difficulty for her.'

But the business of life in the present had a way of pushing aside the past. By the time he was thinking seriously about a search, he had been almost a decade in Parliament as the Member for Grayndler, the whole time in Opposition.

With the Howard Government beginning to fade and the prospect of taking office in Canberra becoming a genuine one, Anthony Albanese, Manager of Opposition Business in the House of Representatives, channelled most of his energy into reaching the leather benches on the other side.

Now and then he would devote time to thinking about Carlo and whether he might still be alive. He confided in a few friends and colleagues and made some preliminary inquiries. But he didn't manage to join up the dots.

For a good while, politics overpowered the search. His party won office in 2007 and Anthony was preoccupied by the challenges of ministerial life and ensuring the smooth running of the Government's legislative agenda in the ruling parliamentary chamber.

It didn't leave a lot of time for genealogical musing.

Early that year, while they were still in Opposition, he asked his NSW Labor colleague and confidant Senator John Faulkner to help. John quietly lodged a request with the National Archives on Anthony's behalf, looking for records of Maryanne's voyage and the steward she met onboard.

'Records held by the National Archives provide little information about this person, apart from the fact that he visited Australia as a crew member of the Fairsky,' the archives' Director of Access and Information Services, Anne McLean, wrote in response to Senator Faulkner.

She had asked around, trying to help further, and suggested some other avenues of inquiry in Australia and overseas, including archives in Britain and Italy.

The research eventually turned up a 1962 crew list for the *Fairsky* that included Carlo's name and position as 'assistant steward', aged 30 – five years older than Maryanne. But beyond confirming he'd had a home port of Naples, there was little in the way of traceable information to go on.

Anthony mined the memories of his relatives, hoping for something to connect all the pieces. While his mother had been a great keeper of sentimental things, there was no correspondence from Carlo nor anything at all which might point to where he was.

Anthony found one black-and-white photograph of a smiling group of young people, dressed up and seated around a table in a ship's dining room.

His Uncle George, known as Johnny, was there with his mate Mel Young, and a young woman, Joan Watkins, who would later marry Johnny and become Anthony's aunt. The voyage produced more than one shipboard romance.

His mother was there in the photo too and standing opposite her, behind Joan, was a steward in a gleaming white jacket. It had to be Carlo.

With both his mother and her older brother no longer living, Anthony asked Joan for all she could remember about the photograph.

She confirmed the smiling steward's identity and did her best with recollections but she had no idea what had become of Carlo. It was all such a long time ago. As far as she knew, as far as any of them knew for sure, after Maryanne came home, the pair had never seen each other again.

Anthony ploughed on, enlisting the help of those trusted few friends and acquaintances, hoping to turn up something more contemporary.

*

Having set the search in motion as best he could, the Honourable Anthony Albanese MP, Minister for Infrastructure, Transport, Regional Development and Local Government, was at the Commonwealth Parliamentary Offices in Sydney's central business district, late on a Thursday afternoon in November 2009, when his phone rang.

He was about to head off to the Hilton Hotel for dinner with state and territory transport ministers – a dinner he was hosting – ahead of one of their regular ministerial council meetings the following day. He was almost ready to go when the call interrupted him.

He recognised the voice. It was one of the custodians of his secret, the one he thought was really his best hope of finding out more.

He knew whatever news she was about to deliver – good, bad or inconclusive – it would be momentous for him.

Seven years since his mother's death, this might be a whole new beginning or it could be the end. She asked if he was ready for some news but he still wasn't prepared for her next three words or how they would make him feel.

'I've found him.'

CHAPTER 2

Maryanne

Until the age of 25, Maryanne Ellery had always stayed close to home.

Fourth among the five children of George and Maynor Ellery, Maryanne – or Mary, as the family called her – was the one upon whom her mother kept the closest eye, after a bout of rheumatic fever in childhood left her permanently weakened and susceptible to illness. Perhaps because of this, she was extremely close to her parents.

The family didn't have much money and, just as her own child would do growing up a generation later, she went looking for an after-school job as early as she could.

Ahead of Maryanne in the hierarchy of Ellery children were Ronnie – short for Veronica – Lenore and George Vincent junior, with Margaret following her at number five.

Maryanne was closest to Ronnie and became like a second mother to her children, according to Ronnie's son, Norm Howett, who was about 11 years younger than his aunt.

She secured her first job at 13 and went on to work in cinemas around Sydney as an usherette. Norm recalls his teenage aunt in a crisp uniform and lipstick, showing patrons to their seats at the big cinema on Broadway, on the edge of Sydney's CBD. To the boy and his two little sisters, it seemed terribly glamorous.

'She used to smuggle us in,' he says. 'You know, she would introduce us to all the other usherettes and they'd all tell us how beautiful we were and they'd find a little seat for us somewhere.'

Norm had a lot of time for his aunt. 'One of the nicest women that you would ever want to meet' is how he describes her.

Maryanne Ellery dreamed of travelling. Once the opportunity presented itself, she single-mindedly squirrelled away her earnings. She was a good saver.

When she decided to go to the other side of the world in early 1962, her parents were glad it was in the company of her only brother, George junior.

At 25, she was hardly a child, but her brother was seven years older and despite having had some colourful adventures in his own youth, his presence on the trip as a kind of chaperone reassured Maynor and George.

For his second-youngest sister, the chance to see the world without having to go alone was too good to pass up. It would be her first and only trip abroad.

Outside the family and eventually inside it too, George junior was known as Johnny.

It was a name he had adopted in the boxing ring, using the pseudonym to compete in bouts around Sydney, to which his parents were initially oblivious.

George had adopted the false name to keep his activities secret but his cover was blown early. One of his father's brothers recognised his nephew in the ring and remarked on the lad's capabilities. An unhappy George senior turned up at the next bout and told his son he had 'better win'.

As 'Johnny', the younger George went on to have dozens more professional fights.

'Johnny was kind of like the black sheep,' Norm says of his late uncle. '. . . He was a nice guy, you know? He'd been married a few times. And he knew everybody.'

Anthony remembers his uncle as the life of the party.

'When I was a kid I just loved him,' he says. 'Just because he was this larger-than-life, funny guy.'

Johnny had gone from the boxing ring to the stage, carrying the new name with him, and was known to the paying public as Johnny Craig. His particular knack for impersonations led to the addition of a middle nickname – 'Rubberface'.

Johnny had also inherited an Ellery family trait – a fine singing voice. He combined it with his talent for impressions and a few dance moves and a stage career was born.

Before their grand adventure abroad, Johnny had been working as an entertainer in Brisbane and Sydney, having gained a reputation as a variety performer and stand-up comic. An American mate and fellow performer, Mel Young, had been working with him in Australia and they had been hired to perform on the ocean voyage.

They weren't the only performers who took up the offer of free passage to England. The Seekers did the same on the *Fairsky* two years later at the beginning of what would be a stellar international career.

When he boarded the *Fairsky*, Johnny was leaving behind a complicated set of personal circumstances he had amassed as George Vincent Ellery.

Before embarking on what became a bohemian sort of life in the entertainment business, George had worked as a truck driver carting bread and getting into occasional trouble because of the company he kept.

At 17, he was before the Metropolitan Children's Court charged with breaking, entering and stealing. As it was his first offence, the conviction earned him a two-year good-behaviour bond, a compensation bill of 93 pounds 19 shillings and presumably a reprimand from his parents, who likely had to pay it.

Five years later, he would face a similar charge. This time, he was out driving with two mates, one of whom decided to break into a house in the well-to-do outer Sydney suburb of St Ives to steal money to cover a child maintenance bill. George stayed in the car.

It wasn't a terribly successful endeavour. The burglars only netted a watch valued at 10 pounds, plus a meagre two pounds in cash. They got caught and ended up at the Hornsby Police Station. George Ellery senior had to put up the 80 pounds bail for his son.

Between them, George junior's two mates had clocked up a list of prior convictions and were found guilty. Their sympathy plea to the judge resulted in a pair of good-behaviour bonds.

George was even more persuasive. He had declared himself not guilty and the judge agreed.

By the time of this second entanglement with the law, 22-year-old George was out of home, living in the eastern Sydney suburb of Edgecliff, married and the father of a daughter.

Maryanne hadn't been especially close to her brother because of the age difference between them. When he had married, aged 19, in 1949, she was only 12.

George's bride, Pat Ryan, was seven years his senior. Their marriage would see the birth of two children – a boy followed the girl – but would fail to survive the mobile lifestyle of the entertainment business, into which he had shifted.

His life became characterised by long periods away from home and he and Pat officially split when he took work in Coolangatta, on Queensland's Gold Coast, in early 1959.

Pat didn't actually file for divorce until early 1962, when she sought financial support for the children. As was the way of things then, she listed his de-facto-wife Pamela White as co-respondent in the proceedings.

Pat was seeking maintenance of three pounds 10 shillings a week for each of the children, to be paid until they reached the age of 16. George accepted his responsibilities and did not object.

By the time the petition was served on him, he was back in Sydney and living in Kings Cross with Pamela. He was served with the petition on 27 February 1962. He left for England on the *Fairsky* a week later.

When the divorce hearing ensued shortly thereafter, he was at sea steaming for Southampton. His lawyers appeared on his behalf and the child-support arrangement was set in place in his absence.

George left the country with his then-current relationship also not in the best repair.

Onboard ship, he met Joan Watkins, a 20-year-old secretary and part-time dancer from Albert Park, in Melbourne. He was almost 33 but told her he was 27. On their return to Australia, he would marry Joan, with whom he would have another son, Jordan, and live the almost 40 years of the rest of his life.

In early 1962, the *Fairsky* was doing laps between Britain and Australia, loaded with hopeful English migrants on the journey over and adventure-seeking young Australians on the way back.

The ship was part of a family of similarly named Sitmar cruise liners which included the *Fairsea* and later the *Fairstar*. The *Fairsky* was the nicest of the three.

The ship was refitted in 1958 as a modern passenger liner after an early career as a World War II British assault ship, and Sitmar promoted it as the first of its vessels to have a revamped interior designed by a professional architect.

The *Fairsky* was equipped to carry 1461 passengers and 250 crew and there was plenty to keep the young travellers amused. There were ping-pong tables, a writing room and library, a cinema and three bars. Should trouble befall anyone aboard, there was a fully equipped hospital with operating theatre and isolation ward.

A teak-floored promenade linked the ship's three passenger dining rooms with the public lounges on its boat-deck. Up on the sundeck, there was a swimming pool with alternative leisure options including deck tennis and quoits.

In the barely-autumn temperatures of early March, heading around Australia's northern coast through the Arafura and Timor seas, it was most definitely still hot enough to be in need of somewhere to cool off.

Sitmar advertised that passengers could 'laze, laugh or let go' onboard and the young Australians and their American friend did exactly that.

The ship was engaged for migrant transport under charter to the British Government, bringing to Australia hordes of English folk hoping for a new life in the Antipodes. Offered assisted passage on dramatically reduced fares, the incoming English would become known colloquially as '10-pound Poms'. Among those who came to Australia on the *Fairsky* was a young Welsh family – parents John and Moira Gillard with their young daughters, Alison and Julia. Looking for a warmer climate to aid Julia's health after a bad bout of broncho-pneumonia, they settled in Adelaide. Julia would grow up to become Prime Minister of Australia.

The outbound fares weren't quite as low as those inbound – usually 50 to 100 pounds – but still relatively cheap. For Australian twenty-somethings, the ticket price made going off to London affordable and therefore the thing to do.

Like Maryanne at her job in Sydney, Joan Watkins saved money from secretarial work and dance performances in Melbourne and she and three friends planned a trip together. But as March approached, the other three all pulled out.

'There were four of us going,' Joan says. 'One bought a car – she didn't have any money then. One got engaged and the other one was broke.'

It was a setback and Joan thought about whether she should stay home too. But she reasoned that she already knew a few people over there in London and she could manage.

'So I said, "I'm going anyway."'

And she did, sailing from Melbourne, minus the friends, on 5 March 1962. She wasn't without travelling companions for long.

Maryanne, Johnny and Mel boarded in the ship's next port, Sydney. Joan can't remember exactly where or when she met them onboard but it wasn't long into the voyage. She thinks maybe it was in the dining room, over a meal. The *Fairsky* dining rooms were configured with round tables rather than the austere oblong numbers on some other ships, which made for more conviviality.

It was in one of the dining rooms that the group, as they quickly became, met a suave assistant steward, Carlo Albanese, a southern Italian who spoke English.

The *Fairsky* was an Italian ship whose home port was Genoa and Carlo had worked onboard since the previous April when he was hired from Naples. He and Maryanne struck up a friendship, which quickly became something more.

Even without cupid's flying arrow, the ship's route, young outbound demographic and onboard festivities meant it was always likely to be a romantic trip, taking in ports in south-east and south Asia, Egypt, Italy and Portugal.

Having offloaded its English migrant passengers and loaded up with (mostly) Australians in Melbourne and Sydney, the *Fairsky* sailed to Brisbane and then on around Cape York, skirting Australia's northern coast and heading up to Singapore, where the passengers made their first shore visit.

Now a group of four, the travellers went to a nightclub and celebrated being young, free and away from home. An excited Maryanne also indulged what would become a dedicated shopping habit, acquiring a set of Chinese dolls and an elegant, fitted silk cheongsam dress in an onshore spree.

After the ship made its way up through the Gulf of Thailand, she honed her shopping skills in the next port, Colombo, the capital of what was then known as Ceylon, now Sri Lanka.

Some of the other passengers wanted to buy gems and Johnny assured them he could tell good from bad, so the group went to a merchant and he advised the would-be buyers on the purchase of sapphires. When they arrived in London and had them valued, they were ecstatic to discover he had indeed known what he was talking about and the stones were worth a lot more than they had paid.

On the way from Singapore to Colombo, the ship crossed the equator and the passengers were treated to a traditional crossing-the-line ceremony – a good-natured hazing of first-timers by a crew member dressed as King Neptune.

Johnny and Joan's treasured photo album captures the occasion in all its camp costumery and mud-flinging, the pictures carefully laid out and captioned by Joan's now late husband early in their married life. Decades later, Anthony would similarly become custodian of Maryanne's many well-preserved souvenirs.

'Mum bought a heap of stuff,' he says, recounting how she had even purchased a set of small tables covered in mosaic, which had ended up in his Canberra flat.

'Oh, she was incredible,' Joan confirms, laughing. 'They'd come along the side of the ship in the Suez Canal selling stuff and Mary would be hanging over the side.'

They weren't short of entertainment onboard, with regular movie nights and variety shows, including performances by Johnny and Mel and the shipboard orchestra. Maryanne was even persuaded to get up and sing once or twice. She was gregarious like her brother and had also inherited a love of music. She was having a great time.

The *Fairsky* crossed the Arabian Sea and sailed up the Suez Canal in the middle of a turbulent decade in the region. It was five years since the failed invasion of Egypt by Britain, France and Israel had sparked the Suez Crisis and strengthened

Egyptian President Gamal Abdel Nasser's nationalist grip. Five years after their voyage, the Six-Day War between Israel and an Arab alliance of Egypt, Jordan and Syria would see the canal close temporarily for only the second time in a century.

On the way up the Suez, the tensions crept aboard. 'None of the Jewish people would get off the ship because they were too frightened,' Joan says.

When it docked at Port Said on Egypt's northern tip where the canal meets the Mediterranean Sea, Carlo accompanied the group of four ashore.

While they were in port, they had a fancy dress gala. It was April Fools' Day and the costumes required improvisation. Maryanne wore the Chinese dress she'd bought in Singapore and Joan went as an Egyptian mummy, with the boys helping to wrap her up.

The port visits became an opportunity for Maryanne and Carlo to spend time together. Some shipping lines had strict rules about crew fraternising with passengers but Sitmar was not one of them. Shipping historian Rob Henderson says the lines' differing cultures were well known and Sitmar was 'typically Italian'.

'There was no great control over stewards liaising with passengers,' he says. 'It's a sort of live-and-let-live attitude.'

Another line, the Orient, addressed the issue differently, to 'protect' the female passengers. 'The Orient Line always made a point of employing, as much as they could, gay stewards because they knew the female passengers would be safe. That was the assumption.'

The Orient Line's owners were so conscious of this that they surreptitiously took note of who among their crew was gay by marking their employment cards. The mark was 'M-A' which – somewhat ironically – stood for 'Mary-Anne'.

Carlo went ashore again when the *Fairsky* reached Naples – his own home port – on 4 April. But this time he and Maryanne went off on their own. They did the same when the ship reached the Portuguese capital, Lisbon – their final port before skirting the Atlantic Ocean and ploughing through the roughest part of their journey, the vomit-inducing Bay of Biscay, and up the English Channel.

Joan says it had been obvious 'kind of straight away' that there was 'a bit of a spark' between Carlo and Maryanne. Maryanne confided on the trip that she really liked him. She'd had boyfriends before, but Carlo was different.

'Carlo was *the* guy,' Joan says. 'He was it. She was rapt in him.'

The ship arrived at Southampton in the first week of April, just before Johnny's 33rd birthday on the 11th. As far as the rest of her travelling party knew at that point, this was where Maryanne and Carlo said goodbye.

The *Fairsky* was only in port long enough to load up the next lot of Poms and then it was off again, taking another month to sail the reverse journey back to Australia and then a month more to return. Carlo was required back onboard and Maryanne and the others headed for London.

Johnny and Mel had an apartment organised for themselves for a few weeks before Mel had to be back in America, where he had shows booked. Maryanne and Joan decided to look for accommodation together and found a house in Shepherd's Bush.

The two blokes quickly looked up their contacts, including English club owner Al Burnett, who Johnny had met back home. Al had two London establishments – the Stork Club, where Mel did some shows, and Pigalle Theatre Restaurant.

Al arranged a night-time job for Maryanne as the cashier at Pigalle Theatre Restaurant – she'd had some cashier experience in the theatres back home – and Joan fell back on the secretarial skills she had acquired in Melbourne.

'I got a proper job,' she says, meaning work outside the nocturnal entertainment business. 'I got a job working for an accountant.'

Mel left for America and, about a month later, Johnny used his connections to swing himself work in Europe. But before he left, he made sure his sister and the young woman with whom he had, by now, struck up a relationship were in safer surroundings. Joan could see the protective Johnny wasn't happy with where they were living.

'He was looking out for me and his sister, I guess.'

He organised via Al Burnett for them to move somewhere nicer. '[Al's] mother had some flats in the West End, right in London,' Joan recalls. 'So we got a really nice, furnished flat. And his mum was lovely.'

Johnny was booked to perform in France. In Paris, he met up with Jeff Patterson, an ex-Australian rules football player who, like Johnny, had been involved with boxing and had also moved into the entertainment industry, as a promoter.

Jeff was touring an American variety act, the Del Rubio triplets – three identically dressed, platinum-coiffed sisters with guitars and go-go boots, who were the great-nieces of the late former United States President Woodrow Wilson.

Born Edith, Elena and Mildred Boyd, the 41-year-old triplets had chosen the stage name Rubio because it meant 'blonde' in Spanish and dyed their hair to match. They had been booked to play at military bases in Germany and Jeff wanted a comedy act to go with them. He offered Johnny the gig.

Johnny agreed to go and because that meant being in Germany for a while, he persuaded Maryanne and Joan to join him. They quit their jobs and flew to Frankfurt on 9 July 1962. Johnny and Jeff picked them up in what Joan's photos reveal as Jeff's rather flash car. 'Oh,' she says, smiling at the memory of it. 'Jeff was always flash.'

They stayed in a hotel and spent the ensuing weeks seeing parts of Germany, as Johnny performed. He would later furnish the family with photographs of himself with Frank Sinatra and other musical luminaries of the era.

Some years later, after they were married, Johnny and Joan would return to Europe and set up in Frankfurt for what became a four-year stint, while Johnny worked the continent.

Back in 1962, Joan had fancied she might chase a ballet career in London or in Europe. She'd studied ballet, tap and other forms of dance in Melbourne.

'I was going to be, you know, Margot Fonteyn all over again,' she jokes. She had ballet certificates, enough to teach, but she never did. Sometimes she dreamed of reviving her cabaret career, too.

'One time I thought, "Oh, it would be nice to go as one of the Bluebells at the Moulin Rouge."' But then she just 'got caught up' with life.

'I guess I was in London working. You know, you're earning a quid, you're just enjoying the town.'

Her stage career didn't end completely. Back in Germany the second time, she and Johnny would occasionally perform together. When Johnny went off once to do shows in Turkey, Joan's friend Vera Mackay came to stay and brought another friend along with her.

Joan complained that she needed a new act, so the visiting girls taught her an exotic trick: fire-eating. She says it took a while to master. 'We half burnt down the joint.'

Part of the drama of it all was running the flames down her body to prove to the audience that they were real. When Johnny came home, he insisted he could do it just as well. 'He burnt every hair off his arms,' she says, chortling.

Her prowess became legendary in the family. Anthony remembers seeing photographs in his youth and thinking it was so exciting.

'[It was] "my aunty the fire-eater",' Joan recalls a young Anthony saying. 'He used to run around telling people.'

But on this first visit to Germany in 1962, it was Johnny performing. The girls were there to watch and have fun.

About a month after they arrived, sometime in August, Maryanne began feeling unwell. Joan suspected she knew why.

Back in June, before they had left London, Maryanne had announced suddenly that she was going away on a short trip.

'Mary says, "I'm going away for three days with some of the girls from work,"' Joan recalls. 'I have a feeling the boat might have been in. I have a feeling – because the dates really do coincide – that she went off to meet Carlo.'

Having left Southampton in early April, the *Fairsky* – with Carlo aboard – had reached Sydney in May. It docked back in England again in early June, around the time of Maryanne's 'girls' weekend.

By August, Maryanne was feeling persistently sick and she asked someone at the German hotel for help. The place was full of English-speaking entertainers and she was directed to a doctor. When she came home from the appointment, she spoke to Joan.

'She went to the doctor and she found out she was pregnant – and she didn't want to tell Johnny . . . She told me she was pregnant but she didn't tell me about Carlo because I would have told Johnny. And he would have gone off hunting Carlo.'

Joan asked her straight out: who's the father? 'I don't think she answered. She wouldn't say.'

Joan was uncomfortable about keeping the secret from Maryanne's brother, her now boyfriend.

'I said, "You know, you've got to tell him. You've got to make up your mind what you're doing." She kind of knew Johnny would be angry . . . But she had to tell. I said to her, "Well, if you don't tell him, I'll tell him."'

A few days later, she did. Joan knew pretty quickly that she had. The news spread fast among their friends. 'I think he told me. Everyone told me then.'

At first, Maryanne refused to tell her brother who she'd been with. As she had barely mentioned Carlo since they got off the boat, he had no idea it was him.

For Maryanne, there was no question about whether or not she would have the baby. She was Catholic and already two months pregnant.

Johnny told her she'd have to go home to get proper medical care and tried to persuade her to fly, to avoid what could be a difficult four-week journey for someone in the family way. But she was determined to return home by ship.

It took a while for Joan to work out why. Carlo Albanese was, of course, going to be aboard.

Crossing the ocean back to Australia, Maryanne had four more weeks with the man she loved, arriving home in Sydney on 11 October 1962. There can be little doubt that Carlo knew she was pregnant, if not before that return journey then certainly with her aboard.

But despite hazy hints to some of her friends that she might have met up with him on one or more subsequent visits, there is nothing to indicate she did.

It seems that after she disembarked that October day, Maryanne never saw Carlo again.

CHAPTER 3

Family

When she came home, Maryanne was almost halfway through her pregnancy. It was not something she was going to be able to keep from her parents. She was tall and slim and four months' gestation is not easy to hide.

It isn't clear whose idea it was to construct the story in which she then cloaked her life, but her parents, George and Maynor, never wavered in their support for their daughter.

For public consumption, Maryanne became a young widow who had married a handsome Italian after a whirlwind overseas romance. It was said that just before he was due to arrive in Australia for the birth of her child, her husband had died in a tragic car accident.

She wore a ring and took Carlo's name, presenting herself as Maryanne Albanese. It would prove to be a pivotal decision – the only way, almost 50 years later, that Anthony was ever able to trace him.

For Maryanne, the truth of it all was almost as sad as if Carlo had actually died. According to the version she gave close friends, she had told him of the pregnancy but hadn't received the response she clearly desired.

She confided her feelings to a couple of her closest neighbours, including Yvonne Miller, who lived over the back.

'That was the love of her life,' Yvonne says. 'I don't think Maryanne had ever been in love before.'

But Maryanne and Carlo had not known each other for long and most of that time he had been at sea working, with only the first and last months – and those few extra days in between – spent in her company.

He told her he couldn't marry her. He was committed to a woman at home in Italy.

When Maryanne arrived back in Sydney, she and her parents made a plan. As she told it to Anthony years later, they decided she would give up her child for adoption, saying publicly that the trauma of losing her husband just before the birth had been so great that it had caused her to lose the baby.

On the night she went into labour, her mother, Maynor, went with her to St Margaret's Hospital and her sister Lenore – whose own marriage was wobbly and would end soon thereafter – raced from her home in Bondi, bundling her two daughters, Lenore junior and Karen Jane, into the car with her.

On arrival, Maynor went down and sat in the car with the grandchildren while the elder Lenore went upstairs to be with Maryanne, hospitals then being not terribly tolerant of extraneous family.

The younger of these two of Anthony's cousins, little Karen Jane, was five. Her nanna put them both to sleep in the back seat but she kept waking up.

'I just remember it was raining and I was thinking, "When are we going home?"' she says. 'My first memory of Anthony being in the world was the day he was born.'

And in another twist, their Aunty Margaret was on a different floor in the same hospital, and would give birth to her daughter, Kim, the next day. Margaret's marriage would also end in divorce, leaving her to raise Kim alone. Their parents' provision of a roof over Maryanne's head while Margaret struggled would later generate some resentment from the younger sister.

Whether or not Maryanne really intended to give her child away, she didn't go through with it.

The practice at the hospital when a baby was being put up for adoption was for the mother to not even hold the child after giving birth. The baby would be taken straight away so the pair didn't bond.

But Maryanne wanted to see her little boy. One of the nuns brought him to her, knowing she was struggling deeply with the adoption plan.

'She knew I could never give you up,' was how Maryanne described it to Anthony, years later. After the nun's compassionate breach of protocol, there was no question. Anthony was not going anywhere.

Those still living among Maryanne's friends and relatives don't believe she ever seriously contemplated relinquishing him, especially those who knew the depth of her feelings for Carlo.

'She just felt at least she had Anthony,' Yvonne says.

Maryanne moved back with her parents into the house on Pyrmont Bridge Road, this time with her baby son. Number 41 would remain her home for the whole of her life. Except for those months she spent on the trip to Europe that set her remaining life's course, she never lived anywhere but there.

George and Maynor accepted her decision. Despite this change in the order of things – having a baby in the household with no father around – again, her parents offered only support.

In some corners of the family, a story persists that once, when Carlo was back in port in Sydney, George paid him a visit.

Johnny told Joan his father went down to the quay and fronted Carlo about Mary, the baby and his responsibilities. Anthony doesn't know if it's true.

As the story goes, the protective father had words with the young Italian steward but it didn't change the situation. Carlo was 'probably lucky he was too old to thump him', Joan says.

Loyalty ran at least as deep in George and Maynor Ellery's veins as did their Roman Catholic faith. Through the trials of their life together and the tribulations of their children, they always stuck. Sometimes seen as a strength and sometimes a weakness, it was a characteristic that would emerge in their grandson, too.

George and Maynor Ellery had known the ups and downs of working life in early 20th century Sydney. After marrying in 1920, they lived in the inner-eastern suburbs, moving around from Randwick to Darlinghurst and Surry Hills before shifting slightly west and settling in Pyrmont Bridge Road, Camperdown, in the early 1930s.

George ran a printing business in William Street, Darlinghurst, not far from Sydney's red-light district. He was the go-to printer for his Labor Party branch and his chapter of the Royal Antediluvian Order of Buffaloes, a men's 'lodge' organisation, with the motto '*Nemo Mortalium Omnibus Horis Sapit*', or 'No man is at all times wise'.

George was installed as the Sydney Buffaloes' Grand Primo in 1958. He was known, at least in the company of fellow Buffaloes, by the title 'Right Honourable Sir'.

He and Maynor had struck trouble during the early years of the Depression. An unfortunate decision to accept a contract to print labels for medicine bottles had brought him into conflict with the law.

In August 1932, 37-year-old George senior was one of six men charged with conspiring to defraud the Sydney Importing Company by manufacturing and selling cut-price fake medicines to wholesalers.

The Sydney Morning Herald detailed in August of that year

how two of the men had discovered what purported to be a recipe in the *British Medical Journal* for a popular brand of laxative, Beecham's Pills. They had used the recipe (which turned out to be incorrect) to have an imitation version of half-a-million pills manufactured from cloves, ginger and aloe.

'By this means, the Crown alleged they obtained some thousands of pounds from wholesale firms,' the newspaper reported.

The case of 'fraudulent conspiracy' earned sensational coverage in newspapers across the country, from the *Northern Star* in Lismore and *The Newcastle Sun* (whose headline blazed 'AMAZING STORY') to Adelaide's *The Advertiser* and the *Western Argus* in Kalgoorlie.

Police had gone to a Bondi house and found chemist Sydney Dunn, 38, and 50-year-old 'cellarman' William Anderson with boxes of pills stacked on the dining table. Alongside them were labels for Beecham's Pills, which the men said had come from 'a printer named Ellery'.

Searches of two other houses unearthed a bowl of loose pink dust and packets labelled 'Steedman's soothing powders', 'Heenzo' and 'Hansen's junket tablets'.

The police nabbed three other men – 23-year-old taxi driver Raymond Kellick, 37-year-old 'traveller' Matthew Doyle and 32-year-old 'business manager' Francis Thompson, who would turn out to be the scheme's mastermind, along with Dunn. They then proceeded forthwith to George Ellery's printing shop.

'Yes, they come here sometimes but I only did business with Dunn,' George protested to the police, admitting he had printed the labels. The six were sent to trial but George was found not guilty and discharged, along with William Anderson and Raymond Kellick. The other three were convicted and went to prison for 18 months.

It wasn't George's only brush with the law, via his printing press. In June 1945, George Ellery was fined a hefty 200 pounds, in Sydney's Central Court, convicted on a charge of printing illegal betting cards. George had pleaded not guilty to printing cards containing a list of horses and another list of betting odds.

On two related charges of printing cards without his name and address on them, the magistrate let him off because only material of a political, seditious or blasphemous nature needed to bear the printer's name and address.

When he printed political material for the Labor Party it seems he generally followed that rule. Even the booklet he printed for his own induction into the Buffaloes' top position bore his details, as printer, on the back.

Police Sergeant Roy Munro told the court that he'd gone to the printing shop in William Street one March afternoon after a tip-off that George Ellery was printing horse cards and a search revealed them. Sergeant Munro said the printer denied responsibility but couldn't explain how they got there.

'Ellery told me that he had not printed any since we caught him last time,' he reported.

The fact that he'd been convicted of the same offence and fined 10 pounds two years earlier in 1943 appeared to undermine George's protestations of innocence. It may also have influenced the magistrate's decision to apply an exponentially greater second penalty.

George argued he was of good character on the basis of his position as Primo of the Buffaloes. 'I am head . . . of the order in Sydney and H. M. the King is a member of the order,' he told Special Magistrate Hardwicke.

'I had no idea it was such an august body,' Mr Hardwicke replied, with perhaps a touch of sarcasm.

George told the magistrate that apart from that prior conviction, he had never been in trouble before, clearly deciding the earlier high-profile charge and subsequent acquittal were best not mentioned.

George's father – Anthony Albanese's great-grandfather – had tangled with the constabulary too, with a less beneficent outcome.

The 11th of 13 children, William Ellery married Elizabeth Mealing in Camperdown in 1888. Two years later, just after the first of his own 11 children was born, William – whose middle name was 'Innocent' – was found guilty of stealing 120 stamps and four letters from the post office, where he worked as a letter sorter.

'Think of my wife and child,' he is said to have pleaded to the post office detective. '. . . I took the letters for the purpose of making up some money to send my wife to the mountains as she is in bad health.'

In the District Court two months later, Mr Justice McFarland told him the offence would normally be punishable by seven years' jail.

The judge couldn't quite come at the mercy that the jury recommended, but he took into consideration that William was only 27 years old, of otherwise admirable character and recently married with an ailing wife. William was still convicted and sentenced to hard labour in Darlinghurst Jail – but only for 18 months.

Upon his release, William had 10 more children with Elizabeth, of whom George Vincent was the second, born in 1894.

The young Ellerys developed a reputation for looking out for each other. As his grandfather had described it to Johnny and Johnny to Joan, if you tangled with the Ellerys, 'It was fight one, fight them all'.

'The local cops knew: don't pick on the Ellerys,' Joan says George senior told his own children growing up.

Not just fighters, both William and his son George were also keen musicians. After his release, William became a clerk and later a piano teacher and stepped up his involvement with the Catholic Church. He secured regular praise in the *Freeman's Journal* for his volunteer efforts in various parishes, both on church committees and in the choir.

George grew up to be an acclaimed tenor in his church

community, singing in the choir first at St Bernard's in Mascot and later at St Joseph's Church, Camperdown.

He also earned himself a glowing review in the *Journal* in January 1924, for punctuating the St Bernard's choir's performance of Turner's Mass of St John the Baptist with a particularly noteworthy offertory rendition of American composer Harrison Millard's 'Ave Maria', sung 'with much devotion and expression'. 'His very fine tenor voice impressed the congregation,' the *Journal* opined, enthusiastically.

George and his wife, Maynor, enjoyed music at home too. After a few changes of address, they were allocated a council house in Pyrmont Bridge Road, Camperdown, and settled down to raise their children, installing a piano in the front room.

As a young boy, Anthony never took much interest in the piano nor indeed in music – at least, not in making it himself.

His mother and her sisters had learned to play the piano in their youth and it was Margaret who played it most often. Maryanne preferred the violin and kept her instrument long after her arthritic hands would no longer allow her to play it.

Anthony's enthusiasm for music extended only to listening and eventually to curating playlists – a penchant that would lead to a curious expansion of his credentials to include amateur DJ appearances in his 50s.

Fortunately for his later career, he hadn't shown much sign of emulating his grandfather and great-grandfather when it came to brushes with the law – at least not in the same manner. But either by inheritance, experience or both, Anthony nevertheless developed the rebellious and pragmatic streak that was evident in a number of his forebears.

As a child, he was keener on sport than music and would sit with his grandpa George watching it on television. Anthony's cousin Norm recalls their grandfather as 'a jolly old fellow' who liked spending time with his young grandson.

'I can remember when we would come down and visit them in Sydney once or twice a year,' he says, 'and Anthony would be sitting in the lounge, you know, with his grandfather watching the cricket or the football or whatever. And you know, I think that's where he got his love of sport and all that stuff.'

Had their grandfather lived longer, Norm wonders if Anthony's interests might have turned in a different professional direction.

'You never know what would have happened if he had stayed alive,' he says. '[Anthony] might have got pushed into sport more.'

As it was, he became a stats nerd with an early capacity to recall the minute detail of a fixture – a general gift of exceptional recall that served him well in later political life.

His grandfather would quiz him on sporting statistics as they watched various matches and tournaments.

'I used to be able to tell you how many Tests people had played and what they had scored,' Anthony says.

He inherited a special, deep interest in one sporting code – rugby league – and one team in particular. Like her parents, Maryanne loved God, the South Sydney Rabbitohs, and the Australian Labor Party – not necessarily in that order. She would pass on at least two of these passions to her son.

With his best friend at school, Lindsay Keevers, Anthony would join his local footy team at St Joseph's Primary School, Camperdown, which was part of the Souths' juniors competition.

Lindsay's dad, Frank Keevers, was their footy coach. The team struggled every which way.

'We had a very poor side,' Lindsay confesses, laughing. 'When I say poor, I mean poor as in *poor*. Not good players. Not very wealthy either.'

When there weren't enough players to sustain the Camperdown team, they switched to play for St Joseph's Newtown instead, where Lindsay then completed his primary school years.

Anthony and Lindsay also played tennis – it was a game that only required two – and they played together at Marrickville, honing their skills on whatever free courts they could find around the neighbourhood.

When they ended up at different schools for their final upper primary school years, tennis kept them in touch. Then, when both attended the same high school – St Mary's Cathedral College in the city – they played football again, too.

Many years on, after life had sent them in different directions, Lindsay and Anthony had sons the same age and discovered their boys were playing in the same Sydney junior football competition. But it was Australian rules, not league – a sign of the successful march north of a traditionally southern Australian game.

Despite the dominance of Souths and rugby league in his life, Anthony had defied the cultural divide in his young years and also developed an interest in the other code which flourished south of the New South Wales border, the one the more hard-line league fans used to lambast as 'aerial ping-pong'.

When he was a child, what became the Australian Football League – AFL – was called the Victorian Football League and Anthony's engagement with it was courtesy of his Uncle Johnny, who lived in Melbourne after he and Joan married.

The task of selecting a Melbourne VFL team had been more complicated for Anthony than his simple inheritance of the Bunnies in Sydney. Not living in the southern city he didn't have any natural geographical team affiliation, but he was also not going to make a random choice. In his mind it came down to a set of other criteria.

No VFL team played in colours matching those of his beloved Souths – cardinal red and myrtle green – and he wasn't prepared to support any team with either colours or a name similar to any of the teams Souths played *against*, even in a different league, lest it seem like betrayal.

So that left him with only one choice: Hawthorn. Its team

colours were brown and gold – a combination he determined was sufficiently different from red and green but just as distinct. What's more, its nickname, the 'Hawks', had no echo in the northern code.

(The Manly Sea Eagles were closest, also being birds of prey, but by Anthony's reasonable boyhood logic, their maroon-and-white jerseys ruled out any confusion.)

He became a Hawthorn supporter and remained so, despite becoming a member of the Sydney Swans, when they relocated from South Melbourne, out of loyalty to his city. Everybody knows one of the unwritten rules of following AFL is that you can't change teams.

Anthony watched the matches of both codes – the rugby league games (when they involved Souths) live, at grounds around Sydney and the Aussie rules matches on television.

After grandpa George died in 1970, seven-year-old Anthony was the only male left in the house. It was the two women – his mum and nanna – who raised him from there.

The only adjustment to this arrangement was Maryanne's brief and turbulent marriage to a man she thought initially might make a good husband for her and a father for her son. Sadly she discovered she was wrong.

In November 1971, 18 months after her father died, Maryanne married James Williamson, at St Joseph's, Camperdown, the church where, as Anthony describes it, 'everything happened' that was significant in the life of his family. He was an altar boy for the occasion and his friend Lindsay remembers attending the wedding.

'They didn't seem to stay together long' is Lindsay's only reflection on the period.

When the couple was dating, Jim – as he was known – had made an effort to get along with Anthony. He had taken him fishing and to the football to see Souths play the Canterbury Bulldogs at Belmore Oval. It seemed like the beginning of a new family life.

When she married Jim, Maryanne changed her surname to reflect her new circumstances. Anthony's name was changed too and he remembers having 'Anthony Williamson' inscribed on his schoolbooks, late in 1971.

In anticipation of this new family situation and, importantly, another income, Maryanne had new, good-quality carpet laid in the house, paid for on lay-by. But nothing would end up as she anticipated.

After a weekend honeymoon at a little house in Umina on the Central Coast offered by Maryanne's neighbour Dulcie Whittingham, Anthony's new stepfather moved into the Camperdown house to live with his new wife, her mother and her son.

But once he was living with them, Jim's behaviour and attitude changed. He refused to allow the boy to sit with them in the kitchen for meals. Maryanne confided to those closest that he was being 'horrible' to Anthony.

'He was nasty and spiteful to Anthony and that broke Mary's heart,' one friend says. 'Mary could not stand anybody that would treat her son like that ... She really loved Jim but she loved her son more. She put her son before anything. She would've moved mountains for Anthony.'

But it was his stepfather's behaviour towards his mother that most upset Anthony.

'It was horrible,' he says. 'The whole thing was horrible. Almost beyond comprehension.'

He recalls his mother discovering that Jim had lost his job but hadn't told her, leaving the house daily as if to go to work and spending his time drinking and gambling instead.

Anthony reflects back on that time with some bitterness on his mother's behalf. His stepfather had brought little good to the family financially or in any other sense.

He declines to discuss that period in any detail.

'I think she was looking for a father for me. He was not a particularly nice man.'

The marriage lasted just 10 weeks. The couple split in late January 1972. Maryanne changed her name – formally this time – back to Albanese.

Her attempt to extract some financial assistance from her former husband resulted in distressing legal proceedings.

Anthony recalls his mother and others fearing Jim would try to hurt him. In the immediate aftermath of the hearings, the nuns at St Joseph's Primary would keep Anthony back after school to avoid having him walk home alone.

'There were real concerns about my safety.'

The terrible shared experience only brought mother and son closer, if that was possible.

Maryanne had been receiving a sole-parent pension but it was stopped once she was married because the family was going to be living off Jim's income – or so she thought. She was soon without either income or husband.

'This was a time – I do remember – when we were dirt poor and there were three of us living on my grandmother's pension,' Anthony says. 'I just remember not having any money and that really distressing Mum for many months.'

Maryanne's health had begun to deteriorate with the worsening of her chronic rheumatoid arthritis. While she had undertaken cleaning and other jobs off and on before that, her capacity to work became less and eventually she was allocated an invalid pension. That and the aged pension Maynor received was what they mostly lived on.

In the council houses, tenants paid rent according to their income. Initially, the rent for number 41 was $3.48 a week, rising in 1975 to $5, in 1981 to $10, two years later to $15 and so on.

After Maynor died in 1976, Maryanne's income was the mainstay until Anthony began earning too. Anthony says that as he grew up, he and his mum didn't have much but they didn't want for much either.

Their house was never untidy and his mother made sure they never got behind in their bills. When he was young, the telephone by the front door always had a jar beside it so each call was paid for as it was made.

Years later, sorting out his mother's estate after her death, he received refunds for her utilities. She'd paid in advance.

Maryanne loved her garden, which she established in a postage-stamp-sized backyard at number 41. Tiny though the space was, she had planted a jade tree, tomatoes and a choko vine with shield-shaped leaves and sticky tendrils that turned the small square emerald green.

The garden was accessed through the kitchen and then the laundry, with a tiny bathroom off to the side that serviced the whole household. Their lounge room was at the front, with windows facing the footpath and Pyrmont Bridge Road. The bedrooms were upstairs.

Maryanne would sometimes sunbake out the back in her bikini, a practice that mortified Anthony, who couldn't bear the thought of his mates in neighbouring houses looking down from their rooms on his mum.

Anthony's own room at the back also looked down on the yard. It was a former verandah enclosed into a sleep-out and had two doors for entry or exit. Using either involved walking through another bedroom, one of which, in the early years, was his mum's.

Like his mother, Anthony inherited his grandfather's boisterous nature. As a youngster, his preferred method of travel down the stairs from his room was wrapped around the bannister, feet first like a fireman.

A small landing broke the journey, where the steep polished-wooden stairs turned 180 degrees towards the front door at the bottom. He would come under mock attack regularly from the family cat, Sheiba, as he landed.

Previously, they'd had a Sydney silky terrier called Peter, but rough treatment elsewhere had made the dog aggressive.

After two biting incidents – he sunk his teeth into Anthony and wouldn't let go – Peter was quietly taken away and put to sleep.

There was a procession of other pets, too. Canaries chirped from a cage in the laundry. Goldfish never lived long and were continuously replaced, and at one stage there was a talking galah, named Andy. He would call out 'Hello, Andy!' repeatedly, until enough was enough. Then it was goodbye Andy and he went to live with Aunty Lenore.

Anthony's room had belonged to his Uncle Johnny before him. Growing up, Uncle Johnny was a more distant figure than his mother's sisters, simply by virtue of his travelling occupation.

On his return from the 1962 Europe trip, Johnny had gone to Melbourne to look up Joan and had subsequently moved there and married her. Later, they had those four years back in Germany.

But despite his long absences, Johnny still played a role in his nephew's life. He gave Anthony his first bike – a Malvern Star – that was smashed up and almost wrecked one afternoon when Anthony was a teenager and a group of local thugs tried to steal it.

He had stopped in at the shop on the corner of Addison and Illawarra roads in Marrickville, on his way home from tennis, when three other kids demanded the bike. 'I wouldn't give it to them for obvious reasons,' he says. 'I wasn't going to get another one. And they didn't get that one.'

He defended the bike with his fists and both he and his transport ended up the worse for wear, with one wheel bent badly out of shape and its rider bruised and bloody.

Anthony can't recall if it was before or after the incident that his cousin Norm gave him boxing lessons in the backyard, lessons he continued at the Glebe Police Boys' Club a few blocks away opposite the Harold Park racetrack – a practice which fostered useful good relations with the police.

Neither occasion was the first time he'd been taught to fight. He recalls getting into a scuffle in the schoolyard at St Joseph's in about Year 1.

'And my mother said, "No, no, I'm not settling it." She sent me back to fight, basically . . . She used to tell people that she hated doing it, but it was to toughen me up.'

On the afternoon of the bike incident, Lindsay's father, Frank Keevers, took him to the Newtown Police Station to report it. The cops, reckoning they knew who was responsible, paid a visit to a certain house in nearby Agar Street, taking Anthony with them.

After a stern conversation, the kids at the address confessed and the police extracted on-the-spot compensation from their parents.

'They just paid cash to fix the bike,' Anthony says, laughing at the effectiveness of the local constabulary. 'Old-school policing.'

CHAPTER 4

Camperdown

When Anthony Albanese was growing up, Camperdown was the centre of his world. The Ellery-Albanese house at number 41 Pyrmont Bridge Road had been modified to turn three bedrooms into four and sat in a row of two-tone brown duplexes known as the Alexandra Dwellings. The houses were owned by the city council and took up most of their block.

His grandparents George and Maynor Ellery had deliberately chosen one of the five pairs of houses facing onto the busy thoroughfare because back when they were moving in, it was more prestigious to live on a main road than a back street.

A footpath and simple railing fence separated each dwelling's front room from the traffic. The Royal Alexandra Hospital for Children was directly opposite and the number 470 and 459 buses stopped right outside it.

Back-to-back with the houses was another identical row, facing the old foundry on Lambert Street behind. Layton Street ran along the bottom of the block and Lyons Road along the top, where a small square of grass separated the council houses from the Johanna O'Dea city council flats.

Together, the houses and flats formed a single residential island, surrounded on all sides by industry – factories, depots and small trade shops on the urban fringes of Sydney's central business district.

Almost 90 years after they were built, most of the Alexandra residences have withstood the waves of modernisation, outlasting many of the business premises that surrounded them. The exception is the two pairs of houses knocked down to make way for a building providing emergency housing and services for the homeless and people in crisis, in between the houses and the flats.

At the bottom of the block on Layton Street sits the only other original premises to survive gentrification – the small Jackson and Perram panel beater's workshop that has operated across from the dwellings since 1930.

Gone is the Weston's biscuit factory that occupied its own block at the other end, opposite the flats on Lyons Road. In the factory's heyday, the sweet smell of baking biscuits would taunt the local kids on their way home from school.

This was a Labor area and these were Labor, mostly Catholic working people. The dwellings' dedication plaque was unveiled on 14 November 1927, by local Labor Party alderman John Harold Mostyn, who also happened to be Sydney's lord mayor at the time, having been elevated to the position almost a year earlier at the age of 34.

Sixty-nine years later, another Labor man – and the block's most famous occupant to date – would be a year younger than that when he gave his first speech in Federal Parliament as the Member for Grayndler.

'Everyone in council housing was Catholic, Labor and either Souths or Balmain supporters,' Anthony says. 'It was just part of the culture.'

It was a point of pride among the Alexandra and Johanna O'Dea residents that unlike some other estates in the inner city, theirs was council – not welfare – housing, with the distinction that at least one occupant in each Alexandra household had a paying job. Many worked for the council itself.

In the days before lucrative rugby league contracts, occasionally the council would support a player by providing a flat at Johanna O'Dea Court and even a job. Some worked as garbage collectors – an occupation so physical it could double as extra training.

When Anthony was young, the decorated South Sydney halfback Bob Grant, who also played for Australia and had been in the premiership-winning sides of 1968, '70 and '71, lived for a time at the flats.

'We used to knock on his door and ask for an autograph,' Anthony recalls.

It was where the Camperdown cultures all came together – Catholicism, Labor and league.

Decades on, the residents of both the houses and the flats would consider their circumstances preferable to those living at the shelter in between – a much more transient population with complex life issues, including mental health problems and drug addiction. The sentiment is a gentle reminder that hierarchy is not the preserve of the rich.

When she was a child, Maryanne Albanese – then Ellery – had gone to St Vincent's College in Potts Point because that's where her older siblings went. She sent her son to another Catholic primary school, St Joseph's, in Missenden Road around the corner and across the busy Parramatta Road intersection from home.

There, Anthony met Lindsay Keevers. Lindsay remembers the school with mixed feelings.

'It was run by nuns,' Lindsay says. 'They were tough nuns, too . . . Horrid.'

The boys spent recess in the playground between the school and the adjoining St Joseph's Church, often playing soccer and chasing runaway balls out onto Missenden Road.

The presbytery, where the priests lived, was out of bounds. The nuns lived in a separate residence around the back and they ruled the school by fear and threat, especially those presiding over the upper-primary classes.

'You knew you'd be punished if you did wrong,' Lindsay recalls. 'It didn't take much to cop it . . . Even though they were supposed to be compassionate people, that's how they ruled – with an iron fist.'

Copping it involved being walloped with a ruler; or worse, the cane, across an open hand.

Girls could attend St Joseph's to Year 6 but boys had to go elsewhere after Year 4. There was a view that after the age of eight or nine, boys were too difficult for the nuns to manage.

The two lads became altar boys, earning them regular passes out of class. They would also sometimes be selected to carry the tuckshop takings down the road and deposit them with the Commonwealth Bank.

'It would never happen today,' Lindsay observes. 'Two little kids leaving school grounds, taking money to the bank.'

Anthony's mum encouraged him to apply himself at school, planning for him to progress eventually to university. Having ended her own formal education part way through high school, Maryanne Albanese was a strong believer in the value of it – for children generally and her son in particular.

Sydney University was only a little way further up the road and Anthony would, indeed, end up in its sandstone surrounds. Its proximity played a big role in his eventual enrolment.

Having used the uni oval as a playground through his childhood and seen students roaming the district, the idea of university wasn't foreign. He wonders if it might have seemed out of reach had he lived further away.

'Proximity made it real,' he says. 'I hadn't met anyone who went to university. You *didn't* meet people who went to university. No one in my family went to university. But I could touch it and see it and it was less alienating because it was a part of our community.'

Later on, as President of Young Labor, he would lead a campaign based on the same principle, to establish what would become Western Sydney University.

In Camperdown, theirs was a close little community and the families on the block were tight. The women would drop in on each other, unannounced, for a cuppa and a chat. They'd take in each other's washing when it rained.

Yvonne Miller and her husband, Barry, lived over the back with their three children, Sherie, Sam and Lynette.

'The neighbours there, the whole lot of us – we were really, really close,' Yvonne says. 'If someone couldn't pay their light bill, everyone would throw money in until they got the money.'

A good number of sons and daughters married their neighbours' kids. Sherie broke ranks and married further afield. Scott Dewstow was from all the way over on the other side of Camperdown Park.

Now the mother of her own three grown-up children, Sherie echoes her mother's warm sentiment about where she grew up.

'That was the type of community it was, you know? If you needed something, someone was there. Someone was always there to help.'

Maryanne was closest with Beryl Anderson, who lived over the back. Beryl and her husband, Barry, were Camperdown through and through. When Anthony was elected to Parliament, Maryanne tried to persuade them to come with her to Canberra for his swearing in. But for a couple who hadn't ventured beyond New South Wales, it was too far.

When Anthony was young, Maryanne was close to Peggy Pincham too. Peggy also lived in a house behind, with her husband, Roy, and sons, Tony and Graham.

Tony, the older brother, was a rough-looking bloke with tears tattooed on his face, long before it was a thing. Both boys spent many of their years in jail. Their father drank himself to death on a bottle of whisky a day.

For all the neighbourhood kindliness, it wasn't completely sweetness and light on the block.

'Cops visiting and people jumping over fences to escape them was not an unknown thing,' Anthony says.

Tony would sometimes drop in and Maryanne would make him a cup of tea and chat, same as she did with everyone else.

Even in their line of work, the Pincham boys observed neighbourly protocols. While other houses in the area were fair game, they wouldn't knock over anyone on the block. If you were from there, you were safe.

Maryanne would visit her various girlfriends after Anthony had gone off to school and her domestic chores were done.

'She'd do her work of a morning,' says Sherie. 'Don't know what she cleaned because it was always spotless anyhow . . . Neat as a pin. Absolutely neat as a pin, that lady.'

Her mother says the same.

When Yvonne secured a cleaning job to help pay the bills after having her third child, Maryanne would mind baby Lynette and do whatever else she thought might need doing.

'When I come home from work – I'm not joking – my house was absolutely spotless,' Yvonne recalls.

Anthony describes his mother as 'a bit of a shop steward' around the place. 'Nothing was ever too much trouble for her,' he says. 'She was very generous in terms of her time.'

As well as living close together, many of the families shared at least a nominal faith.

'Dawn on the end was a Catholic, Joy over the back was a Catholic, Beryl – they're all Catholics,' Yvonne says. '*We* were all Catholics . . . Wendy Whittingham's girls were Catholics. Dulcie next door – when she lived there before Betty – she was a Catholic. Kerry Thomas next door . . . And Mrs See, she was a Catholic, and Beryl Tyler's mother and all her girls. They were all Catholics.'

The Catholic parents were forever trying to encourage their children to go to Mass on Sundays. At one point, a group of the Alexandra parents banded together and devised an incentive scheme to keep their kids close to God – or at least occasionally visiting His house. They promised post-worship pancakes to the lot of them, provided they went to church.

The cooking of the pancakes rotated week to week, house to house, among the scheme's participants and was such a success that one neighbouring child who didn't go to St Joseph's started joining them at Sunday Mass just to get the pancakes. And she wasn't even Catholic.

With limited services and little money, the neighbourhood children had to make their own fun.

Two years younger than Anthony, Sherie counts the total number of kids in the Alexandra houses when she was primary-school age at 56. There were 32 on her side in Lambert Street and another 24 on his.

Looking back, Anthony reckons there were about 20 that he ran around with regularly.

With the boys taking turns on skateboards and the girls on rollerskates, they would fly down the gently sloping Lambert Street – an incline which seemed (like all things from childhood) more dramatic then than it does now. The boards, skates and most other play equipment became communal because money was tight and, like everything else, fun was for sharing.

On Sundays they would meet at the flats and end up in some sort of competitive game, or occasionally mild mischief. Sometimes, they'd beg the migrant workers at Weston's to pass them freshly baked biscuits through the bars of the open factory windows.

On Fridays, the biscuits were coconut and the thick, sweet smell was irresistible. The workers clearly comprehended the agony and the kids' poverty pleadings were regularly successful.

Lindsay Keevers remembers the sweet sensory torture every afternoon. 'You'd get that smell,' Lindsay says. 'You'd stand around after school and some of the workers used to sneak you biscuits, just packets here and there.'

On other occasions they would steal biscuits right off the back of the truck. Wagon Wheels were their favourites – big, round, choc-dipped biscuit sandwiches filled with marshmallow and jam.

'We used to nick Wagon Wheels, boxes of them,' Sherie says. She would distract the drivers while the boys would 'run up the driveway and grab the box'.

'And we used to meet in the park and divvy them all up.'

If they were really lucky the boxes were just sitting there on the driveway and diversionary tactics weren't even required.

The kids ate so many, Sherie swore off them for good. 'I can't look at them. I don't even think Anthony could eat a Wagon Wheel these days.'

She's right.

Weston's was right across from the O'Dea flats, where the laundries were communal and the elevators sometimes got stuck. The 10-storey building of high-density public housing took up the whole of the block's top end, perched on concrete pillars in the style of the day.

The building's roof was a forbidden playground. Anthony's first kiss was planted up there. But it could be a sad place too. Now and then, someone who couldn't see how life might someday be better would climb up there and jump off.

Walking around his old neighbourhood some 40 years on, Anthony notes the trees now dotting the patch of lawn at the flats. A fenced community garden has replaced another corner of grass, with raised beds of flourishing vegetables.

But where some might congratulate the urban beautifiers, he is scathing.

'Where are the kids going to play?' he asks angrily, repeating himself slowly for emphasis. '*Where* are the kids going to play??'

This is where the left-wing Labor man parts company with those he brands as idealists in politics, especially the Greens – the party whose candidates have most often threatened his electoral grip in Grayndler.

He says he is all for sustainable development. But in the end, his working-class upbringing compels a particular determination to put the needs of the neighbourhood children before most other considerations, no matter how worthy.

Anthony's residential surroundings were to have an even more direct impact on his politicisation during his teenage years. He had attended Labor Party meetings since he was small, with his mother and her parents, and at election time they had Labor candidates' posters out front and diligently performed the duties of local branch members.

'There were a lot of Labor Party members in the area – just rank-and-file people – and it was just one of those things. I remember handing out for Whitlam in '72. I would have been nine.'

In the late 1970s, Anthony and his mother joined a rent strike to protest at the proposed sell-off of council housing across the inner city and likely increase in cost to the low-income occupants.

On the Camperdown estate, residents Mavis and Jimmy Johns mobilised the locals and they joined the pushback on privatisation in a campaign that lasted for months. Maryanne quickly became involved and so did her son.

'I was a gopher, distributing pamphlets in the letterboxes and stuff like that,' he says.

His mother's activism earned her a special tribute from the Labor-led City Council when she died in 2002.

Their neighbour Sherie also recalls the residents' determination to resist a move that would have seen many families turfed out.

'They fought and we did a big rally,' Sherie recalls. 'Marched down the street, babies in prams. We did a few of those.'

The campaign was ultimately successful. The Labor Party won control in the city council elections of 1980 and the houses were sold to the State Government for a symbolic dollar, to be retained as public housing. The campaign taught Anthony about the power of collective action – and the vulnerability of being a renter.

'It was something that stuck with me regarding security: that the problem with being a tenant rather than owning your own home is that you're insecure,' he says. 'And that had an impact.'

In 2014, he wrote in *The Sydney Morning Herald* about the effect the proposed sell-off had on him.

'It was our home,' he wrote. 'We cared for it as though we had built it with our own hands, renovating and painting it at our expense to keep it up to scratch. Yet the council was, as my worried mother said at the time, treating us with no respect. It was as though we did not matter.'

The childhood that formed his political consciousness was nevertheless full of fun. The kids played footy on that now-punctured patch of lawn at the flats and cricket in the narrow alleys between the duplexes leading out onto Pyrmont Bridge Road.

His front door faced the door to Tom and Betty Hukins' place. The path between them was so slim it was sometimes impossible to tell from inside which door was being knocked on, and both would fly open.

Skinny as it was, the tiny walkway between those facing doors was unoccupied space ripe for claiming by enterprising kids with a bat and ball. It was just wide enough and long enough for a batter at one end and a bowler at the other, until angry shouts about the noise would send them scarpering to some new game.

The kids who played there learned to drive a ball straight, to avoid the consequences of a broken window and the frustration of watching a ball just bounce from wall to wall. Balls regularly hurtled out into the traffic, with children in pursuit.

'You got four if you smashed it across the road,' Anthony recalls. 'Six if you hit it onto the road on the full. Parents were always worried about their kids getting hit by cars. That happened occasionally.'

He and Lindsay sometimes played in his handkerchief-sized backyard, just the two of them. It was far too small but they turned it into a Test pitch, spinning the ball and emitting the war cry of every bowler looking for a wicket: 'Howzat?!'

It didn't especially bother them that their version of the Sydney Cricket Ground was so small.

'You just did what you did, you got by with what you got by with,' Lindsay says. 'We had good times together. We spent a lot of time together as young kids.'

He and Anthony would adopt the personas of famous cricketers. When it was his turn with the willow, Anthony would pretend he was legendary West Indian batsman Desmond Haynes.

'And then when he'd bowl he'd pretend he was one of the other West Indian fellows. He was very big on the West Indians.'

Lindsay usually opted for an Aussie cricketing hero: '70s fast-bowling legend Dennis Lillee or captain Ian Chappell. He occasionally wanted to take a turn at being one of the supremos of the West Indies – maybe Gordon Greenidge or Viv Richards.

'We'd have to toss to see who'd be the West Indies . . . because they'd win all the time at that time.'

The boys would try to avoid the sweeping over-the-fence, six-and-out shot that only slowed things down.

They played for hours on end. 'I'd look back and go, "Jesus, that would've been boring,"' Lindsay reflects. 'But it wasn't. We always had fun.'

Anthony says he never actually owned a cricket bat as a boy – it was one of those communal commodities like the skates and the skateboards. When he was in his mid-40s, he bought himself a bat for Christmas. His wife, Carmel Tebbutt, queried what was usually a kid's present.

'It was because I didn't have one as a kid,' he says.

He didn't play in a weekend cricket team either. 'You needed a car to play cricket.'

When they played in the alleys between the houses, the boys became accomplished at scaling the walls via window ledges and drain pipes to retrieve lost tennis balls from the wooden porticos overhead which joined each pair of houses to the next and kept any arrivers and departers protected from the elements.

Out on the footpath, the kids would play handball or toss footy cards collected from bubble-gum packets. The cards featured the profiles of rugby league players and their game consisted of tossing them one-by-one onto the ground, facing the wall to reduce the chances of a gust sending them under the wheels of a passing car.

When a flung card touched one or more of an opponent's cards, the flinger secured ownership of the lot. It was a high-stakes game for kids with little cash.

Still, gambling wasn't exactly unfamiliar in the neighbourhood.

There was always a local SP bookmaker – an extra-curricular activity somewhat outside the law. 'SP' bookies were originally so called because they paid out on the starting price of the horses or dogs in a race but the term became a catch-all for illegal betting generally.

One of those providing SP services was Harry Sullivan who lived with his wife, Eunice, down at number 31. In the years before Anthony was born, the Sullivans' granddaughter Anne regularly came to stay. Anne loved the camaraderie of the houses, becoming friends with the then Maryanne Ellery and her younger sister, Margaret. The three girls attended ballet classes together in the city.

'My grandmother was very much the Ena Sharples of the council block,' Anne recalls, referring to the all-knowing keeper of neighbourhood secrets in the long-running British soapie *Coronation Street*.

In those early days, the Sullivans were the only household with a phone – an old one mounted on the wall.

'All the neighbours filtered in and out of there at various times if they needed to use the phone,' Anne says. It also got a good workout on race days. 'So it was a pretty exciting place for a little kid to be.'

The Sullivan family was dedicated Labor too. Eunice and Maynor Ellery were best friends, and before Anthony was born the Ellerys regularly hosted poker nights at number 41.

'The room was full of smoke and they'd be all at the card table but when they weren't concentrating on the game, they'd be talking politics,' Anne says.

In later years, as Anthony was growing up, the local milk bar, Dudley's, around the corner on Layton Street, was also a haunt for those who enjoyed a flutter. Selling sandwiches, newspapers and other necessities, Dudley eventually took over as SP service provider.

The staff from the children's hospital frequented the shop and it was a good place for gossip. The kids liked Dudley's because he had the best lollies. By all reports, Dudley did a roaring trade.

'Everyone knew he was the SP,' Anthony says. 'It was part of the business. Melbourne Cup, once a year, the family would have a bet. I would have a bet or [go into] a sweep but it would be at Dudley's. It was an important part of the local community.'

As the children got older, Dudley employed some of them to help manage his diverse range of goods and services.

'They had afternoon jobs in there,' Sherie Dewstow recalls, 'serving behind the counter while he was doing the bets.'

Some of the kids would traipse across the park to another shop where they could buy loose, single cigarettes – 'loosies' – for five cents each. But while many of the other neighbourhood kids indulged, Anthony never did. He hadn't been around for the smoke-filled kitchen card nights but his mother had smoked when she was younger and returned to it in later life. He hated it.

'She took it up again and it had a terrible effect on her,' he says.

It has made him an anti-smoking zealot.

The kids of the Alexandra Dwellings had their own occasionally flexible interpretation of rules and regulations, surrounded as they were by temptations they couldn't afford. Finding somewhere to swim without cost was a case in point.

Sometimes on a summer evening, there would be a neighbourhood expedition to Bronte beach and kids would grab towels and pile into someone's car.

But despite the communal nature of many of their activities, this was one of the subtle dividers between the haves and have-nots. Without access to a parent's car, you couldn't reciprocate and so you were overlooked. Anthony was never invited.

If you didn't have a car, you didn't go to the beach after school, just like if you didn't have a dad, there was never a work Christmas party with presents for the kids from Santa. They were just things you missed out on.

'At the time I thought nothing of it,' he says. 'You don't know you're missing something if you've never had it.'

More often than not, on those scorching-cement summer days, they all had to employ a local alternative cool-down strategy. A few blocks away, the nurses' quarters for Royal Prince Alfred Hospital had a swimming pool – ripe for sneaking into on a hot afternoon.

The Travelodge up on Missenden Road had a pool too. The kids would stroll in and take up temporary residence on the lounges beside the big, blue oblong of cold water.

Some pretended to be guests and were frogmarched out, busted after over-acting and waving one too many times up at imaginary parents in the windows. Anthony says he never bothered pretending. When the day was hot and money was short, the nearest pool was the answer, public or not. It seemed only fair.

Sherie recalls being particularly indignant after being thrown out of the motel premises yet again one summer afternoon. A quick trip home saw her return with her mother's washing powder and tip the whole box into the motel fountain out front.

Bolting away with a security guard in pursuit, she delighted in watching dismayed motel staff running around in a panic as the suds rose, high as a house.

'There were bubbles everywhere and the 412 bus was coming round the corner and the wind blew and the whole windscreen just got full of bubbles.'

She still roars laughing when she thinks about it. 'We used to have really good times, all of us growing up. We didn't have much but we had a lot of fun.'

CHAPTER 5

Housos and Reffos

Christian Brothers High School at St Mary's Cathedral was one bus ride and a world away from the Camperdown housing estate. If the demographic of his home neighbourhood was rather Anglo, Anthony's high school was anything but.

Adjoining the cathedral itself, the college sits on prime real estate between Sydney's Hyde Park and the parkland of the Domain. Its 1970s student body was drawn largely from what were then some of the less salubrious corners of the inner city. Many came from Redfern, Waterloo, Woolloomooloo and down near the docks at Millers Point, close to the southern end of the Harbour Bridge in The Rocks.

There were Lebanese, Italian, Greek and Aboriginal students, kids from Egypt and Malta and what was then Yugoslavia. Many of their parents didn't speak English and rarely attended parent-teacher interviews. The most dedicated teachers would visit the families at home to try to keep up contact and foster support for the boys after hours. The only school with as rough a reputation in the inner city was Cleveland Street Boys High, in Redfern.

'We took kids who got expelled from Cleveland Street,' Anthony says. '[St Mary's] was a rough school. Now they've got an orchestra.'

Back then, the school and its feeder suburbs had a combined reputation for being composed mostly of housing-commission kids and refugees.

'It's more upmarket now. They've rebuilt it. And the inner city's changed. They were all "housos and reffos" back then.'

Anthony was the only child from his primary school to go to St Mary's but there were kids from as far west as Revesby, out Bankstown way, and even a few from the eastern beachside suburb of Bondi. Some came on choir scholarships, ensuring their school fees were effectively excused in return for their voices being employed during cathedral Masses and on other religious occasions.

In the hope of securing the same arrangement, Anthony's mother had him try out for the choir. 'I tried because my mother sent me along to try,' he says.

The choir kids had a rougher-than-usual time, enduring taunts from their own classmates. He was neither especially enthusiastic nor successful. And he wasn't sorry either.

Maryanne still sent him there to school, pooling her pension with her mother Maynor's to scrape together the fees.

Beyond the school's walls, when necessary the St Mary's students were united against a common enemy: the boys from Sydney Grammar. If the Cathedral lads were from one end of Sydney's social strata, the Grammar chaps were from the other.

The schools were within blocks of each other and when the students streamed out at the end of the day, they often converged on their way to the buses and trains that would carry them home.

The St Mary's boys considered Sydney Grammar and the similar St Andrew's to be – according to Anthony – 'the snooty schools'.

'We didn't like the kids from Sydney Grammar or St Andrew's,' Anthony says. 'They wore boaters, you know? St Mary's kids would be the ones with their shirts out and their ties undone.'

There were some attempts to foster friendship across the social divide. History coordinator Vince Crow had met some of the teachers from Sydney Grammar while monitoring Higher School Certificate exams and would occasionally take his debating students across there for 'friendlies'.

Both the St Mary's Cathedral College kids and those from Sydney Grammar – among whom, almost a decade before, had been a young man by the name of Malcolm Turnbull – considered Hyde Park to be their turf.

Officially, the St Mary's boys didn't have much to do with the boys from Grammar. They weren't Catholic and they didn't play rugby league. Contact was mostly 'to pick on them'. Consequently, there was the odd skirmish.

Anthony recalls the school principal at one assembly reporting a complaint that two Sydney Grammar students had 'ended up in the Archibald Fountain' the previous day. Those responsible were requested to present themselves at the principal's office in what seemed to the boys to be very much a going-through-the-motions request. 'Good on you, lads,' was how Anthony and his mates interpreted it.

'He'd done his duty saying it to the whole assembly. There was no investigation.'

The mutual hostility had developed well before Anthony arrived at the school and, with it, some hostile traditions. Sometimes the Sydney Grammar boys would mock the college students for their poor status and bad English.

In the years before Anthony attended, some St Mary's students developed a buddy system to ensure as few as possible fell victim to bullying. Older Cathedral boys sometimes accompanied the younger ones home, even if it meant going an extra hour or two out of their way on public transport.

But the St Mary's students were hardly saints. When the chance presented itself, the boys occasionally took revenge on the Grammar lads by grabbing their nemeses' straw boater hats and punching holes in them with their fists. It became a kind of unfriendly ritual, passed down through the school generations.

It was what former Christian Brother, now lay teacher at the college, John Iffland, describes wryly as 'a bit of muscular Christianity'.

'In those days, a lot of things would be sorted out at the Police Boys' Club down the road,' John says. 'Sometimes you'd go down there with them and say, "Sort it out here with the gloves on, not fist-fighting." And they'd do that.'

Anthony started at St Mary's in Year 5. Having weighed up the options, his mother settled on the Christian Brothers School at St Mary's Cathedral, later known as Cathedral College, for two reasons related to time.

Although it was further away than other schools, her son could catch either of the two buses that stopped outside the Children's Hospital across the road from home and be in the city in 40 minutes (the 459 being slightly quicker than the 470). But most importantly, at St Mary's he could go all the way through to Year 12 without changing schools again.

Maryanne wanted her son educated in a Catholic systemic school – part of the low-fee, government-subsidised, Catholic education system. Had she chosen to send him to the closer-to-home St Joseph's Newtown, he could only have attended for years 5 and 6 and would have had to go elsewhere for high school – possibly St Thomas' in nearby Lewisham for years 7 to 10 – then switch again for the final two years. Three more sets of uniforms was doubtless a serious consideration on a pensioner's income.

Maryanne was also concerned that facing yet another change of educational institution after Year 10, her teenage son might be inclined to just leave it at that. She wanted him to go all the way through and finish properly.

St Mary's offered a solid, basic education and nothing fancy beyond that.

'At St Mary's, you had very little choice of subjects,' Anthony says. 'There were no languages, there was no music, no art. No creative subjects at all. You did history or commerce and I did commerce. I loved history but I just couldn't do both. And there was chemistry or geography – but that's about it.'

Other than choir for some junior boys, John Iffland confirms the school wasn't big on teaching music.

'The only thing that had anything to do with music in the school was a bass drum left over from the cadet corps in the '40s. It was a rough and tumble inner-city school with no facilities.'

What was on offer in more substantive quantities was sport. Anthony's interest in sport was already well developed by the time he reached St Mary's. Back at St Joseph's, aside from their penchant for backyard cricket, he and his friend Lindsay played tennis games down at the courts near Camperdown Oval. Both boys became good tennis players.

'We played for years and we always used to have good challenges and good games and we'd beat each other,' Lindsay says. 'He'd beat me, I'd beat him.'

The enthusiasm for tennis would survive into adulthood and even decades later, after almost 20 years in Federal Parliament, Anthony was still a keen tennis player, playing in the Sydney Badge for the Marrickville Lawn Tennis Club in his electorate.

Lindsay and Anthony parted ways briefly in Year 5, when Lindsay went to St Joseph's Newtown for the next part of his education. They still saw each other at Mass on Sundays, just no longer at school.

But having travelled the alternative more circuitous educational route, Lindsay eventually also arrived at St Mary's for years 11 and 12. He noticed his mate had become slightly more outspoken.

In Year 12, Lindsay was named the school's tennis player of the year. But the final between Anthony and Lindsay had been rained out and was never completed. Anthony thought it wasn't fair.

'Anthony was very dirty,' Lindsay says, describing how his friend had challenged the teachers that the tournament had been incomplete. In other words, had it been finished properly, Anthony might have won.

'Correct,' says Lindsay. 'And do you know what? I sort of agreed with him. However I wasn't going to [give] the accolades away!'

Lindsay insists he didn't resent his friend challenging the result. 'No, because he was in the right. But it sort of showed me that he wasn't frightened to speak out.'

The teachers dismissed the protest, insisting it was not a big deal. 'It is to a kid,' Lindsay says. 'And it was.'

As children, Anthony and Lindsay were competitive.

'Lindsay was always a good sportsman,' Anthony says. 'His family were.'

Lindsay's dad, Frank Keevers, trained swimmers at the South Sydney swimming club and Prince Alfred Park. Anthony went to swimming training with Frank some afternoons and evenings.

'I did training for a couple of years and swam competitively. I wasn't very good. I was hopeless, but I enjoyed it.'

Football was a greater interest and Frank Keevers had also coached the kids' under 6s and under 7s rugby league teams when Lindsay and Anthony were back at St Joseph's. At that age, it had been about participation rather than success and pretty much all the boys of that age were in the team.

When he moved on to St Mary's, Anthony was encouraged to continue playing footy. In years 5 and 6, Brother Andrew Simpson put him on the field.

'I played football the way I play politics. I always had a crack. I never took a backward step and could be a mongrel on the field.'

He was a skinny kid but Brother Simpson encouraged him and his attitude saw him placed in the under 12s 'A' team. Anthony remembers a moment of childhood glory that propelled him into the captaincy.

'I scored a try out wide,' he says, 'and they weren't going to bother to take the conversion because little kids can't kick a goal from out wide. And I said, "I'll take it." And I kicked the goal from the sideline.

'So they made me the goal-kicker. And the next year they made me captain of the team.'

On playing ability alone, he doesn't believe he was the logical choice, that one starring moment notwithstanding. But he thinks perhaps Brother Simpson – a gigantic bloke who died in 2013 while working in Papua New Guinea – saw other skills in him.

Every week, the captain had to report at the years 5 and 6 assembly on the team's result in the previous Saturday's game. It was Anthony's first experience of public speaking.

'I reckon it was Brother Simpson taking a kid who'd had it a bit rough,' he says. 'Saw some leadership capacity, you know? I wasn't the best player in the team.'

When he started at St Mary's, and with Lindsay at a different school, Anthony had joined up with a group of four other lads: David Brown, Colin Parr, Peter Youssef and Mark Burgess.

Peter was credited with being the smartest kid in the school and went on to study medicine, specialising in rheumatology. Raised in a Lebanese Christian home, he would receive an award at the end of Year 12 for having never missed a single day of school in eight years.

The same could not be said for all of his mates. Anthony describes St Mary's as 'a school full of larrikins', happily also adopting the term for himself, despite some of his old teachers insisting he was never especially troublesome, at least not when he was younger.

'He didn't actually stand out,' says Vince Crow, who taught him directly only in Year 9. 'Even though he was quiet, if you ever challenged him about something – if you asked him why he hadn't done his homework or whatever – he was always very polite. He was never abusive. He was always polite but he always stood his ground. And he was always ready to defend himself.'

'He was a quiet kid at school,' says John Iffland, who was only at the school for the first two years of Anthony's time there and returned much later after stints in the country. 'Not a ratbag. He wasn't kicked out or anything like this – and we had some wild kids here in the '70s.'

But there were a lot of good kids too.

'Really good kids,' John continues. 'You know, they looked after each other. There was no thieving amongst yourselves or anything like that. You could leave things lying around. They wouldn't knock anything off.'

That's not to say there wasn't nefarious activity outside. Anthony remembers one student acquiring a key to the parking meters along St Mary's Road.

'So he'd go and empty all the parking meters at lunchtime. Get all the coins out . . . There were lots of scams.'

Highlights in the school year included the regular trips away to Christian Brothers' retreats in coastal Wollongong and Gerringong. 'We got barred from Gerringong because kids went to the pub,' he says, proudly. They were 15 at the time.

Mark Burgess recalls the games of touch football across the road in the Domain park, which became their playground. 'There were 400 of us all fighting for that one little patch of dirt to play on,' he says.

As a boy, Mark lived down at Millers Point and his dad worked on the wharves. 'You were born there, you didn't *live* there,' he says. 'It was cheap housing for waterside workers and coal lumpers.'

Anthony's friendship with Mark would later see him join campaigns to protect the ageing residents of Millers Point from attempts to force them out or raise their rents to unaffordable levels.

'Albo's always had a good social conscience.'

Anthony's nickname had settled on him well before he arrived at St Mary's. While Mark became known there as 'Budgie', Anthony arrived as 'Albo'. That's what the kids back at St Joseph's and around the Camperdown neighbourhood called him and Lindsay doesn't remember ever calling him anything else.

'Albo's *Albo* – always Albo,' he says. 'He was Albo from five years old. My mum never called him Albo – Anthony, always Anthony – but I called him Albo from five years old.'

It would endure through the formal, if brief, name change during Anthony's mother's unfortunate marriage and the various pronunciations he adopted and to which he continues to answer.

In 2015, 'Albo' Corn Ale even became the name of a beer produced in his honour by brewer Pat McInerney of the Willie the Boatman micro-brewery in his Grayndler electorate.

'Albo' would be the one version of his somewhat pliable surname that would defy alteration.

Throughout their years at different schools, Anthony and Lindsay maintained contact through St Joseph's church. Their junior schooling had cemented a lasting friendship.

'We used to go to church together and we were altar boys together,' Lindsay says. They wore red-and-white robes and battled the other altar boys to win the privilege of ringing the bell by being the first to arrive. They'd been taught to be punctual.

The boys' mothers were friends too, both also attending St Joseph's church and both volunteering to clean the church after hours. Lindsay's mum, Lorraine, was known as Lorrie. She and Maryanne Albanese spoke on the phone regularly and Lindsay recalls his friend's mum's loud voice and 'very loud laugh'.

'For someone who was unwell, she seemed like quite a happy person.'

She was also reasonably devout and worked to create the circumstances for her son to be the same.

The Christian Brothers at St Mary's attempted to continue Anthony's spiritual education. Having taken his first Holy Communion at St Joseph's at the age of seven-and-a-half, he was confirmed at age 10 in 1973, at an evening ceremony in St Mary's Cathedral. He took the confirmation name 'Thomas' after his uncle, Thomas Arthur. His cousin, Norm Howett, was his sponsor.

But while he fulfilled all the technical criteria for a practising Catholic, the faith didn't adhere itself to him. He can't nominate when exactly he stopped regularly going to church, just that it happened gradually as he 'got more independent'.

'You just got on with other things,' he says, describing himself as a 'cultural Catholic'.

But he continues to respect the role non-extreme religious belief plays in other people's lives. That accommodation has, at times, put him at loggerheads with his own colleagues on Labor's left flank, not least when fellow New South Wales left-winger Tanya Plibersek led an unsuccessful push to have Labor MPs subject to a binding vote in favour of same-sex marriage.

Anthony supported same-sex marriage but he also supported MPs being allowed to vote according to their consciences. In the Left caucus, he was the only one to speak out against a binding vote. He lost there but the conference supported his view. Tanya's position was defeated.

*

Though many of the students at St Mary's school were experiencing pretty tough family circumstances, attending there gave them regular exposure to those who were even worse off.

'I say that to the kids today: "You're privileged. You see that every day,"' says John Iffland. 'Homeless people in the tunnels and in the train stations, in the parks and things like that.'

It was like that when Anthony was at school, and more so. When recess ended and the boys streamed back into class, the homeless men would come into the schoolyard and go through the garbage bins.

'[They would] get the sandwiches and things that the kids threw in there that weren't eaten,' John says. 'And they [the boys] were used to that, you know? Used to stepping over bodies coming into the yard, if there were drunks, [there] or in the park.'

At school, Anthony's habit of speaking out against things he saw as unfair was applied at least as much at school as outside it. He was used to having to fend for himself.

When at one point his geography teacher was persistently giving him the same mark for every one of his assignments – seven or seven-and-a-half out of 10, regardless of effort – Anthony accused him of not actually reading them. He argued he had performed considerably better than seven out of 10 in some cases. Mark Burgess remembers the confrontation.

'Albo used to say, "You don't read my work. If I do no work, if I do no preparation, I just write the assignment out – I get seven-and-a-half out of 10. But if I stay home all weekend, really work hard on this assignment, you give me seven out of 10. You do not read my assignments."'

His teacher laughed off the allegation, so Anthony devised a test of his own. His class had been set an assignment on volcanoes, so he carefully crafted the first few paragraphs, and the last few as well, to elucidate the great and notable qualities of mountains that spewed lava and ash. But in-between, he deliberately wrote what Mark Burgess describes as 'just complete garbage'.

'In the middle of it he wrote "fairy floss comes out of the volcano, and marshmallows" and all this,' Mark says. 'And fairies. And the Paddle Pop Lion was in the middle of the earth.'

When he was awarded the same mark as usual – seven out of 10 – Anthony confronted the teacher, both indignant and triumphant. Nothing much ever came of it – and the kids actually thought the teacher was generally a good bloke – but he had made his point.

The kids had teachers they liked and those they didn't. They respected those who managed to outsmart them.

'Brother Simpson was a very good operator,' Mark recalls. 'He used to have this picture of holy-something up above the blackboard and he'd be writing something on the blackboard and he'd say, "Burgess! Albanese! Stop talking!"'

It took the boys a while to work out how he knew they were talking when their whispers were quiet and he had his back to them.

'We didn't realise he was using the reflection on this holy picture. He was watching us.'

Others among the teachers at St Mary's were responsible for shaping Anthony's interest in politics. He had been going along to monthly Labor Party meetings in Camperdown with his mother and grandparents since he was small, but what he learned from particular individuals at school – and later at university – gave his views form and substance.

His commerce teacher, Paul Cheney, pushed his students to keep across current events and discuss them in class. Cheney was a flamboyant man, openly gay at a time when, as John Iffland puts it, 'it wasn't really safe around here to be gay'.

'The kids loved him, he was fantastic,' he says.

Paul Cheney was tough on them and expected a lot. Consuming the contents of the business newspaper the *Australian Financial Review* – daily – was compulsory.

'We had to buy the *Fin Review* every morning – which was a big imposition on us,' Anthony recalls of times when none of his class was exactly flush with cash. 'But we'd buy it and we had to cut out key articles and keep them in a scrapbook.'

Lindsay remembers it too. 'The *Financial Review*, every day. *Every* day. And if you didn't have it, you were done for. He'd pick out passages and he'd pick out things of interest and he'd expect you to be reading it. I could see how he formulated some of the opinions of all of us, not just Anthony.'

Lindsay's dad worked for News Ltd so he could get newspapers for free but other kids had to find the money. In need of cash to help supplement the meagre family income, Anthony took to selling newspapers as well as buying them. From the age of about 12, he was one of half a dozen or so St Mary's kids who sold papers on street corners in the central business district.

'That was part of the reason why he was working – to kick in to help his mum,' says journalist Paul Cleary, who also went to St Mary's and worked alongside him.

Anthony started his paper-selling career down on the corner of Market and Castlereagh streets, where he earned about $7 a week. Eventually, he moved up to Hunter Street where the income was more like $10–$12 plus tips – pretty good money for an under-age, after-school worker.

Paul Cleary joined the group in Anthony's last year running the papers. Two years younger than Albo, Paul was 13. They sold papers for the old woman who ran the newsstand on the corner of Hunter and Pitt streets, Emma Simpson. Emma was an institution in that part of Sydney, having run the newsstand with her sister for decades.

'She was a thousand years old,' Anthony says. 'She was about five foot.'

The group would go to Emma's newsstand and collect papers and little leather pouches and stand on their designated corners from about 3.30 pm. Exposed as they routinely were to the more down-at-heel among the city's occupants, here on the corner of Hunter and Pitt was where the boys also saw the other side of Sydney, the well-dressed office workers who bought *The Sun* or *The Mirror* on their way home.

'We used to call them "suities",' Paul says. 'We were actually mixing it with all the people in the suits. So it opened your eyes to the world of business and these people and how they dressed.'

It taught Anthony something about generosity. He'd had no contact with wealth and he found it was the pensioners with little money who would give him a 3c tip on top of the 10c to 12c cost of a paper. But those who pulled up in their brand new European cars would expect the kids to come over to the window to deliver it and would hold up the traffic waiting for their change.

'We soon learnt the benefit of dropping the change on the ground,' Anthony says.

It opened Paul's eyes to the ways of the street too. He discovered there was 'a bit of a racket going on' among the paper-sellers, something to do with the odd dollar ending up where it shouldn't.

Having been in the business for three years by then, Anthony wound up his paper-selling career soon after.

'I was 15 and then I could get a job legally.'

Paul lived in south-west Sydney. They were long days and the paper-sellers were sometimes late home, but it was lucrative employment. After a couple of years of that, Paul finished up with almost $2000 in the bank.

Like Anthony, he would go on to study economics at Sydney University.

In 2013, Paul would write in *The Australian* about his historical association with Anthony, including their time at university.

'In 1983, I discovered that Albanese had become a fierce political warrior from the Labor Left when I enrolled in the same course,' Paul wrote. '... During these formative years, Albanese was a vehement hater of his political foes, which seemed to be anyone on the right side of the Left faction. When

I once asked him about a political opponent who had died in a car accident, he had no kind words to say.'

Unlike many of the St Mary's students, Anthony's small group of close friends would go on to uni too, one of them almost by mistake.

Mark Burgess recalls that one day at the end of Year 12, he discovered the rest of the group was headed down into Martin Place, in the centre of the city.

'And I said, "Where are you going?" And they said, "Oh, we're all going to enrol in university." The thought had never crossed my mind. It was not like a career path that anybody from Millers Point or the inner city ever did.'

He went with them and applied for accounting at Macquarie University.

'Got in too,' he says, laughing. 'Surprised everybody.'

Anthony almost didn't get there himself. Indeed, he almost didn't complete his schooling at St Mary's at all.

In July 1976, his grandmother, Maynor Ellery, died. In the months leading up to her death, she had had a stroke that had seen her hospitalised for a long time at what was then Eversleigh rehabilitation centre in Petersham. It cost her entire pension for her to stay there and some of Maryanne's too.

'Mum went there every day and worked with her in terms of occupational therapy to get feeling and movement back and getting her to walk again and all of that to get her home,' Anthony recalls. 'And Mum was absolutely determined that that would happen.'

It did and they adjusted the sleeping arrangements to account for his grandmother's impairment.

'We moved the bed into the lounge room because she couldn't get up and down the stairs. So that became a bedroom. And she didn't last very long at home. She had another stroke and that was it.'

Like nearly every other significant family event, her death was marked with a funeral at St Joseph's.

The bereavement left Maryanne Albanese facing a financial crisis along with the personal loss. The three of them were suddenly two and the two pensions they had lived on, only one. Inflation was rising but pensions were not.

Maryanne notified the school that she could no longer afford for Anthony to attend. She faced the prospect – terrible after such an effort thus far – that he might have to leave school altogether.

The principal, Brother 'Lex' Hall, asked her to come to the school for a meeting. As sometimes happened when such circumstances prevailed, he exercised his discretion and waived the boy's fees. Anthony would continue there to the end of Year 12 and scrape into economics at Sydney University by just two marks – which was, he notes, at the top of his class.

The other threat to his mother's plan that he would complete his schooling came from his mother herself and her state of health. In Anthony's early teenage years, Maryanne's arthritis became so chronic that she was regularly hospitalised for long periods while doctors tried to manage the pain. Sometimes, her son would stay with relatives or friends.

Once when Maryanne was in hospital at Meadowbank, in Sydney's north-western suburbs, Anthony spent time with family friends Georgia and Russell Gear at their home in West Ryde, and caught the train for the 15-kilometre journey in to St Mary's and back every day. At one stage, when no alternatives were available, he stayed at home alone for weeks, organising his own meals, washing his clothes, paying bills and getting himself off to school.

It wasn't school policy for teachers to be told of students' particular home circumstances, but in Anthony's case his teachers were aware of his mother's affliction.

In his social science and history classes, Vince Crow took it into consideration. 'If he didn't get his homework done . . . I assumed it was because he had been helping his mother at home,' Vince says.

It seems he mostly did get his homework done, in history at least.

Vince taught Anthony history in 1977. The records show the boy ended his third year of high school – and fifth at St Mary's – second out of 74 students in Year 9 in that subject. As usual, Peter Youssef was first.

But in Year 10, Anthony beat him at something. The school had the chance to send students to appear on the educational television game show *It's Academic*. The kids competed for a place on the team by doing a general knowledge test and Anthony was made captain, with Peter Youssef and another student, Paul Bailey, as his teammates.

Maryanne was part of the Channel Seven studio audience as a series of episodes were taped. The St Mary's boys won the first round against two other teams but were relegated to second in the next.

'It was a big deal. Mum was really proud. It was my first TV appearance.'

It was a triumph for St Mary's too, which had never had its students on the program before.

Although he was a diligent student and an avid reader, there were times when Anthony's schoolwork suffered. In Year 7, his maths marks fell dramatically. After starting out on 83 per cent in term 1, he scored 90 per cent in term 2 and was placed second in his class. But in term 3 his marks plunged to 71 per cent. He missed three textbook chapter tests and ended up seventh in the class overall.

His teacher, John Iffland, was puzzled at the drop.

'No-one else was like that.'

Doubtless his grandmother's ailing health and his mother's illness contributed to the situation. But something else also proved a major distraction from Anthony's schoolwork. The year was 1975 and 11 November fell right in the middle of term 3.

On that Remembrance Day Tuesday afternoon, Vince Crow came bursting into the Year 7s' Room 13 with news from Canberra.

'I remember him coming in and telling us that the Whitlam Government had been dismissed,' Anthony recalls.

Vince, who taught at St Mary's from 1972 until he retired in 2009, certainly remembers how he felt.

'I was so incensed and annoyed that Whitlam had been dismissed,' Vince says. He went into the various history classes, announcing the news. He hadn't advertised it at school – teachers weren't encouraged to parade their politics – but he'd been a member of the Labor Party since 1969.

Teaching a separate class that afternoon, John Iffland marched his boys outside and down to the school fence. The news of the dismissal had also stirred an angry response from the wharfies down the hill on the docks at Woolloomooloo.

'The men dropped tools and walked off the site and they came up St Mary's Road past our school and they were chanting,' John remembers. 'They were really angry. I said to the boys, "Come down, guys, we're coming down to the fence. We're watching history being made here." And we took the kids down . . . I stood them along the fence and said, "You'll tell your children you were here that day. You saw them."'

When Anthony heard of Gough Whitlam's dismissal, he walked out of school and went down to the Stock Exchange, where a protest was building.

'I got home really late that day.'

It would be three more years before he was old enough to formally join the Labor Party. The event was galvanising.

Three years earlier, he and his mum had handed out how-to-vote cards for Whitlam at the 1972 election. The dismissal was devastating.

A few days later there was a huge demonstration across the road, just metres from his school.

'On the Friday, the big demo in Sydney was across the road, basically in our school playground at the Domain, and a whole lot of us went across to listen to the great man,' Anthony says. 'We just wagged school. No one ever asked any questions.'

It could have been what cost him 20 per cent in maths. His focus was on the political price his party had paid. He and the more activist among his friends were angry.

'Our team had finally won – and we understood that – after 23 years in opposition,' he says. 'We'd won two elections and then people had intervened to chuck us out. In terms of incidents that politicised me, that was one of them. That sense of injustice.'

He felt it when he looked at people like his own mother, for whom the Whitlam Government's changes to health and social security policy had been essentially designed.

Gough Whitlam and his colleagues had introduced the Supporting Mother's Benefit for single mothers. The revolutionary national health insurance scheme, Medibank, had only begun operation that year.

During high school, Anthony watched his mother's health continue to deteriorate. Afflicted by vicious knotting in both hands and feet from her rheumatoid arthritis, Maryanne would sometimes have to haul herself downstairs from her bedroom to the kitchen or the house's only bathroom on her backside.

Until a painful, lengthy operation to straighten out her curled fingers and toes with metal rods, there were some things she couldn't do for herself. Her young son cut up her food, occasionally bathed her, paid all the bills, washed the clothes and hand-wrote any necessary correspondence in his teenage script.

After a heater malfunction set the lounge-room curtains on fire and no assistance to replace them was forthcoming from the Housing Department, he penned a complaint letter under her instruction.

It all activated a sense in Anthony Albanese that life wasn't designed to be easy, you had to fight for what you believed was right and nothing much ever came for free.

CHAPTER 6

Pragmatism, Principle, Protest

Somewhere between high school and university, Anthony got angry. Before that, the frustration about his mother's circumstances – and his own – had just been percolating, quietly.

But once he started spending more of his days in his own Camperdown neighbourhood again, this time as a member of the student body of the prestigious University of Sydney, Anthony began to experience fully the difference between the haves and the have-nots. With that transition came the uncomfortable confirmation that he and his mother were in the second category.

When he went to enrol for his Economics course, Anthony felt completely out of his depth. He knew his way around the campus a bit, thanks to the full-time job he'd snagged at the Commonwealth Bank, just as high school was winding up. The job was his fallback in case the university application was rejected and his employers had assigned him, usefully as it turned out, to the university branch, close to home. But he still didn't know anything about how things were actually done at university itself.

'I hadn't read the handbook or anything and you had to pick subjects,' he says. 'No one I knew had gone to uni. I just thought I was doing Economics so I'd do Economics – tick the box and that would be it. But there were all these subjects and I had no idea I had to do that.'

At enrolment, he found a helpful lecturer who quizzed him on why he had chosen Economics and suggested he do Accounting as part of his degree. Armed with this input, Anthony selected Accounting and an accompanying Law subject. There were two Economics units to choose from – Economics 1 and the progressive Economics 1P, which was known as Political Economy.

A controversial subject as it turned out, Political Economy was designed to put the study of Economics in a broader (largely left-wing) political context. He decided to enrol in both.

'So I was doing the full gamut of economic theory and I'm glad I did that because I got to do everything from Milton Friedman to Marx.'

His participation in the course, which had been under longstanding threat of abolition from the conservative university leadership, would lead him later into a full-scale political protest in its defence.

Having joined Young Labor back in high school, Anthony bemoaned the lack of a Labor Club on campus and, with others, went about setting one up. Also known as the 'ALP Club', it became a vehicle for his political activism and he would use it to funnel enthusiastic student activists into the Labor Party proper.

Even before he held his own membership ticket, Anthony's Labor Party involvement had exposed him to the ideological and personality divisions that made up its infamous factions.

In the party as a whole, both nationally and in his home state of New South Wales, the power of numbers lay with the Right. Anthony might have been expected to go that way too.

Maryanne Albanese and her parents were active in the party locally that had been controlled by the Right, particularly in politics around the inner city. Anthony's grandfather, George Ellery, had printed electoral material for the local MP and then-Labor leader, the Right's Pat Hills.

Although it was assumed she would, Maryanne didn't always vote with the Right. Anthony's first encounter with then-ALP organiser, later NSW state party secretary, John Della Bosca was when he arrived on their Camperdown doorstep with a pre-prepared statutory declaration for Maryanne to sign, saying she had voted for sitting MP and right-wing candidate Les McMahon in the 1981 preselection for the seat of Sydney. Maryanne waited upstairs while Anthony told him she wouldn't be signing anything. She hadn't voted for McMahon at all.

As Anthony became more involved in the Labor Party in his own right, his ideas began to take a slightly different shape. He drifted away from the working-class Catholic ideology that had informed the views of his mother and grandparents and found his own sympathies lay with the Left. And in Young Labor, the Left ruled.

The main Left faction in Young Labor was known, somewhat melodramatically, as the Radical Leadership Group. Centre Unity represented the Right and other smaller and narrower sub-groups existed on the fringes of both. Their battles were as fierce with each other as with the Liberals, the Communists and whoever else wasn't one of them.

At university, Anthony's political and social networks merged, as his high-school friendships faded. His childhood mate, Lindsay Keevers, had been accepted to university to study business but got a job at an accounting company, became accustomed to the income of a full-time worker and, apart from the odd TAFE course, decided against further study. After Year 12, he and Anthony drifted apart. But Anthony would check in with Lindsay's parents occasionally, as they aged. The senior Keevers were still living in Camperdown when Anthony went into politics and became his constituents. Lindsay doesn't believe Anthony did it 'for the politics'.

'He'd always buy them flowers,' Lindsay recalls. 'He remembered them. Maybe they'd done some good things for him, I don't know. He'd send them cards. Very thoughtful guy.'

When Frank died in 2008 and then Lorrie a few years later, Anthony attended their funerals. Maryanne had died before them and Lindsay had done the same for him.

At university, Anthony's comrades in the ALP Club became his mates outside of it. Alex Bukarica was one of those whose friendship with Anthony would begin in the university years and outlast them, withstanding the subsequent vagaries of party politics.

Alex and Anthony came from different quarters of the education system – Alex was a public-school kid from Leichhardt High – and although they figured their paths must have crossed around the streets before then, it wasn't until university, where Alex was studying Law, that they met properly.

Hailing from neighbouring Annandale, his first recollection of Anthony was on the bus. In the era of the Sex Pistols and The Clash, Alex had fashioned himself as a bit of a punk. Anthony wasn't.

'He was a bit sort of scruffy and wore nothing but Dunlop Volleys and a denim jacket and T-shirt,' Alex recalls. Dunlop Volleys were the commonest kind of Australian tennis shoe and they were not cool. Not punk cool, anyway.

Anthony was agitated at the gentrification of his suburb and had begun resenting anyone he thought might be participating in it. Having lived for decades surrounded by industry, he and the other residents of the Camperdown council-housing block were finding the new landscape even less comfortable. The factories were being turned into apartments as the middle class moved in.

So when they finally met through the ALP Club, Anthony had formed a judgement about Alex. 'He thought I was one of those inner-city wankers that had moved in.'

It turned out, he wasn't. Alex's parents, Jovan and Katica Bukarica, were Yugoslavian migrants of meagre means. Both worked at the Children's Hospital across the road from the Albanese house on Pyrmont Bridge Road, Katica in the kitchen and Jovan as an orderly.

'Years later, I found out my dad knew Maryanne – used to pass her and have a chat to her on his way to work,' Alex says.

Unlike Anthony, Alex's family wasn't much into politics. But he'd developed an interest in it in high school, falling in with 'the Trots' – the Trotskyists. When he arrived at university, he joined the first left-wing group he could find.

Adjusting his first impressions, Anthony discovered quickly that he and Alex had financial deprivation in common and they became great mates. Alex had been finding the tertiary transition strange, too.

'In those days, Sydney Uni – I suppose it still is – was fairly alienating if you were from a working-class background.'

Fellow student and ALP Club member Paul Murphy arrived the year after. Paul also experienced a kind of culture shock.

'I came from a working-class Catholic background and landed in Arts Law at Sydney University and it was just people from a world that I never even knew existed – people from some of the big North Shore schools,' Paul says.

He and Anthony also quickly became friends.

'I think the reason I warmed so quickly to Anthony was there was a lot more to him than just politics. I mean people saw that political activist but he was someone who was genuinely passionate about music – and the same type of music I was into – and you could have a laugh, a conversation about sport, play a game of pool. He was fun to be around as well.'

Paul would become part of Anthony's closest circle and – almost 20 years later – would serve as best man at his wedding.

Like Alex, his career would lead him into the union movement and he would go on to become secretary of the Media, Entertainment and Arts Alliance.

In their new surroundings at university the working-class boys stuck together. But university also provided Anthony's first large-scale social interaction with those whose upbringings had been significantly more privileged than his own and whose political leanings were different from those of his neighbourhood.

'Almost everyone would have voted Labor,' he says of the Alexandra Dwellings and the flats nearby. 'And I didn't know anyone – I'd never met anyone – who voted Liberal. That was what rich people did. No one I knew was rich. That was the way that we saw politics – in those simple class-based terms.'

Suddenly he was mixing with the people from the North Shore and the eastern suburbs. It was very different from the church school for poor kids at the top of St Mary's Road.

While he would never quite shed the tribalism inherent in NSW Labor politics, Anthony learned to get along with all kinds of people – and found he was pretty good at it. It was an ability that would serve him well throughout his professional life. There would be occasions when he didn't especially feel the need to demonstrate it with individuals who'd crossed him.

In such cases, Anthony's remarkable, almost savant-like memory for detail would be fully employed.

'He would certainly remember how you voted,' Alex observes. 'Forever!'

And those who voted against him would be left in little doubt about how he felt.

As he began university, Anthony knew just one person whose earlier economic circumstances had been markedly different from his own. That friendship had been forged towards the end of 1980, his final year of high school, when a member of the

Young Labor Left had knocked on his door in Pyrmont Bridge Road around eight o'clock one night.

Craig Sahlin was a Swedish-American Australian, born in Pennsylvania, who had migrated to Sydney with his family when he was 14. The Sahlins were liberal – with a small 'l' – and middle class and Craig's politics were inclined seriously Left. He had been to university and done honours in Anthropology, lost his American accent, become a Trotskyist, joined the Labor Party and gone back to university as a mature-age student to study Industrial Law.

Craig had become associated with what was known then in Labor circles as 'the Gould Group', a far-left collective that had formed around prominent Sydney anti-conscription, anti-censorship activist and bookseller, Bob Gould.

In 1980, the Gould Group was running a ticket for the election of delegates to the then-upcoming Young Labor conference. Playing off the name of the more prominent Radical Leadership Group, it was calling its ticket the 'Socialist Leadership Group'.

The Gould supporters had divided up among themselves the list of Young Labor members eligible to vote and were going door-to-door visiting them, recruiting for their sub-faction and lobbying for votes to get their candidates elected.

When he turned up on the doorstep of number 41 in the winter of 1980, looking for 17-year-old party member Anthony Albanese, Craig was 25 – barely still eligible to even be in Young Labor himself – and living in Glebe, a few blocks from Anthony's Camperdown home.

'So I knock on the door at eight o'clock at night,' Craig says. 'He comes out, I think, in his pyjamas from memory.'

It was their first meeting and also Craig's first encounter with Anthony's mother, Maryanne.

'The welcoming! Just a wonderful, wonderful person. We were used to getting not a great reception when we knocked on people's doors.'

Craig was invited in for a cup of tea.

'We go through our spiel – he should really throw his lot in with us – and what we're about. We're better than that other fake Left, the Radical Leadership Group, the RLG.'

The ensuing conversation convinced Craig the young Anthony was already developing political skills. The older man had no idea where they could have come from but was impressed.

'It was clear we had a livewire here and we certainly wanted him.'

They didn't get him. His support went to the majority Left group. But what grew from the encounter was a longstanding friendship.

Despite the difference in age, the two had a lot in common politically and were both on student timetables.

'We would sit up until all hours talking politics,' Craig says. 'We saw things the same way. But he was always someone who would go more to the mainstream. He wanted to be in places where he could make a difference and do things. And I think he found the sort of Trotskyist groups too ultimately ineffective.'

Craig liked Maryanne as well as Anthony and both were quickly introduced to his partner, Jeremy Fisher. Maryanne was completely unfazed by the fact that they were a gay couple and it was only years later that Craig realised how significant that was for a woman of her background at that time.

'It was just not an issue,' he says. 'I think she was naturally a tolerant, warm, loving person.'

He wonders if her own experience as a young devout Catholic, pregnant and unmarried in the early 1960s, might have informed her attitude.

'Maybe that gave her a kind of unconscious insight that just made her totally non-judgemental. And maybe that's rubbed off on Anthony as well. It's the non-judgemental matter-of-factness about it all.'

Craig and Jeremy would drop in to number 41 regularly, accompanied routinely by Craig's dog, Hugo.

Eventually, Hugo started also dropping in on his own. From Glebe to Camperdown was a fair distance for a dog but he was smart. He knew how to find his way there – where there would be snacks – and back.

'In those days you could have a dog that lived its own life and wandered around,' Craig notes, a bit nostalgically.

Anthony reserves a special affection for dogs and he loved Hugo, a shaggy, collie-coloured, mixed-breed 'bitzer'.

'Hugo used to come down sometimes to Mum's place and just stay – he'd knock on the door,' he says, demonstrating how the hound would nudge at the screen. 'Mum kept dog food, even though we didn't have a dog. And when he was ready to go home he would just go to the door.'

Hugo would also often join Anthony and Craig in the social activities that student schedules allowed.

'We'd go to the pub and play pool and Hugo would wait outside,' Craig recalls.

For a few years, Craig and Anthony were close companions.

'He was fun to be with. We had a great time.'

Their flexible hours sometimes involved playing music long into the night at the Glebe house with perhaps inadequate consideration for Jeremy, who was working full-time and trying to get some sleep.

Occasionally, Craig and Jeremy would invite Anthony and Maryanne over for dinner.

One such night when they were talking about music, Maryanne mentioned she liked the violin. Craig had a set of reel-to-reel recordings he had made of a performance of Bach's six Sonatas and Partitas for solo violin.

'I played it and it was the soundtrack for the evening. And Maryanne just loved it. Loved it.'

Her hosts weren't aware she had previously played the violin herself until her arthritic fingers could no longer manipulate the strings. It was a good night with much laughter and well past midnight when the guests finally left, heading off with Maryanne insisting she was well enough to manage the kilometre-or-so walk on crippled feet.

Later, her son wanted their hosts to know how happy they'd made his mother.

'Anthony rang me up and said Maryanne danced on the way home.'

On less cheerful days, when she was in hospital, Anthony's mates would go with him to visit her. Craig, Alex and others have stories of trips to nearby Royal Prince Alfred or St Vincent's in Darlinghurst.

Once, as Anthony and Craig were on their way to St Vincent's on Craig's motorcycle, a Telecom service van turned illegally in front of them. Anthony remembers the date: 19 May 1982.

As they collided, Craig had the handlebars to steady him and was miraculously not too badly hurt. His pillion passenger was catapulted into the air.

'We hit the van and I went over,' Anthony says, describing the spot outside the Clock Hotel in Crown Street, Surry Hills, where the crash happened.

'I went literally a block. Bounced up and down on the road. Thank God I had my helmet on.'

He ended up with a damaged left sacroiliac joint – the bone on either side of the pelvis that acts as a shock absorber for the spine. He made it to St Vincent's – in an ambulance.

Anthony didn't see his mother but instead was examined and treated, unbeknowns to her, in the casualty department a few floors below. With a diagnosis established, and no further useful immediate treatment recommended beyond bed rest, he was sent home.

The sheepish son waited several days for the bruising and severe gravel grazes to improve before going back to see his mum, hoping he might get away with avoiding a full explanation.

'But as soon as I walked in, she instantly of course knew and said, "What's happened?"'

He ended up having months of physiotherapy. An ensuing court case secured a compensation payout and after all the medical bills were cleared he was left with around $27,000 – and a dodgy back.

In what might be described as a substantial case of bad luck, he would find himself in a second accident five years later when he was travelling in the back of a Commonwealth hire car in Canberra, where he was then working as an electorate officer to Minister Tom Uren.

The car was T-boned while crossing an intersection in the suburb of Narrabundah, near Parliament House, and Anthony was knocked unconscious, sustaining head and back injuries. There was another trip to hospital, another compensation case and another payout.

The two accidents left him with permanent damage to his back. But the money, which he banked, transformed his financial circumstances.

Respectively, and combined with savings from his job, the payments would eventually help fund an overseas trip and the deposit on a house – the second being something his mother had never been able to afford.

Anthony's closest friends became devoted to his mum. She used to refer to Alex, Craig, Jeremy, Paul Murphy and others as her 'boys'.

'She was just a really witty, engaging woman who just adored Anthony,' Paul says. 'And her house was always open.'

Alex also remembers her with great affection. He becomes emotional talking about her.

'She was a lovely, warm person. We used to go see her Christmas morning before we'd have family lunch. Or Christmas Eve. We'd always make a point of seeing her.'

Maryanne loved Christmas and hosted an orphans' Christmas lunch every year. Paul also made a point of swinging by.

'I used to drop in there at some point on Christmas Day after my own family things,' he says. 'She loved everything about it – all the decorations, getting the food ready. It was a really big, big thing for her, Christmas Day.'

When various among Anthony's friends visited them at home, the conversations would swing between the political and personal, canvassing life, relationships and the freedoms of youth. Now and then, Maryanne would talk about her travels abroad.

Anthony supposed she was keen to seem worldly among these exuberant young people and whenever she mentioned her shipboard romance with the dashing Italian steward, her son would listen carefully.

After her kitchen-table revelation of a few years earlier, they had never really discussed his father and it wasn't a subject he felt comfortable raising.

It became a source of frustration in his later teens and 20s that what his mother told the various visitors on those afternoons and evenings was not always consistent. He excused that, on the grounds of her illness and her medication and perhaps just a little of the rosy tint which time can add to a tale.

Uncharacteristically, Anthony hasn't retained – or perhaps has jettisoned – the detailed content of these conversations and his friends' recollections are even less precise. Unlike him, they weren't trying to forensically cross-match the details she offered.

For Craig, the stories dissolved into the blur of garrulous nights and spirited exchange.

His sense from Maryanne's descriptions of the Italian, Carlo, was of a European man with 'continental manners', very different from the Australian blokes she knew. Whatever the emotional truth of their relationship might have been, Craig didn't need to know.

'I think Maryanne wanted to exist in a thought world where she focused on the positive – which was that she was a girl swept off her feet by a dashing continental Italian with manners and style and it was romantic,' he says. 'And it was a period of her life that she would treasure – and especially because Anthony came out of it.'

For all of Anthony's insistence that having no father didn't bother him, some of his old friends are convinced it did. Alex is among them.

'I came from a big family and a fairly loving family. And I think when he would visit my parents – our house – he would miss a bit of that. It was a big absence in his life. And although he is and he was an extremely emotionally strong person, I think at various times of his life it was fairly keenly felt. The guy has got a tough exterior when he wants and I think that comes from having a bit of a hard time in your early years.'

Anthony's friends knew not to ask him about his dad. Some viewed his 'I'm fine' attitude as a defence mechanism – hardly surprising given the sense of rejection that must dwell deep in a child when an absent parent has never come looking.

Those early years – and the welling anger others sensed, which he turned into politics – shaped Anthony's development in a very direct way. At university, he found his voice – frequently with the help of a loudhailer. His political interest became a passion and eventually a vocation.

He and his 'comrades' on the Left took up the causes of the downtrodden and fought for them hard and loud: Aboriginal land rights, Palestinian human rights, opposition to South African apartheid. And they learned how to fight with and against others in the Labor Party and the labour movement to advance those causes and their own faction, sometimes for its own sake.

While he learned to pick his battles and fight them to win, something in Anthony's upbringing – possibly the imprint of Catholic social justice – also drove him to speak up for things that were neither popular nor in his own particular interests, if he thought they were important. His critics question the portrait of altruism but his supporters insist.

'This is the funny thing about Anthony – he's a pragmatist but there's principle there,' says Craig. 'He will take a position regularly that's not going to get up and he will do it publicly. And he picks his things. He's not going to do it at random but he does it.'

No doubt in part due to his friendship with Craig and Jeremy, one of those issues was gay rights. He had also been conscious back in high school that kids who were gay got a rough time.

'There was a group of students at school, one of who went on to become a drag queen,' Anthony recalls. 'And I just never had any issues with them. They were friends. They got picked on a bit as a group and they were obviously gay.'

He says some of the teachers singled them out for attention too. 'Not in a good way.' And at home, his mother 'just treated people as people, regardless'.

'She knew about Craig and Jeremy – couldn't care less – and never worried about her son – I was still at school – spending time with them all.'

Early on in Anthony's time at Sydney Uni, another of his friends in the Left, Chris Gration, came out. Chris and others formed a lesbian and gay collective on campus.

'Anthony, strikingly, spoke out for gay law reform,' Chris says. 'It wasn't popular. And so at the time, for him to speak out about it meant that people sledged him for being a poofter. He never bothered to respond to that.'

More than a decade later, as a Member of Parliament, Anthony would become one of the most outspoken early advocates for changes to allow same-sex couples the same legal rights to each other's superannuation as heterosexual couples.

He saw it as something that could make a real difference – a publicly saleable measure that could herald other changes, including same-sex marriage eventually, too. He was playing the long game.

'It was easier to win support for the logic of that because it was people's own money,' he says of the superannuation change. 'But once you did that, once you got into the debate and that logic, the principle of "people should be treated the same" was easy to be extended.'

Chris says Anthony's causes were all 'kind of woven together' by his upbringing. 'You knew he lived in and came from housing commission and was a working-class kid and proud of it.'

Among his closest friends and associates from that period, one word surfaces repeatedly about Anthony Albanese's political emergence.

'He was always a charismatic personality,' says Alex, working in 2016 as legal and industrial director in the mining division of the Construction, Forestry, Mining and Energy Union.

'He would always make his way in any group of people. He never felt – what's the word? – second class. I don't think he ever felt inferior in terms of those eastern suburbs, North Shore born-to-rule types that dominated the university.'

Maryanne had instilled in her son a healthy sense of who he was.

'She instilled confidence in me that I could be somebody,' Anthony says. She wasn't specific about who or what that might be. 'She always said you could do anything you wanted to do.'

Among former associates who are more critical of him and his trajectory, that common word still arises.

'Even as a student, he was very charismatic,' says one. 'But he was possibly the angriest person I had ever met on campus. He had so much anger about the class system . . . and the situation of his mother . . . It was very sparse, very poor. There was nothing in the fridge.'

Chris Gration calls the young Anthony 'fearless'.

'He was really charismatic at university. He wasn't a great orator, he was just a very charismatic man. He was very good at putting ideas together . . . There's something very warm in his interaction. He has a great gift for friendship.'

Anthony had to learn to contain, as well as maintain, his rage about the class divisions he observed.

'He's spent decades learning how to do that,' says Chris. 'That's how he managed to form really good relationships at Sydney University with all those middle-class people that were moving in and destroying his suburb.'

Left-wing colleague and friend Mark Butler, with whom Anthony would serve in Parliament, initially in opposing parts of the Left but later together, also says Anthony is exceptional at keeping channels open.

'He's a very good person, but he's a very good organiser as well,' Mark says. 'So he never burned a bridge, no matter what fight I'd end up on. He always kept a line of communication going. He'd always ring me, talk through the merits of the case, keep a relationship. [We'd] have a drink every now and then when we were in the same town.'

Through the ALP Club, Anthony drew Chris, Alex and others from non-aligned groups like the harder-left Left Action into the Labor Party.

'I always believed Labor was the main game for progressives.'

Looking back, Chris describes student politics as 'great training at debating, at understanding how the rules work and the application of power through the rules'. 'But also the understanding of relationship. It's all about relationship.'

Chris speaks from bitter experience. In 1986, a political confrontation would see his own relationship with Anthony fracture dramatically, delivering a decades-long and, by his own admission, self-inflicted estrangement from a man he admired greatly.

For all the headiness of student politics, the factional manoeuvrings and power plays within Young Labor were, at times, deadly serious.

CHAPTER 7

Political Economy

If Anthony Albanese had followed another of his options for tertiary study, his life might have been dramatically different. Rather than his militant period, the early 1980s might have been his military period instead. Fleetingly – and unlikely as it seems – Anthony considered joining the army because his university expenses would be covered.

Even before the dismantling of Whitlam's free-education policy, going to university wasn't completely without cost. Low as they would seem once full fees became the norm, there were still expenses that had to be met: student union fees, textbooks and just the cost of living (and beer).

By the time he finished high school, Anthony was juggling after-school and weekend jobs to supplement his mother's pension and help meet their financial commitments, including those associated with her chronic health problems.

As soon as he was old enough to find something better, he'd given up selling newspapers and started working at McDonald's in George Street, where he would do shifts after school and on weekends. Sundays were especially lucrative, paying well above the standard hourly rate.

Anthony's job was in the kitchen, frying chicken, filet o' fish and apple pies, and doing the cleaning. The job came to an end when he worked a double shift one afternoon to cover for someone who hadn't shown up – something McDonald's ordinarily tried to avoid because it cost them more – and then copped criticism from a supervisor for his cleaning effort after standing at the fryer for hours.

'I remember the boss – who was about 18 – coming in and complaining that it wasn't clean enough. So I handed him the mop and said, "Do it yourself, I'm out of here."'

By then he could afford to take a stand. He'd also started working at Grace Bros department store on Broadway on Thursday nights and Saturday mornings.

The combined income from Anthony's casual jobs still wasn't a lot. As the prospect of university and its associated costs loomed, he became concerned about how he was going to be able to afford it. So when army recruiters came to St Mary's towards the end of Year 12, talking about how he could be paid to study, he took a brochure.

'I remember going down to the place near Belmore Park and getting the forms and stuff about Duntroon,' he says. 'I never went through with it, but I thought about that, about what options I would have.'

The military option was discounted quickly and he pursued entrance to a more familiar institution, closer to home. Ensconced as he became on the most politically active of Sydney's then-three university campuses, he discovered militancy – or at least robust activism – instead.

In his first year at uni in 1981, Anthony juggled the study with work, political activity and a solid schedule of socialising. Having been a member of the ALP for almost three years and already active in Young Labor, he and others set about re-establishing the defunct campus Labor club – named the 'ALP Club' – to represent the views of left-wing students. He discovered university was a fertile recruiting ground.

Along with the casual jobs, he was also working full-time at the Commonwealth Bank, where he had started the Monday after his last HSC exam.

The bank was introducing a newfangled product known as the 'keycard' and Anthony was given the task of persuading customers to abandon their old passbooks.

'Because I was young they thought, "Oh, he'd know how a computer works,"' he says.

He had to convince customers to try the new hole-in-the-wall technology, the Automatic Teller Machine, 'which they weren't sure would ever catch on'.

His bank bosses would sometimes let him leave a bit early to get across campus to the Merewether Building where his Economics classes were held. But he missed a fair few too.

He'd also picked up weekend work at Pancakes on the Rocks – mostly the overnight shift on Saturdays, 11 pm until 7 am, which paid triple time. He did the dishwashing. The gluey pancake mix stuck to everything. 'You used to stink of the stuff.'

Saturday nights paid the best but they could get a bit wild, with people pouring out of the bars and clubs in the Rocks, looking for a feed.

'There weren't many people not affected by something or other,' he recalls. 'Who wants a pancake at 3 am?'

When he realised he could earn as much in one night at Pancakes as he was earning in a week at the bank, he quit the bank. However, even the good money wasn't worth those long, smelly Saturday nights and although he enjoyed the camaraderie, eventually the hours, unpredictable customers and layers of liquid mixture on the skin became too much.

'I hated it. You stunk. For days.'

He lined up other work and left.

Among his next clutch of casual jobs was babysitting for the Teachers' Federation, arranged by someone who knew someone in the Camperdown ALP branch.

'They used to have pretty regular conferences and I'd go up to Kings Cross and they'd put all the babies in a room at the Crest Hotel,' he says. 'I'd look after the kids.' Two of the children belonged to Janelle Saffin, with whom he would go on to serve in Parliament.

He liked children and there would usually be three or four to look after at any one time in the hotel room until their parents returned from a long conference dinner, sometimes at 1 or 2 am. They paid him separately so it was lucrative.

Anthony also picked up odd jobs from the casual-employment board at the university. Once, he and a bunch of other students were hired to clean out a warehouse at Walsh Bay for a glamorous corporate retail event. The contractors whose job it was to decorate the space were offering each of them $50 to make it clean and functional in a single day.

'It was this old warehouse that hadn't been used forever and it was just full of pigeon shit,' Anthony says. 'We had these high-powered hoses and they were huge big roofs, right up.'

The pigeons, which had apparently been roosting in the high ceilings since close to the dawn of time, had left them a mammoth task and the contractors were angry it couldn't be completed in a day.

But the excrement was caked on and rained down on their heads. The floors also had to be scrubbed. It was a three-day effort.

Anthony nominates this as the worst job he ever accepted. 'We were basically hosing pigeon shit for days.'

He pocketed $150 but, once again, walked away caked in muck.

Eventually the multiple jobs – combined with the generally nocturnal existence of a first-year uni student – started taking their toll. Despite a slightly patchy attendance record, he was at least motivated enough to keep up with the reading. And he read more than was required.

'I read Keynes' *General Theory* and Milton Friedman's *Free to Choose* and Marx's *Capital* – all of which I still have at home – and everything in between.'

He read about Joseph Schumpeter's theses on evolutionary economics and 'creative destruction' and the Marxist Paul Sweezy's ideas about monopolisation, stagnation and financialisation in the capitalist system.

And he managed not to fail anything.

University life had both opened Anthony's intellectual world and widened his social circle and he began to meet more people whose financial backgrounds differed wildly from his own.

While he found some of it strange and inexplicable – like the fact that at Sydney Uni, the blokes from the most prestigious private schools, 'Joeys' (St Joseph's) at Hunters Hill, Riverview and Kings, would wrap their old school ties around their beer steins while drinking – his skill with a pool cue became a great equaliser.

'I got on with people because I played pool and I drank and I was gregarious,' he says.

He would be invited to parties at houses in Killara, on the North Shore, with their own tennis courts. He'd never seen anything like it.

'There were people who I liked and I got on with and I went to these places I just never knew existed . . . It was like, "What?! Wow!"'

He would go to college balls, escorting various girls. Sometimes a girl's parents would look askance at the young man with long hair and an earring wearing something that was not a dinner suit, who was purporting to be good enough to go out with their daughter.

It all taught him about social status. He learned not to judge on background alone and to appreciate not being judged the same. But he also learned what making the right connections could do.

In second year a uni mate, Mark Lyndon Jones, came over to Anthony's place for dinner one night. Mark came from Hunters Hill, where his father had been the mayor. Hunters Hill was hardly a hotbed of socialism.

'He wasn't a Labor Party mayor,' Anthony says, explaining the difference between them. 'There's never been a Labor mayor of Hunters Hill.'

As Mark ate and chatted to Anthony and his mum, he was horrified to see how badly crippled Maryanne's hands were, how she could barely manage utensils and sometimes couldn't cut her own food.

'He was shocked and said, "How long has that been like that?",' Anthony recalls.

After questioning his friend about the situation, Mark revealed his own mother worked for an orthopaedic surgeon, Dr David Champion, and asked for permission to discuss Maryanne's condition with her. Anthony agreed and he did.

Mark's mother in turn raised the issue with Dr Champion and then, at their urging, Anthony talked to Maryanne about the possibility of surgery.

'We lined up an appointment,' Anthony says. Dr Champion took her on as a patient in the public health system.

'It changed her life. He reconstructed her hands and her feet . . . so she could use them.'

In a different way, that experience changed Anthony too. He realised that social classes existed, but that good did not rest in only one.

'There were rich people who were good people,' he says. 'They were wealthy people who were good, generous, nice people.'

And it affirmed a favourite old saying of his mum's: 'It's not what you know, it's who you know.'

When Mark's mum died, Anthony went to her funeral out of respect for her and deep gratitude for what she'd done.

'Without that, I probably would never have been able to move out of home,' Anthony says. 'She was healthier when she was 60 than when she was 40, which was pretty amazing.'

As Anthony's university life progressed, politics began to occupy an increasingly large space in it. He became secretary of the Young Labor Association in the electorate of Sydney, an activity that took up time and attention after hours. The resurrection of the uni's ALP Club shifted some of his political activity onto campus as well. That's where he and Alex Bukarica met.

'With supporters, he filtered those people into the ALP proper,' Alex says, 'firstly into the Young Labor Association branches and then into the ALP. I suppose that was the start of his political machine in a way.'

Student politics were highly factionalised. There were groups representing the Labor Left, the Communist Left, the Labor Right, Jewish students, the Liberals and a raft of others.

Internationally, the Cold War was still in full swing. The events and political identities overseas were shaping the views of passionate, young Australian students. The example set by Prime Minister Margaret Thatcher in Britain and President Ronald Reagan in the United States fired up conservative students and drove those of socialist sentiment to the barricades. Like-minded groups from different campuses banded together to fight their ideological battles.

The Left-led Australian Union of Students was trying to get campuses to affiliate. Its President in 1982 was future Prime Minister Julia Gillard, followed in 1984 by Michael O'Connor, who would become a prominent union leader. The ALP Club supported affiliation.

By the end of first year, the ALP Club was in full swing and the following year, 1982, Anthony and his comrades set about running candidates for the university's Student Representative

Council, on the first ALP ticket for some years. Their campaign was hardly original.

'We ran under the slogan "It's Time". Who would've thought of it?!' (In 2016, the Labor Party resurrected the slogan yet again in its campaign for same-sex marriage.)

Anthony was elected and served alongside Belinda Neal, who represented the Labor Right's Centre Unity group and would become a NSW senator nine years later. Neal married John Della Bosca, with whom Anthony would work under testy circumstances in NSW ALP headquarters a decade on.

Also elected to the SRC was Christine Abbott, a member of the conservative Democratic Club who was the younger sister of future Prime Minister and former SRC President Tony Abbott. She would eventually go into politics herself at the local government level. Anthony set about recruiting from other groups into the ALP Club, primarily Left Action, persuading Alex, Chris and others to abandon it in favour of his group and ultimately the Labor Party.

In 1983, he stood for the SRC presidency against Belinda Neal and the leader of the extremist National Action group, Jim Saleam.

National Action had been active on campus and the ALP Club, which supported the African National Congress and its efforts against apartheid in South Africa, strongly opposed its activities.

Anthony and Alex had tangled with Jim Saleam late one night when they discovered him pasting up anti-ANC posters on campus.

'We almost got in a punch-up,' Alex says. 'There was a push and shove and so on and so forth. And ultimately these uni security guards broke us up.'

The SRC election involved a hard-fought campaign, and Belinda Neal beat both Anthony and Jim.

The ALP Club alleged irregularities with the ballot so an investigation was set up, headed by then-lawyer Anna

Katzmann, who would eventually become a Federal Court judge. At the end of that lengthy process, the election was voided and the SRC was disbanded until new elections the following year.

But 1983 became more notorious at Sydney University for a separate political event – the student protests in defence of the Political Economy course.

Political Economy had been the subject of controversy for years, symptomatic of the struggle between left-wing and right-wing academics in the Economics department under a conservative university leadership.

The standard curriculum was based on neoclassical – meaning traditional – economic theory, concerned primarily with supply and demand and the workings of the market.

But the proponents of what became known as 'Political Economy' argued that a wider view was necessary and economics should be seen in its social context.

They relied on Marxist and other left-wing theory to analyse the distribution of wealth within the economy and the role and influence of the most powerful – especially the state and private corporations. In their more modern form, Political Economy courses take account of social movements such as feminism and disciplines like environmental economics in explaining how the organism that is an economy works.

But back in the '70s and early '80s, before the course existed in its own right, those who supported this approach were seen as undermining the orthodoxy at Sydney University. As the left-wing economists pushed to have their part of the Economics course expanded into a course all of its own, the university leadership – backed by the more conservative economists in the faculty – was trying to scale it back to just a few electives.

The moves prompted those students who supported the left-wing course of study to mount protests in its defence. Those that erupted in 1983 became Anthony Albanese's first genuine political fight. But the fight itself wasn't new.

The Vietnam era had seen a push for more critical thinking on university campuses, including at Sydney Uni. Within the department of Economics, a debate had begun about what constituted a good, well-rounded education in the subject.

In the 1960s, the course was a combination of traditional, mathematically focused economics – micro and macro – and elements of broader economic policymaking.

But a course review – and the arrival of two new professors – sent it in a more conservative direction. The study of the social dimensions of economics was jettisoned in favour of purer, drier curriculum.

The shift angered the left-wing academics within the faculty, led by Ted Wheelwright and Frank Stilwell and later Gavan Butler. It also angered many of the students, who complained that their subjects had become interminably boring with less relevance to other related courses, such as politics.

In mid-1973, Economics students held a day of protest and began referring to the school of economic thought they were demanding to have incorporated as 'political economy'. The following year, a repeat of the day of protest was recast as a day of 'outrage' and the dissident students became increasingly militant.

The university's professorial board eventually endorsed the introduction of Political Economy units which would become known as Economics I(P) and Economics II(P) for 1975 – within the existing department.

But the courses were only offered for first and second-year students. The academics wanted to expand them into third year and honours. They also complained those teaching the controversial courses were being overlooked for promotion. A conservative academic was brought in and Ted Wheelwright was passed over for a professorship. Left-wing tutors were sacked.

More protests followed. Students burned an effigy representing 'professorial power' and when Vice-Chancellor Bruce Williams was away at a Reserve Bank board meeting, they broke down the doors to his office and occupied it for several hours, drinking the contents of his liquor cabinet.

On return, the vice-chancellor called the police to evict them. They left peacefully but the move ensured that 'cops on campus' would be a sensitive issue from then on.

While the unhappy students and their supportive lecturers had made gains in adjustments to the curriculum, traditional thinking continued to dominate and the Economics department was split.

Beyond its sandstone walls, the university was gaining a fair bit of adverse publicity from the seemingly intractable Political Economy dispute. In late 1975, an enterprising and confident young Arts Law student who had nothing to do with the Political Economy course offered to try and mediate. His name was Malcolm Turnbull.

Now-retired professor Frank Stilwell remembers the exchange. 'One time he appeared in my office and almost offered himself to be a Henry Kissinger go-between, between the rival factions.

'He said, "Oh, I think this dispute needs someone to be a peacemaker, a negotiator. I'm willing to play that role." I said to him at the time, "Good luck to you, Malcolm."'

Two decades later when a journalist asked Malcolm Turnbull about his mediator role, he said he couldn't remember much.

'I don't recall the details of it,' he told ABC Radio's Catherine Freyne. 'It's a long time ago. But if I played a mediating role, that is obviously a good thing to do. I am after all a man of peace and moderation.'

In 1975, Turnbull was on the SRC and was also a student representative on the university's professorial – renamed the 'academic' – board. His efforts in shuttle diplomacy had mixed results.

'He wasn't particularly successful,' Frank Stilwell says of the efforts of the man who would become Prime Minister. 'But he did one thing that was quite memorable and quite powerful.'

Malcolm Turnbull persuaded the board to set up an inquiry under then history professor John Ward – who would rise to become vice-chancellor a few years later and, like his predecessor, find his office full of unwelcome student visitors, too.

Among other things, the inquiry recommended establishing a unit of Political Economy within the department of Economics to provide partial autonomy. It would assist in the eventual entrenchment of the course.

But in the short-term, the vice-chancellor did not follow the recommendation. More protests ensued.

In their 2009 book *Political Economy Now!*, left-wing lecturers Frank Stilwell, Ted Wheelwright and Gavan Butler said the 11-day 1976 strike involved 4000 students and 100 staff.

Ted Wheelwright had declined to support the strike, telling one of the tutors he thought it was an outdated mode of protest.

Off campus, the vice-chancellor's university-owned residence, the stately mansion *Wybalena*, in Hunters Hill, was spray painted with student unhappiness. For the next five years, the course – and the tensions – continued as another student who would become Prime Minister emerged on the conservative side of the fight.

In 1979, then-SRC President and Economics student Tony Abbott railed on campus radio against Arts and Economics courses that focused on issues like feminism that were 'so much nonsense'.

'Quite frankly, I think that these courses are trivial,' Tony said at the time. 'Certainly Political Economy and General Philosophy are thinly disguised attempts by unscrupulous academics to impose simplistic ideological solutions upon students, as it were; to make students the cannon fodder for their own private versions of the revolution.'

Tony and other opponents of Political Economy argued it lacked rigour and discipline. He told ABC Radio there were Marxist academics at Sydney University trying to destroy the moral and intellectual standards of the elite to undermine liberal democratic society in Australia.

The battle over the kind of education that Economics students received raged on. Restrictions on Political Economy staff numbers put a strain on resources and in 1981 another application for full third-year and honours PE courses was rejected.

John Ward had taken over as vice-chancellor and students demonstrated outside his office, seeking to present a petition with hundreds of signatures calling for the changes. Having started university that year, Anthony Albanese's signature was among them.

'At the time that the young Anthony was a student at Sydney University it was a struggle about simply defending and extending these courses in PE that were so unwelcome to the more mainstream economists,' Frank Stilwell says.

The Political Economy stream attracted students from a range of backgrounds.

'I suppose a class analysis would lead you to think that PE might appeal to people from Struggle Street, like Anthony, whereas mainstream economics might appeal to the social elite or those aspiring to join. But I don't think it was ever that simple. I mean, we had very articulate young people attracted to PE because it seemed to be more interesting, more lively, more controversial, more fun. Less mathematical.'

One of those was David Re, an Arts Law student from Armidale in northern New South Wales, whose background was distinctly different from Anthony's and who also became politically active in defending Political Economy.

Re would go on to become an international lawyer and trial judge, serving on international criminal tribunals in The Hague and elsewhere in Europe.

In mid-1982, the angry students pitched a tent in the quadrangle and stayed overnight in protest. When there were moves the next year to abolish the Political Economy course, and a student-run referendum result in favour of retaining it was ignored, the protests erupted again.

In early June 1983, the dissident students towed a caravan onto the university's front lawn, took the wheels off to make it harder to shift and hung a banner naming it the 'Faculty of Political Economy'.

With cross-campus activist politics thriving thanks to the work of Young Labor and the Australian Union of Students, students from other universities joined the rallies on the lawn. Bob Hawke's Labor federal election victory in Canberra only made them more enthusiastic.

University of New South Wales activist Malcolm Larsen recalls attending one of the rallies and hearing a young Anthony Albanese speak. He found him enigmatic, impressive and, yes, charismatic.

'He always had charisma, particularly at that point,' Malcolm says. 'He really had that young leftie firebrand style about him.'

On 15 June, during one of these rallies and after students had marched to the main quadrangle, a small group of the protest leaders, including Anthony Albanese, Chris Gration and David Re, plus Alex Bukarica and two other student activists, Paul Porteous and Peter Collie, climbed onto the roof and up the clock tower.

'I was a ring-in,' Alex says. 'I wasn't even a Political Economy student. I just thought, "There's a good protest."'

At David Re's instigation, the hands on the clock face were changed to just before 12, in what was meant to be a dramatic minutes-to-midnight statement signifying the urgency of their fight. The clock face sustained minor damage.

'The vice-chancellor was really angry about all of that,' Chris recalls. 'They had undercover people in the planning meetings and they had photographers every time we went and did anything.'

On 29 June, students occupied the staff common room in the Economics faculty's Merewether Building and, despite face-to-face talks with the vice-chancellor, refused to leave.

When they were still there (or some of them) the next day, an exasperated and enraged Vice-Chancellor John Ward did what his predecessor had done years earlier, and called in the police. This time they were not just the regular blue uniforms but the Tactical Response Group. The students were shocked. The university was an independent jurisdiction and police did not just venture onto campus.

Those inside made out that their numbers were much greater than the small group actually left and continued to refuse to move.

'There were 15 people in the room,' Anthony says. 'It was absurd. They didn't know that. And we were pretending there were more. They would have burst in if they thought there were 15.'

Some were frustrated by the lack of a plan to end the sit-in.

'Students are getting very pissed off because they can't get to their lectures,' Chris Gration recalls. 'So we're sitting around inside . . . in a circle, passing the talking stick.'

There was – literally – a stick.

Anthony concurs. 'You had all these, I guess the forerunners of the Greens and people, wanting to all hold hands and go "kum ba yah".'

David Re had his baby daughter, Rebecca, with him, so the group wanted to get out without a physical confrontation. When the police came across the roof, negotiations began through an open window.

'They were like "You've got to go now" and we were like "Nope, we've got to have a meeting,"' Anthony recalls. 'So that was my first-ever negotiation. And we shut the window on them.'

Describing how the group stalled for time by insisting they needed to discuss things further, he laughs. 'It was because we were waiting for the media to get there.'

After a few phone calls, reporters, photographers and TV camera crews arrived and the students agreed to come out. But as they went down the stairs inside the building, the police were waiting – out of sight of the cameras.

'In the stairwell, we got basically jostled – kneed as we walked down the stairs – because they were on both sides. There were a lot of cops.'

The confrontation didn't end there. As the sit-in students emerged into the crowd outside, passions were running high. Chris Gration, who'd declared his homosexuality on arrival at university, had decided to share his liberation with the armed visitors, in the form of a large badge pinned to his shirt that said 'GAY'.

It was only five years since police had roughed up and dragged off those who would become known as the '78ers', the founders of Sydney's Gay and Lesbian Mardi Gras, for attempting to march through Darlinghurst and little had changed.

In 1983, public declarations of homosexuality still didn't exactly garner congratulations from the constabulary and especially not when they were being made by a student who also happened to be screaming through a police-car window: 'Pigs off campus!'

The officer sitting inside didn't much appreciate any of it.

'He says to me, "So you're a fucking poofter too," when he sees the badge,' Chris says. 'I, of course, instead of stepping away say, "You're fucking right I'm a poofter." He gets out and arrests me.'

Chris' friends tried to help. Anthony jumped in front of the car – something he's sheepish about now – as he and others tried to extract their detained comrade.

'They put him in one side of the car and we tried to pull him out the other. I was shocked that Chris had been targeted because he was gay.'

Their endeavours weren't terribly successful and Chris was, indeed, arrested.

He was charged with a common law offence – 'serious alarm or affront'. But when he appeared at the Newtown Court of Petty Sessions, the police contradicted each other's evidence and the magistrate found there was no case to answer.

With the benefit of three decades of hindsight, Chris sums up his own actions in a single word: 'stupid'.

The vice-chancellor decided to take disciplinary action against nine of the protesters: Chris, Anthony and David, plus fellow students Adam Rorris, Tony Westmore, Daniel Luscombe, Maria Barac, Marijka Conrade and Paul Porteous.

He wanted them suspended. To add insult to the day's events, according to Anthony, Vice-Chancellor Ward had summons documents delivered to their homes while they were at the protest.

With the confrontation between students and police leading the nightly news, Maryanne Albanese was served with the papers at her front door and made to sign for the registered letter. That made Anthony even angrier.

The vice-chancellor's decision to call in the TRG had already enraged the students. A week later, the Merewether common room was once again the scene of an occupation.

At one stage, the students expanded their occupation down a corridor, leaving the university leadership puzzling over what they assumed was a strategic manoeuvre. It was certainly strategic but not in the way they had assumed.

'It was just so they had access to the showers,' Anthony says, laughing.

The second occupation dragged on and after several days it had turned into a kind of festival. The vice-chancellor wasn't calling in the police a second time and the students just stayed, tag-teaming between the sit-in, their lectures and visits to the pub. Some would go home and sleep in their own beds and return early in the morning. Others just stayed day and night.

The core group held an endless discussion about what to do next. Buoyed by the success of the Franklin Dam protests in Tasmania, the anarchists and others on the far-left political fringes had instituted consensus decision-making, and with all the comings and goings, the conversation simply never reached any kind of conclusion.

It drove the pragmatists in their midst crazy, foremost among them the members of the ALP Club.

'They'd sit in a circle and they'd keep talking until everyone agreed,' Anthony says. 'So no-one ever made a decision ... It just never started and never stopped. It was just a continuous meeting.'

The protest had become an end unto itself.

'They had no strategy for it to end. And what was clear was that for some of them the sit-in was the objective. It was literally a place to live!'

A group from the ALP Club, including David Re, Chris and Anthony, cooked up an escape strategy. As the protest was entering its 10th day, they arrived early in the morning and interrupted the never-ending discussion, demanding an immediate vote on finishing the protest.

'We stacked it basically,' Anthony says. 'To end it.'

And it ended. Anthony reckons that explains why he's in the Labor Party. 'I want outcomes rather than just process.'

There was certainly an outcome for the nine who faced disciplinary charges at the hands of the university's proctorial panel. The students first faced proceedings before the proctorial board and later a formal disciplinary hearing before a three-member panel headed by Justice James Staunton, who was then chief judge of the District Court. To the students' maximum inconvenience, the hearings were held in November, during exams.

The university operated under its own rules and the students weren't allowed to bring formal legal representation. But they were allowed to bring a friend.

'I brought Greg Woods QC who happened to be my friend,' Anthony says, smiling. They also organised for a sympathetic solicitor, Jack Graham, and a junior barrister to attend as 'friends' of the group. Labor people in high places provided references and the Transport Workers' Union threatened action against the university.

'I was suspended for two years but the suspensions were suspended,' Anthony says. He was also slapped with a $100 fine.

'The university backed off basically is what happened. It was a disaster for them. Having a judge and QCs and all this expense for a bunch of students saying we just want to keep our course was ridiculous.'

By the time the case was resolved, they had attended numerous protests but missed months of class. Anthony fell behind in his studies, which involved a double major in Industrial Relations and majors in Government and Economics.

Having also devoted so much attention to politics, becoming national President of the Council of Australian Labor Party Students along with his involvement in Young Labor, he dropped one subject and took an extra year to complete his degree.

He did not fail anything.

'I was no great student. I certainly wasn't a university medallist – except in political activism.'

Frank Stilwell recalls him as a roughly credit-average student. Frank is one of the few who gets away with referring to his former student as 'Tony'.

'I think Tony would be the first to say he wasn't an intellectual high-flier,' he says. 'A very decent student, getting pretty good results.'

He describes Anthony as 'a very prominent student' who was 'fully engaged in university life' in an academic, political and social sense. 'He was someone who had the political gene.'

In the end, Political Economy survived, if not exactly as they had hoped.

Anthony rejects the suggestion that the fight they won on campus was lost in the wider economic and political world, with neo-classical economics now the standard. In a 2013 interview with ABC Radio National, he argued that the Rudd Labor Government's economic stimulus in response to the global financial crisis proved his point.

'There you had an example of the philosophical view that economic growth isn't the end in itself. It's about jobs. It's about living standards. It's about protecting the vulnerable.'

At Sydney University, the radical economists and their generations of supporters claimed success, with the Political Economy course entrenched in the curriculum.

In 2008, they finally saw the establishment of a Department of Political Economy – not in the Economics faculty, but in the School of Social and Political Sciences, which sits alongside the School of Economics in the Faculty of Arts.

In fact, the Sydney University Economics Faculty no longer exists. In what the market capitalists may claim as proof of their own ultimate victory, it has become the School of Business instead.

CHAPTER 8

Liberty Street

Through much of his time at university, Anthony lived at home with his mum. But whenever he needed a bolthole, there was Alex's place in nearby Enmore, in the aptly named Liberty Street. Alex lived at number 11. It was lefty central.

In its 19th-century heyday, the place had been a grand gentleman's house – six bedrooms in a freestanding street-front residence with more rooms in a two-storey terrace behind, where the servants had lived upstairs.

By the late 20th century, it had become an extremely dilapidated, long-term group house, inhabited by a constant procession of students living on a shoestring and having a good time.

'It was a fairly derelict place,' Alex says, 'owned by an absentee Greek landlord from Melbourne who didn't care how the place was, as long as the rent kept coming in.'

Alex Bukarica lived there for almost four years and Anthony – who by then was 'Albo' to just about everybody – was a regular visitor, hanging out in the main living room that boasted a pool table and little else.

For left-wing student activists, the house at 11 Liberty Street served as a social hub and alternative to the various pubs where they also spent time – the Sandringham, which ran free music gigs, and the Courthouse in Newtown, the Southern Cross Hotel, later renamed the Strawberry Hills, in Surry Hills and the Trade Union Club.

'It's where people would meet before they went out,' Anthony says of Liberty Street. 'We had a pool table there that I helped pay for. You'd chip in money for things even if you didn't live there.'

The walls of the poolroom were decorated with music posters and postcards. The postcards came from one of the few former residents sentimental enough about his time there to keep in touch with the strangers who had succeeded him.

A hippie bloke with the memorable double-barrelled surname of Garfit-Mottram, the cheerful correspondent's first name has been lost in the mists of time and wafts of smoke. His cards would turn up at random intervals, postmarked Germany.

'He was in a commune in West Berlin and he was just sending us postcards for years and years,' Alex recalls. 'And we'd sort of wait for his postcards.'

The housemates thought they were hilarious, even though they didn't say all that much. 'Just weird hippie sort of messages of love and resistance.'

Former resident Garfit-Mottram had apparently been one of the founders of the Liberty Street set-up. They had certainly left a legacy of communal living.

At any given time, there were about a dozen people residing at number 11 and sometimes more, if you included girlfriends, boyfriends and more casual overnight guests.

Paul Murphy was among the regular visitors too.

'It was a huge house,' he says. 'I don't know how many rooms there were in that house but there were a lot.'

It wasn't the only house the group of friends spent time at but it did have a certain reputation. The household's traditions, dubious though some were, added to the character of the place. Room vacancies were handed down through the networks of the Left. New arrivals did not try to change things. It was a prerequisite to just fit in.

The residents shared food and chores, more or less.

'The standard of food wasn't great,' Alex confesses. Like all students, they ate and drank whatever was cheap. 'A lot of lentils, a lot of mince. Casks of wine. And cheese.'

It was an egalitarian sort of existence, again more or less. 'If you did the cooking you wouldn't have to clean the bathroom or do the shopping.'

The bathroom was its own special place, one of the more memorable areas of the house. The floor was rotten so the group put a wooden palette down as reinforcement and walked on that instead.

A horizontal pipe ran along the wall with just enough space to suspend toothbrushes in the gap between pipe and plaster. The pipe became home to a considerable historical collection of the toothbrushes of housemates past and their assorted guests, like a sort of unsavoury art installation.

'The house of a million toothbrushes' is how Paul Murphy remembers it. There weren't quite that many. But Alex admits there were a lot.

'We had literally, I don't know, dozens of toothbrushes around and no-one could throw the toothbrushes out because you didn't know who they belonged to,' he says. 'It was quite gross actually.'

Liberty Street was an important social centre if not a terribly salubrious one. They kept it as clean as they could but it was, by Anthony's description, 'a hovel'.

At the time, the British TV sitcom about four dreggy undergraduate housemates, *The Young Ones*, was screening in Australia. Although there were a lot more than four living at Liberty Street, its residents felt a certain affinity with Vyvyan, Rick, Neil and Mike.

'It was like us looking at ourselves on the TV,' Alex says.

Number 11 was a party house. Anthony and the others confirm there were some memorable nights.

'I had my 21st birthday there. We had a band in the lounge room.'

On the detail of what went on at Liberty Street parties, they're deliberately vague.

'They were the days when things were a bit more relaxed,' is all Anthony will say.

As was pretty standard in group houses of this kind, the police had occasion to drop by now and then, usually in response to a noise complaint. One particular night, a cop arrived at the unlocked front door on this regular mission but couldn't attract anyone's attention over the music.

'We didn't hear it – the knocking – but he must have knocked first,' Alex says.

When there was no response, the policeman walked in. The front room was scattered with mellow partiers, lolling about in beanbags. The cop just stood there, looking at them, and shaking his head.

The police officer took matters into his own hands.

'He literally stepped over me where I was lying on a beanbag, went to the stereo and turned it down and said, "Keep the music down, will you?"'

And then he left.

'He just saw paperwork.'

The housemates were an eclectic bunch, representing the broad sweep of the political left.

'We had everything from lesbian separatists to communists to Labor Party types . . . hippies, you name it.'

The turnover was reasonably high and fairly swiftly Alex Bukarica became the longest-serving housemate. As such, he had the pick of the rooms and claimed two in the servants' quarters upstairs out the back, at a total cost of $27 a week.

'Which was pretty good.'

Anthony thought so too. Sometimes Alex would loan his quarters when Anthony needed to spend quality time with a companion.

During these university years, the social and political lives of the young leftists became inextricably linked. Fellow activist and 1984 SRC President Helen Spowart recalls it as 'a romantic, left-wing time'.

'Weekend camps that we would go on, the meetings, the conferences – they were a lot of fun in a lot of ways,' Helen says. 'We went to the beach and had meetings down in Newcastle and went to the pub and spoke about politics and went out dancing.'

Anthony's first serious girlfriend was another young activist, Heidi Brown. Heidi was a Science student from Hunters Hill, and before Anthony she had gone out with David Re. After he and Heidi broke up, David went out with Helen.

When Heidi had the opportunity to go interstate to study, Anthony faced a dilemma. 'I toyed with going to Melbourne. She was in Melbourne studying for the last year.'

Anthony applied for a job with the Melbourne-based national office of the Plumbers' Union. It would have been difficult to move, given the distance from his mum and the state of her health, but that particular job would have allowed some work from Sydney.

He didn't get it.

By the time the union offered him an alternative position, he had accepted a job in the office of federal Minister and leading Left figure Tom Uren, in Sydney.

Heidi went south to do a PhD through the Walter and Eliza Hall Institute.

When she moved, the relationship ended.

Anthony's closest mates were all also in the Labor Party. Despite Alex's initial doubts about Anthony's musical taste (a judgement based on his attire that day on the bus – and especially those tennis shoes), the group of friends formed through the ALP Club found they had a love of music in common. They all liked punk.

The Sex Pistols. The Clash. The Jam. They banged their heads to all of it.

There were lefty, folkie artists who were favourites too – The Pogues, Billy Bragg – and good Aussie, indie rock, much of which passed across the stage of the infamous live music venue, Selinas, in the beachside Coogee Bay Hotel.

'Paul Kelly was really emerging then,' Paul says. 'We saw Hunters and Collectors so many times. We saw [them] at Selinas, with Do Re Mi opening.'

Anthony was out two or three nights a week at gigs, venturing as far afield as Punchbowl and Dee Why, as well as to venues nearer home in the inner west.

'When we weren't attending political meetings I was seeing live music,' he says. 'This was a time when there was a vibrant live music scene in Sydney.'

It was a time when some of the gigs were free too – a boon for impoverished university students. They knew there was at least one failsafe gratis good night out each week at the Southern Cross, where the Cockroaches played, every Friday night.

Anthony and friends were also fans of a certain group of protest rockers gaining a strong following: Midnight Oil.

He had first seen the Oils play back when he was still at school at St Mary's. A teacher asked him and his three closest classmates to go along to her younger sister's high-school formal to help make up the male numbers.

'We didn't mind,' says Anthony's school friend, Mark Burgess. 'A few bottles of Passion Pop and we were having fun.'

The shindig was being held at Sydney University and the then newly emerging band Midnight Oil was the entertainment. They quickly became a favourite. 'Albo' developed an 'interesting' dancing style, curiously similar to that of one tall, bald lead singer.

'He idolised Peter Garrett when he was a kid,' Alex says.

Two decades later, Peter would be serving alongside him in Parliament as the federal Labor Member for the seat of Kingsford Smith, after the National Executive fast-tracked his preselection.

Alex and Anthony saw the Oils play at Selinas, too. After one gig, they missed the last bus home and slept on the beach.

Sometimes he made it to the footy to see his beloved Souths play and whenever he got to Melbourne for Australian Union of Students or Young Labor conferences, he'd go to see an Aussie rules match. Despite being a Hawks fan, he would go wherever his Melbourne mates were headed, having struck up a friendship with the likes of Lindsay Tanner, with whom he later also served in Parliament and in the ministry, and Andrew McKenzie.

Anthony would often stay at Lindsay's place in the inner-Melbourne suburb of Carlton. It all helped in forming a political network beyond NSW.

More than a decade later when he was first elected to Parliament, Anthony shared a flat in Canberra's satellite town, Queanbeyan, with Lindsay and Alan Griffin, who co-owned the place, and Alan's adviser Daniel Andrews, who would become Premier of Victoria.

(He didn't stay in the share house for long. When he asked for a key, he was told it wasn't necessary because the door didn't lock. There was nothing worth stealing.)

Those days and nights hanging out at Liberty Street were a good time in their lives. Anthony sums it up. 'Politics. Music. We lived hard, campaigned hard, partied hard, worked hard.' Not always in that order.

There were sometimes deep personal conversations. But in talking to Albo, Alex recalls there being lines he wouldn't cross.

'Not having a father – that was a thing I probably didn't have a decent conversation with him about until he started looking for his dad.'

Having come from a big family himself, Alex sensed it was something Anthony missed.

After Anthony's break-up with Heidi, there were other girlfriends.

He met Joanne Scard through student politics – she was studying Law at Macquarie University and was also active in Young Labor.

Jo Scard, who would eventually run her own government relations and PR agency, had grown up in the Sydney suburb of Arncliffe and went to St George Girls' High School, in the city's south.

Her parents were working-class intellectuals and political activists who worried that the selective state school would expose her to middle-class people who would turn her into a Liberal.

Jo's dad was a trade union official and her mum's side were communists from Scotland.

'We spent a lot of time talking about politics and yelling at the television,' Jo says, 'getting angry about Margaret Thatcher and Ronald Reagan and Malcolm Fraser and the bosses and the whoever else.'

Her parents were members of the Communist Party. 'I mean they weren't radical crazy revolutionary communists. They were democratic communists or democratic socialists . . . They had a dislike for mainstream politics.'

But like her boyfriend, Jo was more attracted to the Labor Party because it had the capacity to form government. She, Anthony and the others in Young Labor threw themselves into the fight.

'There were lots of passionate discussions about politics,' Jo recalls. 'That was sort of what consumed us for years, all of us. We were all in there together. We were all fighting the good fight, whatever that was at the time. That week, that moment, that month, that year.'

And Anthony was a fighter.

'He wanted to fight the Right, he wanted to fight the Liberals, he wanted to fight the people on the council he didn't like,' Jo says. 'He wanted to fight people who made life harder for his mum. He wanted to fight people at university. It was always about fighting . . . It wasn't a vindictive fight, it was a fight with an agenda. It was fighting with a higher purpose – to achieve something.'

All the fighting – by more than just Anthony – sometimes became an end unto itself and obscured those higher purposes for which the fights were being undertaken.

Looking back, many of the group of friends roll their eyes and laugh at their own intensity in those days and at the battles they fought, sometimes for things that actually were important and sometimes because it just seemed that way at the time.

Jo thinks Anthony's fighting instinct came from his upbringing. 'He had to fight from an early age. From the moment he opened his eyes, life was a fight for the whole family.'

In their student world, the young friends all found much to fight for and against.

'It was all that insurgent Left politics,' says Damian O'Connor, another of Anthony's Young Labor colleagues and the one who would succeed him as assistant general secretary in NSW and eventually work in his office.

'It was all about nuclear disarmament and a whole load of causes that aren't so prominent today.'

There were endless meetings. Helen Spowart recalls long, dedicated nights.

'I can remember having meetings around at my house till all hours of the morning and people drinking endless cups of coffee and writing leaflets and writing manifestos and talking about issues and running off pamphlets to hand around at university. It was a really unique, really interesting time.'

Helen had grown up in Annandale, also in the inner west, and moved with her family to Concord while still at school.

In her second year at university, she moved out of home and into a house in Enmore, not far from Liberty Street, and then to another in Newtown. She calls it an 'incredibly formative period'.

Despite the volatility of student politics, for activists on the Labor side in NSW, Young Labor was the main game.

'We were all really idealistic and we wanted to change the world, we wanted to change the Labor Party,' Paul Murphy says. 'We were passionate about Young Labor. We wanted to develop a generation of activists who could achieve some change.'

Anthony was always in amongst it.

'If there was a march, he was there,' says Helen. 'If there was a rally, he was there. If there were elections he was there lobbying, he was there campaigning. He was involved. I suppose we all were, this group of people. Perhaps there were people who disagreed with him on the Left or didn't like him, but I wasn't one of those people. He encouraged me to run for the SRC President and supported me. And I really valued that.'

With his help, Helen both ran and won.

Getting active in Young Labor was what eventually catapulted Anthony into the political big league. Helen wasn't surprised.

'I thought his passion and commitment was inspiring. He inspired me to want to become more involved and I thought he was a lot of fun to be with. When he was around we always had a good time. He could be very wily and rigid about political ideas and that could be a bit frustrating at times when he wouldn't perhaps listen to dissenting views. But overall he was always going to succeed in politics because of that great passion and commitment and ability that he had.'

Along with all the passion and commitment, they still managed to have a laugh.

Paul Murphy recalls how, years later when Anthony had become Assistant General Secretary of the NSW Labor Party,

Paul dared him to include part of a quote from the early-20th-century Italian Marxist Antonio Gramsci in a Labor Party conference speech.

'I think he actually name-checked Gramsci – I think he said "as Gramsci said",' Paul recalls, still amused at the games they played.

Although the challenge was frivolous, Anthony was serious about his interest in Gramsci, who he had discovered in his reading at uni.

'He was particularly interesting as somebody who had gone literally to prison for fighting the fascists, for fighting Mussolini,' Anthony says.

The quote that was the subject of the dare is his favourite.

> How can the present be welded to the future so that while satisfying the urgent necessities of the one, we may work effectively to create and anticipate the other?

He believes it summarises the Labor Party's two main challenges.

'We have a task to deal with things that are immediate – to improve the living standards of people, to look after people's health care, to look after people's education, to look after people's jobs. But the second task while you're doing that is to look to the long term . . . It's the job of government and the state to fulfil both of those things.'

The immediate task Paul had assigned his friend was to get some of the quote into his conference speech. Anthony won a case of Tooheys Old for his efforts.

In the structure of the Labor Party overall, Young Labor had a place at the table. Even if the wider party didn't always take its youth wing seriously, that official place gave Young Labor status. And in NSW in the early 1980s, aside from the Labor Women's organisation which had less influence, it was the only corner of the Labor Party in which the Left ruled.

The Left faction had controlled NSW Young Labor since 1973 and its dedicated adherents fought hard and sometimes bitterly to keep it that way. The party was highly factionalised and the battles between the Left and Right were legendary.

The 1980 bashing of senior Left member and state MP Peter Baldwin in his home in the inner-west suburb of Marrickville was one of the things that had galvanised a young Anthony Albanese to become more involved.

The attack on the NSW parliamentarian, for which nobody was ever charged, was attributed to his campaign against right-wing corruption within the Labor Party in the inner city. It was said to be payback. Allegations of branch stacking were levelled in both directions.

The attack became the symbol of the genuine viciousness of the factional war in NSW Labor.

Until that incident, Anthony hadn't really belonged to a faction. He had joined the Labor Party in his own right as a non-aligned teenage member in 1979 and initially had kept pretty much to himself.

'I went along to Young Labor conferences. Didn't really know anyone. Sat at the back.'

But in that factional atmosphere, nobody gets to sit at the back for long without being lobbied by the various factions and sub-groups always looking to boost their numbers.

Anthony was inclined to vote with the Left and mostly he did, despite his family's connections to the Right through his grandparents' friendship with Pat Hills, who had variously been Sydney Lord Mayor, Opposition Leader and Deputy Premier between the 1950s and 1970s.

'I wanted to make up my own mind rather than just go with the crowd,' Anthony says. 'I certainly voted primarily for Left candidates from what I remember, as a delegate to Young Labor.'

Craig Sahlin's doorknocking exercise in Pyrmont Bridge Road in 1980, which led to his long-term friendship with Anthony, was the far-left's attempt to win the young man to their cause.

In fact, he refused to join any part of the Left for quite a while. Asked why, he laughs as he answers for his teenage self: 'Because I'd met them.'

Back then, he hadn't found the Left leadership – including Peter Baldwin – very inspiring. At the same time, he had been horrified at what had been done to him and horrified all over again when he saw how his own party colleagues treated him afterwards.

Despite the fact that Peter Baldwin was a parliamentarian – a member of the Legislative Council – who had been brutally attacked, at the first Young Labor conference after the incident, he was jeered.

'He went up the middle through the crowd of delegates and the right wing were booing him and carrying on,' Anthony says. 'He had been bashed basically and almost killed and for them to treat him with absolutely no respect was pretty shocking, I thought.'

Peter Baldwin would later shift into federal politics and serve there in Parliament until 1998, when he retired and helped devise an online tool for modelling and mapping public-policy debates, known as Debategraph.

On the Debategraph website, he mused about his decision to leave representative politics after 22 years.

'The experience of Opposition led me – belatedly – to the conclusion that politics was an occupation for which I was cognitively and psychologically ill-suited,' he wrote. 'So I left.'

He then adds: '(a bit reminiscent of the scene in a film about Soviet master-spy Kim Philby, where his fellow-spy Guy Burgess is depicted agonising about the rightness of his support for communism while in the process of defecting to the Soviet Union after a long spying career).'

Despite what he'd had to endure, it wasn't Peter Baldwin who most impressed Anthony at that conference, but the state's then Attorney-General and Housing and Aboriginal Affairs Minister, Frank Walker.

Frank gave a speech on Indigenous land rights, housing and equality. Anthony thought it was fantastically progressive.

'He was the first person at the senior level that I'd seen in person in the party that I was impressed and inspired by. He was a big reformer. He wasn't just occupying the space.'

It made him want to engage more with the party and its activities. In 1982, as Anthony entered his second year of university and ran for the Student Representative Council on campus, he also put his hand up for a role in Young Labor.

He had joined the Young Labor Association in the inner-city electorate of Sydney and the previous year had served on Young Labor's economic committee, which fed ideas into the party's statewide policy debate. He was elected convenor of the economic policy committee and began what would become an upward trajectory through the complicated structure that was the Labor Party's left wing.

Anthony's eventual alignment with Frank Walker and his associates would see him positioned on one side of an enduring split in the Left, with some of his best friends – and others who would become his long-time enemies – on the other.

CHAPTER 9

Father Figure

When Anthony interviewed for a job on Tom Uren's electorate staff, he was nervous. Tom was a towering figure in the Left and beyond – a true Labor hero who had endured the deprivations of a prisoner-of-war camp in World War II and then gone into politics, fighting doggedly for causes from nuclear nonproliferation to urban infrastructure.

Anthony had first met him when Tom doorknocked number 41 Pyrmont Bridge Road, seeking support for fellow left-winger Ann Catling in the 1981 preselection contest against Peter Baldwin for the electorate of Sydney, into which Camperdown fell.

Three years on, when Anthony finally completed his university degree a year later than he anticipated, a vacancy arose in Tom's office. It wasn't advertised. Through the networks of the Labor Left, he was urged to apply.

At the time, Anthony's mind was on Melbourne. He'd been trying to work out if he should follow Heidi south, but the path wasn't proving simple or smooth. Suddenly here was an amazing potential opportunity in Sydney in the office of someone he admired. He couldn't miss the chance and put in an application.

'I was very overawed,' he says of the job interview. Leaving Tom's office, he wasn't sure how he had fared. As he was heading for the door, Tom's adviser, Frances Rees, asked, 'When can you start?'

Suddenly it dawned on him that he wasn't in a competitive situation at all. He was 'just being checked out'.

'I don't think other people were being interviewed,' he says, 32 years later. 'It was just to see whether Tom thought I was okay. And clearly he did.'

Looking back, it all seemed a bit pre-ordained. And that's because it was.

In the early 1980s, the elders of the NSW Labor Left used to meet regularly to survey the national political landscape and sort out collectively whatever problems needed addressing. They were the faction's old guard and came to their task from four powerful corners of the party.

Tom Uren was in the House of Representatives for the Western Sydney seat of Reid and in the federal ministry. Arthur Gietzelt, in the Senate, was organisational leader of the national Left and on the ALP's national executive. Jack Ferguson, a Labor man with solid working-class roots (and who headed what would become a political dynasty involving his three sons Martin, Laurie and Andrew), was Deputy Premier of NSW under Neville Wran.

And Bruce Childs, also in the Senate, was the former Assistant General Secretary of the NSW ALP – the inaugural occupant of the sole position that the Right-dominated branch had conceded to create for the Left in the party's administrative headquarters in Sydney's Sussex Street.

The four men would meet weekly, on a Friday, often in Jack Ferguson's office at State Parliament or in a local restaurant, their location being chosen for the convenience of whoever was busiest that day. A federal ministerial travel schedule meant Tom didn't always make it but got there when he could.

Among their regular agenda items, the men discussed who was showing promise in the Left among those youngsters coming up through the universities or the trade-union movement. They would analyse the various skills and struggles of these emerging leaders and talk about what they could do to nurture them.

'If you're not training your apprentices, then you're not a proper leadership,' the last surviving member of the quartet, Bruce Childs, observed in 2016.

As Anthony Albanese began to make a name for himself in Labor circles in the early 1980s, he was one of the up-and-comers they discussed.

The young Albanese lad was a firebrand they felt was showing great potential. But they all believed he needed guidance. Aware of his family circumstances, the men talked about how the absence of a father meant Anthony lacked a good, strong, male role model.

'He had the problem in that he was living with his mother and he didn't have a father, in practice,' says Bruce. 'So the real danger was he was just a bit too fiery and he needed a father figure.'

They decided to provide one, to keep him on track. 'We agreed that Tom was just the right person.'

Tom Uren was a big bloke. In his younger life, he'd been a competitive swimmer and professional boxer and had played rugby league for Manly Warringah. As Bruce puts it, he was 'a man's man, physically' and that helped.

'But the main thing is that he wouldn't stand any nonsense.'

Imbued with the toughness and resilience which had seen him survive hellish deprivations at the hands of the Japanese on the Thai-Burma railway, Tom set out to hire Anthony and school him in politics and in life.

Tom had three children: Heather and Michael with his first wife, Patricia, and Ruby, through his marriage to Christine Logan. After starting out as his research officer, Anthony became a de facto fourth.

'Anthony was like his son,' Bruce explains. 'But his political son.'

Working for Tom opened yet another world to the now-twenty-something young man from Camperdown. Soon he was researching and writing reports and policy proposals, from snapshots of the economy for Tom's electors through his Federal Electorate Council to a Left position paper on dividend imputation, ahead of the tax summit Prime Minister Bob Hawke and his Treasurer Paul Keating were to convene in 1985.

Anthony would also attend meetings of two of Labor's caucus committees – one on foreign affairs and defence, the other on economics – either with Tom or on his behalf, taking notes and summarising the issues of special relevance to his boss.

He was gainfully employed, on a mountainous learning curve and taking early steps on the path to what would become his vocation, something about which his boss had a more structured idea than he did. Initially, Anthony was just focused on the experience.

The first time he had to go to Canberra to accompany Tom to committee meetings as his note-taker, a Commonwealth car came to collect him in Pyrmont Bridge Road. Nothing like it had ever happened to him before – or to the neighbourhood.

'A white car out in Camperdown, picking up a bloke and taking him to the airport!' Anthony says. 'No one in Camperdown went to the airport.'

It was also his first time on a plane. Upon arrival in the national capital, he was whisked off to the white wedding cake of a Parliament – the original one – with its view across the lake to the War Memorial, the line of sight arranged by Walter Burley Griffin's prize-winning design. Anthony was dazzled by the grandness and importance of it all and struggled to focus on the job he'd been brought there to do.

When Anthony walked into the committee room, Tom called him over to take a seat and asked how he was.

'I just blurted out this big spiel about how exciting it was to go on a plane – and a car to pick you up,' Anthony says. 'I told him about how exciting it was – that my mum and all the neighbours came out to look at this car.'

Anthony remembers his manic burbling as a turning point in their relationship, if a slightly embarrassing one.

'He thought I was okay from that point. By the fact I was just this excited kid.'

In his 1994 memoir *Straight Left*, Tom wrote about taking on the young protégé with his militant reputation.

'When I first put him on my staff some of my comrades on the Left said, "Oh, you're putting a young Trot on your staff",' he wrote.

But Tom, more pragmatist than ideologue, wasn't convinced the young man was as far Left as that.

'I told them: "I haven't! I don't think you're right." For the first year or two I never really badgered him. I would have a talk with him occasionally, and just observe him, but I watched him a lot more than he realised.'

What he observed prompted Tom Uren to predict big things for the young man, of whom he became deeply fond.

'I think that for someone still in his late twenties, he has enormous maturity,' he wrote ahead of his book's publication. 'And I feel that, in time, he will be a very great leader of the Labor Party and particularly the Left because he has such a balanced understanding of the labour movement.'

Anthony speaks of his mentor with deep affection.

'He led such an extraordinary life and was a window into a previous generation that had done it so tough,' he says of Tom.

'He was wise. He would counsel me that "you have to improve yourself and learn every day".'

Tom also grew very fond of Anthony's mother, Maryanne Albanese, with whom he had some things in common. After the war and almost two decades before Maryanne had done the same, Tom had made a sea voyage to the United Kingdom. He had worked for his own shipboard passage, hoping to resurrect his boxing career in England, a dream that gave way to politics in the end. Tom understood what that adventure was like.

He was especially conscious of Maryanne's struggles, both with her health and as a single mother. With his labourer father becoming unemployed as the Depression struck, Tom's own mother, who worked as a barmaid, had carried much of the burden of raising her sons, who grew up in working-class Balmain and later at Harbord on the northern beaches.

Like Anthony, Tom reserved special wells of love and admiration for his own mother. While he also loved and was proud of his father, he credited her with making him who he was.

'I've always felt that my mother has given me that strength and that tenacity and that drive and that warmth and affection and love in my life,' Tom told interviewer Robin Hughes, for the Australian Biography project in 1996.

As he and Anthony became closer, Tom would sometimes stop in to visit Maryanne and share a cuppa. He was full of respect for the sacrifices she had made for her son.

'He comes from an Irish-Italian working-class background,' Tom wrote of Anthony in *Straight Left*. 'He is very considerate to his mother who reared him, and I suppose I have a kind of fatherly love for him.'

The feeling was mutual.

'Tom was tough as they come but so gentle,' Anthony says. 'He spoke of love unlike any other man I have known. Given his war experience, I found it remarkable that he lived by Martin Luther King's creed, "There is no progress in hate." He loved his fellow humans. And I loved him.'

When Tom died in the early hours of Australia Day, 2015, Anthony already knew he was expected to be master of ceremonies at the funeral service to honour his exceptional life.

In fact, he had known it for some time, long before the visits to the hospice to spend time with the man whose mental agility was barely diminished – and who was still having friends assist with in-bed workouts and throwing cross-chest air punches at the age of 93.

'He told me I would be MC at this celebration more than a decade ago,' Anthony told those gathered at the Sydney Town Hall on a melancholy February afternoon in 2015.

Through two hours of speeches and songs, Anthony wrestled down the tears that came and went. In attendance were the Governor-General, NSW Governor and former Governor, three former prime ministers, one fellow former prisoner of war in Sir John Carrick, and senior Labor figures of current and past generations. Anthony's partner, Carmel Tebbutt, and son, Nathan, were there, and Tom's beloved family, supported by hundreds and hundreds of comrades, both friends and strangers.

In contrast with the uncontrollable collapse in his composure at the service for his mum at St Joseph's 13 years earlier, this time Anthony determinedly did not break down.

'We've gathered here to celebrate the life of a truly extraordinary man,' he told the gathering. 'A big man in stature, a big man in ideas and a man with a big heart. Those closest to him loved him dearly. For me, of course, he was not just a political mentor but the closest I have had to a father figure in my life.'

There had been other men who had stepped in to fill whatever father-shaped gap there may have been at various stages in the life of the young Anthony. As a child, he'd been invited away for weekends with local families keen to help out when his mother's illness or hospitalisation was making life especially hard.

Among them were Harold and Dot See, who lived a few doors up with their daughters, Lorraine and Christine. Harold's brother Bobby was a neighbour too, living alone at the other end of the dwellings, around the corner near Dudley's shop.

When Anthony was seven or eight, the See girls – who were then in their early teens – would babysit.

'They were [among] the people who introduced me to music,' says the MP and amateur DJ of his teenage babysitters, more than four decades on.

Harold and Dot were Labor Party members and the See family would sometimes go up to the Central Coast and take Anthony with them. Other neighbours would do the same.

Bill McMillan was an alderman on the Sydney City Council and he and wife Edna lived in the flats. They had no children of their own and they, too, would offer to take Anthony up the coast when they were going away.

In March 1975, three weeks after Anthony's 12th birthday, they took him up to Gosford for what was to have been a two-night stay. But the day after they arrived, 51-year-old Bill collapsed. They knew there was a nurse in the house across the road and a panic-stricken Anthony was sent to get her.

'I had to run for a neighbour, to a nurse and yell,' he recounts. 'I said, "There's something wrong with Bill."'

They couldn't revive him.

'It was incredibly traumatic. The ambulance came. He died.'

Anthony was taken back to Sydney, distraught. His surprised mother found him knocking at the door, puzzled as to why he was home a day early. He had to explain that 'Uncle Bill' had died in front of him.

They went to his funeral at the Catholic church in Pyrmont, and by then word had spread about Anthony having witnessed the alderman's passing.

'People were going, "Is he okay?" People were worried about me.'

The incident had a searing impact on him. He has never forgotten it.

Aside from his aunts and cousins and his Uncle Johnny, who visited his nephew and was responsible for the prized Malvern Star bicycle, one other man made a particular effort to take on some father-type duties for the young boy who didn't have one.

Georgia and Russell Gear lived in the north-western Sydney suburb of West Ryde, about 15 kilometres from Camperdown across the Parramatta River.

A friend of Anthony's Aunt Lenore, Georgia had moved in with the Ellerys at number 41 during the early 1960s, after splitting up with her first husband. Her temporary stay of two weeks stretched to months and she grew close to the family, including her friend's sister's little boy, Anthony.

Even after she moved out and remarried, Georgia stayed in touch. She and husband Russell didn't have children of their own and they enjoyed spending time with the lad.

'They were very good to me,' Anthony says.

Russell was a mechanic and a volunteer with the coastal patrol. He and his brothers, who all lived around the same area, built their own boats.

'They were all very blokey, so it was quite good,' Anthony says. Now and then, Russell would take him out on the harbour when he was on patrol. It was pretty exciting for a little kid.

'They used to take me to the Sydney-to-Hobart yacht race. I'd go out on the boat.'

Their job on the water on Boxing Day was to keep the spectator craft away from the competing yachts. He loved it.

When he reached his early teens, they would take him for weekends away. On one trip to Bathurst, a regional centre two-and-a-half-hours' drive west of Sydney through the Blue Mountains, Russell and his mates taught Anthony to ride a motorcycle.

'They had this little Bridgestone 100,' he recalls. It was

a trail bike, like the one Mike and Mal Leyland had on the popular TV series *Ask the Leyland Brothers*.

'I learned to ride a motorbike on that.' He pauses and smiles. 'My mother didn't know about that.'

It was just as well. They were crazy weekends. While the women cooked and caught up, the blokes went off and played their own version of Demolition Derby, taking Anthony with them.

'I just remember them being complete maniacs. They were these blokes – they were all truckies – and they'd go up there and deliberately smash into each other. And I just remember it being very male . . . I went a couple of times and I remember there were always accidents – broken legs.'

He survived largely unscathed and was glad for the adult male company.

It was around this time that his mother told him the truth about his parentage. He concedes that, at that point, his heart hardened against his absent father.

'My father I didn't give a second thought to,' he says. 'I didn't have one. I thought he was dead and he wasn't discussed. We didn't mark his birthday. There weren't any photos of him. Before and after the discussion with my mother, the significance of my father was not something that I thought greatly about. I'm not saying I never thought about it but it was not a factor in my life.'

When it came to that subject, a protective layer was forming itself around the young Anthony's emotions.

'He'd shown no care for me,' he says. 'I was a pretty damn tough 14-year-old.'

Not, though, when it came to his mother, the person he calls 'my light'. He adored her.

'Her love was very unconditional.'

In a similar way, he would grow to love his boss and mentor, Tom Uren – the man who had most successfully filled the empty space Anthony denied existed but others could see, the space left by the absent man he only knew as a name: Carlo Albanese.

While Tom's influence cemented Anthony's values and ways of practising his politics, the values themselves were already there, courtesy of his mother and the way she'd brought him up.

In political terms, Maryanne Albanese was a progressive who didn't much heed factional delineations. That didn't mean she was unaware of their influence or of the need to steer clear of certain people.

Anthony recalls noting this as a child, while attending a meeting of his mother's Camperdown branch, held on the second Wednesday night of the month at Chrissie Cotter Hall in Pidcock Street, near Camperdown Oval.

It was a small branch – no more than 30–40 members – and mostly focused on local issues. If a local councillor attended, that was a big night. Members of Parliament hardly ever did.

'I was fascinated,' he says of the goings-on in the inner-city branch. 'And at a meeting very early on, Tom Domican was [there]. It was one of the first meetings I went to. And I remember Mum saying, "Don't go near that man."'

Tom Domican worked for Marrickville mayor John Harrison as a driver and enforcer of sorts. He was a member of the notorious Enmore branch, whose falsified membership books Peter Baldwin would uncover and force action upon – a move that, along with the Left's own efforts at branch-stacking, is believed to have led to his bashing. Domican would be accused of involvement with the bashing – something he would continue to categorically deny – with the culprits never being identified.

This particular appearance at the Camperdown branch meeting was years before that and Anthony can't remember what the man with the violent reputation was doing there, just that even then his mother wanted her son to stay away from him.

Maryanne was a woman of strong convictions. Her faith was at the heart of her views and while that faith didn't necessarily embed itself in her son's heart, the belief system did.

'Principles of Catholic social justice are very strong and progressive,' Anthony says. 'The rights of women and Aboriginals and standing up for the battler. And my mum's values were you treat everyone with respect.'

Anthony is dubious about some of the doctrines of the church and some of the biblical details of the life and activity of Jesus underpinning the Christian faith. Asked if he believes in God, he doesn't give a yes or no answer.

'I have a belief in some form of spirituality but I think that's something that's really private. I've never gone on about it publicly.'

He reserves special praise for the pontiff. 'I do believe that Pope Francis is the most outstanding voice for the poor and marginalised to emerge this century.'

As for his faith in the Labor Party, Anthony had a less benign view of factionalism than his mother. He had watched the warfare erupt at branch level over corruption in the inner city, as the '70s gave way to the '80s. And he had come to the conclusion that you had to fight faction with faction.

By the time he took the job with Tom, Anthony was already in the Left. It was Bruce Childs' son, Stephen, who had finally persuaded him to join.

Some time after Craig Sahlin had come doorknocking on behalf of the far-left Gould Group, Stephen Childs talked Anthony into a more mainstream factional allegiance.

'We sat in a car outside my house for about an hour and a half,' says Anthony, 'and he convinced me to join the Young Labor left faction, the Radical Leadership Group as it was called.'

Despite its name, the RLG was less radical than those on the Left fringes and was the junior faction of the NSW Left.

Arthur Gietzelt had driven the formation of the Left in the 1950s in the wake of the Labor split, to counter the rise of the industrially dominated Catholic Right in the form of the Democratic Labor Party and National Civic Council.

The Left's administrative body became known as the Combined Unions and Branches Steering Committee, or the Steering Committee for short.

It developed a complicated structure designed to keep its base in touch with its leadership, a system of zones from which delegates were elected to attend conferences and fill administrative positions within the Left, Young Labor and the state party. From there were chosen those who would represent the state and the faction in the Labor Party nationally.

While at times Anthony was frustrated with his faction in both its junior and senior forms, he insists he was never tempted to move further Left to the more fringe groups.

'No,' he says. 'I couldn't relate to them at all.'

He was also never inclined to leave altogether to join one of the other smaller parties claiming space on the Left spectrum.

As the Member for Grayndler fighting for re-election after two decades in office in 2016, he would put his greatest latter-day electoral enemies, the Greens, in the same category as those fringe groups.

He has held to a principle he considers fundamental to his politics: you don't change teams.

'Labor is a part of who I am. It's not just a sort of belief. It's part of who you are. Like you didn't contemplate going for a team other than South Sydney either.

'Labor are the party that can form government. Why wouldn't you want to be a part of determining the policy of people who can actually be in government, rather than just protest? That to me was just an absolute gut instinct that was always there.'

*

Along with mentoring him in the ways of politics, Tom encouraged Anthony to gain life experience too, including travel. When his friend Jeremy Fisher made plans to go to Vanuatu on holiday in 1986, Anthony decided to go with him. He could get leave, and with a full-time income he could afford a trip.

Jeremy's partner, Craig Sahlin, wasn't able to go. (The two eventually broke up and, as friends do in such circumstances, Anthony had to navigate the complexities of remaining loyal to both.)

It was his first trip overseas, 10 days in a non-English-speaking country that was poorer than the worst of what he had seen of his own.

The two stayed at the Le Lagon resort in Port Vila on a package deal, availing themselves of the complimentary drinks on the flight over and the hotel's pool facilities once there.

Echoing Craig's observations of Anthony's non-judgement on matters of sexuality, Jeremy says it didn't faze Anthony that he was sharing a room with a gay man. 'He didn't have any issues about that at all.'

In a neat twist on all those nights that a boisterous Anthony and Craig had kept full-time-employee Jeremy awake with their student lifestyle back at university, Anthony proved keen on his sleep.

'Anthony had been working very hard so he was sleeping in,' Jeremy says. 'I was keen to do other things so I was always pestering him to wake up early.'

They did manage a few holiday adventures, sampling the fare at local restaurants including, at one stage, flying fox – sweet and gamey.

They climbed the Tanna volcano, flying from Port Vila in a tiny aircraft that landed on a grassy cliff-top airstrip and took off again, straight out over the edge and into the air in a dramatic, stomach-turning manoeuvre.

They also had a day on the golf course. Their game shouldn't have taken as long as it did, but neither was terribly good and

Jeremy insists he was worse. 'We had taken most of the day to play about nine holes,' he says.

The enterprising local children were hanging around the golf course, collecting up the balls and selling them back to hapless tourists.

Jeremy and Anthony observed the country's poverty and lack of the most basic infrastructure. Jeremy had travelled before – to the Philippines, Indonesia and Sri Lanka – but Vanuatu was less well-equipped than any of them. 'The villages were very basic and just were lacking in a lot of what we'd take for granted,' he says.

Anthony's second opportunity for travel was into Asia and would come courtesy of his work and of Tom himself. In 1987, the veteran former soldier and politician arranged for Anthony to accompany him on what would be his final trip before he left the ministry for the backbench ahead of retirement three years later. It was a visit to Singapore, Thailand, Laos and Vietnam.

That privilege and responsibility would normally go to someone more senior than the young researcher. But Tom insisted that Anthony should go.

'He wanted me to have the experience,' Anthony says. 'He very much took the need for me to grow and develop – that mentoring role – very seriously.'

In *Straight Left*, Tom would record the trip as having cemented their personal relationship. And it was another eye-opening experience for his young charge.

'The trip . . . brought us much closer and opened and developed our understanding of one another,' Tom wrote. 'We are true comrades. I will never forget smiling at the young class-conscious Anthony breakfasting at Raffles hotel in Singapore.'

In Bangkok, Tom represented Australia at a meeting of the Economic and Social Commission for Asia and the Pacific, where he delivered a speech he'd asked Anthony to write.

The speech, peppered with typically forthright language, caused tension between Tom and the Department of Foreign

Affairs officials also attending, because it replaced the more benign version they had prepared.

Tom had a particularly strong view about the role of the Khmer Rouge in Cambodia, which was then operating out of Thailand as a government in exile. He wanted to express it.

Key Khmer Rouge officials had fled to Thailand when the Vietnamese army had toppled their government in 1979, ending the four-year genocidal rampage of Khmer Rouge leader Pol Pot.

In 1985, the Vietnam-installed government in Phnom Penh had given way to the government of the Cambodian People's Party, led by former Khmer Rouge commander Hun Sen, but the UN did not yet recognise it.

So, one of the Khmer Rouge's most powerful exiled officials, Khieu Samphan, was attending the conference as his country's representative. He would be convicted 30 years later of crimes against humanity for his role in the Cambodian genocide.

When Khieu Samphan rose to speak, Tom walked out. That didn't go down well with the nervous Australian officials either.

'We had argy-bargy over whether we should do that,' Anthony says. '[Tom] said, "I'm not listening to murderers," and he walked out. A few other countries walked out too.'

The Thailand leg of the trip was especially important to Tom, but for a different reason. They were to attend the ANZAC Day commemorations and the dedication of the newly rediscovered Hellfire Pass on the Thai-Burma railway, where Tom and his fellow soldiers had suffered at the hands of the Japanese army and where so many of his mates had died.

'That was quite a remarkable emotional experience, Hellfire Pass and all the diggers,' Anthony recalls.

On the plane on the way over, Tom had told Anthony about his experience there during the war. It was an extremely intense and moving conversation and the only time Tom ever talked to him about the realities of being a POW.

'It was an enormous privilege to develop a close relationship with Tom,' Anthony says. 'You learn from history and Tom was living history.'

From Bangkok, they travelled by car to Kanchanaburi, taking with them Tom's fellow former POW and former Liberal MP, Sir John Carrick, who had travelled to Thailand for the ceremony. On the way, the two men talked about the war. Anthony listened to their stories.

On ANZAC Day, they all joined the other veterans at the dawn service at Kanchanaburi War Cemetery, and the following day attended the commemoration at Hellfire Pass. The men shared a drink at the site of Tom's former camp.

Anthony was honoured to meet some of the men with whom Tom had served, including 'Blue' Butterworth and their famous leader, the surgeon Sir Edward 'Weary' Dunlop. Anthony was struck by their strength and, at that moment, their vulnerability.

'They weren't angry,' he says. 'They had just come through such extraordinary hardship without bitterness. They were just remarkable. I think you had to have a real strength of inner character to survive and these were the ones who did.'

It felt like a window on history.

'You just had that sense of moment. It was an extraordinary event.'

More than a few of the former POWs who attended told Anthony they owed the ultimate debt to Tom Uren.

'One after the other, [they told] extraordinary stories that he hadn't told me about. One said, "I was about to be bayoneted and Tom stood in between the guard and me" . . . He was regarded as a hero amongst heroes.'

During the visit, the young researcher accompanied Sir John Carrick on a trip up the River Kwai and they talked for hours about what it had been like in those terrible years.

Anthony recorded some of his thoughts in a travel diary.

'It was hard to imagine conflict in such a peaceful, tranquil environment,' he wrote.

Thereafter, he reserved a particular respect for the revered Liberal Party elder statesman.

Anthony would recall that day as he singled out the then-frail Sir John for special acknowledgement at Tom's funeral 30 years later, in sincere thanks for his attendance.

Back in the Thai capital in 1987, Tom and Anthony also attended the local premiere of the Australian blockbuster movie *Crocodile Dundee*, at which Tom introduced Anthony to Ingrid Hayden, whose father was Tom's friend and colleague, the Foreign Minister, Bill Hayden. Bill had arranged in advance with Tom for Ingrid to tag along on the Vietnam leg of their journey and to make a short side trip to Cambodia.

Australia's non-recognition of the Hun Sen Government meant Cambodia was somewhere Tom, in his official capacity, couldn't go, so it was suggested that Anthony might like to join her. His only previous overseas experience having been largely by a resort pool in Vanuatu, he was happy to grab an opportunity to get to Cambodia. Their visas were organised before they left home and before they had even met. They would visit Phnom Penh and Siem Reap and then return to Ho Chi Minh City to meet up with Tom for the homeward journey.

From Bangkok, the official party plus Ingrid headed north, first to Vientiane in Laos and then on to Hanoi. After spending 30 April in Hanoi, the day the Vietnamese call Victory Day or Reunification Day marking the 1975 fall of Saigon, and then May Day the day after, Anthony and Ingrid left Tom to fly on ahead to Ho Chi Minh City.

Because of Ingrid's father's status, the Cambodian Government had insisted on making the travel arrangements for their side trip and seizing the opportunity for some international PR by hosting the young travellers as official guests.

If the Foreign Affairs officials had been upset about the speech and the walkout, they must have had a coronary over this.

Oblivious to any diplomatic palpitations, Anthony and Ingrid travelled from Ho Chi Minh City to Phnom Penh by road in a four-car convoy, complete with armed security. The road had a bad reputation for rebel activity.

The two Australians were put in separate cars for the trip.

'In case one of us got blown up, I think,' Anthony says decades on, a bit incredulous at his own laissez-faire attitude. 'It was pretty serious.'

In Phnom Penh, they were given the red-carpet treatment and shown to a government guesthouse. Their official guides took them to see the notorious Tuol Sleng prison, which would later become the genocide museum, and the area known as the killing fields, then only a few years old.

The next day, they were flown to Siem Reap to see the world-famous temples at Angkor Wat. They would also be taken to a crocodile farm, where the bones of child victims of the Khmer Rouge had been found – extra reinforcement of the new government's message about the horrors that were past.

When Anthony inquired about the duration of the flight on what was to be a single-day round trip, the answer began with the words 'if we land'.

'If?' he queried.

The guides explained that now and then, Khmer Rouge guerrillas would take the airport.

'How do you know if they've taken the airport?' he asked, mildly alarmed at the prospect of landing amongst murderous insurgents.

'They let us know,' came the unfazed reply. The plane landed without drama.

As they toured the temple site inside a four-point security cordon, they heard the unmistakeable sound of automatic rifle fire.

'What's that?' they asked their guides.

'Mosquitos,' one replied. 'We have big mosquitos.'

'And they just laughed,' Anthony says.

On return to Phnom Penh, they were taken to meet the Cambodian Prime Minister, Hun Sen, who upon taking office in 1985 had been the world's youngest head of government at just 32.

Anthony looks back now and it all seems bizarre. Here was a 24-year-old research officer and the Foreign Minister's daughter, a year younger, invited over to the presidential palace for a chat with the 35-year-old leader of a government with whom Australia was not friendly.

'It was an amazing experience,' he says. 'It was very cordial. I remember I had to make it very clear that I wasn't the Australian Government's representative.'

They spoke for over an hour and Anthony took copious notes, which he handed to Bill Hayden's office on return.

It wasn't the only skill he honed in the office of Tom Uren.

CHAPTER 10

Enemy of My Enemy

Under Tom Uren's watchful eye, Anthony's rise in the Labor Party continued. He had become more and more active in Young Labor – the breeding ground for many who would go on to representative politics at the local, state and federal level.

While the Right ruled the Labor Party overall in NSW and federally, the Left had dominated NSW Young Labor since 1973. The early '80s saw the Left-Right divisions explode.

They also heralded the emergence of divisions within the Left itself, with two groups emerging, galvanising around Frank Walker on one side and Jack Ferguson on the other, later to be succeeded by fellow state parliamentarian and Wran Government Minister Rodney Cavalier. These groups would become known respectively as the 'hard' and 'soft' Left.

Among their differences, they held contrasting views on the role and influence of unions in the ALP. (Whether the differences were ever genuinely ideological or mostly about personalities and power is the subject of ongoing debate.)

Frank Walker's 'hard' Left was more closely associated with the unions and campaigned more on contentious international issues, while the 'soft' Left was based more around branch members and domestic concerns.

The 'hard' Left had the backing of the Amalgamated Metal Workers' Union while the Federated Miscellaneous Workers' Union supported Jack Ferguson and Rodney Cavalier's 'soft' group.

Members of the hard Left accused the soft Left of running an intellectualist agenda inside the faction and not properly representing the interests of working people. Some in the soft Left believed then – and in 2016, still – that this argument was little more than an excuse to increase the hard Left's power by persuading small, obscure disengaged unions to become involved and back its candidates.

Through his association with Frank Walker, Anthony Albanese was part of the hard Left and became Frank's natural successor as its leader. Among those on the other side were the sons of Tom Uren's mate Jack Ferguson: Laurie, Martin and Andrew. Martin was secretary of the FMWU.

Anthony's first direct clash with the Ferguson sons had come via a 1984 ballot for the position of assistant secretary of the Combined Unions and Branches Steering Committee in which the eldest Ferguson, Laurie, was a candidate.

Laurie was running against the assistant secretary of the Printed and Kindred Industries Union, John McCarthy. At the time, Laurie Ferguson was a state parliamentarian. It was the closest possible result. Laurie lost 52 to 51.

'I went along to this meeting and I voted for John McCarthy and he won by one vote,' Anthony says. 'And because I voted the wrong way in a ballot for an obscure position that I thought about for two seconds, Laurie Ferguson has been an enemy ever since. Thirty years.'

Curiously, Laurie Ferguson remembered the contest as having been against Anthony directly. (In 2016, he concedes his memory is faulty on that point and it was John McCarthy who beat him.)

In any event, he clearly associates Anthony directly with his loss. Anthony says he knew little about either man before the vote, but what he knew of Laurie had not especially impressed him. He insists his decision was motivated by little more than that.

Laurie isn't convinced. He believes it was a part of what would become the hard Left's pro-union agenda. The soft Left's rejection of arguments that it was anti-union was not helped by Rodney Cavalier's rhetoric on industrial issues when he became NSW Education Minister in 1984.

'They were able to further personify us as against the unions, against the workers,' Laurie says.

He attributes the hard Left's strategy to Ian Macdonald, a left-winger Arthur Gietzelt had recruited from Victoria in the '70s, who was then working in Frank Walker's ministerial office and would eventually enter State Parliament himself, rise into the ministry and in 2012 face an Independent Commission Against Corruption investigation which would lead to findings of corruption against him.

As a result of the inquiry, Anthony's factional association with Ian Macdonald through the hard Left would be scrutinised publicly and in more detail.

In 1987, Tom Uren would have his own run-in with the Fergusons, when Martin sought a meeting with him and told Tom he had to quit Parliament to make way for his brother Laurie in the seat of Reid.

In his book, *Straight Left*, Tom details how Martin told him he had heard that Tom had been rubbishing him, Laurie and their father, and that if it came down to a direct contest, Laurie could muster enough support in the branches to defeat him.

According to Tom's written version, he dismissed the 'gossip', saying Laurie would not have been his choice for Reid but would probably win preselection when he retired (which, by implication, he did not intend to do just yet).

Tom wrote that Martin told him, 'The family will decide.'

'I was so appalled I ended the discussion there and then,' Tom wrote. '. . . I thought he was talking about some mafia decision. I was deeply hurt.'

The Ferguson version is that Tom left part of the conversation out of his book – the part in which he retorted to Martin that he had friends in the Right and that there wouldn't be a preselection contest.

Despite Martin's demand, Tom Uren would remain the Member for Reid until February 1990, when Laurie Ferguson would succeed him, as he predicted.

In his memoir, Tom wrote that the incident created 'aloofness' between him and the Ferguson clan, except Andrew with whom he had no quarrel.

It didn't help relations between the Fergusons and Anthony Albanese, either.

As the internal ructions were stirring within the Left, relations with the Right weren't exactly rosy. In 1985, as Anthony was preparing to run for President of NSW Young Labor, the Right began stacking the upcoming annual conference with right-wing delegates in an all-out bid for a hostile takeover.

When the NSW Left faction's executive, the Combined Unions and Branches Steering Committee, met ahead of the 1985 Young Labor Council's conference, secretary Delcia Kite reported as a fait accompli that the faction was going to lose control of the party's youth wing.

'She said, "Oh, you know we've lost Young Labor,"' Anthony recalls. 'And I was sitting there and I went, "Hang on."'

Anthony was to be the Left's candidate for NSW Young Labor President, standing against the Right's John Hatzistergos, who would go on to become Attorney-General in the NSW Government and later a District Court judge.

Anthony rejected the Left leadership's predictions of certain defeat. He thought they were giving in too easily.

'I stood up and said, "No, we're going to win." And I had an argument where she said, "No, no, we've had a look and you're not going to win." And I said, "Well, we will."'

In order to do that, they had to respond to the Right's rise in numbers by getting more Left sympathisers credentialed to the council and ensure they voted the Left's way.

The council was comprised of delegates from ALP branches across NSW, Young Labor Associations (YLAs) and affiliated trade unions. Each branch and association was entitled to send two delegates. Each union could send four.

Some had so few members who were young enough to qualify that those who fitted the bill were arbitrarily elected with little say in it. The process didn't always generate the enthusiasm required to actually attend, particularly among those who didn't know other members or faced long-distance travel to get there.

Provided they had the right credentials beforehand, all of the delegates were entitled to vote. But not each of these institutions always filled its delegate quota, for reasons ranging from lack of motivation to lack of money. So the Left went into overdrive to get as many of the Left-leaning among them as possible to turn up.

'We got onto all the country people who they didn't think would come and we encouraged them to come,' Anthony says. 'We offered them places to stay.'

As they dragged in every youth delegate they could find in the union movement, the branches and the YLAs, they counted their numbers, listing each potential delegate in one of four categories: category one was a solid vote for the Left; category two, probably Left; category three, a swinging vote which could go either way; and category four, gone to the Right.

But not knowing exactly how many delegates the Right would rustle up made it an only-vaguely-educated guessing game.

One Left member from the eastern beachside Sydney suburb of Bondi, Ted Plummer, recalls Anthony and his colleagues making a concerted effort to campaign for individual votes.

'In politics, some people – particularly people running for public office – take people for granted in a preselection or the like,' Ted says. His Bondi branch was a left-wing branch and Anthony would have known he could assume support from any delegate representing it.

'But despite that he came around . . . he came to see me in Bondi, came to my house, and he actually made the time to introduce himself and say why he was running for President. So it's always struck me that he doesn't take people for granted . . . The only time I've been in a position to vote for Anthony, he's never done that. He's come around and argued his case.'

Years later when a journalist asked Anthony Albanese what advice he would give to anyone seeking public office, he responded that there was one basic thing people sometimes forgot to do.

'You have to ask people to vote for you.'

On the eve of the 1985 presidential vote, the right-wing NSW Labor Party leadership used the credentialing process to strike out up to 40 of the Left-recruited delegates and arbitrarily declare them ineligible.

'They thought they'd got rid of enough to win,' Anthony says.

The showdown inside the ALP's youth wing had found its way into the newspapers. Ahead of the vote, journalist Andrew McCathie reported in the *Australian Financial Review* that the characteristics on display were familiar.

'The battle for control of the youth wing which has unfolded in the past few months has all the hallmarks of the factional warfare which takes place with the over-25-year-olds in the ALP,' he wrote on 13 August, just before the conference. 'A series of charges and counter charges has been levelled by both sides.'

He described a Young Labor executive meeting two months earlier which had 'erupted into rowdy scenes, with one right-wing member jumping up on a table to deliver a few sharp words about the Left'.

By the time the conference convened, delegate numbers had more than doubled, from the just-over-200 who had voting rights the previous year, to 454.

'We worked on a strategy and we just worked bloody hard,' Anthony says.

In the final ballot for the presidency at the conference, Anthony won 223 to 211. Jo Scard was elected Senior Vice President and the Left's candidate, Patrick Dwyer, became secretary.

But the Left's battles didn't end there. The Right's determination didn't, either.

The Left's Radical Leadership Group was still running Young Labor, but had to be in a permanent state of readiness to fight a rearguard action against their factional enemies, whose members still wanted control.

After the 1985 victory, the Left set about laying the groundwork to ensure they hung onto their prize. They began a concerted drive to recruit new members from the far corners of the NSW ALP. After Young Labor Associations had been established in the electorates of Parramatta and Werriwa and on the Central Coast in 1984, they went further afield in 1985 to towns like Broken Hill, encouraging sympathisers there to establish a Young Labor presence.

At a 'political skills forum' later that year, the Young Labor Council listed first among its priorities to 'promote and encourage youth to join the ALP'.

The handout attendees were given describes recruitment as 'a continuing task of all Young Labor associations' in 1985. Target groups were the 'unemployed, young workers, school students, TAFE and uni students' and those in local branches. And the advice for producing posters, leaflets and press releases was to 'keep it simple'.

'A press release is not the place for esoteric theorising,' the handout reads.

It was International Youth Year and the Young Labor leadership harnessed the focus on young people to promote itself and its ideas throughout the ALP and in the wider community.

In September 2013, a circa-1985 photograph of Anthony in an IYY T-shirt would emerge via Fairfax newspapers and go viral on social media, after writer and broadcaster Marieke Hardy published it on Twitter under the capitalised line, 'OH DEAR LORD HAS EVERYONE SEEN THIS PICTURE OF HOT ALBO?' The photo, and the '#hotAlbo' tag, would turn his younger self into a pin-up in young Left circles, cause eye-rolling among his friends and teach him a lot about the power of the internet.

In 1985, the Radical Leadership Group produced an Action for Youth policy kit and had their own T-shirts printed, bearing the socialist rose – Socialism International's symbol of a red rose in a fist – over the Eureka flag.

The Left candidates appealed to members to support 'a progressive, active and independent' Young Labor Council – a dig at the Right's reputation for rorting.

The Left didn't come to every ballot with entirely clean hands either. Some took the view that they had to play the game by whatever rules the Right set for itself.

After the Left's audacious 1985 win, the Right raised the bar, using its control of the state branch overall to change the rules the following year. Credentialing of delegates for the Young Labor conference was restricted severely. Accreditation was normally allowed for two weeks leading up, but the deadline was dragged forward without warning.

Ahead of the 1986 conference, the then Assistant Secretary of the NSW ALP, the Right's John Della Bosca, called in the Young Labor President and Senior Vice President – Anthony Albanese and Jo Scard – and told them credentialing would close in two days.

By now, Jo and Anthony were not only colleagues but a couple, in a relationship which would last three years.

The head office credentials ruling was an arbitrary decision made by – and therefore favouring – the Right. It was expressly designed to stop the Left stacking the conference with its own supporters. Having orchestrated the early closing date, the Right had already been hard at work dragging in delegates and getting them credentialed to vote in its favour.

The Left was then in an almighty rush to do the same, recruiting delegates from the dozens of tiny unions which had never sent anyone to anything much before. The new credentialing deadline sent NSW Young Labor's left-wing leadership into overdrive.

'We had about 48 hours to send people out to all these obscure unions to say, "These awful right-wing people in head office are trying to undermine democracy,"' Jo says.

They set out to contact every non-aligned union they could find. Jo jokes that they went to the equivalent of the 'chairmakers union of Australia and the pencil-sharpeners' union' – or their real cousins, the Pastrycooks and the Marine Stewards unions – asking them to each find four young delegates to send to the conference, apply for credentials and vote for Anthony and the Left ticket.

Another Right stipulation for the '86 conference was that it be held in the Trades' Hall auditorium, on the corner of Goulburn and Sussex streets, in the same building as ALP headquarters.

On the day of the conference, the Left's scrutineers challenged a number of the Right's delegates on the grounds that the ALP membership cards they produced to verify their identities were suspicious. They were smudging.

The cards appeared to have just been printed, allegedly in head office upstairs. The ink wasn't even dry.

On another occasion, Ted Plummer was one of the Left's delegates that the Right ruled out – on what he says were spurious grounds.

'I was actually excluded on grounds that I was too old, even though I showed them my birth certificate,' Ted says. 'There were shenanigans involved.'

The combination of the Left's concerted engagement efforts over the preceding 12 months, and the last-minute drive for more delegates, saw the 1986 conference's numbers swell even further.

The Left increased its margin and again held the Right at bay. It would do so for five more years.

But inter-factional relations were at a very low ebb. The pressure – and the passion of the players – often led to belligerent, personal exchanges, sometimes worse.

'In Young Labor we were all very angry,' Jo says. 'We had to chair meetings of 600 to 700 people. And we had to be very aggressive. It was abusive. The Right was standing there yelling at you. It was like trying to organise . . . competing rugby fans or something. It was full on, so you did have to get angry.'

Very occasionally, it got physical.

At a Young Labor country conference at Gan Gan Army Base at Nelson Bay on 2 March 1986 – Anthony's 23rd birthday – Jo was speaking when a female delegate from the Right began heckling her, shouting allegations to the effect that she was only in her deputy's position because she was sleeping with Anthony Albanese, who was chairing the conference.

Chris Gration whispered in the heckler's ear that she was a bitch (with an expletive prefix attached) and she grabbed him by the throat. A bit of what might be called untidiness ensued. Belinda Neal became involved and then so did Paul O'Grady. Order was restored, just before it broke into a full-blown brawl.

The Right-controlled leadership from NSW Labor headquarters in Sussex Street tried to have Paul suspended. The suspension didn't proceed but the incident said a lot about the state of relations.

In its report to the membership for the 1985–86 year, the NSW Young Labor Council made no mention of the incident, describing the country conference as 'the best for many years'.

*

The events of 1986 highlighted that in NSW Labor, alliances were formed according to need and a friend in one context could be an enemy in another.

Although Paul O'Grady and Anthony Albanese were both members of the Left, they were on opposite sides within it.

Already a significant Left figure who would become a member of the State Parliament, Paul was aligned with the soft Left, pitting him against Anthony and the others who lined up with the Walker group.

Earlier in 1986, Paul – who was then in a relationship with the activist Anthony had met at Sydney Uni, Chris Gration – executed what became seen as a treacherous manoeuvre during a vote of the Young Labor Left caucus.

In Chris' mind, their move was never meant to undermine Anthony. By his version, it backfired. But Anthony believes Paul knew exactly what he was doing.

Young Labor's left-wing groups were meeting to elect three delegates to the Central Steering Committee – the Left's governing body in NSW – among the 50 or so from affiliated unions and other groups that would comprise the committee's membership.

Anthony was the faction's overall leader and, as the then-President of Young Labor, headed the ticket for the Radical Leadership Group within the Left and expected to be victorious.

Chris was not in the ballot. As the caucus secretary, he was supposed to be Anthony's right-hand man and that's how he says he saw himself.

Just before the vote, Paul O'Grady – who was aligned with the Ferguson Left – decided to add his well-liked boyfriend Chris' name to the candidates list, along with two other 'soft'-Left-aligned candidates on a new ticket.

A large number of previously unseen members had also turned up to the Sunday-morning vote in Parramatta, prompting Anthony to ask what was going on. He was told it was nothing, not to worry and everything was fine.

Chris insists the move was only meant to make room for him by knocking off one of the other two RLG candidates – and not Anthony. As was – and is – so often the case in Labor politics, the purpose of Paul's manoeuvre may have been simply to prove he had the power to do it. Anthony isn't convinced he meant it to be as dramatic as it was. Unfortunately, Paul can't answer for himself – he died in 2015.

Whatever Paul's intent, Chris was a naïve proxy.

'I was absolutely critical to the strategy because people really liked me,' he says. 'And they trusted me. People asked me, "This is not about getting Anthony?" And I, hand-on-heart, said, "No. Obviously not."'

But that's what happened.

Because it was a winner-take-all ballot, all three of the alternative-ticket nominees were elected. Anthony and his two running mates, Jo Scard and Pat Dwyer, missed out.

Beyond student politics, it was the first significant vote Anthony had lost. He was shocked.

'I was hurt by it,' he says, looking back. 'I got personally hurt and I shouldn't have been.'

Chris was shocked too. Anthony rejected Chris' immediate offer to stand aside, saying the ballot had been held. The next day, the then-ALP Left Assistant General Secretary John Faulkner offered to have the Steering Committee overturn the ballot.

'And I said no,' Anthony says. 'It was a ballot. Make your bed. Lie in it.'

Chris was devastated.

'He was my best buddy and I was personally loyal to him and yet I had executed this fuck-up,' Chris recalls. 'It wasn't a deliberate betrayal on my part, but nonetheless it was a betrayal. Shocking behaviour and I should have known better. But I didn't.'

Some who were around at the time think Chris is rewriting history, convinced he must have known what he was doing.

He insists he didn't. But he speaks about it with a present grief that suggests whatever was intended at the time, he regretted deeply what happened – and still does.

It shattered relationships – for years. Chris' role particularly stung because of those assurances and because it was Anthony who had recruited him to the Labor Party in the first place.

'I then left NSW,' Chris says, 'went and worked in Canberra and just swore off factional politics because I thought, "I'm not cut out for this. I'm not cut out for it." His relationship with Paul O'Grady also would not survive.

Eighteen years later, to his surprise and relief, Anthony would contact Chris and seek to repair the friendship.

Curiously, Anthony and Paul did not fall out over the incident. They remained personally close.

'For Paul, it was just business, not personal,' Anthony says. 'And I understood that.'

But he did not let the move go unanswered and his response would end up shaping his political future and that of the whole NSW Left.

Anthony set about ensuring that he was elected via an alternative path – through one of the multi-electorate regional zones that also sent delegates to the steering committee. Each zone sent one delegate per electorate.

Camperdown branch fell within zone two, covering the inner west and eastern suburbs, which had five electorates within it. At the next meeting, Anthony nominated 130 new members to the zone.

When the annual general meeting came around, he was duly elected a zone delegate along with four other supporters, defeating the soft Left's senior nominees, including federal Minister Peter Baldwin and state parliamentarian Sandra Nori.

Until then, Anthony had not been interested in the organisational machine politics of the Left and had not served on any of the faction's structural bodies.

But his response to Paul O'Grady's manoeuvre did not end there.

'I did that and voted the ticket against the people who did that [to us] at the next central meeting and the one after that and the one after that and the one after that. And the Young Labor delegates from that point on for the next decade were bloc votes against that group.'

In terms of the faction's power balance, it had a huge knock-on effect.

'That's what changed the power balance in the NSW Left.'

Having installed hard-Left supporters onto the steering committee, his own unexpected ascendancy into head office three years later would be made that much easier.

It also would motivate Anthony to ensure that in every future ballot, from party positions to preselections, he would seek to replace a soft-Left candidate with one from his own group.

While he may sometimes forgive betrayal, Anthony Albanese doesn't forget. Personal loyalty matters enormously to him.

'I think this is a characteristic I got from my mum,' he says. 'People start off at 100 per cent and work their way down to zero.'

He sticks by those who have been loyal – sometimes to his detriment and occasionally beyond what some of his friends think is reasonable.

He says he prefers to assume the best of people.

'And that can often be a mistake, particularly in politics . . . You assume people are going to tell you if they're not going to vote for you. You assume that people will, because I do that. If I'm not going to vote for someone, I tell them. So I assume a reciprocal arrangement.'

The legacy of that Young Labor vote was more than broken personal friendships. It would form what Chris calls 'the tinder to the fire', which was an already emerging split in the Left in NSW that would still exist, 30 years on.

*

Also feeding into the Left's unrest was the demise of the peak student body, the Australian Union of Students, which had struggled through its final years and was eventually disbanded.

In 1983, a former Adelaide University Law student turned Melbourne University student and activist had taken over as AUS President, a young woman by the name of Julia Gillard, who would go on to become an industrial lawyer, member of Federal Parliament for the Victorian seat of Lalor and, in 2010, the 27th Prime Minister of Australia.

In the early 1980s, AUS was facing an existential crisis. It had formed and flourished through the early 1970s, when it became a vehicle for students to join the moratorium marches and protest against the Vietnam War and its direct impact on them through conscription.

But as the war ended, the union lost its focus.

A member of Labor's Left who would move from South Australia to Victoria, Julia and others had taken over the leadership of the union to try to change its direction.

'We came in as a reform generation to try and clean up the act, to get AUS out of international policy, to get it back into education policy, education lobbying and student services, including cheap travel,' Julia says in 2016.

She argues what they wanted was to revive it and save it from a downward spiral.

'With the benefit of hindsight, it is clear we were on an impossible mission, because we were trying to rebuild a union that had been too profoundly weakened in the late 1970s.'

During that period, some students on major campuses had formed the view that the union's purpose had been lost, as a more radical left-wing leadership had shifted focus to causes further away from home.

'There was a generation of radical Left activists that tried to keep the spirit of the moratorium alive,' Julia says. 'And they tried to keep it alive particularly around international causes like Palestine. And of course, students were desperately interested in the Vietnam War because they didn't want to get conscripted. The vast majority were a whole lot less interested in these other international causes, which didn't touch their day-to-day lives.'

The push-back came from right-wing students, both inside and outside the ALP, Jewish students and others who – as Julia puts it – 'thought, "I don't know why I pay money for this boutique international lobbying outfit."'

At the time – and in some cases, still – others including Anthony believed the new AUS leaders were being played, used by right-wing groups who wanted to weaken the Left's influence wherever they could.

'The Right were trying to destroy AUS by getting campuses out [of the union],' he says.

As a member of the Sydney Uni Student Representative Council, Anthony went to his first AUS conference, held at the Australian National University in Canberra, in 1982.

But although that is how he and Julia came to know each other, he was far less involved with the student union and its associated politics than was she.

'He was very young,' Julia says, 'very working class, indeed welfare-class kind of proud – proud of his single-mother and housing commission background, and very keen to point fingers at university wankers and people who came from more upper-income backgrounds.'

Anthony's primary cause was the Labor Party and, via campus politics, he directed his energies to supporting it.

'He had a particular disdain for people who had lived lives of privilege as children but then became interested in Left politics,' she says. 'He was pretty "boyo" – keen to give it to people, an argumentative type at that point.'

She jokes about his transformation over three decades. 'He's mellowed a bit since. Though some would say that mellowing's taken quite a while.'

Back in 1983, when Anthony was ALP Club President and a member of the Sydney Uni SRC, the SRC held a referendum on formally affiliating with AUS. The council's left-wing leaders recommended students vote yes.

But the Australian Union of Jewish Students, or AUJS, involving some who would go on to become leading figures in the NSW Labor Right, were strongly opposed to affiliation.

'AUJS were very active and motivated by Middle East politics as well as domestic politics,' Anthony says. 'They were very political.'

For ALP-linked students including Anthony, affiliation to AUS was important symbolically as much as practically.

'It was a very defining issue – whether you supported a union or not – because it was seen as [that] you couldn't be in the Labor Party and not support the existence of a national student union.'

But the student body voted against affiliation. That defeat prompted him to get involved in the Left-led Council of ALP Students – or CALPS – which gave him another way of linking up with AUS. He secured the CALPS presidency and other like-minded students from non-affiliated campuses won other key roles on the CALPS executive. They continued to campaign for affiliation to AUS, Anthony writing a paper to argue his point, entitled *Fight or Flight*.

That same year, he went to the AUS conference in Melbourne. It was his first trip beyond NSW and the ACT and it confirmed what he had discovered previously: conferences were not all about work.

'There was a big social element to it,' he says. 'People partied hard.'

But the serious element was the fate of AUS. At the Melbourne AUS meeting in 1983, Anthony recalls his right-leaning rivals Eric Roozendaal, who was President of Macquarie University SRC, and Belinda Neal turning up to a meeting of the CALPS caucus on the sidelines of the conference. As they had opposed affiliating the Macquarie and Sydney University SRCs with AUS – and then turned up at the AUS conference – they didn't receive a terribly warm welcome from the largely left-wing CALPS leadership.

'We expelled them,' he says.

Julia Gillard recounts that, as its President, she tried to shift AUS' focus off the international issues – including the controversial subject of Israel and the Palestinians – and onto students' more immediate domestic concerns.

Anthony, and those who shared his view, opposed the kinds of controls that were being applied to the union's scope and what they saw as restrictions on the issues it could address.

They were unhappy that Julia's successor as AUS President, Michael O'Connor, who would rise through the union movement to lead the Construction, Forestry, Mining and Energy Union, continued in the same vein.

In the end, whatever their motivations, the union didn't survive.

'The decay had gone too far for remedying it, to bring AUS into viability,' Julia says. '. . . There was an endeavour to transition AUS into a new body, so to shed the AUS sins of the past by creating a new organisation. But it wasn't successful.'

The fallout from the demise of AUS was felt throughout student politics and across the arenas of Young Labor. At the Australian Young Labor conference in 1986, which was delayed from January to the Easter weekend in late March, it was still reverberating.

The Left controlled the AYL executive but only by a whisker: 24 votes to a combined total of 23 from the Centre and Right.

At the '86 conference, the executive had to elect a delegate to represent AYL at the ALP's national conference in Hobart, the party's supreme policy forum. Across the entire party nationally, 99 delegates would be accredited to attend. Only one of those would be from Young Labor.

The delegate election was against the backdrop of some factional strong-arming in the Labor Party at the federal level. The

Hawke Government was nearing the end of its second term and the Right was seeking to gain overall control of the conference and therefore the party's policy direction through its platform, heading into an election year. The faction was doing all it could to capture as many of the Left's delegate spots as possible, including the one from Young Labor.

As President of the powerful NSW organisation, with reasonable interstate support networks established through his role within CALPS, Anthony was expected to be the Left's nominee and, if all the numbers fell where expected, to win the representative spot by a single vote.

But at a meeting of the Left caucus at the Metal Workers' Union offices in Chalmers Street, Surry Hills, on the eve of the weekend gathering, Anthony discovered that one of the Left's representatives – Perth delegate Bonita Mason – was abandoning the faction.

More than that, in an apparent attempt to divide the Left, Bonita was making it personal. Without warning, she submitted a letter saying she was prepared to support an alternative Left candidate, but not Anthony. He and others in the Left believed the Right and Centre had put her up to it.

'We adjourned for 10 minutes to have discussions between ourselves with some of my supporters and decided we weren't going to be blackmailed,' Anthony says. They held a ballot on the spot, pitting Anthony against her nominated alternative, Victorian delegate Andrew Scott. Andrew secured support from some in his home state and from WA, but Anthony won 17–6.

The group then adjourned to what Anthony describes as the 'traditional Friday night lefty sort of party' at someone's house to discuss the bigger problem: his victory had confirmed his candidacy but also the Left's loss of that all-important extra vote. They were one short.

If they lost the ballot, they would be boosting the Right's numbers in the party's national policy-making forum and paving the way for it to take control of Young Labor. They needed to somehow find a replacement vote among those listed for the other side. Amidst the usual drinking and pre-conference frivolity, they hatched a plan.

One of those whose vote Anthony might normally have been able to count in his favour was Andrew Mitchell, a Left delegate from Tasmania, but for the fact that Andrew couldn't get to Sydney for the ballot because he was getting married in Tassie over Easter.

The rules in Young Labor dictated that if someone couldn't make it to the conference to cast a ballot, their place went to a proxy. Proxy delegates weren't under any obligation to vote any particular way. They could do with their vote whatever they wished.

Andrew Mitchell's spot had gone to fellow Tasmanian and former Left member Dale Raneberg, who had joined the middle-ground faction, the Centre-Left. Raneberg was the Right and Centre-Left's choice for national conference delegate, so he was expected to vote against his old faction and for himself.

As the original delegate, Andrew would outrank Dale and be entitled to take back the spot and cast a vote – if he turned up. The leader of the Tasmanian delegation, left-winger Ian Rogers, proposed they contact Andrew and try to persuade him to come. Three decades on, Ian explains their thinking.

'If we can get hold of Andrew,' he says, 'and we can come up with the money – and then we can persuade him – we can bring him up for the day and he'll be there for the vote.'

They would have a whip-round to cover the airfare. It was a genius idea.

Ian got Andrew on the phone and explained the situation. Without his vote, the Right would be representing Young Labor at national conference. Could he come? If they could pay for his fare and get him back home in time, he said, yes he could.

The crazy manoeuvre wasn't only about ensuring the Left's ideas prevailed. Just a little bit of it was about spectacularly wrong-footing the Right. Or maybe a lot of it.

Many of those at the conference were working for MPs and senators, including for the Right's federal heavies Graham Richardson from NSW and Victoria's Robert Ray.

'I'm working for Uren, there's Richardson staffers, there's Ray staffers,' Anthony says. 'There are proxy wars going on.'

It was an intense scene with very passionate players. Jo Scard, who was working in Frank Walker's office, recalls the whole period in Young Labor as being like that.

'To some extent, Young Labor was as close as I got to being involved with a church,' she says. 'Coming from an atheist family, that's the closest I'll ever get . . . It sort of takes your soul.'

That particular Saturday, for some it was just as much about achieving a spectacular victory as salvation.

'We were all up for a bit of monkey business and mischief,' says Ian Rogers, now a Melbourne-based business journalist and website publisher.

Fortuitously, there was an early direct flight from Hobart to Sydney with seats available. They booked Andrew Mitchell on it.

By Ian's recollection, the airfare went on Paul O'Grady's credit card, with the promise of eventual reimbursement via their hasty collection. Anthony remembers jubilation at their own audacious plan.

'We fly this guy in,' he says, laughing again. 'We get someone to meet him at the airport . . . [And] we take him to the pub.'

They hid Andrew in the bar at the Royal Exhibition Hotel, also in Chalmers Street, down the road from the Metal Workers' Union offices and just across from Central Railway Station.

To its regulars, the pub had become known affectionately as Platform 26, named after one of the disused or 'ghost' platforms beneath the station, because a railway worker or two had been known to slip away there for some respite during a work day. When a missing worker's absence was noted, the boss would be told he was 'on Platform 26', while a mate scooted across the road and hurried him to finish his beer.

On that Saturday morning, Andrew was stashed at the pub until just before the vote and then ushered down the road and into the conference room in time to answer when his name was called, collect a ballot paper and gazump his proxy, Dale.

Anthony barely knew Andrew but was fairly pleased to see him.

'He goes up and gets his ballot paper and all hell breaks loose,' he says of the Tasmanian's sudden emergence. 'They thought he wasn't coming. They thought it was over. Bang!'

An original delegate outranked a proxy. There was nothing the Centre and Right could do. Andrew cast his vote and delivered victory to Anthony, by the narrowest margin, 24–23.

The newly endorsed Young Labor representative to national conference wasn't the only one happy at the outcome. Ian Rogers was elated that Dale Raneberg, who he considered to be a rat, had been done over.

'I was happy to have smacked him in the face in front of his new right-wing friends,' he says, still unrepentant after three decades.

Anthony chalked it all up to useful experience for the career he didn't know lay ahead.

'All this stuff put me in good stead.'

At the national conference he would lead the charge to expand the ABC's Sydney-based youth radio station Triple J into a national broadcaster and force changes to party policy to ease back some harsher elements of the Hawke Government's work-for-the-dole program.

And he would remember the trick employed to secure his spot – how to outfox his opponents by using the rules against them. It wouldn't be the last time he used it.

It also wouldn't be the last time people on the Left chose to support a right-wing candidate to avoid voting for Anthony Albanese.

CHAPTER 11

To the Barricades

In the late 1980s, NSW Young Labor had one eye on events overseas and the other at home. It kept close track of international issues, maintaining solidarity with the African National Congress in its battle against apartheid and taking anti-nuclear campaign cues from the then-ongoing Cold War.

But it was also becoming extremely active domestically, especially in the industrial arena. Among its higher profile activities during Anthony's time as NSW Young Labor President was to lobby hard for the creation of a university in Sydney's western suburbs, presenting a petition of 10,000 signatures to the State Government in late 1985.

The idea had come from the Young Labor Association around the Blue Mountains, Penrith and St Marys and the statewide body took it up, arguing that tertiary participation rates among Western Sydney's youth were shamefully low and quoting statistics showing that while Sydney overall had 26.9 tertiary places taken up per 1000 people, in the west there were only 1.7.

Young Labor centred its campaign on high schools, TAFE colleges and shopping centres across the Western Sydney region.

Having learned a thing or two in student politics about gaining media attention, Anthony and his colleagues maximised the opportunity their petition provided. Ahead of presenting the petition to the Education Minister at State Parliament – who by then was Rodney Cavalier – they stuck the pages of signatures together into a long roll for dramatic effect, unfurling it for photographers and TV crews. It ran the full length of the building's Macquarie Street balcony.

Their efforts would eventually contribute to the establishment of a new university in 1989. Young Labor had wanted to call it 'Whitlam University' but the State Government wasn't prepared to go quite that far. Given the more benign title University of Western Sydney, it would be renamed Western Sydney University in 2015.

Young Labor also ran a campaign for higher youth wages, targeting the McDonald's food chain with which Anthony was so familiar.

He had been concerned about what its employees were paid since he had worked there himself through high school in the 1970s. Back then, he had tried to mobilise fellow Maccas workers around the Camperdown flats to join the union and push for better conditions. He didn't have a lot of success.

At the time, his back-fence neighbour Yvonne Miller's daughter Sherie was among his fellow golden arches employees. Yvonne remembers asking Sherie what young Anthony's union campaign was all about. She ended up phoning the union direct for more details.

'I rang up and I said, "Well, how much would it cost them [to join]?"' Yvonne says. She explained the kids were only working casually and wanted to know if there was some kind of part-time membership rate.

'And they said, "Oh no, you've got to join for the full thing." It was something like a hundred and something dollars at that stage, and I went, "Oh no, thank you."'

She decided they could do without it. Years later, when Young Labor was using the 1985 International Youth Year to kick off its campaign on youth wages, it zeroed in on McDonald's. They were chosen because they were big. And Anthony and his comrades knew exactly what their workers were paid.

'They were symptomatic of the large employer,' Anthony says, acknowledging targeting the company's attitude more than any specific individual sin.

'They were anti-union at that time. And there was a campaign by the "New Right" as they were called at that time to drive down wages, to say, "The way that you employ young people is that you should abolish any minimum wage at all."'

In late 1985, the NSW Young Labor Council's quarterly journal *Young Labor Voice* made it clear the campaign was designed to unionise the McDonald's workforce.

'McDonald's is probably the perfect example of an American corporation with a Neanderthal approach to industrial relations,' it declared in a front-page feature.

'The prime objective of McDonald's management strategy is to totally exclude trade unions from their premises, thus leaving their workers totally disorganised and open to exploitation.'

Anthony's Young Labor colleague Damian O'Connor, who had been active in student politics at the University of New South Wales, ran the campaign. It lasted for months.

In the same journal edition, Damian wrote about the youth wages campaign and warned of a resurgence in 'hard right' politics.

'This resurgence has the potential to return Australia to the rules of the economic jungle, where the weak lose and the strong win,' he wrote.

They put up posters and distributed stickers and pamphlets declaring 'Stop the McRipoff' and ran protests, stationing activists dressed like Ronald McDonald outside stores to hand out pamphlets. The first protests were held in Sydney city,

Parramatta and Tamworth, but its leaders were also aiming to influence events in Western Australia, where employer groups were applying to cut youth wages by 10 per cent and McDonald's hoped to use a cut-rate trainee scheme, which it said would assist 20 unemployed people.

'It was always peaceful and it was just outside handing pamphlets to people,' Anthony says. 'But McDonald's didn't like it.'

The fast food giant was so unhappy, it threatened to sue Young Labor. Its then chairman Peter Ritchie announced in October 1985 that the company had sent a legal letter.

'To some extent we did threaten them that if they go too far, we will stamp on their toes,' Ritchie was quoted as saying. 'If they do anything really damaging [we] wouldn't hesitate to.'

Damian O'Connor recalls that the letter was delivered to the NSW ALP's head office.

'Because we were unincorporated, they wrote the letter to Sussex Street,' Damian says. 'So we got hauled into Sussex Street, the implication being they would sue the party for actions in our name.'

It probably didn't help relations that the campaign also advocated a boycott of McDonald's products. There are scurrilous rumours that the occasional dedicated campaigner may have engaged in late-night cheating at the drive-through after a hard day putting up posters.

Damian laughs at the suggestion.

'Well, I haven't heard that,' he says. 'Nobody would dare mention that in my presence.'

Anthony also denies any knowledge of campaigners breaching the Maccas ban. He insists he had no trouble sticking to it, having previously worn the constant smell of burgers and fries deep in the pores of his skin.

The McDonald's campaign also served as a vehicle for attacking the then Liberal-National Opposition federally, whose leader John Howard was on a drive to end what he saw as the union movement's stranglehold on the industrial landscape and to dismantle the prices and incomes Accord which Bob Hawke's government had introduced.

'Ultimately, you have to create a situation where there is a decline in union membership,' the *Sydney Morning Herald* quoted John Howard, then deputy Liberal leader, as saying in March 1985.

John Howard was also floating the idea of a youth wage in response to rising levels of youth unemployment. That made him a popular target among the members of NSW Young Labor.

'We had a poster with him on it,' Damian recalls. 'We did a lot of this sort of stuff.'

For NSW Young Labor, it was not just a consciousness-raising exercise about youth wages. The campaign added Young Labor's voice to the defence of trade unions generally, issuing a pamphlet entitled 'Some questions young people are asking about trade unions', addressing whether or not they had too much power, were too greedy, were above the law and ran too many strikes. Unsurprisingly, the pamphlet answered all of its own questions with a resounding no.

In his President's report in the journal, Anthony acknowledged that International Youth Year was providing the vehicle for Young Labor to press its ideas onto the wider party, in the form of an Action for Youth policy document. At the same time, it was a chance to raise its profile and recruit more like-minded members.

Throughout 1985 and 1986, he and the rest of the leadership continued to encourage the establishment of Young Labor Associations – including one in the inner-city electorate of Grayndler – until the whole of metropolitan Sydney was covered, along with key regional population centres including Newcastle.

'There is every reason why Young Labor should be in the forefront of the emergence of a politicised, active and progressive youth movement in Australia,' Anthony's journal report reads. Mal Larsen, who would follow Anthony as NSW Young Labor President, recalls the Left-led youth wing taking its critical cues from senior members of the faction.

Those were days when the Labor Left would be at least as outspoken in attacking the Hawke Government's policy moves as the conservative Opposition parties.

'After Keating brought down a budget, it was Bruce Childs who would hold a press conference and condemn the Government,' Mal says.

Bruce Childs and fellow Left convenor Gerry Hand would blast their own government's budget measures, using briefing notes prepared for them by young Left staffers, including a certain research officer working for Tom Uren. The advisers would begin combing through the budget as soon as it was handed down.

'We would stay up all night – literally all night,' Anthony says.

Young Labor would also launch critiques of its own government, if with slightly more youthful brashness.

'Much of Young Labor's activity in that time was condemning the Hawke Government for horror budgets cutting government spending and welfare and the introduction of HECS,' Mal says, of the then-controversial Higher Education Contribution Scheme.

At the ALP's NSW state conference ahead of Paul Keating's 1985 tax summit, Young Labor delegates seated in the galleries above the Sydney Town Hall stage listened carefully as the Treasurer explained his reasoning for proposing to pay for income tax cuts with a consumption tax – option C among a list of tax options the Government was considering.

As soon as he uttered the words 'option C', the air in the hall filled with fluttering paper money, collected from personal Monopoly sets and tossed down by protesting activists above.

'That was one of the actions that didn't endear Young Labor to the party leadership,' Anthony says, chuckling.

The NSW Young Labor Council had established a committee to scrutinise the Federal Government's youth strategy Priority One. Ahead of the 1986 ALP national conference, it had persuaded Australian Young Labor to join its opposition to Bob Hawke's work-for-the-dole scheme. The Left and Centre-Left factions joined forces against the policy and in a significant defeat for the Prime Minister, it was overturned at the July conference which Anthony attended after his faction's successful manoeuvring back at Easter.

The Right-led Federal Government was regularly frustrated that the Left was not more supportive of its own party in government. The Left was unrepentant. In fact, after policy victories like the one at the 1986 conference, it was jubilant.

The report Anthony presented to Young Labor on the national conference outlined his concern that ministers, including the Prime Minister, had indicated that platforms 'would be ignored', which he said undermined the conference's policy-making role.

'The danger with this shift in focus was exemplified by the void in discussion of Labor's long-term objectives and aspirations,' he wrote.

He wrapped up his report with a rallying cry about building a truly socialist future. And he ended on that favourite quote – the one from Antonio Gramsci that he would employ again later on the floor of state conference to earn himself a case of beer.

The McDonald's campaign also earned Anthony airtime on radio, where he came up against an aggressive broadcaster by the name of Alan Jones. Despite Alan's exponentially higher profile and lack of sympathy for the cause, Anthony opted for a forward defence, demanding to know how much Jones was paid and could *he* survive on a youth wage?

Hardly in the same league as the long-time radio man when

it came to public discourse, Anthony was unfazed by the combative style.

His own take-no-prisoners mode of engagement won him strong support in Young Labor.

'He was enigmatic, I guess,' Mal Larsen says. 'You wanted to be with him. He was very popular.'

Anthony's social circle continued to consist of those with whom he had Labor politics in common. With himself as NSW Young Labor President and his girlfriend, Joanne Scard, as Senior Vice President – and destined to become President of Australian Young Labor – the personal and political became so finely interwoven, there was nothing to separate them.

Anthony's friend Craig Sahlin recalls being part of that Left-aligned social network long after he had outgrown Young Labor and moved on from the Gould Group, occasionally visiting the Liberty Street house and other gatherings with Anthony, his mates and sometimes their parents as well.

'There'd be a barbecue at Alex's parents' place at Annandale and his father would bring out his good, home-made red wine,' Craig says. 'There was a social circle that was probably pretty congruent with the Labor circle. It was the same people largely but it was broadened to their families and relatives and also people like me who might have been in the party or in politics but not in Young Labor.'

On Friday nights, members of the broader Left would gather at Sydney's Criterion Hotel, in Pitt Street just near the town hall, for a drink.

That was where Macquarie University academic Meredith Burgmann met Anthony. Those Friday nights attracted an eclectic group of drinkers.

'All the Left gathered,' Meredith recalls. 'Aboriginal activists, builders labourers, prison activists, civil libertarians – all the different groups. Even Trots would turn up and drink there on a Friday night. It was a huge meeting place – very important politically.'

Anthony had developed a wide circle of lefty friends and could hold court easily when the occasion warranted it.

'I was very impressed that at an early age, he had such self-confidence,' Meredith says.

A fellow left-winger, member of the Glebe branch of the ALP and President of the Academics Union – who at Anthony's instigation would go on to serve in the NSW Legislative Council – Meredith recalls asking him how he came to be so self-assured.

'I think he might have said to me, "It's because I brought myself up."'

He had explained about his mother's ill health and the long periods he'd had to spend on his own, attributing his independence and confidence to the circumstances of his childhood.

He and Meredith would go on to become great friends, a friendship punctuated by some fantastic political arguments. They were robust and on at least one occasion, ended with both of them in tears.

'If you're in an argument with Albo, he will destroy you,' Meredith says. 'There is nothing in his make-up which says, "Oh, agree to disagree or let sleeping dogs [lie]."'

Despite such rip-roaring debates and his natural self-confidence, Anthony drew on the wisdom of his elders through those Young Labor years.

Meredith and her Labor friend Ann Symonds, then already an MLC, offered him free advice on some of the little things, like the social skills he would need at public events.

As he became more prominent in the Labor Party, they talked to him about table manners.

'I remember once telling him to his horror that you don't butter the whole of the bun at the table,' Meredith says. He thought to butter repeatedly was 'very time wasting'.

While the socialising was important and enjoyed for its own sake, it was very frequently combined with work. Paul Murphy describes Anthony as 'a driven person', even during those nights out at the Criterion and elsewhere.

'I clearly recall one night, walking to someone's house from the pub, I think, and he was reciting names and telephone numbers of delegates,' Paul says.

It's a skill that has served Anthony well throughout his career. He can recite his Sydney University student number and the telephone numbers, long disused, of people from those Young Labor days. And he remembers the final count in every significant vote he has ever won – or lost.

He modelled his political character on Tom Uren's example, as the Left elders had hoped he would. Paul Murphy says his friend's socialist characteristics existed well before he went to work for Tom, but that the older man's influence gave them structure and meaning.

'He was such a consistent person, capable of being very forceful in prosecuting his views but always wrapped in incredible humanity and tenderness,' Paul says of Tom's approach to politics and life.

Anthony became a lot like that. An emotional young man, prone to tears but taught that it wasn't anything shameful, he also learned how to ruthlessly avenge a perceived political wrong.

He was a bloke with a soft side, climbing the ranks of the so-called hard left.

For all that his personal experience brought to his defence of the unemployed and low paid, by the late 1980s Anthony was doing much better himself financially. His mum and their circumstances had taught him frugality and he'd worked hard and saved well.

On top of that, his bank account received a couple of sizeable deposits, courtesy of the two nasty road accidents he'd had the misfortune of being involved in, the second of which – involving a Commonwealth hire car in Canberra – was in 1985.

In both cases, he was a passenger. He hasn't been on a motorbike since the Crown Street crash in 1982. The accidents didn't keep him off the roads but from then on, whenever possible, he preferred to be in charge of the vehicle himself.

'I always drive,' he says. 'I'm a nervous passenger.'

Having finally learned to drive in 1985, he acquired his own car – a metallic gold Holden Gemini, which he bought from his friend Jeremy Fisher for $800.

In the socialist manner of share and share alike, his jalopy was occasionally employed on the odd long-distance mission, in the service of Young Labor country recruitment, which in 1985 was considerable.

'For months we chased delegates, got them elected in branches, locked them in,' Damian O'Connor says of that drive to hold off the Right in 1985. 'We went and doorknocked them. This was a really considerable logistics effort. This was all of NSW . . . This was all we did for months. It was an incredible result given that clearly we needed to have done it. We only won by 12 votes. If we hadn't done it, we would have lost. And [the Right] didn't come back again and try it until 1992.'

With the victory margin out to 100 votes by 1986, Anthony held the presidency again and then Mal Larsen took over in 1987, winning comfortably.

Among the things instigated during Anthony's tenure, he encouraged the Left faction to change its name. He had privately thought the 'Radical Leadership Group' was not the right kind of statement. In the vein of calling it what it was, it became the less grandstandy 'Young Labor Left'.

In order to get what he wanted, the young 'Albo', as he was by then universally known in Labor circles, would turn on the charm. Like others, Mal Larsen uses that other 'c' word: charisma.

'He really had that young lefty firebrand style about him,' Mal says. 'What was notable about Albo was when that changed and he also became pragmatic ... Most firebrand lefties don't know how to do deals.'

Mal observed Anthony's approach changing as his position at the helm of NSW Young Labor threw him into the orbit of some of the party's heaviest characters.

'That's when Anthony started to, I suppose, have to deal with serious people as opposed to just all the other kids. At some point he learnt. And it became obvious that he started to not just have conflict with the Right but was able to work with them.'

One of Anthony's final campaigns as President was in favour of democratisation of the party's decision-making in the wake of what Young Labor argued were policy breaches by the federal Labor Government.

'There is an urgent need for the Government to implement policies which go beyond making working-class people bear the brunt of our economic problems,' Anthony wrote in a letter addressed 'Dear comrades'.

He and his council colleagues launched a petition declaring that ALP policy was not made by directives from on high, but 'by resolutions originating from branches affiliated unions and individual party members'.

In later years, there would be those who would suggest his drive to give the rank and file greater influence in party decision-making was a very late conversion after years of convenient deals.

His response is to point to that campaign. And he insists that any cross-factional deals to preserve his own group's power and keep others at bay were – and are – for the greater Labor good and don't contradict that at all.

Once he was no longer Young Labor President, Anthony decided it was time to take a substantial break. He was keen to go off and see more of the world than his past short trips had allowed. His relationship with Jo Scard was waning. It was the right time to make the break. He decided to travel further afield, this time to Europe.

For each of his two previous trips, someone else had made the bookings. He didn't really know where to start.

'I knew nothing about travel. I went into the Commonwealth Bank travel agent and said, "I want to go to Europe. I want to fly Qantas. Where do they fly via?"'

One of the options was Harare, in Zimbabwe.

'I thought, "Oh that'll be interesting." So I went via Harare.'

He decided to make the most of the African sojourn and explore beyond Zimbabwe to Zambia and Botswana. Then he would go on to Europe and take a 30-day Contiki tour, followed by two months' independent travel on a Eurail pass. After that, he would go wherever the circumstances took him.

'I booked it and paid for it all on the spot.'

He did it that way because although he really wanted to go, he also knew there was a risk that if he went home to think about it, he would focus on his mother's situation. The guilt at leaving her at home alone for six months might be too much.

But he knew he needed to get away.

'The only way I was going to go – it was a big deal leaving Mum for that period of time – was to go and book it . . . and pay for it. And it was done.'

He left on 10 March 1988 – a week after he turned 25, the same age his mother had been when she set sail for England in 1962.

The night before he flew out, he celebrated with a combined birthday and farewell dinner at Effa's Indonesian restaurant in King Street, Newtown. His mum was there, along with a dozen friends. She would miss him but she wasn't going to hold him back.

'She thought it was a good thing that I was going on a grand adventure,' he says.

Arriving in Harare, Anthony joined a 10-day tour that took him through the Chobe National Park in Botswana and the Hwange National Park in Zimbabwe and then on to Victoria Falls.

When the tour ended he stayed on at the falls for a couple of days, sleeping in a hut in the campground for less than $1 a night. He crossed the river into Zambia.

'I went whitewater rafting down the Zambezi,' he says. 'Amazing.'

He caught local buses to Kariba Dam before looking up a friend of a friend back in Harare and staying there for a few more days.

After just over three weeks in Africa, he headed for London, staying with the former head of the British National Union of Students – the United Kingdom's equivalent of AUS – Scotsman Neil Stewart, whom Anthony had met at an AUS conference.

From there, he joined the Contiki tour he'd booked from home, following a well-worn path across western Europe. He travelled through France, Austria, West Germany, Switzerland and the Netherlands.

The Contiki tour also took him to Italy. He saw the northern cities of Venice and Florence and the capital, Rome. The route took the tour group south to Brindisi, where they caught the ferry across to the Greek island of Corfu.

Sailing away from the Italian coast, Anthony had no idea he had been less than two hours' drive from his father's front door.

After the organised part of his trip, Anthony ranged further afield. He didn't return to Italy. He had nothing to which he could anchor the Italian part of himself, so it was just another country on the itinerary.

Instead, he got a cheap flight from London, where the tour disbanded, back to Paris and then activated his pre-purchased Eurail pass, taking the train to Spain.

He had arranged to meet some people from the tour in Morocco and spent five days there before heading back to Spain and Portugal, back up through Paris and on to Luxembourg. He went on to Amsterdam, Brussels and Bruges and up to Copenhagen, then to Sweden and Norway, where he travelled the Oslo-Bergen railway. Backtracking across Scandinavia, he arrived back in Stockholm and phoned his mum.

'I rang home and spoke to Mum and she said, "Oh it's great you're seeing Jeremy next week,"' he recounts.

At his farewell dinner three months earlier, his friend Jeremy had suggested that they could meet up in Greece in the northern summer.

He had enthusiastically encouraged the idea but in all the excitement of new adventures overseas – and without having made any formal plans or had any further contact since he left home – he had forgotten.

This was the pre-mobile-phone era and Jeremy had left messages for him along his anticipated route – none of which he had received. He asked Maryanne to let Jeremy know he'd meet him but would be a little late.

'I had the Europe guide book and I just named somewhere,' he says. He nominated a day and a location. I'd be around the main square around 12 o'clock.'

And then he headed south, through Germany and Yugoslavia, to Greece where he managed to meet up with Jeremy in Athens.

'I spent about 48 hours on a train.'

They went to Ios and then Santorini where Anthony met a Swedish traveller, Christina, who lived in a fishing village, Havstenssund, outside Gothenburg. Christina then met up with them again in Paros, where the group was kicked out of their hotel for being too rowdy.

When Jeremy went home, Anthony travelled on to the then Yugoslavia, where he caught up with more Australian friends in another meet-in-the-town-square arrangement.

Eastern Europe proved much more amenable to a backpacker budget and he went from Croatia to Budapest, in Hungary, and Prague, in what was then Czechoslovakia.

'Eastern Europe was cheap to travel,' Anthony says. '. . . But by then I was starting to run out of money.'

He went on to Berlin, which then was still a divided city, arriving into the eastern half.

Bruce Springsteen was playing at the Berlin Olympic stadium on the other side of the wall and Anthony crossed into West Berlin to try and go to the concert.

'I just stood there and announced to everyone loudly, "I've got ten bucks. One of you is going to sell me a ticket eventually for this." When it got to the third song I got my ticket.'

He made his way down to the front and a bunch of US soldiers stationed in Berlin shared their beer with the Aussie backpacker.

By the time the show was over, the border crossing had closed. Anthony found a youth hostel for the night, realising belatedly that he only had a single-entry visa for the east – and he'd already used it.

'I then had to talk my way back across the border the next day. I remember being asked, "Why were you across in West Berlin?" And I said, "I wanted to see what it was like on the other side."'

It was a lame attempt at the chicken joke but the English-speaking guard let him through.

He went back up to Sweden, where, by no coincidence at all, he spent a few days in a certain fishing village, Havstenssund.

After saying goodbye to Christina again, Anthony headed back to London and met up with some of the Australians from his Contiki tour. They hired a car and drove through Scotland before he crossed the Irish Sea for a few days in Dublin – his final stop – where he stayed near the Guinness factory and saw Australian punk rockers The Celibate Rifles play.

'It was awesome.'

Back home, one of Anthony's friends let slip some of the details of his holiday to Jo and how much he'd been enjoying himself overseas. She hadn't exactly been staying in every night herself, but she wasn't happy at the news.

Their relationship was definitely done.

Not long after that, some of the Young Labor women got together for a night out. Jo told them her relationship with Anthony was over.

One of those Jo recalls being present would soon find herself interested in Anthony Albanese. Her name was Carmel Tebbutt.

CHAPTER 12

The Long Game

Anthony Albanese and Carmel Tebbutt had known each other for a while before he decided to ask her out.

Carmel was a year younger than Anthony and hadn't joined the Labor Party until her final year of study, in 1985. Like him, she went to Sydney University; however, despite the campus notoriety he gained through Student Representative Council elections and defending the Political Economy course – in which she was also enrolled, a year behind – she had been only vaguely aware of him there. His name was on the posters. But their paths didn't cross.

'I wasn't involved in student politics,' Carmel says. 'I wasn't interested in getting involved in student politics. It wasn't my world.'

Carmel hailed from the Shire, local shorthand for the Sutherland Shire, the 370-square-kilometre area south of Sydney's central business district that reaches east to the beach-side suburb of Cronulla, west to the Georges River and south to Bundeena and the Royal National Park. She was one of seven children in a close, Catholic family.

Carmel's dad, Bede Tebbutt, was interested – but not active – in politics and was a supporter of the Democratic Labor Party. Her Mum, Marcelle, rated other interests higher.

The fourth child after a sister and two brothers, Carmel was born in Sydney. When she was nine months old, her parents moved the family to Forbes, in the central-west of New South Wales, so her father, who was a meat inspector, could do his necessary country service.

'I think their plan was to go for a couple of years and then come back,' Carmel says. 'But they liked it.'

Bede and Marcelle enjoyed the town so much they stayed for a decade – and three more kids.

'[We were] a big family. There were seven kids. It was a good lifestyle for a big family.'

When Carmel was 10 and her older siblings were heading for high school and beyond, the family returned to Sydney where the opportunities would be greater.

They moved in to the gentrifying but still affordable Shire suburb of Caringbah. The family had enough to live on but not much more than that.

Socially, Carmel found herself in what she came to know as the middle class, among friends whom she discovered had more than she did.

'I think I grew up with a sense that people sometimes had a lot more or an easier life just because of who their parents were,' Carmel says. 'And that sense of inequity was something I found difficult to deal with or didn't like – thought it was a bit unfair.'

Before she went to uni, she was focused on the normal stuff of beachside teenage life.

'I wasn't interested in politics. I was interested in going out and having a good time. I had a big circle of friends who did the same sort of stuff. So I was very much in that world of being a typical Sutherland Shire teenager.'

But she noticed the economic divisions in her community and her observations stayed with her. As she grew up, and they began to take shape, she became increasingly motivated to do something about it.

Reaching university, Carmel found a community of knowledge and ideas that shaped her views further, giving her a philosophical and ideological framework for that experience of the social divide.

'It helped me make sense of some of the things I had thought in my life didn't seem fair,' she says.

Her dad took a conservative approach to political engagement and Carmel was aware of his views. As many parents are when their children head out into the world, her mum and dad were conscious their daughter was moving into surroundings at university that would expose her to a range of political views.

They warned her against getting caught up in the trendiness of the radical Left. She was determined to set her own course but also mindful of their advice and guidance. It made her think seriously before choosing her direction.

'I really had to justify to myself that I was getting involved for genuine reasons of my own beliefs, rather than getting caught up with what other people thought.'

Towards the end of university, she decided to join a political party. Initially, she wondered if Labor was radical enough. But after looking at the options, she decided that for expressing her ideas and values, it was the best vehicle available.

Beyond university, Carmel and Anthony separately became members of the Federated Clerks' Union – he through working for Tom Uren and she as an employee of the AMP Staff Association. That meant each added monthly union meetings to their various other Labor-linked commitments.

Within the union, they were also both members of the Clerks' Reform Group, a collection of left-wing members concerned about the union's direction and trying to take over its leadership.

Carmel had begun to be active in the Labor Party, but had taken a different path to Anthony, bypassing Young Labor initially and just joining her local branch.

'I'd left uni – I thought I was too old for Young Labor,' she says. 'I wasn't interested in getting involved.'

It was her branch secretary who persuaded her to join the youth wing. By then, she was 24. The age cut-off for Young Labor was 26.

'I think I probably went to a couple of meetings when Anthony was President but really wasn't that involved.'

By 1988, Carmel had become the Junior Vice President. She was becoming more involved with Young Labor and, by late that year, with Anthony too.

Carmel had met Anthony at Young Labor and at Federated Clerks' Union meetings and they had been to the occasional group dinner. But he wasn't especially on her radar until a night in late 1988, just after he had returned from Europe, when they were both at a party in the inner-west suburb of Enmore. They got talking.

'Anthony was much more mature, much more politically mature than the rest of his peers,' Carmel says. 'And he was really recognised as a leader. And I could certainly see that.'

After the party, she gave him a lift home to Camperdown, where he was still living.

Anthony thought she was attractive, smart, funny, interesting. She impressed him.

'I rang her up and asked her out,' he says.

The night he called her at Caringbah, she wasn't there. He left a message and her younger brothers, who didn't have a reputation for absolute reliability on the message-passing front, eventually conveyed it.

'It was quite serendipitous,' Carmel says. 'We might never have actually ended up together.' She pauses, slightly, and smiles. 'Well, maybe we would have.'

They eventually spoke and arranged a date to see Australian jazz singer Vince Jones at Kinselas on Taylor Square, just off

Oxford Street in Darlinghurst, with dinner first at a Thai restaurant. A very private person, Carmel sums up the night without resort to extraneous detail.

'We went out and it was good and it developed from there,' Carmel says.

The conversation was easy. Afterwards, Anthony was determined there would be more outings with Carmel Tebbutt. Soon after, there were, including a night seeing the Go Betweens at Paddington Woollahra RSL.

Things were going well.

Anthony talked to his mates about Carmel. As his friend Mal Larsen puts it, he was keen enough to play 'the long game'.

'I think she meant a lot to him [well] before they got together,' Mal says. 'He liked Carmel. A lot.'

She was also part of a slightly different circle, having joined Young Labor later than him. He liked that too.

'It just seemed like a relationship that developed quite effortlessly really,' his friend Paul Murphy says. 'And it's sort of funny because they are different personalities. And they work really well together.'

She got on well with his friends.

'What you see is what you get,' says Alex Bukarica. 'She is a really lovely person . . . just a really top woman.'

Craig Sahlin says it was clear from early on that this relationship was different for Anthony.

'I certainly remember the general sense that something was going to happen with Carmel,' Craig says. 'It quickly became "Anthony and Carmel" . . . Anthony had met his match. Carmel was just as politically adept. She was just as capable.'

In fact, their involvement with the Labor Party and political issues meant their time together was squeezed between the many meetings that filled their weeks. The parallel career paths that were to come would ensure it would be that way for a long time.

On many of the nights when others their age were socialising, they were in meetings. Little wonder that many in their Labor-linked peer group paired up. It was the only guarantee of spending time together.

'Looking back, it seems ridiculous,' Carmel says. 'We used to spend nearly every night of our life going to a meeting, doing some mail-out. It was very intense.'

But they also worked hard to find time for other things. They shared an interest in going to the beach and seeing live bands and movies.

As their relationship and their careers progressed, Anthony and Carmel would continue to try and prioritise time away from the work pressures.

'When we took holidays it was often overseas to have a complete break from day-to-day political engagement,' Anthony says.

Over the years together that lay ahead, they variously would take trips to Europe, India, Vietnam, Indonesia and the United States – escaping the constant intrusions of politics.

Carmel developed a reputation among her friends as a committed, dedicated person.

'She was straightforward and hardworking, incredibly hardworking, very serious,' says Nareen Young, who also grew up in the Shire, around Cronulla, and would become one of Carmel's closest friends.

Nareen is married to Anthony's mate, Paul Murphy, but the women have also known each other since their youth. Both found their political grounding in the Labor Party and the labour movement.

'She's a very serious person,' Nareen says. 'She's also a very strong person. And very mindful and thoughtful.'

'Thoughtful' is also the word Nareen uses about Anthony's mother, Maryanne, whose affection extended beyond her son's friends to their partners and children.

Nareen and Paul have two – Harry and Roisin. Maryanne adored them.

'She was just an incredibly loving woman,' Nareen says. 'She loved all of us. When she passed away, Anthony found a card that was on her sideboard that was for Harry – for Harry's birthday. It was addressed to him and it had $5 in it.'

She'd died just a couple of days before his birthday.

Nareen describes the same qualities in Carmel. She says sometimes people mistake her soft, quietly-spoken demeanour for weakness.

'Because Carmel's quiet, I think sometimes people underestimate her. But she is a strong, smart, hard-working, thoughtful woman . . . They think she's not assertive. But she's assertive and she's strong.'

She would demonstrate that in what would become an 18-year political career, culminating in her election as Deputy Premier of NSW.

Within months of starting his relationship with Carmel, Anthony's professional life shifted gear dramatically. Returning from Europe to resume work with Tom Uren, he had not given a great deal of thought to his future career path. But another opportunity opened up. Against expectations, he seized it.

In 1989, senior left-winger John Faulkner was vacating the Left's only position in the managerial structure of the NSW Labor Party. One of the two Assistant General Secretary jobs allocated to the major factions, the dominant Right had grudgingly created the Left's post 18 years earlier.

John had spent nine years in the position, only the second person to serve in the role after Bruce Childs, who had moved out of it when elected as a NSW senator in 1980.

John was more sympathetic to the 'soft' Left which was aligned to the Federated Miscellaneous Workers Union and its officials, including Martin Ferguson, and was now also moving into Parliament, filling the Senate vacancy created by the mid-term retirement of Senator Arthur Gietzelt. The faction was preparing to elect his replacement.

The Cavalier-Ferguson group was dominant so its candidate was expected to hold sway – Jan Burnswoods, a long-time Left member 20 years Anthony's senior. But some in the faction believed there should at least be a ballot.

Senior figures among the Left unions and factional elders suggested Anthony should be the hard Left's candidate. They thought it was important to send the soft Left a message about assuming its own candidate would sail through. They certainly didn't expect the 25-year-old brawler to beat her.

Having become a pathway into federal Parliament, the Assistant Secretary job was prized within the faction as much for the future opportunities it presented as the influence it brought.

Before then, Anthony had not participated in the administrative side of the party machine at all.

'I had never held a position on the machinery committee, credentials committee, disputes committee – nothing,' he says. 'Unless you were part of the inner circle of the group around Martin Ferguson then you just didn't get a look in.'

Decades later, as he marked his 20th anniversary in Federal Parliament, some of his critics within the Labor Party would make the same complaint privately about him.

Back in 1989, when it was proposed that he put himself forward to run against Jan Burnswoods, he talked it over with Tom Uren. With Tom's encouragement, he agreed to do it. But he was determined he wasn't going to be a token candidate.

'I clearly indicated to them. "If I'm running, I'm running to win,"' Anthony says. And they [said], "Oh yeah, sure."'

He went away and threw everything at it. He secured support from corners of the party that had had no contact with the Cavalier-Ferguson group, including young left-wing members in the Blue Mountains zone, whose idea for a Western-Sydney university Anthony had picked up and pushed hard as President of NSW Young Labor.

In the lead-up to the vote on the Assistant General Secretary position, the contest became fairly heated. The week of the ballot, Federal Parliament was sitting and Anthony was in Canberra, in Tom's office. During the week, he was summoned to Arthur Gietzelt's office to a meeting with Arthur and Bruce Childs.

'And I thought, "Oh, here we go,"' he says.

His sense of foreboding was prescient. They were going to tell him he was pulling out.

Paul Murphy, who was working for Peter Baldwin and also in Canberra that week, went with him to the meeting. Beforehand, Tom Uren approached him in the hall. Tom was ropable.

'I know you're not with those dirty dealers, Paul,' he told Anthony's mate, embracing him. 'Stick with Anthony and help him through this.'

At the meeting, Arthur and Bruce told them they were concerned the contest had become heavy and divisive. They were putting up a compromise candidate – one that both sides could live with – and Anthony would be standing aside. They expected Jan Burnswoods to agree to do the same.

The candidate would be then-recently-retired Wran Government Minister, Ken Gabb. It wasn't a negotiation.

'Arthur said the deal was in,' Paul recalls. He and Anthony were not impressed and it showed.

Arthur turned to Paul and said, 'What are you looking so angry for? Do you think the revolution can be won in a day?'

Paul told him no one had a problem with Ken, who he describes as a progressive and 'one of the most ethical and genuinely decent people' he has ever met. But they certainly had a problem with this 11th-hour intervention.

'I told Arthur that the activists in Young Labor wanted to see change,' Paul says. 'We wanted a more aggressive approach to the NSW Right and we knew Anthony would never take a backward step.'

Anthony protested too. He ran them through his numbers and told them he was going to win. Arthur just kept talking about the deal. The conversation went round and round.

In the end, while the elders might have admired his gumption, they didn't think he was right. The deal was already done.

As Parliament rose that Thursday evening, a furious Anthony returned to Sydney. The next day, ahead of the weekend ballot, he was in Macquarie Street and ran into Paul O'Grady, who was by then a member of the NSW Legislative Council. The two had managed to remain good friends, despite Paul's ambush of Anthony in the Steering Committee vote several years before, which had so damaged both men's relationships with others and exacerbated the intra-factional split.

Three years on, something else was testing the friendship. Paul had been organising the numbers for Jan Burnswoods' campaign against Anthony's challenge, the challenge that had now been put down from within.

But Anthony was about to be surprised. Paul told him the soft Left had knocked back the compromise deal. The Jan-versus-Anthony contest was back on.

He couldn't believe it. He asked his friend why.

It seemed Paul was suspicious and thought his side was being played. He thought the hard Left leadership knew it was going to lose with Anthony and was just trying to find another way to install someone of its choosing.

'He said to me, "You wouldn't have agreed to the deal if you thought you could win,"' Anthony says.

Anthony was incredulous. Paul's advice to Jan was based on the mistaken assumption that Anthony had agreed to the compromise deal, when actually it had been foisted upon him against his will. It seemed nobody had divulged that piece of information to the soft Left.

Anthony told him, 'Well, you don't know me very well then. I will win.'

*

The man vacating the job, John Faulkner, was voting for Jan. His closest ties lay with her group, largely because he was appalled by one of those who had emerged as a key backroom figure in the hard Left, a man who had since moved into State Parliament in the Legislative Council, Ian Macdonald.

Ian had been lined up to run against him in 1980 when he'd stood for the same position Anthony was now contesting and some of his colleagues saw that as the basis of his animosity.

But John argued it was always about integrity – Ian Macdonald's approach to politics and the methods he used to achieve his objectives.

With Anthony, however, John Faulkner got along well.

'He stood out from the crowd as being a really capable young guy,' John says, in 2016. 'And he was. Time has proven that to be the case. He still stands out from the crowd.'

John and Anthony spoke before the vote. It was the first and only time since the position had been created that the Left had actually held a ballot for it.

John said, 'So, looks like you are going to win.'

'Yep,' Anthony replied. 'I've got 50.'

Laurie Ferguson tried to ensure he had one fewer vote, attempting to have Bruce Childs ruled ineligible. He was overruled. John Faulkner says he knew Anthony would win before hearing the 26-year-old outline his numbers.

'He was very honest with me about how much he was going to win it by,' John says. 'He was right.'

On 10 March 1989, a week after his birthday and exactly a year to the day after he'd left Sydney to head overseas, Anthony won the ballot, 50 votes to 43.

'And afterwards,' Anthony says, 'I remember [John] saying to me, "Well, you said you had 50. You got 50." From that day, he always knew that I could count.'

That ballot convinced Anthony's friend Paul Murphy of the same.

'He's genuinely gifted with numbers,' Paul says. 'Genuinely gifted.'

After their meeting with Arthur and Bruce, Anthony and Paul had discussed those numbers again. Anthony had pulled out one of Tom Uren's 'with compliments' slips and begun scribbling.

'I remember Anthony . . . just scrawling down the numbers from each delegation, from each union, from each zone and the totals,' Paul says. 'And it was absolutely [accurate]. Not a single vote variance.'

After the ballot, Paul sent him a note observing that two big events in Anthony's life had occurred on 10 March, a year apart. Remarking that his friend had been off overseas one year and off to Sussex Street the next, Paul wrote, tongue firmly in cheek: 'Do you ever question your direction in life, comrade?'

Anthony would face one more challenge before the result was settled. Although he started the job in May, he still had to be confirmed in the position by the party's annual state conference in June.

On the conference floor, the soft-Left-aligned former state MP Peter Crawford stood against him as an independent candidate. Enjoying the Left parading its dirty laundry, the Right lampooned the process which had seen Anthony elected, devoting a front-page report in its factional newspaper *Labor Leader* to free character assessments of both candidates.

It was a bruising encounter but, in the end, a useful one.

Anthony had to get around to introduce himself to as many of the 900 or so conference delegates as he could, among those he didn't already know.

'I got to sit down with them and ask them for their support,' he says.

He won comfortably and made some new connections among the delegates.

'I got to know them and that helped me do the job for the next six years.'

It also served to reinforce the divisions within the faction.

Winning the ballot was a huge political development in Anthony's life, the first big change since he and Carmel had become a couple.

'I didn't really appreciate the significance of that job,' Carmel says. 'I mean, I knew it was important but I didn't really recognise *how* important it was . . . how important that position was in the overall party and within the Left in particular. But I certainly knew it was a huge deal for Anthony to get it because he was so young and it was such a battle.'

For Anthony, it was enormous. It meant a likely future in representative politics. It was a serious job with serious implications for his future and it made him think about his life.

Along with acquiring a suit to wear to work, he decided he needed to do something about his living arrangements. He had to buy a house.

He'd already decided on his return from Europe that it was time to look for his own place. He had spoken to his mum about it – an essential first step.

Anthony had been careful with his spending while travelling, leaving money with his mother to pay the credit card bills and totting up his expenditure every 10 days or so in the back of a meticulously kept travel diary, so he could warn her how much each bill would be. It ensured he kept track of his finances and didn't overspend. He didn't want to return home skint.

It meant he still had enough money, with the rest of his compensation and savings combined, to be in a position to look at putting a deposit on a house when he got home.

'I was busy in the new job, trying to get on top of everything. But I was wanting to get into the housing market and Mum encouraged me to. She was always conscious of the fact that she'd rented and that the family had rented that house from 1930 until 2002 – for more than 70 years my family lived in that house.'

Maryanne had been acutely aware of her own father's struggle.

'He wasn't wealthy – he was a printer,' Anthony says. 'But he owned a business. He employed people but never owned his own home. She was always conscious [that] if they had bought a place, all the rent that they paid – they could have owned something many times over.'

For several reasons, Anthony was also focused on where he should live. He says he wanted somewhere that would not give rise to speculation that he was positioning for future preselection.

'I looked for a place that I could afford and also – ironically – that wasn't politically contentious. I wanted to concentrate on being Assistant Secretary and I didn't want to be seen to be looking for the next move.'

He says 'ironically' because the location of the house he ultimately chose – in the electorate of Grayndler – would eventually become highly contentious. Grayndler was then a Labor Right stronghold and in future years he would oversee a Left takeover of the branches in the electorate and orchestrate a series of manoeuvres that would see this become his vehicle into Parliament in 1996. He liked the area and it was near his mum.

Anthony was grateful for Carmel's understanding in willingly accommodating his closeness to his mother and his need to see her often. It wasn't a standard mother-son relationship. They were more like equals who looked after each other.

He realised it must be difficult for his girlfriend sometimes, given Maryanne's emotional dependence on her son as her physical health suffered.

'Carmel was very good to her,' he says.

Maryanne's condition meant he called in to see her a lot.

'More than the average 30-year-old calls in to see their mother . . . And Carmel was always really understanding of that.'

Carmel saw it from Maryanne's point of view.

'She was an extraordinary woman and she was so warm and welcoming to me,' she says. 'Under the circumstances where you've only got one child, I'm not so sure every mother would be so welcoming of their son's girlfriends.'

Fitting into Carmel's immediate family was not hard for Anthony either, although he sometimes found the sheer size of it daunting, compared with his own minimalist version.

Maryanne Ellery in the cheongsam she bought in Singapore on her grand adventure.

George Ellery senior and Maynor Ellery, Anthony's grandparents.

Maryanne (on the right), her brother Johnny and friends Joan and Mel in the *Fairsky*'s dining room. Carlo Albanese is standing behind Joan.

Above: Maryanne (L-R) and her sisters Veronica and Margaret.

Right: Anthony, aged two, and Santa at Grace Bros, Christmas 1965.

Anthony and Lindsay Keevers at their First Holy Communion lunch, 1970.

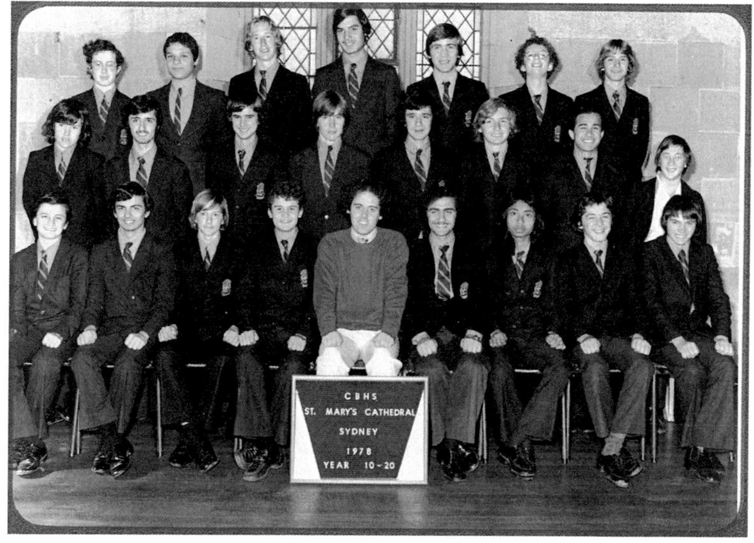

Year 10 school photo, St Mary's Cathedral College. Anthony is third from the left in the front row.

Anthony, Craig Sahlin and the dog Hugo, Nambucca Heads, January 1982. (PHOTO: JEREMY FISHER)

Anthony at a Young Labor conference in Bellingen.
(PHOTO: MALCOLM LARSEN)

Anthony and comrades in Young Labor, Pat Dwyer and Jo Scard.
(PHOTO: ALEX BUKARICA)

The Political Economy protest in 1983 took to a roof on the campus of the University of Sydney, Albo on the walkie-talkie, with Paul Porteous, Alex Bukarica and Chris Gration.

The now infamous 'Hot Albo' photograph taken in the International Year of Youth, 1985.

Carmel Tebbutt, Anthony Albanese and his mother, Maryanne, at their wedding, Taronga Zoo, June 2000.

Anthony with Jeannette McHugh and Tom Uren on his wedding day.

With Carmel and Gough Whitlam, 2000.

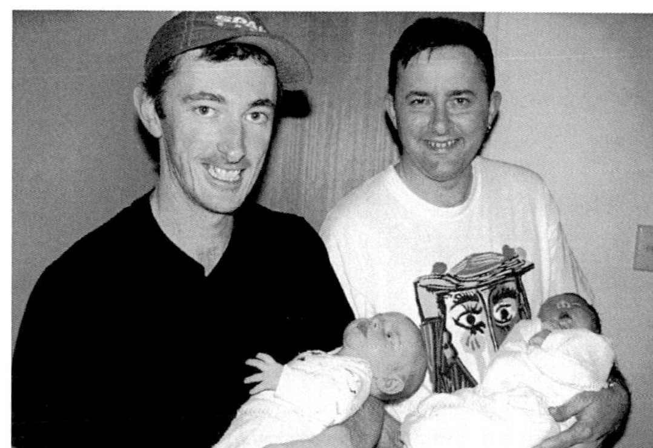

Proud dads: Paul Murphy and Roisin, born in December 2000, only days before Nathan Albanese, held by Anthony.

Anthony, Carmel, cousin Norm Howett and baby Nathan on the couch at home in Newtown, 2001.

Anthony, Andrew Denton and George Piggins in their Souths scarves celebrating victory, 2001.

Anthony, Kristina Keneally, Russell Crowe and Peter Holmes a Court, at the 2010 South Sydney season launch.

V for Victory, on same-sex superannuation rights, at the 2001 Mardi Gras parade.

Anthony and then leader of the Opposition, Kim Beazley, Federal Parliament, 2004. (DAVID FOOTE – AUSPIC/DPS)

Kevin Rudd, Wayne Swan, Julia Gillard and Anthony Albanese in 2008. (FAIRFAX SYNDICATION/ANDREW MEARES)

Anthony at the dispatch box, Budget Day 2009, with Kevin Rudd and Stephen Smith paying close attention. (MICHAEL JONES – AUSPIC/DPS)

Anthony with his father, Carlo Albanese, Barletta, Italy, 2009.
(PHOTO: LISA GOLDEN)

Anthony, Carmel, Nathan and Carlo Albanese, Barletta, Italy, 2011.
(PHOTO: LISA GOLDEN)

Tom Uren speaking at an Albanese campaign event in 2010.

Above: Anthony takes to the crease in a match with junior cricketers, Mackey Park, 2010.

Left: Celebrating turning 50, with a Bunnies cake, of course, in 2013.

February 25, 2012, Anthony at a press conference explaining he had just called the then Prime Minister, Julia Gillard, to tell her he would be voting for Kevin Rudd. (FAIRFAX SYNDICATION/LEE BESFORD)

Chris Bowen, Kevin Rudd and Anthony Albanese after their swearing in at Government House, July 2013. (DAVID FOOTE – AUSPIC/DPS)

Carmel, Tom Uren, Meredith Burgmann and Anthony, celebrating Tom's 90th birthday in Balmain, 2011. (PHOTO: MEREDITH BURGMANN)

Rousing the party at the 2013 campaign launch. (PHOTO: MICHAEL BOWERS)

Above: Anthony with Blanche d'Alpuget, Bob Hawke and Carmel at his 20th anniversary celebrations, 26 February 2016, in Hurlstone Park.

Left: Anthony and Carmel both looking hot at the Midwinter Ball in Canberra, June 2015. (FAIRFAX SYNDICATION/ALEX ELLINGHAUSEN)

Election 2016 and News Ltd is onside. It wasn't always thus, 11 May 2016. (NEWSPIX)

The Daily Telegraph

WE'RE FOR NSW

$1.50 // WEDNESDAY, MAY 11, 2016

SAVE OUR ALBO

True believer in the fight of his political life with Greens radical who wants to overthrow capitalism

ANDREW CLENNELL

ONE of NSW's most accomplished politicians faces being kicked out of federal Parliament by a Greens extremist who champions the "overthrow of capitalism".

Labor's former deputy prime minister Anthony Albanese is caught in the fight of his political life to prevent far-left union boss Jim Casey seizing his inner Sydney seat of Grayndler for the Greens at the July 2 poll.

Labor has been frantically pouring extra resources into the seat in a desperate bid to save its most popular politician, as Greens leader Senator Richard Di Natale hit the streets to personally campaign in the electorate. The Daily Telegraph today editorialises in favour of Mr Albanese's re-election because of his commitment to NSW and the Greens' extreme policies.

» FULL REPORT PAGES 4-5

» KEEP ALBO IN PARLIAMENT PAGE 27

ROGER: I'M THE VICTIM

Rogerson lashes out » PAGE 12

STITCHED UP BY WALEED

What outed star really thinks » PAGE 9

Farewelling dear comrade Alan Griffin, 2 March 2016, Parliament House. (PHOTO: MICHAEL BOWERS)

DJ Albo at a fundraiser for Reclink which aims to rebuild lives through sport and arts, 22 June 2016.

Paul Keating brought a bit of humour to Albo's campaign as he launched a withering attack on the Greens, 25 June 2016.
(PHOTO: JOHN TASS-PARKER)

'I think he found it quite interesting and a bit of a challenge at family events,' Carmel says.

'We got on very well,' Anthony says of the Tebbutts. 'I found it from time to time a bit overwhelming.'

Finding the right house took time and opportunities came and went. None in his price range were exactly what he wanted but he wasn't especially bothered. He was in no rush. In late 1989, after he'd taken up the new job, he found a place up for auction in Marrickville. The vendors wanted more than he bid and the property was passed in.

It was a tough time in the economy and an especially tough time to be borrowing money to buy real estate, with Australia sliding into recession and interest rates up around 17 per cent. But Anthony was still living happily in Pyrmont Bridge Road and he wasn't in any particular hurry to move out.

Quite a few months later, the real estate agent contacted him to say the same house was still on the market – a little two-bedroom semi-detached place he'd been really keen on – and if he upped his offer he could have it.

After some back and forth, Anthony bought his first home in a quiet part of Marrickville. He would sell it five years later to buy a better house a few blocks away, but move back to the original street, to a different address with his family 20 years on, because he had liked the area so much.

When he bought that first house, a friend from Sydney Uni and Young Labor, David Bourne, moved in to share with him. By then, Carmel had left the Shire, also for the inner west, and was living with friends in Stanmore.

The following year, about 18 months after she and Anthony began seeing each other, her group house was breaking up and she needed somewhere else to live.

David moved out of Anthony's Marrickville house and Carmel moved in.

CHAPTER 13

On the Numbers

The ninth floor of 377 Sussex Street was not an entirely welcoming environment for whoever was the left-wing Assistant General Secretary of the NSW Labor Party. The arrival of 26-year-old Anthony Albanese did nothing to change that.

'It was a very difficult role and a very difficult job and extremely stressful for Anthony,' Carmel says. 'And the pressure on him was immense.'

The first to hold the job, Bruce Childs, had also found it a challenge to carry out his duties among his unfriendly right-wing colleagues and things really became ugly in John Faulkner's time, in the aftermath of Peter Baldwin's bashing.

At the more benign end of shenanigans, John famously was excluded from the office Christmas party. His Left colleagues came in and held an alternative festive celebration with him in his personal office instead. It got a lot worse than that, but he does not care to discuss exactly what happened.

Anthony was therefore well aware of the hostility awaiting him among his colleagues in the Right when he won the position. From their point of view, he hadn't exactly held out the hand of friendship either. So they made sure to make him feel deeply unwelcome.

For a start, his office key opened only his own office door. The party's important documents, along with its administrative equipment, were kept in a separate room. He was locked out.

'I didn't have access to the photocopier or the fax machine,' he says.

The NSW ALP's membership records – including those of people from his own faction – were not accessible to him either, also stored in the admin room.

The then General Secretary John Della Bosca says that during his time 'the party records or at least the roll of members was fully computerised', making their physical location less relevant. He says access to the office where all the administrative records were kept had been restricted severely after a notorious earlier state preselection battle, during which two party officials had accessed the files after hours and 'improperly varied' them.

'Anthony had the same access to those records as me,' John says.

Nevertheless, it was, as Anthony puts it, a 'very unusual work environment'. He operated on the correct assumption that his right-wing colleagues would take any opportunity to undermine him, including rifling through his office whenever he wasn't around.

'I used to leave absolutely nothing behind,' he says. 'Except the stuff I wanted them to find.'

He was told subsequently that a junior staff member had been assigned to the rifling task, on Friday nights after he'd gone home. John Della Bosca says that was absolutely untrue.

'No one was ever assigned to search Anthony's office regularly or otherwise,' he says. 'I have no knowledge of this occurring and Anthony never complained to me about it at the time.'

But from the Right's point of view, Anthony was certainly a foe. John Della Bosca says it was his aggressive approach to party politics that generated suspicion in response.

'I think at the time Anthony was regarded as more of a super militant,' John says. 'A tear-down-the-house type of guy.'

Anthony treated this situation like any other political contest – as a challenge requiring a strategy. He made sure he was courteous to the administrative staff, when some of his right-wing colleagues didn't bother.

'They made a mistake,' he says. 'Always be nice to workers.'

It had its benefits. The receptionists would find ways to alert him if they had been instructed not to put incoming calls through to his phone. They developed a code when he passed by the desk.

'The young women who were at the front of the office would often say to me, "Oh, you haven't had any calls today?"' he recalls. 'And I would say, "Right, okay. So you're not allowed to put them through?" And they would say, "Oh, can't say." They'd let me know.'

Eventually, he acquired a key to the admin room. He is deliberately vague on exactly how.

'I just found it. As you do.'

He made good use of both the files and the photocopier, copying the entire membership list.

'I mean, why shouldn't I? I was the elected Assistant Secretary and I had a right to know who the membership was.'

A couple of factional allies then typed up the data offsite so the Left could mail out direct to the whole membership, just as the Right did. But he needed to ensure his right-wing colleagues didn't find out.

'I had to keep complaining about not getting access to anything,' he says. 'Long after I had a key.'

At his first Administrative Committee meeting at the Sussex Street office, Anthony was the only member of the Left who turned up, among 20 members of the Right.

Right-wing powerbroker and NSW Legislative Council President 'Johno' Johnson was there and furnished his right-wing colleagues with a warning that they weren't to cooperate with the lone lefty.

'I said, "Oh, I haven't even got a seconder,"' Anthony recalls. 'And Johno said, "If anyone seconds any of his motions, you're expelled."'

It was a joke – more or less. The first item of business was endorsing the minutes of the previous meeting. The defiant young left-winger was fast.

'Moved!'

It took a moment for the rest to realise they'd been snookered. No seconder, no proceedings. They had to laugh. Score one to the young smart-arse.

'That broke some of the ice,' he says.

His double-headed tactic proved both the power of humour as a political weapon and the value in being a step ahead of your opponents. Anthony would learn to employ both of these throughout his career in politics, sometimes with devastating effect.

The year Anthony moved into Sussex Street, the split within the Left widened. Having seized his job by defeating the soft Left through ballots both in the Steering Committee and on the conference floor, Anthony and the hard Left group he was leading struck again at a Steering Committee meeting on 10 November 1989.

Before the meeting, a number of proposals had been put forward to restructure the NSW Left to broaden the participation in the peak body. The proposals from the soft and hard Left differed on who should qualify to vote in internal Left ballots. The soft Left wanted a more flexible approach to eligibility.

A soft Left proposal was defeated, 52 votes to 39, and

Martin Ferguson's Miscellaneous Workers' Union representatives walked out in protest.

The hard Left's proposals were adopted, including changing the name of the committee to the 'Socialist Left', the name by which it was known everywhere but NSW.

It happened to be the same day that, a world away, the Berlin Wall fell in Germany. The irony of moving to formally embrace socialism just as one of its most famous global symbols was being torn down was not lost on some cynical observers.

Among those alongside Anthony at the top of the hard Left in 1989 was Amalgamated Metal Workers' Union secretary George Campbell, who would succeed Bruce Childs in the Senate in 1997. George's elevation would be at Bruce's expense, with the hard Left insisting the latter retire and make way.

Because he was reluctant, a compromise was negotiated so he would remain on the Senate ticket for the 1996 election but resign later, creating a casual vacancy for George Campbell to fill.

Anthony's support for the changeover would generate the only real argument he ever had with his mentor and former boss, Tom Uren, who believed he should have showed more loyalty to Bruce Childs.

'He was really cross about that,' Anthony says. 'Tom expressed very directly that he was disappointed, that I was wrong.'

It was an emotional episode. Bruce Childs was widely respected and both men came from the same union.

'It was one of the most difficult ballots I've been involved in,' Anthony says. 'I respected Bruce and had been close to him for a long time. Carmel had worked for him and supported him strongly in the ballot. I was desperate to get a resolution that didn't force people to choose between the two, who had been friends and comrades for a long time.'

Nevertheless, George Campbell would be installed and would retain the seat, from second position on the NSW Labor Senate ticket, at the 2001 election.

But ahead of the 2007 election, when he hoped to be re-endorsed, George too would experience the abandonment of his factional colleagues – including Anthony – when they switched their preselection support to another left-winger, George's union protégé Doug Cameron.

In 2016, George declines to speak about Anthony. Once a close associate – George was one of the few federal colleagues who attended Anthony's wedding in 2000 – a decade and a half on, the two are no longer friends.

As the '80s gave way to the '90s, another who was becoming more prominent in the NSW hard Left after Anthony's elevation to Assistant General Secretary was Meredith Burgmann.

Meredith's involvement in the Labor Party pre-dated her association with Anthony but was stepped up under his patronage. In 1990, he would persuade the then senior lecturer at Macquarie University and head of the Academics Union to seek preselection – successfully – for a seat in the NSW Upper House, where she would then go on to serve for 16 years, including as its president.

'He just turned up one day when I was marking first-year essays,' Meredith says. '. . . And I said, "Don't be silly, I'm an academic."'

But he took her to a Friday lunch at her local pub, the Friend in Hand, in inner-city Glebe, talked her through it and asked her to think about it over the next few days.

At home, faced with having to spend her weekend marking 500 first-year politics essays, she started to think maybe it wasn't a bad idea. When he came back to her on Tuesday, she said yes.

The other main Left candidate was someone with whom both she and Anthony were familiar – the woman he'd defeated to secure his own job in head office, Jan Burnswoods.

The Right was a lot less enthusiastic about the idea. In the end, Meredith and her backers prevailed. Jan Burnswoods was also preselected, further down the ticket, and both were elected to State Parliament in the Legislative Council.

Anthony says he encouraged Meredith's greater participation because aside from seeing her as a good candidate, he believed her involvement sent an important message to those with progressive politics operating outside the ALP.

'Meredith more than anyone else was a part of the Vietnam, anti-apartheid, activist generation,' he says. 'She sent a huge message to the Whitlamite Left, if you like, that you should be *in* the Labor Party. She was a radical. Meredith was a genuine radical in the feminist movement, in the movement outside the Labor Party. And that was one of the distinctions with the groups in the Left.'

There was a division between those left-wing activists within the Labor Party and those operating outside. Far from denying his influence in identifying and assisting fellow left-wingers – and especially women – into politics, Anthony celebrates it. It means he has also conveniently established a network of people beholden to him for their success.

He puts it in far simpler terms. 'Political power is defined by its use.'

Anthony not only antagonised those in the soft Left by manoeuvring himself into an influential position in the party, he antagonised the Right as well. And that antagonism was not confined to his role in head office.

Having bought his house in Marrickville, Anthony had joined his local ALP branch, Marrickville West, within the federal seat of Grayndler.

His Camperdown home had been in the seat of Sydney, which was held by the Left. But this other electorate was a right-wing-Labor stronghold.

His new local branch was struggling so badly it had become almost non-existent, and in 1991 it was merged with the powerful and notorious The Warren branch.

Anthony went along to the first annual general meeting of

the newly amalgamated branch and quietly lodged a written nomination with the returning officer for the branch's most senior position: secretary.

His form was dropped in among others' nominations for various positions and buried in the pile. Apparently assuming he was nominating for some lower-ranking administrative post, the branch's right-wing powerbrokers did not bother lodging their own paperwork for the secretary's position.

When nominations closed, Anthony's was the only formal one for the job. The branch's senior figures were shocked and asked him to withdraw.

'That's fine,' Anthony replied, claiming he was more than happy to pull out – as long as someone else had nominated on paper as per the rules. He knew very well nobody had.

The branch's leaders generally didn't bother following the actual rules too closely. Having always had the numbers to do whatever they liked without anyone much to challenge them, they had been planning to sort it out on the floor of the meeting, as usual. But written nominations overrode verbal ones and Anthony stood his ground.

'So somehow, without really having the numbers in this branch, I became secretary of what was on paper a big branch in what was then a pretty safe right-wing area,' Anthony says. 'I became effectively secretary in charge of the books of two branches which – on paper – had lots of members.'

He was, he concedes, 'a bit lucky'.

The Warren branch's reputation was that its written membership lists did not always match the identities of actual human beings who had joined of their own volition.

Historically, it had been a hotbed of stacking. In the period before Peter Baldwin had been bashed in 1980, he had been accused of stacking numerous Left supporters into branches across the inner west. As one of his fellow left-wingers put it in 2016, Peter was 'a huge recruiter of members in his day'.

In the aftermath of that period, Fairfax journalist Mike Steketee offered perhaps the most accurate summation of how things worked.

'Branch-stacking is something the other side does,' Mike wrote. 'If it's your faction, then it's called things like "recruiting new members to broaden the base of the party".'

In 1991 and '92, Anthony set about 'recruiting new members' ferociously for the Left. He'd become accomplished at the task through his activities at Sydney University and in Young Labor.

'I used to use cricket analogies,' he says. 'You turned singles into twos, twos into fours. So if you recruit someone – "who's your partner? Are they in the party? Have you got a brother? A sister? Who do you work with?" There were a lot of members in Grayndler.'

They recruited anyone progressive they could find. Progressive Greeks. Progressive Italians. Lebanese. Palestinians. The Right was employing the same tactics, looking for anyone who was prepared to vote their way.

'I had a view that if they brought 100, I'd bring 150,' Anthony says. 'It was exhausting.'

The Left's numbers in Grayndler grew. Former Keating Government Minister Jeannette McHugh, whose parliamentary career was extended with Anthony's help, insists the distinction between his activities and stacking in the classic sense is his attachment to the branches and their members.

'Branch-stacking usually means you rope a whole lot of people into the branch and then you just use them to vote,' she says. 'Anthony could no more do that than fly. If a person is in a branch and he's got them into the branch . . . he knows them very well forever. He's very close to the branches.'

Along with The Warren branch, his faction gained control of other key branches in the inner west. Then at the beginning of 1992, something serendipitous happened which delivered more power over the seat into Anthony's hands.

In January, the Australian Electoral Commission completed a review of federal electoral boundaries in NSW – a redistribution process undertaken Australia-wide every few years, to take account of shifts in population. The review covered Sydney city seats, including Grayndler.

As is normal practice, the political parties lodged submissions arguing exactly how the boundaries should be adjusted. Unsurprisingly, each party generally sought an outcome most favourable to its chances of victory in as many seats as possible. Each usually sought to persuade the commission to group together the areas that tended to vote its way and exclude those that didn't.

The AEC weighed up the arguments, seeking compromise boundaries that would fit its brief to give all electorates nationwide roughly equal populations.

Early on the morning the final result of the 1991 NSW redistribution was to be revealed, Anthony was in his office in Sussex Street when former NSW ALP education and research officer, the Right's Shane Easson, appeared. He was clutching the new electoral map showing the boundaries of Grayndler, a safe Labor seat, redrawn.

Shane was the redistributions expert, responsible for preparing all the submissions to the Electoral Commission for NSW, both state and federal. He spread the map out on Anthony's desk, exclaiming at the young left-winger's apparent good fortune, 'They've drawn a seat of Albanese!'

And indeed, they had. The newly drawn seat of Grayndler took in part of the old seat of Sydney and included Anthony's old stomping ground around Camperdown, as well as the part of Marrickville whose branches he and the Left now controlled.

'It was my turf,' Anthony says. 'Where I'd lived my whole life. My old base. My new base. And I had the numbers.'

His faction had been moving in, right across the electorate. Left-winger Barry Cotter had been elected mayor of Marrickville, ousting the seven-year incumbent, the Right's

Barry Jones, who was a personal friend of the federal Member for Grayndler, the Right's Leo McLeay. The Right correctly smelled a wholesale Left takeover in the making.

It was not in the habit of simply making way. When Anthony and his comrades established a Young Labor Association in Grayndler, things began to get really unpleasant.

At the first meeting of the Grayndler YLA, on the night of Tuesday, 11 February 1992, the sons of some of the area's most prominent figures from the Labor Right were among the dozens who suddenly took a keen interest in Young Labor.

Leo McLeay's son, Mark, was elected secretary of the new association. The membership numbers swelled dramatically to 60 and among the newcomers was a group of young thugs who turned up largely to disrupt proceedings at Marrickville's Alfred Frede Hall.

The intruders commandeered the membership book and when Anthony was called down from the back of the room to try to retrieve it, he was surrounded. One intimated he had a knife.

'See what I've got in my pocket, mate?' is what Anthony recalls one of them telling him. 'You're going to feel it . . . I'm going to slit your throat.'

A member from the Right intervened and told them to cool it, that if they actually hurt him they would be in big trouble.

But things weren't calm for very long. Young women, some of them teenagers attending their first political meeting, were being subjected to aggressive sexual taunts. When the verbal attacks on one female office-bearer became so bad that another young woman stepped in to defend her, they turned on her as well. Her boyfriend leapt up and both were set upon and chased out the back door, down the stairs and along Illawarra Road.

The incident found its way into *The Sydney Morning Herald* after Anthony made a report to police and to the party's Administrative Committee, forcing General Secretary John Della Bosca to also ask police to investigate.

Anthony gave a police statement. He was shown mug shots and identified the man he said was responsible for the knife threat. Nothing ever came of it.

The Right assumed Anthony's Grayndler takeover was because he was lining himself up to run for preselection in the seat – which would involve seeking to overthrow right-wing incumbent Leo McLeay – ahead of the 1993 election. That was the expectation being expressed privately and publicly around the area at the time.

Just over a week after the knife incident, *The Sydney Morning Herald* ran another report on the factional tensions, quoting alderman and former mayor Barry Jones urging observers to 'look at this in context'.

'Anthony Albanese has been telling everyone that he will be the next member for Grayndler,' he was reported as saying.

Along with securing more turf for his faction, Anthony doesn't deny he was also looking ahead. But the pundits were wrong on the timing. He is a master of forward planning.

'I wasn't ready to run,' Anthony says. 'I was just trying to get it for the Left.'

At 29, he believed he still had work to do as Assistant Secretary – and hadn't yet identified an obvious sub-factional successor in the job, something he would rectify before he eventually moved on.

Having secured the numbers to command a Left majority in Grayndler, he began work on a plan to wrest it from Leo McLeay and put someone from the Left in instead. The electoral redistribution paved the way.

The redrawing of boundaries may have helped deliver Grayndler to the Left but it had robbed the faction of another seat. In its submission to the Electoral Commission, the NSW ALP – in other words, the Right – had recommended the abolition of one of its own party's seats, the eastern-suburbs seat of Phillip, held for the previous decade by the Left's Jeannette McHugh.

The Right was so motivated to weaken the Left's numbers on the leather benches in Canberra, it was prepared to sacrifice a Labor seat to do it. After considering all advice, the commission had indeed slated Phillip to disappear, leaving Jeannette facing compulsory retirement.

Another Labor-held Sydney seat was also abolished, the southern-suburbs seat of St George, held by the Right's Steve Dubois. A new seat of Watson replaced it, covering largely the same area, with some of the old Grayndler incorporated.

Anthony had a solution to the abolition of Phillip that was bound to enrage the Right: shift Jeannette to Grayndler and force Leo to move. It would salvage her political career and secure an extra seat for the Left. He also happened to believe she deserved saving.

'Jeannette had been the first woman to get elected to the House of Representatives from NSW from any political party,' Anthony says. '. . . And they'd abolished her seat in a *Labor* submission.'

He calls that 'incredible'. Meredith Burgmann agrees.

'She was clearly important – she was iconic,' she says. 'And the Right supported a redistribution that got rid of her. And Albo organised a way to fix that.'

He arranged to have lunch with Jeannette and her good friend, left-wing MLC Ann Symonds, at the Spanish Club in Liverpool Street, a favourite lunch spot for the Left. There, he suggested to Jeannette that she put herself forward for preselection in Grayndler for the 1993 election, opposing Leo McLeay. She was initially incredulous.

'Don't be ridiculous! People wouldn't support me.'

'Yes,' he insisted. 'They will.'

Jeannette lived in the eastern suburbs and was far more genteel and softly-spoken a character than the inner west usually endorsed. But like Anthony, she was a committed, old-style campaigner who believed in turning up to meetings, answering to the branches and getting to know members personally.

They all knew she would need to work hard to get the inner-west branches onside and some of them were not going to be easy, The Warren foremost among them. Add to that the fact that there were others interested in contesting Grayndler, including Marrickville mayor Barry Cotter, and the whole thing would take some finessing.

But Jeannette was the one Anthony was supporting and that counted for a lot. He proposed her for a range of reasons, among them, as she puts it, that after another three-year term in Parliament she would be 62 and likely more willing than others might be to move aside.

She was also a hardworking representative in her existing seat and he knew she would put in the effort. And with the Left having risen to prominence and then dominance in Grayndler, once the faction formally anointed her she would have a very good head start.

When he put the proposal to Jeannette over lunch, she thought he should run. He told her he wasn't ready.

But eventually, he would want to run. What was unspoken was that when that time came, she would have to retire.

It was a plan to advance both her interests and the interests of the NSW Left, he said. Jeannette was a team player. She agreed.

But this was only the first stage in an audacious one-two manoeuvre that would infuriate and gazump the faction of then Prime Minister Paul Keating, the NSW Right.

The Member for Grayndler, Leo McLeay, was also the Speaker of the House of Representatives, one of a group of powerbrokers known as the 'mates' in NSW. His factional colleagues were moving to ensure his preselection was secure.

Labor has a rule that ministers are immune from any preselection challenge. But the Speaker was not a Minister and so wasn't similarly protected. The Right's leaders could see the shadow of the Left falling across Grayndler. They started to push to have the protection rule extended to the Speaker as well.

They attempted it through the party's national executive but failed, thanks to the efforts of John Faulkner, who also secured the votes of the Right's Gareth Evans and John Button from the Centre-Left.

In the middle of all this, Senator Graham Richardson – another of the hard men of the NSW Right – was forced to quit the Cabinet after revelations he had used his ministerial influence to seek to help out a relative.

Ministerial vacancies were subject to negotiation between the Labor factions and a deal had been struck between Left and Right after the 1990 election to allow then Prime Minister Bob Hawke to promote two colleagues from the Right into the ministry.

At the time, the Left agreed to give up one of its ministerial spots to accommodate his wish. In return, Hawke promised the Left would fill a future vacancy – not the first that arose, but the second.

After his failed leadership challenge in June 1991, Keating's resignation as Treasurer created the first vacancy. Eleven months later, on Monday, 18 May 1992, Richardson's resignation provided the second. Immediately, the Left was calling in the debt, claiming it was entitled to the ministerial spot as promised.

Paul Keating was now Prime Minister and, having won some support from the Left to get him there, he and his faction reluctantly agreed to uphold the deal. The only question became who in the Left would get the job.

The Left's leading figure in Parliament, Victorian Gerry Hand, wanted it to go to Northern Territory MP Warren Snowdon. But Anthony, with his state-based colleague Paul O'Grady and other factional leaders in the NSW Left, came up with an alternative plan.

The next day, a Tuesday, Jeannette McHugh was in a lounge at Sydney Airport heading to Albury-Wodonga to deliver a speech to a union dinner and visit the Trade Union Training Authority, when she was called to the phone. It was Anthony.

'You're running,' he said.

The idea that she might fill the ministerial vacancy was so far from her mind, she thought at first he was suggesting she was late for her plane.

'Running for what? What do you mean?'

He explained that he and others had decided she was the best candidate for the ministerial vacancy. She was gobsmacked a second time.

She certainly thought it would be good for a woman to run – Keating only had two in his ministry – and she'd even rung her friend and colleague Carolyn Jakobsen to see if she might be interested in nominating. But it hadn't occurred to Jeannette that it could actually be her.

For a second time, Anthony was proposing the unthinkable and asking her to step up. There would doubtless be blowback from those who didn't think she was up to it.

'The reason I was able to do those things is I was always part of a group, part of a team,' Jeannette says in 2016. 'And Anthony was the one organising that team.'

Barry Cotter, the mayor of Marrickville, was doing some work at the Training Authority office in Albury, the regional city separating NSW and Victoria. From his office, Jeannette made phone calls on Anthony's instruction – to a furious Gerry Hand, who was on his way to Indonesia, and Brian Howe, his fellow Victorian and faction leader and the Deputy Prime Minister, and others. She was sensitive to the fact that Barry, who would have liked to contest Grayndler himself, was now graciously helping her.

'He was the most supportive person in the world.'

He was also attending the dinner. By the time they arrived, she had spent much of the day on the phone. But it wasn't over yet.

'A waiter came to the table and said, "There's a phone call for you in the kitchen,"' Jeannette recalls.

It was *The Sydney Morning Herald*'s Alan Ramsey. She wasn't sure exactly what to tell him. But clearly he found others to fill in the gaps, because the next morning his front-page story revealed her candidacy for both the ministry and for Grayndler. There was no backing out.

She returned early to Sydney and a Commonwealth car collected her from the airport. The driver turned on the radio and the ABC's AM program announced she was to be the Left's candidate for the Keating ministry.

'I knew the driver very well and we're listening to AM and they said, "Well, a bit of news. Jeannette McHugh . . ."' she says, laughing. 'And the driver looked round at me and I looked at him.'

And that was that.

Securing Jeannette the ministerial post not only restored the Left's numbers on the frontbench, it also protected her from any head-office attempt to stop her running for Grayndler.

A Minister trumped the Speaker when it came to preselection. As long as she won the support of rank-and-file party members, she was home free in her new seat.

Once she had Grayndler, then the Left had Grayndler. And provided the Left kept its grip on the electorate – and a majority of voters there continued to support the Labor Party – Anthony also had Grayndler whenever he decided he wanted it.

His chess-like manoeuvres had triumphed. It was a checkmate strategy and one of the reasons colleagues many years his senior would defer to him on such matters.

'He's incredibly good at [it],' says Meredith Burgmann. 'The number of times we've been in a situation and he's said, "We've just got to keep dancing." And I've said, "What do you mean by that?" And he's said, "Oh, we've got to keep moving."

He's the best strategist I've ever come across. I always used to pride myself at being three steps ahead. And he used to laugh because he's always 10 steps ahead.'

Once Jeannette McHugh was officially a frontbencher, Anthony did not muck around.

Jeannette and the rest of the reshuffled ministry had been sworn in at Government House, and within 24 hours she had faced her first Question Time as one of those having to answer rather than ask the questions, followed by her first parliamentary debate as a Minister on a Matter of Public Importance, both fairly robust affairs.

Just before she headed for the airport at the end of a head-spinning week, Anthony rang.

'Get home,' he said. 'You've got to run a preselection.'

Telling the story 24 years later, she laughs. 'It wasn't "Well done, Jeannette! Good on you, Minister!"' she says. 'It was "Get home, you've got to run a preselection."'

When she sat down on the plane, Leo McLeay was sitting behind her, the man with whom she was about to have a showdown over the seat. 'And I turned round and said, "Well, Leo, we'd better set some ground rules."'

He just glared at her and said nothing.

Once back in Sydney, McLeay had a decision to make. Would he fight it out with Jeannette in an ugly battle for Grayndler where the Left now held sway, or would he seek to move to the new seat of Watson where his seniority would ensure he was given priority over incumbent Steve Dubois?

Leo insists he had already made his decision. He had paid a quiet visit to the newly included parts of Grayndler.

'As soon as that redistribution came out, I went and had a cup of coffee in Newtown and said to myself, "Those people are never going to vote for me,"' he says.

Then aged 47, he had already served 13 years in Grayndler. But he argues that his support base – or those who most resembled it – had been shifted via the redistribution into Watson.

'The three groups that I was always comfortable with were the Greeks, Arabs and working class,' Leo says. 'And in the electorate of Grayndler after the boundary change, there weren't too many of them at all because they'd all gone to Watson. And so I was off with them . . . It would be pretty hard for me to get out there and sign up to the agenda of latte sippers and chardonnay spillers in Newtown.'

He maintains he wasn't unhappy. 'That was the best thing that ever happened to me in my life.'

He and Anthony would eventually overcome their differences.

'We were like enemies,' Anthony says in 2016. 'It was a war. And then we became friends.'

In 2016, as he marked 20 years in Parliament with an anniversary dinner at the Canterbury Hurlstone Park RSL, Anthony would pay tribute not only to the Left's surviving elder statesman, Bruce Childs, but to both of his immediate predecessors in Grayndler, Jeannette McHugh and Leo McLeay. He said they 'have far more in common than they would like to acknowledge'.

'I was friends with Jeannette,' he told the gathering, referring to those hectic days in the early '90s. 'Wasn't always friends with Leo and that's the truth. But the truth is also that mentors like Leo, who was the Chief Whip at the time [I went into Parliament], took me under his wing and I learnt a lot off him.'

In 1992, things weren't quite so congenial. And for Jeannette, regardless of Anthony's support, there was still the challenge of introducing herself to the inner west. At one of the early branch meetings, a row of men sat, just staring at her.

'They had their arms folded and looking at me as if to say, "What's she doing here?"' she says. They weren't used to their local member routinely turning up to their meetings.

She persevered. The following month she was running late for the same branch's meeting, having rushed there from the airport. When she arrived, the same blokes – who had apparently come around to the idea of a more involved local member – said, 'Where have you been?'

The Warren branch, however, was in a league of its own. The branch was named for the area of Marrickville South in which it first resided, originally the site of a Victorian Gothic mansion called 'The Warren', built by business tycoon Thomas Holt in 1857. The castle-style home sat on 100 acres, located between the modern-day Unwins Bridge Road, Illawarra Road and Warren Road.

Eventually sub-divided and sold off, the property had been a landmark in the area, its name living on separately in the form of both the Warren View Hotel in Enmore and the most notorious Labor Party branch in the inner west.

In the early '90s, The Warren branch had swollen to more than 400 members, so big its meetings had to be moved to the auditorium at the Marrickville RSL.

'It was absolutely terrifying and they were so hostile,' Jeannette says.

One man sized her up and demanded to know why she didn't just go back to the eastern suburbs – only he used a slightly more four-letter turn of phrase. It was the first time she had realised just how significant a divide there was between east and west in Sydney. It was more than just mistrust. It bordered on hatred.

'You couldn't get less wanted than that, to be from the eastern suburbs,' she says.

At The Warren branch meeting, another bloke sneered at her, 'You married a judge.'

Her husband, Michael McHugh, was indeed on the bench. But he'd left school at 15 and done manual work before putting himself through night school to obtain his leaving certificate and going on to study Law. She was having none of it.

'I married a fellow working in the rod mill in the BHP in Newcastle,' the demure Jeannette responded, refusing to retreat. 'The fact that he's now a High Court judge should make you very proud.'

As she left the meeting and crossed the street, Anthony came running out.

'You got them!' he told her. They thought she had guts.

But the hostility didn't end there. The Right continued to load new members into Grayndler to try to wrest back control. One night at a branch meeting with both Anthony and Jeannette attending and Carmel Tebbutt among those on the door checking credentials, several unfamiliar men turned up, saying they wanted to join. As is standard procedure, they were asked for identification.

'They said the only ID they had was gun licences,' Anthony says. '*Get the message?* And they produced their gun licences – with an address outside the electorate, by the way.'

Carmel didn't recognise them personally but knew they were linked to the Right. She asked them for some other form of identification.

'And they insisted and said that was the only identification they were going to provide,' Carmel says. 'I was pretty shocked at that. I can remember I wrote to the General Secretary about my concern.'

Later, to make the point, Anthony put a motion to The Warren branch and the Grayndler Federal Electorate Council that gun licences be prohibited as ID. It was acknowledged but not adopted.

The incident shook them all up, just as it was meant to.

With Anthony's career progressing, Carmel had been making her own way in politics and also becoming more engaged locally. As their personal partnership strengthened, Carmel's professional path became clearer too.

She had risen quickly through the Young Labor ranks and become NSW President herself in 1991 at the age of 26, serving one year before the age limit on Young Labor membership would force her out of the organisation.

As President, she continued the frenzied activity for which NSW Young Labor had become known. It was part heady excitement, part achievement.

'We thought we were making a real difference,' Carmel says. 'We were recruiting people into the Labor Party. We were developing policy. We were running campaigns . . . Some of it was just getting caught up in the activity for activity's sake. And some of it was real.'

Two years after she stepped down, control of Young Labor finally fell to the Right. But Carmel herself was held in high regard across the party. As of 2016, NSW Young Labor – still controlled by the Right – was showcasing Carmel's photograph on its website as one who had risen to be among 'Australia's greatest Labor figures' through that organisation. Among those named with her were former Prime Minister Paul Keating and former Premier and Foreign Minister Bob Carr.

Carmel was a former Deputy Premier and the first woman to have held that role. Hers was the only left-wing name among seven singled out for special mention on the Young Labor site. Her husband and fellow former NSW Young Labor President, Anthony Albanese – whose past positions by then included Deputy Prime Minister – was not mentioned.

At the time she left Young Labor, Carmel believed her professional future was in the union movement. She resigned the Young Labor presidency in 1992 and, at least partly to escape the factional aggro of the local neighbourhood, set off on her own grand solo travelling adventure – four months in Europe. Anthony's Sussex Street job and the vigilance required in Grayndler meant he couldn't join her. While she was away, another of his left-wing mates, Luke Foley, moved in to help with the mortgage.

Two decades later, Luke would become leader of the Labor Party in NSW. Back then, Luke says he and Anthony kept things fairly 'tame' at home. Any raucous partying tended to be done elsewhere.

Carmel flew to London and stayed with an Australian friend who was living there. Together they went to Spain and after that she went on to Greece, with an old school friend who'd flown over to meet her.

'I had periods of time when I was with people and then I had the big block of time when I was on my own,' Carmel says. It gave her some welcome distance from all the political upheaval back in Marrickville and in the Labor Party. 'I think it was really good for me.'

They were the days before email and mobile phones and she carried bags of coins with her, so she could phone home. Like other backpackers, she also used the Post Restante system, nominating towns to which friends and family could send letters and then dropping in to each town's post office to collect them.

For young travellers, this kind of big backpacking trip was a wild adventure far from home. The other side of the world felt very distant.

'I think it was good in a way because you really did immerse yourself in another world,' Carmel says.

After four months of exploring Europe, Carmel headed home via Thailand. While she had been away, Jeannette had been preselected, so with things slightly calmer Anthony managed to snag two weeks off. He flew to meet Carmel for a beach holiday. They stayed briefly in Bangkok and then headed for Koh Samui to relax and catch up.

When the couple returned, it was Carmel's turn for an unexpected change of direction.

CHAPTER 14

Moving On Up

In 1993, there was a vacancy on Marrickville Council, the heart of local government in Anthony and Carmel's part of the inner west. The left-wing mayor, Barry Cotter, approached Carmel to see if she'd consider running.

She had dipped her toe into local politics once before, with an unsuccessful tilt at the Sutherland Shire Council. Feeling like she wanted more in her political life than just her union work at the AMP Staff Association, she decided she was ready to try again and told Barry she'd do it.

Her community support was so strong she did something virtually unheard of at the local level. Securing more than 50 per cent of the primary vote, she won the seat without the need for preferences.

'The result was much better than anyone thought was possible,' Anthony says.

When she joined the council, Carmel found she loved it. 'I was interested in local government but I can't say I had this huge passion for representative politics as a long-term career,' she recalls. 'But I think it was my experiences once I went onto council that really drove a greater desire to get more involved in representative politics.'

The opportunity for that came soon enough. Marrickville lay within the state seat of Ashfield and Carmel and Anthony became involved in the seat's State Electorate Council.

There was local dissatisfaction with the sitting Labor Right member, former Minister Paul Whelan. The state seat overlapped the federal seat of Grayndler and the Left saw it as equally ripe for a takeover.

Leading Left figure Andrew Refshauge had suggested to Carmel previously that she should think about moving to state politics. He thought she had something to offer.

'That was quite influential because I don't think up until that point anyone of any great seniority had given me that sort of encouragement to aspire to go into Parliament,' she says.

She nominated for Ashfield in 1994 and began campaigning for preselection, ahead of the '95 state election, along with several others. But they were seeking to challenge a sitting, senior right-wing member. Once again, the Right was not happy.

Shortly before the preselection ballot, the NSW ALP's Right-controlled administrative committee intervened, indicating it would not allow the Ashfield preselection challenge to go ahead. According to Anthony, there was only one reason.

'Because she was going to win.'

A protest was arranged outside head office and the angry would-be candidates and their supporters succeeded in shutting down Sussex Street. But they didn't sway the party's Administrative Committee and Paul Whelan was installed as the candidate.

Carmel's compensation was to come three years later, in the form of a vacancy in the NSW Upper House, the Legislative Council, upon the retirement of Ann Symonds.

In 1995, at the same time as the thwarted challenge in Ashfield, another similar preselection challenge was underway in the state seat of Liverpool, where the Left's Paul Lynch was running against right-wing incumbent and former Minister, Peter Anderson.

But that challenge was ultimately allowed to proceed. The struggling Labor leader Bob Carr let it be known he was happy to see Peter Anderson – a possible future leadership rival – replaced and Lynch won the ballot and ultimately the seat.

The then NSW ALP secretary John Della Bosca concedes that while the Ashfield intervention was to protect an incumbent with ministerial experience, there was also a touch of putting a 'bolshie' Left in its place. He concedes that the other experienced incumbent, Peter Anderson, eventually went unprotected.

The concurrent but different outcomes in Ashfield and Liverpool demonstrated a core principle of NSW Labor politics: that in the hierarchy of protecting interests, both Left and Right and the sub-groups within will identify their primary interests and preserve and advance them first.

Circumstances determine the best way to do that. Whether those interests always align with the party's broader interests or even the national interest is sometimes a matter of debate.

Beneath the Left-Right manoeuvrings over state preselections was an undercurrent: John Della Bosca and Anthony Albanese worked in the same office for the same political party, but they did not trust each other.

Anthony and Della Bosca had first met on the doorstep of 41 Pyrmont Bridge Road in 1982, when John had been sent to interview Maryanne Albanese about a controversial ballot, just completed, for preselection in the federal seat of Sydney.

Peter Baldwin had defeated incumbent Les McMahon for preselection and Les was trying to mobilise an appeal and seeking support.

When John turned up to see Maryanne, Anthony intervened and gave him an earful on the doorstep, insisting she did not want to see him. He didn't want his mum being put under pressure or dragged into the Left-Right brawl.

John accepted his word and left. He had grown up in Marrickville and his own mother was also a hard-working woman who had struggled. He could understand Anthony being protective.

'Standing up for your vulnerable mum against perceived political trickery and emotional intimidation was a badge of honour to me,' John says. 'Though I could have done without the accompanying profanities at the time.'

Anthony's Labor upbringing had schooled him in the inner workings of the Right before he'd even joined the Left, and he saw its leaders as the frontline enemy. Because of how provocatively he practised his politics, the Right saw him the same way. The suspicions eased over time, but at that point they were very real.

'When we didn't trust one another we probably deceived one another – either accidentally or on purpose,' John says. 'I think Anthony [was] – and maybe still is – very clever in what he doesn't say, when he's negotiating. So [he] leaves a loophole.'

John felt like Anthony had misled him – unintentionally or otherwise – ahead of the previous state election, in 1991. In Labor's quest to defeat the incumbent state Liberal Government led by Premier Nick Greiner, John Della Bosca was casting around for candidates who could win in vulnerable Liberal seats. The Left and Right had been negotiating in a fairly civil manner, carving up the candidacies between them.

Among those allocated to the Left was the seat of Blue Mountains, which left-wing former Minister Bob Debus had held for seven years until he was defeated in 1988. John had lined up a quality candidate from the Right, in case nobody better from the Left could be found. But he believed Debus would be Labor's best chance to regain the seat, if he was prepared to run again.

Based on conversations with Anthony, John became persuaded that Debus was willing – something he concedes in retrospect was 'probably a bit silly', given others were telling him otherwise. Taking Anthony's observations as an assurance, he told the right-wing candidate to stand down and waited for Bob to nominate.

But he didn't. Anthony insists there was nothing duplicitous about it: Bob had indicated he would be prepared to run, then changed his mind. Instead, the Left put up another candidate – Jim Angel.

John was furious. Liberal incumbent Barry Morris achieved a two per cent swing in his favour against Angel and held the seat. Labor lost the election narrowly and some in the Right grumbled that with one more seat, they could have come close to denying the Liberals government.

'It sums up the communication deficit that sometimes occurs,' John says, in an understatement that demonstrates his point.

The 'communication deficit' had already reached a flashpoint in a very public way. On the ledger of victories, Right versus Left, the Left was ahead.

The Right's Stephen Loosley had become General Secretary of the NSW ALP in 1983, following Graham Richardson who moved into the Senate. In 1989, Stephen also became the party's national Senior Vice President, resigning from his NSW secretary's position when he secured his own Senate seat in 1990 but retaining the national position. Anthony, John Faulkner and his colleagues in the Left would eventually see him forced out amid a controversy over the NSW party's finances when he was at the helm.

After a ballot in which he tied initially with Labor MP and former *Pick A Box* TV game show champion Barry Jones, Stephen was made national President of the ALP in 1991.

Just before he resigned as NSW General Secretary, Stephen Loosley had overseen the purchase for $3.8 million of a building at 291 Sussex Street named Labor Centenary House. The building was to become a financial burden so great that the state branch almost went under. A subsequent valuation put the building's worth at only $1.8 million, finding it also required a $1 million upgrade.

The party's debt had spiralled. An audit report prepared in late 1991 revealed the parlous state of its finances in the wake of the building's purchase. Its other assets included Newcastle radio station 2HD, which the NSW Labor Party and its industrial wing, the Labor Council, had bought jointly in 1945 and would retain until 1999.

Among the debts in '91, the party's political wing owed its own Labor Council more than $1.5 million. The unions had become so frustrated with what they saw as a failure of political leadership that they were threatening to take legal action to recover the money.

The Left was blaming Stephen Loosley and wanted him to resign both as national President and from the Senate. Ahead of the state conference in December '91 where those demands were due to be put directly, Stephen issued a statement.

'Any fair examination of the purchase of Labor Centenary House will demonstrate beyond doubt that the matter was handled on the basis of due process, sound commercial advice and unanimous decision-making at all appropriate levels of the ALP,' his statement read.

But the Left – and some in the Right – were also angry that a severance package had allegedly been arranged for Stephen. It emerged in a newspaper leak – in *The Sydney Morning Herald* – that the NSW party itself had not actually covered the cost of the payout, or indeed the wage and salary costs of either Stephen or his personal secretary when they had been employed there. All had been paid through the radio station 2HD, under a long-standing arrangement in which the

General Secretary was also the station's nominal managing director.

The 1991 state election had forced a delay in holding the annual conference, pushed back from June to December. On 7 December, as it got underway, the *Herald* quoted unnamed sources saying the arrangement had 'recently been terminated'. Stephen's successor, Della Bosca, was being paid directly by the party.

At the conference, Stephen won the backing of his faction, which dismissed calls for his resignation. Graham Richardson led the defence of his Senate colleague, vowing the leadership would raise the money to pay off the debts and blasting the Left for persistently failing to contribute to fundraising efforts or take any responsibility for the lack of scrutiny of either the building purchase or the arrangements at 2HD.

Della Bosca reported that another valuation proved that the building had been worth what the party had paid for it at the time. Anthony returned fire, insisting the issue wasn't whether the building had lost value during the recession, but that the party should never have bought it because it was never going to be able to service the debt.

In his speech on the conference floor, he blamed the party leadership for the situation.

'This debacle is an inevitable product of a complacent, pompous, arrogant, lazy machine,' he said. 'Johno [Johnson] once told me that the General Secretary had "papal infallibility" – that the disciples of the machine always fell into line, right or wrong. It is time the white smoke was raised for the last time.'

The Left's John Faulkner also mounted a blistering attack on Loosley, accusing him of buying an 'uninhabitable, rat-infested fire trap' and turning the party's centenary – which the purchase was supposed to celebrate – into 'an absolute debacle'.

'Our party as a whole will suffer because of this for a generation,' John thundered.

In the end, the Left didn't bring up the salary package arrangements at the conference. But it did manage to secure extra positions on the party's powerful oversight committees.

With 1993 scheduled as a federal election year, the 1992 state conference was returned to its usual June timeslot – just seven months after the last one.

The Left remained dissatisfied with the response to the party's financial situation, and with Stephen Loosley in particular, and stepped up its campaign for his resignation.

On the eve of the conference, *The Sydney Morning Herald*'s front page repeated the salary-package story and added a new allegation – that Stephen had continued to receive his General Secretary's salary via 2HD for two months after he resigned, and while he was also being paid as a senator.

Journalist Paul Cleary – the same Paul Cleary who had sold newspapers on street corners with Anthony back in high school – wrote that details of a $99,000 severance payment and a further $30,000 in ongoing salary were included in a letter from Della Bosca to senior Left figure and former senator Arthur Gietzelt, who was one of the NSW party's trustees.

The report said the severance package was comprised of unclaimed holidays and long-service leave and that Stephen had used very little of his recreational leave, taking paid overseas study tours instead.

The next morning, Saturday, the stand-off between Left and Right delayed the conference's opening at Sydney Town Hall. With the pressure mounting, the Right made an offer. Graham Richardson was dispatched as emissary to convey that if the Left dropped its planned public lambasting, Stephen would quietly resign at the July meeting of the ALP national executive.

But the Left didn't want to wait.

Six leading left-wingers gathered in a small meeting room under the Town Hall stage to consider the Right's offer. Arthur Gietzelt, John Faulkner, Bruce Childs and Anthony were there, with George Campbell and Junior Vice President Chris Raper.

They weren't inclined to accept. Bruce said he'd been up late writing a speech tipping a bucket on Stephen and he didn't especially want to waste it.

In the middle of their conversation, the toilet in the corner of the room flushed, the door opened and out came Graham Richardson. After surprise gave way to jokes about strategic leaks, they took the opportunity to explain to him again and plainly that they expected Stephen to announce his resignation immediately.

Graham didn't need it spelled out. He knew from what he'd overheard that if Stephen resisted, the left-wingers were prepared to add to their case with more allegations on the conference floor.

When the proceedings opened, Stephen took to the microphone and announced his resignation. From his factional opponents and those in the Right disillusioned at the party's financial predicament and reputational damage, cheers filled the hall.

In head office, they thought the Left had had one too many victories. It was only a matter of time before the Right struck back.

'We were the enemy,' Anthony says. 'It was the culture.'

The hostility at Sussex Street came to a head spectacularly in 1993, when Anthony went overseas for a month on a US-Government-sponsored young leaders' study tour. Nicknamed 'the CIA tour', it was an opportunity routinely offered to emerging leaders from across the Australian political spectrum.

Once he was gone, his colleagues in the Right hatched a plan to put him – literally – in his place.

While Anthony was away, Carmel had been dropping in to head office to collect his mail and generally keep an eye on things. She had become more involved in the organisational side of the party, and as a member of both the Administrative and the Credentials committees – and as Anthony's partner – she had legitimate reasons to be swinging by.

But on the eve of his return, she went to his office at party headquarters to discover it was no longer there. His right-wing colleagues had commandeered his solid-walled corner office just inside the main entrance on the ninth floor – a position that made it a refuge for disgruntled party members who wanted to complain about something – and turned it into a library.

His desk had been moved into a newly constructed, small glass office wedged in the middle of a row of junior officials' rooms along the side and towards the back of the room, where everyone coming and going would be clearly seen.

Carmel was horrified. 'I knew that this was a really inappropriate action and something that we just couldn't accept,' she says.

She rang George Campbell, the secretary of the left-wing Metal Workers' Union, Senator Bruce Childs and a few others and told them what the Right had done. With Anthony due home a couple of days later, they held a phone hook-up and hatched a plan to put it back.

'There was a view that Anthony shouldn't have to come back from this study trip and confront this,' Carmel says. 'So the plan was that we would go in early the [morning after he got home] and we would move his office back. And that's what we did.'

Anthony arrived home on a Thursday morning, the day before their planned renovation raid. To avoid spoiling the end of his trip, Carmel had not told him what had happened while he was away. He was enraged at what his right-wing colleagues had done.

'It was a brutal act,' he says. 'It was an attempt to humiliate me. "You have so little power we can move your office, turn your office into a library." I mean, what a joke.'

John Della Bosca says none of the books had actually been moved in and a joke was all it was meant to be.

'The office thing was a childish stunt,' he says.'I think it was at the level of a practical joke that got taken very seriously. It was a practical joke that got out of control, I think, is the best way to describe it.'

They had had the new library approved through the Administrative Committee, without stipulating where it would be located. Anthony never found out exactly how much their joke cost but he figured it had been 'a substantial amount of money to remodel the office just to put me in a goldfish bowl'.

Early next morning, Anthony, Carmel, Bruce Childs, George Campbell, Ian Macdonald, Meredith Burgmann and a group of others from the union movement met at 377 Sussex Street.

'I love a bit of direct action,' Meredith says.

It was before normal business hours – around 7.30 am. The only person already in the office was the accountant, Trevor Williams, who was not a participant in any factional shenanigans. When Anthony and his posse appeared, Trevor nervously greeted them, saying, 'Something's happened . . .'

That part was already clear. They then discovered his colleagues had also changed the locks. Anthony couldn't get into either his old office or his new one.

He knew the accountant had not been involved in any of it and he felt sorry for him.

'He wasn't political at all,' he says.

Anthony told Trevor that, as an elected official, he was entitled to access these rooms.

'Why don't you go and get a cup of coffee?'

Trevor took the hint. Once he was gone, the group retrieved the keys and got to work. Meredith insists she was the only one among them who turned up with tools and she laughs as she describes the scene.

'I had a wrench and a hammer . . . and it was because I was the one who was married to a plumber. So the President of the Academics Union turned up with the tools . . . And we had a wonderful time, early in the morning. No one was around.'

George Campbell struck the first blow, swinging the hammer to dislodge the bookcase, which had been drilled into the wall. They then set about dismantling the new 'library' and moving Anthony's desk, chair and other office furniture back.

'But we kept some of the nice things that they'd put in the library,' Anthony says. 'They had a nice coffee table and a nice lounge to sit on. So [my office] became nicer than it was before.'

Word soon reached the Right that their changes were literally being undone, a communication assisted by the fact that Anthony had alerted the media. A TV crew and radio reporters had arrived to capture the action.

John Della Bosca concedes the publicity made the joke somewhat less funny.

'They [the Left] put out the kind of idea that this is an outrage and then it was very embarrassing for everyone,' he says.

The right-wing officials arrived and met in the basement car park to work out how to respond. They sent a delegate upstairs to negotiate. Carmel recalls that by the time they walked into the office, it was all done.

'They weren't happy but they just all had to accept it,' she says. 'I think they realised that to continue on with their view of the world that Anthony's office should become a library just would've looked ridiculous. So they recognised they'd lost and moved on.'

There was a mid-morning meeting in the general secretary's office involving the senior figures from both camps to discuss the incident and the way forward. The NSW party President Terry Sheahan arrived and suggested they convene another meeting on Monday.

'And I just said there's no need for a meeting,' Anthony says. 'It's fixed. It's done. Move it and I'll move it back.'

He regards that incident as the turning point in his relationship with his colleagues from the Right.

'From that point on they never tried again to say, "We're in charge. You're just the Assistant Secretary."'

Graham Richardson was Senior Vice President of the NSW ALP at the time. Later that morning, by Anthony's version, Graham telephoned the triumphant left-winger. According to Anthony, he said, 'I told them not to do it.'

Anthony says Graham also claimed to have told his colleagues: 'This is going to end very badly. He's not just going to cop this.'

More than two decades later, Graham professes to recall only scant details of the incident. He reiterates that he had nothing to do with organising or executing it, insisting that if he'd plotted it, the outcome would have been different.

'If you're going to do something you've got to make it stick,' he says.

Graham acknowledges the Right sometimes played – and still plays – hard.

'I don't think we've ever played it as hard as the Left have played on us but, yeah, I'll plead guilty,' he says. 'We play hard when we have to. Why not? It's a hard game. It's not a game for the weaklings.'

He came to respect the young 'Albo' for his intellect and his fight.

'He was still the young Left warrior and a good one – a worthy opponent,' Graham says. 'He had real balls, Albo. He had real balls. I admired him because he knew how to fight. You know he's one of those guys – it doesn't matter if he's down, he doesn't give up. He keeps going.

'He's like the boxer on his knees and the count's begun and he's still swinging. He can't lie down. Whatever happens with Albo, you will never see the white towel thrown in.'

For all the Right's protestations that Anthony couldn't take a joke, the one other characteristic which Graham says set him apart from others in the Left from very early on was his capacity for humour.

'He was a different kind of lefty for these reasons. It wasn't just that he was hardworking and obsessive, which he was.

There were a lot of them in that category. But he could smile. The Fergusons were notorious for never smiling. No one ever laughed. They were the humourless Left.'

For all that divided Left from Right back then, Graham Richardson says that he – and a number of his NSW Right colleagues – have much more in common with Anthony than is sometimes acknowledged.

'He's a far more normal person [than some of the others],' Graham says, insisting that the members of the NSW Right are also very 'normal'.

'We drink beer, we eat pies, we go to the football, we go to the cricket. We're pretty normal Aussies. And Albo does all of the above . . . You could relax talking to him. You could never relax talking to the others. You were always on your guard because they were on their guard.'

Interestingly – and perhaps because their different positions required different levels of engagement – John Della Bosca takes another view. In contrast to Graham's experience with Anthony, in the first few years of his time in head office, John found almost exactly the opposite. He found communication with other members of the Left a lot easier than with the then Assistant General Secretary.

'It just seemed to be a lot easier to talk to those characters than it did to talk to Anthony, who was just a very aggressive kind of character at that time,' John says. 'He's somewhat different now. He's much more amenable, much more accommodating. He takes himself seriously, but not seriously in the same way.'

The young, angry man would gradually give way to a more mature, still-sometimes-angry-but-often-more-reasonable man, who saw increasing value in a cool-headed response.

But whether striking hard in the moment or planning a longer-term manoeuvre, Anthony would not be a passive participant in politics or in life. Ask him why and he refers to the experience of his mother, whose poor health and circumstances forced her to live a limited life.

'And so, it's a thing of value every day,' he says. 'Squeeze everything you can out of every ounce of life.'

The 'library' incident heralded a shift in relations between Anthony and some members of the Right. But the battles between the two parts of the Left would continue, following Anthony into Federal Parliament where Martin Ferguson would arrive at the same election, and where his older brother Laurie had been serving since 1990 after six years in the NSW Parliament.

In both number and influence, ultimately Anthony and the hard Left would end up the dominant force within the faction as a whole.

'Up until a decade ago, it was still a contest between Albo and the others,' says Graham Richardson. 'But he was always going to win, in my view, because he's far more engaging.'

Anthony, he says, is not 'some aloof, elite person'.

As the '96 election approached and Anthony began to contemplate his own move into representative politics, the influence of his non-Aussie heritage on his Aussie character would begin to weigh more heavily on his mind.

He was an Aussie as Graham described – raised by a mother of Irish-Catholic stock, carrying around an Italian name. As his public profile grew, Anthony began to feel that there was a space where his Italianness should be, a vault labelled 'Albanese' that everyone could see but that he could neither open nor fill.

CHAPTER 15

Making a Name

Since he was a kid, Anthony had been known among his friends as Albo. But whenever his surname was pronounced at its full length, it was always 'Alban-eez' – rhyming with knees. It was how his mum said it, how all of his mates said it and how he said it himself.

But before he formally sought preselection for Grayndler as he became more engaged in his local electorate – including and especially around the suburb of Leichhardt, a centre of Italian language and culture in Sydney – the name and its pronunciation became more of an issue. The Italian community tended to pronounce it 'Alban-ee-zee', or even 'Alban-ay-zee'.

When he introduced himself, people would sometimes pick him up on his own lack of verbal flourish, so gradually his pronunciation became more flexible, subtly adjusted as required to account for expectations.

Those of Italian background would also ask about his Italian family and especially his father.

'I remember at some stage thinking he was from Naples,' Anthony says. 'It wasn't an issue really until I went into public life and then people want to know, "Where's your family from?"'

It wasn't an easy subject. He couldn't answer with any certainty and the assumptions of those asking were sometimes hard to deflect. The questions also reminded him constantly that he was missing knowledge of half of his heritage.

Not only did he not know where his family was from or how they pronounced their name, he didn't even know who they were.

In the wake of the library incident at the Sussex Street office, things became slightly more inclusive within. John Della Bosca was a dedicated and effective campaign strategist and less interested in factional conflict than some of his colleagues, so he began to encourage the party as a whole to harvest Anthony's talents.

The ALP national secretary at the time, Bob Hogg, brought him in to work on the national campaign for the 1993 federal election. It was a step up from the tasks members of the Left had been assigned in the past. He was asked to actually contribute ideas.

'Not just to print the how-to-votes,' Anthony says.

Anthony's engagement with the branches in his local area naturally brought with it an engagement in local politics. Whether an election was local, state or federal, the party members – and therefore the preselectors – were the same in all three jurisdictions for Marrickville and the other councils; the then state seats of Ashfield, Marrickville, Canterbury, Heffron and Port Jackson; and the federal seat of Grayndler.

Anthony had maintained close contact with the Labor-linked members of local councils in the inner west and continued his practice of advising and assisting those in the Left who he saw as being able to serve the community, the party, the faction, or all three.

His engagement was rooted in his own history, growing up in the Alexandra Dwellings in Pyrmont Bridge Road.

'Stopping my house being sold was my first big [political] campaign,' he says. 'So I always had an affinity with the council because it had a direct impact. They were our landlords.'

In his final year in head office, he was drawn directly into the municipal politics of Sydney's inner west through the mayoral election in Leichhardt and what was to become a wildly successful if slightly unwelcome documentary film on the contest, *Rats in the Ranks*.

The film by Bob Connolly and Robin Anderson, in which Anthony played a reluctant off-camera bit part, exposed the ruthlessness of politics even down at the local level, charting the lead-up to the controversial September 1994 poll.

The Leichhardt Council fell within the state seat of Port Jackson, a Labor-voting area that included Anthony's sphere of influence. The colourful mayor, ex-Labor councillor turned 'community independent' Larry Hand, was fighting to keep hold of the ermine robes. The 12 councillors allowed the cameras to film every meeting, manoeuvre and conversation in the lead-up to the election, in a rare fly-on-the-wall glimpse of what it's really like behind closed doors.

Larry faced a challenge from the Labor Party but its four councillors were divided over which of them should be the candidate. Labor councillor Neil Macindoe wanted the job and so did Kate Butler, who was then the deputy mayor. In the end, Larry faced two challengers. Neil put himself forward without the support of Kate and Trevor, who opposed his tactics.

The other nominee was one of Larry's former allies among the community independents, Kath Hacking, who had split from his team to be even more independent.

Through a matrix of internecine wheeling and dealing, Larry was victorious, convincing two of the four Labor councillors – Kate and Labor caucus secretary Trevor Snape – to rat on their Labor colleague Neil Macindoe and support Larry instead. In return, Kate secured the backing of Larry and his group of independents to stay on as deputy mayor. She was expelled from the Labor Party for her treachery. It fell to Anthony to move the expulsion motion.

He was then still the Left's Assistant General Secretary in Sussex Street and featured in the film by reference only. Larry Hand was filmed speaking on the phone to a *Sydney Morning Herald* journalist, leaking the fact that Neil Macindoe had been to see Anthony in head office to try and get him to pull Kate and Trevor into line. Larry said he knew about this because Anthony had told him. Anthony denies being the source.

The Labor councillors had asked Anthony to come and mediate. He met the group at a café in Norton Street, advising them to resolve their dispute by drawing names from a hat. He refused to be filmed. It was a prescient decision.

Waiting for Anthony before the meeting, Kate told the camera she'd had a visit from Neil the previous Saturday night. 'And he is so desperate to become the mayor,' she said. 'He might be okay. He could be.'

She then smiled and said rhetorically, 'How can you hit somebody on the head when they have such a burning desire to be mayor of Leichhardt? And I don't have the burning desire. I wish I had it.'

Nevertheless, metaphorically, she gave Neil the feared headache.

Rats in the Ranks would spend 14 months in pre-production and its release would come three months after Anthony's election to Federal Parliament. Soon after the film's release, Larry Hand told Fairfax journalist Ben Hills that it was naïve for people to suggest elected representatives should pay more attention to policy-making than politicking.

'You have to fight to get to a position where you can put those policies in action,' Larry said. 'You have to fight to get the numbers, you have to fight to become mayor. You have to fight to make sure the bureaucracy doesn't fuck it up. This is not a teddy bear's picnic.'

Larry would go on to rejoin the Labor Party and become a ministerial adviser to Anthony in 2012.

The film's exposure of the power games of politics would strike a chord so resonant that it would also screen in the United States and across Europe. In 2016, Anthony would attend a reunion for the film's cast, marking 20 years since its release.

The eight months between filming and its arrival in cinemas would see a few political developments back home. Unsurprisingly, Jeannette McHugh announced she would retire from politics at the coming 1996 election and Anthony secured preselection for her seat unopposed after Marrickville mayor Barry Cotter was persuaded, once again, not to contest.

The leaders of the Right weren't unhappy to see Anthony move on and likely head to Canberra. 'For God's sake, get him out of head office!' is Anthony's take on their attitude.

Before his preselection was confirmed in May 1995, the would-be candidate for Grayndler did what he hadn't been in a position to do three years earlier. He oversaw the succession for his job.

The following month, the state secretary of the energy division of the Construction, Forestry, Mining and Energy Union, Damian O'Connor, was elected unopposed.

'Anthony suggested to me that I might like to think about doing it,' Damian says. 'Others did too. I thought about it and eventually ran.'

The other potential candidate, Anthony's former housemate Luke Foley, who would go on to lead the NSW Labor Party, tested his support for a possible run but ultimately decided not to contest.

'Damian was a bit older, had a bit more experience, had probably closer connections with the unions at the time and so I deferred to him,' Luke says in 2016.

Once the pair of them had indicated interest, Anthony stayed out of it. He didn't want to choose between his mates.

'Anthony was neutral when Damian and I expressed interest, because he was and is close to both of us,' Luke says.

Both candidates canvassed the Left delegates to state conference who would decide the issue, on the understanding that if one clearly had the numbers the other would withdraw. The outgoing Assistant Secretary kept an eye on the process. For a Labor Party ballot, it was unusually civilised.

'I recall a conversation with him [Anthony] where he said he thought Damian had the numbers,' Luke says. 'And he could always count and I thought he was probably right. So I backed off.'

Damian O'Connor shared his predecessor's politics but his practice was quite different.

'It used to be fairly bare-knuckled fighting stuff,' he says. 'Anthony's got that good fighting character that appeals to delegates.'

Anthony's personality and changes in the party necessitated a different style from the man succeeding him. But Damian respected his skills.

'I think he's pretty direct but he's also got a really keen sense of timing,' Damian says. 'Good ideas can fail because of timing. Good strategies can fail because of bad timing. It's one thing to have a good idea. It's another thing to pick the right time to float it and bring it into play. I think he's got a remarkable strategic mind.'

The two shared the view that the Left needed to seize every opportunity for victory, no matter how small.

'The Left was never going to win a ballot whilst the Right remained strong,' says Damian. 'So it was really about your performance in losing effectively and how well organised you were and how many moral points you could make against the majority. We created space for the Right's inherent tensions to emerge.'

Damian would become an exception among the Left assistant secretaries, the first to not proceed directly into representative politics.

He has no regrets. In 2016, having served as a ministerial adviser when Labor was in government, he was Anthony's chief of staff.

'I think you've got a whole lot more freedom when you're involved in politics but you're not at the front line,' Damian says. 'I don't need the limelight to motivate me. And you certainly don't have the pressure and the relentless after-hours activity and the requirement to be a role model all the friggin' time.'

Also on Anthony's electorate staff in 2016 were two former Labor mayors of Leichhardt, Darcy Byrne and Kris Cruden. Anthony's choice of staff would reveal both his habit of nurturing and promoting talented factional colleagues – a habit commonly practised on all sides of politics – and his ongoing links to local government, links which *Rats in the Ranks* would also put up in lights.

After experience on Sydney City Council and as deputy mayor, another of Anthony's former advisers, Verity Firth, would win preselection for the state seat of Balmain ahead of the 2007 NSW election. Niece of Meredith Burgmann, Verity would serve as a minister under premiers Morris Iemma, Nathan Rees and Kristina Keneally.

Another of Anthony's protégés, Jo Haylen, would enter state politics upon Carmel's retirement from the seat of Summer Hill in 2015.

The formal transfer of the Left Assistant General Secretary's mantle from Anthony to Damian came at the NSW Labor Party's annual state conference, normally held mid-year but delayed until October in 1995 because of the March state election.

In his six years in the job, this platform above all others had highlighted Anthony's capacity for invective at the microphone and garnered him national attention. In his final conference speech before stepping down, he joked about the hostility in head office, telling delegates his had been essentially 'a shit job'.

He also warned his successor that he should not expect any friendlier treatment from the Right. 'There is already a shit-sheet out on you!'

Nevertheless, he paid tribute publicly to John Della Bosca's strategic skills and told the party President, the Right's Terry Sheahan, that even though he'd never voted for him, he respected him. In a funny sort of way, from most of the key leaders in the Right, the feeling was mutual.

'I don't think I'm particularly well liked but I think I've got respect,' Anthony told Fairfax journalist Michael Sharp afterwards. 'They don't respect you unless you're prepared to take a stand. It's the nature of the NSW branch.'

For the five months between officially handing over his Sussex Street job and his election as the federal Member for Grayndler, Anthony would serve as a 'senior policy adviser' to the NSW Premier, Bob Carr – a warehousing arrangement that also allowed him to step up his campaigning efforts.

The '96 federal campaign in Grayndler had effectively been underway since before the '95 state election, thanks to the single issue overshadowing almost all others in Sydney's inner west: the ear-splitting noise from the city's only jet airport, situated on the edge of Botany Bay and ringed by densely populated suburbs.

Sydney's Kingsford Smith Airport is one of the oldest continually operating commercial airports in the world and Australia's busiest. As the 1990s approached it was operating two runways – one running north–south and the other east–west. But it was struggling with its workload.

There had been longstanding bipartisan support for a second airport to be built at Badgery's Creek, in Sydney's west, but the likely timeline meant there was increasing pressure for some kind of relief at Kingsford Smith in the meantime.

The southern end of the north–south runway jutted out into the bay and its northern approach sent low-flying aircraft directly over Marrickville and the suburbs around it. Running perpendicular, the east–west runway spread the noise burden around, sending aircraft in and out over Sydney's south-west and the more expensive beachside eastern suburbs.

In 1989, the Hawke Government had approved the construction of a third runway running north–south, parallel to the original and designed to increase capacity ahead of the 2000 Sydney Olympic Games.

The decision so angered junior Minister Gary Punch, the Member for the electorate of Barton, to the airport's immediate west, that he quit the front bench. Having had Aviation Support among his portfolios, he felt his position was untenable.

When the third runway opened in 1994, matters worsened. With a second north–south runway in operation, the Keating Government shut down the east–west runway to contain the noise problem. The reality of extra air movements over the inner west enraged the local residents, many of whom were traditional Labor voters.

At a protest on 7 December 1994, organised by 11 local councils in the airport's surrounding areas, an estimated 10,000-strong crowd gathered at Leichhardt Oval, demanding that then Prime Minister Paul Keating sign a charter to entrench a curfew, expand proposed compensation to residents and open a new main airport at Badgery's Creek within three years. Land had been set aside at Badgery's Creek some years earlier but nothing had been done about it.

Marrickville mayor Barry Cotter addressed the crowd. Anthony was among the protesters. He had joined the Sydney Airport Community Consultative Committee as a community representative, already the second incarnation of the group, which had been established in 1988 in response to the agitation over the Government's plans.

By 1994, the emotions among residents of the inner west were running higher than the jets seemingly skimming their garage roofs. Some of their anger was directed at the then Transport Minister, Laurie Brereton, whose electorate of Kingsford Smith took in the airport and the eastern suburbs. Laurie's constituents had been relieved of their noise problem when the east–west runway was shut down.

When the protesting residents' demands weren't met, they descended on the airport itself two weeks later, right in the middle of the pre-Christmas summer holiday season. This time, an estimated 15,000 protesters disrupted flight schedules and the local councils sent garbage trucks to ring the airport in a supporting blockade.

Out of the protests, a new political party was formed, turning on the Government and Labor in general. It proved so popular, it undercut Labor's hold on some of the councils.

The No Aircraft Noise Party launched candidates in the 1995 local government elections, securing council seats in Marrickville and the mayoralties of Leichhardt, Hunters Hill and Ashfield. At the state election the same year, they achieved a 23.65 per cent primary vote in Marrickville, but didn't win.

Some of the party's prominent members would go on to join the Greens. Separately and together, these two political forces would become Anthony's nemeses for the next two decades, challenging him repeatedly to fight for his electoral life.

As the '96 election approached, Anthony appointed a campaign manager, a 25-year-old colleague he knew through the Left, Tim Gartrell. Tim, who would later become Labor's National Secretary, admired Anthony and was chuffed to have the job.

'He was a very important mentor to our generation of activists coming through NSW Young Labor,' Tim says. 'He motivated people through his own personal courage and tenacity in a nasty, tough internal party environment – the old days of hard factional warfare in NSW Labor. But he also built a deep relationship with us younger activists, encouraging us and being generous with his time – letting us in on his thinking. It was genuine but also very canny leadership. As a result, we'd have walked over broken glass for the bloke!'

There are many in the Labor Party and labour movement who say similar things.

'You constantly come across them,' says National President Mark Butler. 'They've learned a lot from Albo . . . One of the rarer things in this place, in this business, is his ability to nurture and mentor other people. Now sure, there's a return on that investment, but, like Tom did to him – that's what keeps the movement going. That's why it lasts more than 100 years. You've got that mentoring relationship as part of our culture.'

In 1996, the aircraft noise issue completely dominated the campaign for Grayndler. The No Aircraft Noise Party was a formidable opponent.

'They were well organised,' Tim says. 'There were some smart operators in NAN but there were also a lot of very unhinged people too.'

He recalls one elderly protester biting the finger of a security guard at the ALP state conference – and drawing blood.

'But they tapped into this fury about how the runways were being operated. The constant parallel runway operations (were) a nightmare. It was a huge problem for the campaign.'

It was the kind of fight that suited Anthony.

'And so I think a softer gentler candidate – I'm not sure they would have survived it,' Tim says. 'He was absolutely courageous in that campaign and he still is this way.'

Anthony's campaign team ordered around 10,000 corflutes, corrugated plastic all-weather campaign placards to put up in people's yards, plus thousands of other campaign posters, which they attached to every available surface, flat or otherwise.

'They just went up, got ripped down, went up, got ripped down again,' Anthony says. 'No telegraph pole was safe.'

Some houses that had Anthony's posters in the front yard were doused in black paint. At a public meeting at Sydenham Town Hall, the panels on Barry Cotter's mayoral car were kicked in.

'It was very emotional and heavy,' Anthony says of the campaign.

Tim recalls one particularly heavy community meeting at the St Peters Tempe Neighbourhood Centre. It was massively hostile. But Anthony went and addressed the crowd.

'It was really going into the lion's den. He was courageous, passionate – the only time I was worried that he was going to lose it was when someone had a go at his mum.'

It was just one of those throwaway jibes from the audience: 'Your mother would be ashamed of you!' But any reference to his struggling mum cut Anthony deeply. His eyes welled.

'You could see him slightly tear up,' Tim says. 'And then he just said, "How dare you attack my mum!"'

As well as the candidate himself, Tim also admired the relationship Anthony had with his mother.

'She'd had a rough trot,' he says. 'She was completely proud of him.'

And he knew Anthony was equally proud – and protective – of her.

'As his campaign director, I urged him to push out the story of how tough it was for him and his mum,' he says. 'I thought it would hit a note with many of the older inner-city voters and demonstrate his authenticity. But I didn't express the idea sensitively and he pulled me up. He made it clear that while it had been very tough for them, there was love, dignity and pride in their life. He was worried his mum might feel ashamed or be embarrassed.'

Tim thought he made a good point.

'A more cynical candidate might have let it go,' he says.

The aircraft-noise controversy was stealing the oxygen from almost every other issue in the battle for Grayndler. The Keating Government had agreed to an acquisition program, buying out and demolishing the worst affected homes, which were in the suburb of Sydenham.

'The No Aircraft Noise Party [and] Greens campaigned that [the houses] should be left there as a monument to government incompetence,' Anthony says. He thought it was left-wing politics gone mad and would create a rat-infested health hazard.

'It reinforced some of the fundamental differences between my politics and the Greens',' he says.

There were also mitigation measures to insulate against the noise and Anthony and others pushed to have them all increased.

The No Aircraft Noise supporters turned on Labor candidates because it was their party that had caused the problem. During the campaign, they produced a CD *Songs from the Heartland*, featuring musical protests about the airport issue. One of the songs was about the candidate for Grayndler and his Labor colleague, Laurie Brereton.

It featured a choir of small children. The chorus went: 'Laurie has a lapdog, lapdog, lapdog. Laurie has a lapdog, he calls it Albanese.'

The next line left Anthony even less impressed. 'They say that he's a Shih tzu, Shih tzu, Shih tzu . . .'

'These were little kids they had singing this,' he says. 'As in, "Ha ha, *you* know, '*Shit*-zu.'" Brilliant . . . They produced posters that had me as a dog.'

At one community meeting, there was so much anger at the Labor Party that someone moved a formal motion that their federal Member, Jeannette McHugh, be shot. And she was sitting there.

The noise was literally driving people crazy. During the campaign, Anthony showed then Treasurer Ralph Willis around Sydenham, where an arbitrary line had been drawn excluding some residents from the acquisition arrangements. The Xidias family, in Rowe Street, were on the wrong side of the line.

'[They had] huge cracks in their home,' Anthony says. 'Literally in the walls. The place just shook when the planes went over.'

Ralph agreed to expand the scheme.

'It was about helping people,' Anthony says. 'That of course meant they left the area and didn't get to vote for me. So there was no electoral benefit, but there was immense satisfaction.'

But when Laurie Brereton held a news conference to announce the expanded assistance, anti-Labor campaigners blockaded the Cyprus Community Club in Stanmore, where it was being held.

In the volatile campaign climate, all sides employed whatever tactics they could to get attention and gain an advantage. At a gathering of candidates outside a Marrickville childcare centre, No Aircraft Noise's Kevin Butler cried in front of the television cameras.

'What about the children under the flight path?' he asked. The centre was already being moved under the assistance scheme.

As the poll approached, Kevin would be on the receiving end of some psychological warfare. After nominations closed, the one thing he had told others would be his worst nightmare had indeed come to pass. At the electoral office for the draw of ballot paper position, Kevin discovered that among the candidates he faced was another Butler, K.

Out of nowhere, the ex-Labor deputy mayor of Leichhardt and chief 'rat' Kate Butler, whose Machiavellian moves before the mayoral elections had been captured on film in *Rats in the Ranks*, had decided to run as an 'independent'. She'd had no burning desire to be mayor but suddenly wanted to sit in Federal Parliament.

The colour of her campaign material was remarkably similar to that of No Aircraft Noise. The chances of some of NAN's would-be voters becoming confused and accidentally voting for her instead seemed fairly high.

Anthony denies any involvement in Kate Butler's candidacy.

'It was her idea, clearly,' he says. 'She decided to run. Spontaneously.'

Making it even worse for Kevin, Kate had drawn the spot just above him on the ballot paper – they were at seven and eight respectively, with Anthony at number three.

In the end, Kate Butler only secured 751 votes among 78,815, or 1.01 per cent. But her preferences mostly flowed on to Anthony and it was one per cent that did not go to Kevin Butler. Anthony won on primary votes, without the need for preferences. Kevin ran third.

On election night, Anthony and his supporters gathered at the Portugal Madeira Club, in Marrickville. With the Labor Party nationwide being swept from office after 13 years, many of its MPs were feeling the misery of defeat. But the party at the Madeira Club was an exuberant, against-the-tide, victory celebration.

Addressing the crowd, Anthony thanked them for their hard work and support. He'd had four years to prepare for the moment, ever since he'd secured Grayndler preselection for his predecessor, Jeannette McHugh.

In some ways, this was not actually as big a step as winning the ballot for the job in head office seven years earlier, which would be the vehicle for delivering him here. But it was still a big night and with his mother, Maryanne, in the room, it was also an emotional moment.

'I said how proud I was of her . . . and of my background,' he says. 'To be able to get into Federal Parliament was a big deal. She cried.'

He cried too. It also happened to be his 33rd birthday and there was a cake and singing, as they gradually relieved the establishment of its liquid stores. The beer on tap went first, then the bottled beer, then the wine.

'We drank them out of beer then drank them out of wine, until all that was left was spirits,' Anthony says. 'That was one hell of a bar bill.'

Arriving in Canberra as a Member of Parliament was a far more sobering experience. It was only early autumn but there was a definite chill in the air when he turned up to see the Opposition Whip, whose job it was to allocate him an office.

Unfortunately for Anthony, the Opposition Whip was the man he had forced out of Grayndler three years earlier: Leo McLeay.

'I said, "Oh, I'm told I have to find out where my office is,"' Anthony recalls. 'And he got out the map. And he said, "I think I'll have you here. It's the furthest office away from me."'

The message was clear.

Having found his office, Anthony spent the next few weeks finding his feet, before standing up on them on 6 May 1996, to give his first speech. He was already an experienced public speaker, having graduated from the loud hailer many years before.

'But speaking in Parliament is something different again,' Anthony says. 'I think you are very conscious of the fact that every word is written down in Hansard and I had a sense of history. It was quite overwhelming. I think it is a very humbling experience to be one of the few people, relatively, who have been elected to Federal Parliament.'

His speech was passionate and, as they mostly are, punctuated by the issues he cared most about. When the time ran out before his words did, the Government granted him the extra minute he needed to finish up. As it was an occasion for setting enmities aside, his soft-Left opponent Laurie Ferguson was among the first to shake his hand.

In his speech, Anthony noted that he had defied the predictions of those who said that No Aircraft Noise would defeat him and condemned the decision makers, including those in his own party, who had so disappointed the residents of Sydney's inner west in their deliberations on the airport by failing to 'look beyond the bottom line' in the monthly and annual accounts.

He said he wanted to feature the airport issue in his first speech not only for its own sake but 'as a noisy reminder of the need for vision and proper environmental assessment in the provision of public and social infrastructure'. He advocated increasing spending on infrastructure to boost public sector growth, a call that would go unheeded by those in the newly elected Howard Government shaping the federal budget.

On a normal parliamentary timetable, the following day would have been budget day but the March election had pushed it back to August, when the Treasurer, Peter Costello, would announce brutal spending cuts across the board, including to the public sector. The budget would also mothball the plans for the Badgery's Creek airport and bank as savings the billion dollars set aside for it.

In his speech, Anthony spoke about the need to fund community services both to support those on low incomes and to create jobs. He spoke about wages, pensions, superannuation, multiculturalism, reconciliation and urban planning, and the need to do better at all of it. He vowed to defend the unions and the working class.

'They're the sort of issues that you could change a few words around and talk about the current government,' Anthony says, dryly, in 2016.

In his first speech, he also acknowledged his constituents, his predecessors in the seat and his campaign director, Tim Gartrell, as well as the people most important in his life, including the man who had stood in as father, Tom Uren.

His mother, Maryanne, and Carmel had flown to Canberra to be there for the occasion and watched with pride from the galleries. As the two women reviewed the events on their homeward flight together, Maryanne unexpectedly spoke about Carlo Albanese. It was one of the very few times Carmel ever heard her discuss him. She took it as a sign of how much the day had meant to her.

'I think it was a very emotional day for both of us,' Carmel says. 'There is that connection or that bond that you form when you experience something like that and often in those circumstances you become more open with each other.'

She made sure she told Anthony what his mum had said. From the floor, he had thanked them both – Carmel for her 'constant support, advice and outstanding political judgement' and, before her, his mum for having raised him 'under very difficult economic circumstances', instilling 'a strong sense of social justice and fairness'.

In acknowledging Maryanne he had used her full name – and pronounced it 'Alban-ay-zee'.

CHAPTER 16

In the House

Having won his seat promising to keep fighting aircraft noise, Anthony's focus on the issue only increased when he got to Canberra. There were those in the Liberal Party who shared his anger and the noise issue flung together some who would otherwise have been opponents, working in public and behind the scenes.

A moderate Liberal by the name of Joe Hockey was among them. Joe had won the blue-ribbon seat of North Sydney, just across the harbour as the crow – or the plane – flies from the inner west. North Sydney was also under the flight path, as was part of John Howard's seat of Bennelong.

'[The planes] had to go over Labor seats before they went over Liberal seats,' Anthony says. He repeats one of his favourite sayings of the time: 'Sensitivity to aircraft noise is not determined by income.'

Another Liberal, the conservative Paul Zammit, who represented the seat of Lowe, neighbouring Grayndler, was also pressing for action on behalf of his constituents. Likewise, the

Labor representative for the seat of Watson, Leo McLeay, was on board.

After the election, Prime Minister John Howard had made Joe Hockey chairman of the latest incarnation of the community airport committee, renamed the Sydney Airport Community Forum. Joe had proposed it be a bipartisan affair and that as a previous member, Anthony Albanese also be included.

'Anthony had a number of the inner-city councils,' Joe recalls. 'And at various moments we were able to galvanise those councils in protests before and after the election, to send a message to Sydney Airport and others that we were serious about redesigning the flight paths.'

Despite their differing political allegiances, Joe and Anthony began to work together on the noise abatement problem, using whatever leverage they could muster.

'We both wanted the outcome which was to share the airport noise fairly over Sydney,' Joe says.

Anthony invited Joe to visit Sydenham residents to better understand what they were going through, courtesy of the traffic from the third runway.

'No media, just us and some officials,' Anthony says. 'He genuinely cared about their plight.'

Joe was shocked at the volume of noise from the jets passing overhead.

'They were genuinely disadvantaged people doing it tough and the noise was just ridiculous,' he says. 'I had a lot of sympathy. I ensured that we extended the insulation program to families and shopkeepers that were most severely affected in Sydenham and other places. And I convinced the Government to extend the levy and extend the noise abatement measures.'

His Labor colleague appreciated the effort.

'It was soon after the election and from that point, there was a respect, even though we had different politics,' Anthony says.

Before the 1996 election, John Howard had promised to reopen the east–west runway that the Labor Government had closed, to spread the noise burden around once again.

A month after the election, he made good on the promise. But the runway's operating hours were restricted and its traffic was light, leaving most flights still travelling over the inner west. Like Anthony and Leo McLeay, Paul Zammit, Joe Hockey and all of their affected constituents believed more was required.

In Parliament in November 1996, Anthony introduced a private member's bill aimed at capping the air movements at Kingsford Smith Airport to 80 per hour. He was determined to take every opportunity to increase the exposure of the issue at the heart of his bill and put pressure on John Howard to support it.

Anthony's unpleasant experience at Sussex Street had taught him a useful skill: to always study the rules carefully and then stretch them as far as you could. It was pretty good training for being in Opposition.

'You read the fine print, you get down to details,' he says. 'How do you make a difference without having the numbers?'

So he studied the standing orders and worked out a way to use Question Time to do it. Normally, the questions in each daily session are directed to the government frontbench, answered only by ministers or the Prime Minister. But strictly speaking, if another Member – even one on the Opposition backbench – had introduced a private member's bill, the standing orders permitted that he or she could be asked about it.

So, on the day his bill appeared on the notice paper, and with no guarantee the Government would even allow the bill to proceed to debate or a vote, Anthony organised a stunt. His co-conspirator was his former factional enemy turned noise collaborator, the Chief Opposition Whip, Leo McLeay.

Never mind that Anthony had arranged Leo's overthrow in Grayndler, or that Leo had retaliated by duly allocating the young warrior an office so far from the chamber he needed to take a packed lunch.

The pair had managed to set aside their ugly history and they were now bonded by common foes: the scream of jet engines (and their own constituents) and the Coalition Government.

Declaring he was seeking 'a proper answer on aviation', Leo rose in the middle of Question Time, turned to his own backbench colleague and asked Anthony if he could please explain the merits of his bill.

Anthony was determined to enjoy the irony of this collaboration, and to make sure nobody else missed it either.

'I thank the Member for Watson,' he replied, as the place descended into pandemonium. 'I am particularly pleased that *he* got to ask this question today, as my colleague and friend over many years . . .'

John Howard would eventually agree to cap air movements in Sydney at 80 per hour – but he had separate legislation drafted to do it, so the Government would get the credit.

Once ensconced in Parliament, Anthony also joined as many committees as he could – economics, transport, Aboriginal affairs. He saw them as an opportunity to extend himself.

'In my first term I wanted to broaden out my knowledge,' he says.

Joe Hockey was also on the economics committee and both found it invaluable working alongside more senior and experienced members of Parliament, including the former Treasurer, Ralph Willis.

This is the committee that grills the Reserve Bank Governor quarterly and receives briefings on the state of the economy, an invigorating training ground for young ambitious MPs.

'It was an incredibly high-powered committee,' Joe says. 'We were there and we were both pinching ourselves.'

Anthony found the other committees and their subject matter equally engaging, especially Aboriginal Affairs. Until then, his contact with Indigenous Australians had been restricted to his St Mary's schoolmates from Redfern.

He had never been to far north Queensland, the Northern Territory or the Kimberley, and on committee work he visited them all.

'I think every parliamentarian has a responsibility to be conscious and aware of issues affecting Indigenous Australians,' he says.

It was also through the Aboriginal Affairs committee that he met maverick Queensland ex-Nationals MP turned independent, Bob Katter. The larger-than-life Katter and his ten-gallon hat were well known across northern Australia and Anthony was struck by the high regard in which he was held, especially in Indigenous communities.

'He had a real connection with people in Torres Strait,' Anthony says. 'I developed a relationship with him that I still have. I actually like him, whilst I don't agree with all his views. And I think that kind of experience is quite useful as well.'

His friendship with Bob Katter would prove doubly valuable years later, when Anthony would find himself as Leader of the House in a hung Parliament dealing closely with the crossbench on which Katter still sat.

Twenty years on, he advises new MPs to throw themselves into committee work, especially in Opposition, both for what they learn and the people they meet.

'You're here for a while, one would hope. Learn. Expand your horizons and make sure you're a stronger parliamentarian for it.'

Anthony's provocative politics were also well employed in the post-defeat environment of a crushed Labor caucus. At their first meeting after the massive loss, Labor MPs and senators were contemplating what would clearly be a yawning, disillusioning stretch out of government. Its new leader, Kim Beazley, had the job of trying to pull it all back together.

Kim told them they needed to regroup and be robust but responsible as Her Majesty's loyal Opposition. But when the meeting finished, he called over the new young lefty from NSW. As Anthony tells it, the big man fixed on him and said, 'Not you. I want *you* to give them hell.'

Anthony was designated one of the chief bomb-chuckers.

'His reputation was that he was a brawler,' Kim says. 'But you know the thing about him was – and I always thought this – he was an incredibly intelligent brawler. He was not going to conduct himself as a moron but he'd conduct himself strategically. And he always did.'

The Opposition Leader needed a few people to get right up their ribs.

'Kim certainly encouraged him to do a bit of occasional bomb-throwing,' says Anthony's left-wing former colleague Lindsay Tanner. 'This happens with party leaderships pretty routinely where there are individual backbenchers they can rely on to get under the skin of the other side, that are sufficiently at arm's length from the leadership that if it doesn't work they are deniable.'

Kim viewed Anthony as a person who could 'do what needed to be done'.

'And if what needed to be done was to go to the mattresses, he was perfectly able to do that,' he explains, borrowing a phrase from *The Godfather* about ruthless combat. 'But also able to switch off and approach intelligently what he needed to do to get things through or to get the right positioning of any sort of argument, so that we weren't completely fruitless [in Opposition].'

Kim Beazley says whatever acknowledgement there might have been of the Howard Government's mandate dissipated fairly quickly.

'We were cooperative not really on much except national security,' he says. 'In the Parliament of '96 to '98, when we were really on the bones of our bum basically – a much worse position than the current bunch [in 2016] – we took a pretty hard line. That was the time when Howard was doing the GST. So we went into very solid opposition.'

Anthony's twin habits of audacity and failing to know his place became one of the useful weapons available to a shattered Opposition and he took his chances whenever they came to launch verbal barrages against his opponents. He would make one of his most infamous interventions in a grievance debate on the afternoon of 6 April 1998.

In 1997, just over a year into his first term, John Howard had lost six ministers and his chief of staff in a controversy over parliamentary travel allowance claims. It had begun to dawn on the Labor side that the next election might not be unwinnable after all and its MPs had found a bit of fight.

Aiming to encourage a bit more, Anthony took the gloves off, declaring his grievance was with John Howard 'for his failure to provide leadership'.

'You can trim the eyebrows, you can cap the teeth, you can cut the hair, you can put on different glasses, you can give him a ewe's-milk facial for all I care,' he sprayed, standing in the House of Representatives.

'But to paraphrase a gritty Australian saying, "Same stuff, different bucket." In the pantheon of chinless blue-bloods and suburban accountants that make up the Liberal Party, this bloke is truly one out of the box.'

His 10-minute derogatory character analysis mocked John Howard's middle name, Winston, and accused him of having left the inner-western Sydney of his youth to move 'across the harbour'.

He blasted the Prime Minister's views on Aboriginal reconciliation, multiculturalism and the role of women, describing him as 'a weak little man without courage or vision' who had been oblivious to the social change of the 1960s.

'Here is a man who lived at home until he was 32 – you can imagine what he was like,' Anthony continued. 'Here were young Australians demonstrating against the Vietnam War, listening to the Doors, driving their tie-dyed Kombi vans – and what was John Howard doing? He was at home with Mum, wearing his shorts and long white socks, listening to Pat Boone albums and waiting for the Saturday-night church dance.'

Even by robust parliamentary standards, it was an utterly insulting speech, made more so by the fact that the speaker was a 35-year-old MP with two years' service – who also happened to spend quite a bit of time at home with his mum – and his subject was a man 23 years his senior who had sat in the House since 1974 and achieved the highest elected office in the land.

To observers, it looked like a young, headstrong MP had gone completely rogue. But Anthony insists that's not how it was.

'Some more senior people knew that was coming,' Anthony says. And by 'more senior people', he means a few colleagues. 'That was not an unauthorised break-out although I wouldn't have discussed it with Kim.'

Kim Beazley's recollection is that it was all Anthony's work.

'I don't think I turned him loose on that,' Kim says. 'He arrived at that position all by himself, I suspect. Basically he's always his own man. It's one of the strengths of the guy, I think. In the end he is his own man.'

Two decades on – and having since had his own teeth fixed and changed his own glasses – Anthony concedes it was 'not a respectful speech'. He pauses when asked if he regrets it, then declares himself unrepentant.

'I was a first-term MP,' Anthony says. 'Labor had been decimated and we needed to show that we had some fight. Is it a speech I'd give now? No.'

But equally he doesn't resile from what he insists was the speech's underlying point.

'It was my speech and I take responsibility for it whether people like it or not . . . The political point to it was that Australia, as we approached the end of the century, needed to embrace diversity and modernise.'

Some of the speech's contents had been fed to him by a few of John Howard's own disgruntled colleagues. The Prime Minister found the speech deeply offensive. He raised it in his weekly party-room meeting with coalition MPs but otherwise maintained a public silence.

Others did not. The Government whip, Alan Cadman, had been the next speaker to his feet in the grievance debate, decrying the offering as an amazing example of class warfare from a former Labor Party official 'who claims to be an intellectual'.

'Despite the wearing of your heart on your sleeve here in the Parliament, there is no courage in you whatsoever,' Alan fired back. 'When it comes to your own people, you are quiet and you are compliant. You will toe the line no matter what the circumstances.'

The following sitting week, the Liberal Member for the marginal South Australian seat of Makin, Trish Draper, rose in Parliament's parallel debating chamber, the Main Committee, calling the Member for Grayndler's speech 'the most extraordinary, vicious and personal attack' she had ever heard on an MP.

'The Member's comments obviously demonstrate that he missed the very essence of what the flower-power children of the 1960s were trying to convey,' Trish Draper said. 'Much of their sentiment and the movement of the 1960s was a backlash against people being judged and excluded on the basis of gender, disabilities, religion, age, race, economic status and, yes, appearance. Perhaps the Member is a little bitter and envious because he missed the era of the flower-power children.'

She declared John Howard's vision and leadership was clear: 'solid, fiscal and economic management to lead Australia into the 21st century'.

'There is nothing wrong with caring for family values and Christian ethics,' Trish said in conclusion. 'Australia could do with some more, which is an improvement, may I say, on the stoned, tie-dyed Kombi van driver of the '60s.'

John Howard would go on to serve another nine years as Prime Minister.

Anthony maintains that he failed to prepare Australia for the future and that the speech reflected on the conservative view of an Australia 'that no longer existed'.

'Compared with the actions of Margaret Thatcher or others on climate change, he was way behind – on all of those issues of modernisation. I think a leader should lead. And on the range of social issues I think he didn't do that.'

But he does praise John Howard for his achievements in gun control in the wake of the 1996 Port Arthur massacre.

'It was the right thing to do,' he says. 'He deserves unqualified credit for it . . . He didn't have to do it and he showed courage.'

But, Anthony adds, it was also good politics.

Despite the angry rhetoric regularly flung around, Parliament also had its social side. Anthony's political network meant he already had friends in Canberra when he arrived in early 1996.

Like all parliamentarians, in sitting weeks he needed to find accommodation. Logically, he turned first to the people he knew.

Anthony had met Victorian left-wingers Lindsay Tanner and Alan Griffin through his involvement in the reform group within the Federated Clerks' Union. Similar to the movement in NSW through which Anthony and Carmel had met, the Victorian Left had its own, more successful reform push, aimed at seizing power over this and other unions still controlled by the Catholic Right. The Victorians conferred regularly with their colleagues north of the border.

Lindsay and Anthony had also known each other through Young Labor, going back to when Anthony was a teenager and Lindsay a young activist in his 20s.

Lindsay and Alan had both been in Parliament since 1993 so it was logical Anthony would link up with them. They had a three-bedroom flat just across the NSW border in the satellite town of Queanbeyan where they stayed when Parliament sat. Anthony moved in.

He arrived in Canberra with an earring and a reputation.

'He was quite flamboyant,' Alan says. 'He was seen as someone who was basically standing up to the Right and articulating positions on issues and being a bit of a focal point for dissent within the NSW branch . . . He was a bit larger than life. So all of that I suppose created a bit of a persona.'

Alan and Lindsay had bought the flat together to avoid always staying in hotels. To describe their residential set-up, Alan used to borrow an analogy from the 1970s American TV show, *The Odd Couple*, in which two divorced blokes shared a house, one a neat freak and the other a slob.

'He said it was a household with two Oscars and no Felix,' Lindsay Tanner recounts. 'And he was pretty right. We used to have things like cartons of off milk sitting in the fridge and half-eaten pizzas in trays two weeks old lying on the floor and ashtrays of cigarette butts lying around. It was a pretty low-rent kind of establishment.'

He didn't just mean it was cheap.

'It should have been a warning sign, when I asked for a key to the flat I was told it wasn't needed,' Anthony says.

It became known as 'Grozny' because, like the Chechen capital during the war a year earlier, it was a scene of utter devastation.

'We all had enormous resilience and therefore the number of days when we'd front up to work in Parliament House only having a few hours' sleep the night before were quite substantial,' Lindsay says.

It wasn't always from carousing (although sometimes it was). In those days, Parliament regularly sat until 11.30 pm. Wide awake when they got home, the trio and others who variously slept on their couch – including one of Alan's staff, Daniel Andrews, who would become the Premier of Victoria – would often sit up talking about the interesting factional goings-on in their home states, until the early hours.

Having moved in with them, pretty soon Anthony moved out again. He eventually bought his own flat in Canberra.

Similar in age and outlook, Anthony and Alan would become especially close mates and their funny-voiced banter, unofficial comedy routines and schoolboy humour made them hilarious company. They became a familiar, almost hyphenated duo – 'Albo and Griffo'.

'Our offices were just near each other,' Alan says, of the far reaches of the second floor which they called alternatively 'Siberia' or 'Red Square'. 'And we established the fun faction.'

The 'fun faction' was formed at Anthony's suggestion, late one night in the downstairs bar of the National Press Club after a Labor caucus dinner. It was a dinner for those Alan calls 'the walking wounded', who had 'survived the Armageddon' of the 1996 election.

The fun faction became an imaginary splinter group that usually held its meetings after Parliament rose, wherever its members could get a drink.

It also became a way of poking fun at their whole environment and themselves. Albo and Griffo would have the imaginary 'fun faction awards' which they called the Baldwin Awards, named after their parliamentary Left colleague Peter Baldwin, who they designated the most serious person in Parliament.

'I would argue that the fun faction became a way of explaining the nature of things we ended up doing in this place,' Alan says.

For a while, their housemate, Lindsay Tanner, was a member too.

'I was officially a member of the fun faction but I think I eventually got expelled,' Lindsay says. 'I think I got too boring.'

There were many nights, though, that were far from boring. The three of them were renowned for performing renditions of one of Cold Chisel's most famous songs at caucus parties – at about three in the morning.

Lindsay believes Anthony's capacity for fun is one of the things that sets him apart.

'In an era of plastic politicians, he stands out because he's real,' he says. 'And he knows all the words to "Khe Sanh".'

'The truth is,' Anthony says, 'Opposition backbenchers have a bit of time on their hands.'

They would also form the Parliamentary Poets, a cross-party musical group of MPs established to sing parodies. The Poets had the express purpose of serving it up to the press gallery, whose own a-cappella satirists, the House Howlers, had until then commanded a fairly merciless solo billing – and a captive audience – at the annual parliamentary Midwinter Ball.

For a few years, the duelling songsters were a feature at the end of the ball's festivities. At their peak, along with 'Albo and Griffo' and their Labor colleague Kelvin Thomson on guitar, the Poets featured a somewhat bipartisan line-up. Once, they even included both the eventual Liberal Speaker Bronwyn Bishop and the former Midnight Oil front-man, Peter Garrett.

But as the prospect of a change of government loomed in 2007, the coalition's choristers would receive word from on high that their permission to participate was withdrawn and the Labor MPs became distracted by the anticipation of victory. Sadly, the band broke up.

It was fun while it lasted. And, says Anthony, 'as an added bonus, I can say I got to sing in a band with Peter Garrett'.

Relationships across the aisle were less common and harder to maintain but they did exist. And back then there were certainly a lot more 'Tories', as Anthony likes to call the coalition, than there were of any other brand of MP.

On arrival in '96, he had discovered that the exhilarating wind in his face was actually the whoosh of departing Labor colleagues.

'I well remember they had orientation day and overwhelmingly I think there were 40 Liberals and Nats – or maybe 50 – and half a dozen of us,' he says.

There was fellow newly minted NSW MP Joel Fitzgibbon, and Jenny Macklin and Kelvin Thomson from Victoria. And there was a familiar face, a bloke who had left Sydney to take up a job as secretary of the Australian Council of Trade Unions and then also chosen a pathway into Parliament in the safe Labor seat of Batman: his old factional enemy, Martin Ferguson.

On the other side, he already knew fellow newcomer Joe Hockey from the airport campaign. Anthony and Joe found they had more than Sydney Airport in common, including that Joe's relationship with the Government Whip, Alan Cadman, was no closer than Anthony's had been with Leo McLeay. On arrival, Joe had had even more trouble securing an office.

'He hated my guts,' Joe says of Alan Cadman.

Roomy though it had been when it opened in 1988, Parliament House was full, with all Lower House offices occupied until someone moved into the Speaker's suite, later that week. Joe was told he would have to bunk in with fellow newcomer, Nationals MP Ian Causley.

'So he said, "You can share an office with Ian Causley until we elect a Speaker." And I had my family down there and so did Ian Causley. So I went crazy and they cleared the boxes out of a storeroom . . . The first day of Parliament I had my family sitting in an ex-storeroom.'

Joe and Anthony became friends, checking in with each other and sharing a drink now and then.

'We've always had shared moments and exchanges and we've talked to each other – had a beer in each other's offices,' Joe says.

Their personal association strengthened on a parliamentary trip to the Middle East – and particularly the Palestinian territories – in 1998, as part of a delegation which also included Leo McLeay and helped foster a further thaw in relations between Leo and Anthony.

The Palestinian representative in Australia, Ali Kazak, had organised the trip, which businessman Said Meshal had agreed to fund. Inquiries were made about the backgrounds of both men, to ensure the MPs would not find themselves compromised.

'Everyone said [the hosts] were fine and we should do it,' Joe says.

Liberal MP Peter Nugent was leading the delegation and the Nationals' Peter McGauran was its fifth member.

Joe decided to pay for his father, Richard, to go too. Born in Bethlehem to Armenian parents, Richard had come to Australia in 1948 as a 21-year-old post-war refugee, anglicising his surname, Hokeidonian, and determined to make a new life. Joe thought making the trip together would be good for both of them. He also introduced his father to his mate from across the political divide.

'Albo got on really well with Dad,' Joe says.

Anthony and Richard had an element of upbringing in common. Both had grown up without a father around, Richard's dad having walked out the day he was born. And both men completely adored their mums.

When the group went to a beachside refugee camp at Gaza, they were all deeply affected.

'Seeing the extraordinary conditions that people lived in,' Anthony says. 'Seeing the queue to get access into Israel for the workforce in the morning. The extraordinary security that was there – and this was a relatively peaceful time.'

As they stood in a tiny shed where eight people slept, Joe remembers his father's comment.

'He said, "There but for the grace of God, I would have gone." He stood there and he looked at Albo, and Albo had, I remember, tears in his eyes.'

For Anthony, the emotion came from observing a father and his son experiencing that profound moment together.

'It was a privilege to see a man bond with his dad in the way that they did, over what was a very emotional experience for them both,' Anthony says.

On their return to Australia, the two MPs founded the Parliamentary Friends of Palestine, Joe as its chairman and Anthony as secretary.

'It wouldn't have worked if it was just a Labor group,' Anthony says.

Over the years, they would occasionally confer or swap stories.

'We were honest with each other about people on our own side,' Joe says.

When, after years in Opposition, Anthony would finally go into government as a Minister in 2007, he received congratulations from Joe. And some advice.

'We traded notes about people in the business community,' Joe says, laughing. 'The ones that had sucked up to us in government were now sucking up to Albo. The business community think you don't talk to each other. So we always talked about public servants, about departments, about people in the business community who run with the hares and hunt with the hounds.'

Retiring from Parliament in 2016, Joe reflects on the value of the kind of friendship he has shared with Anthony.

'That's one of the relationships that was genuine and I'm sort of sad that I didn't put more effort into it.'

Anthony's factional ally, ALP National President Mark Butler, notes that not all the relationships forged in politics – especially federal politics – are genuine in a traditional sense. They're unusual because they're forged in a kind of vacuum, away from home.

'Often people talk about "How about your kids?" But really, they don't know them,' Mark observes. 'They've never met your kids. It's not that they don't care – it's just that they're not the sort of friendships you have with people where they're invested in your personal life.

'At the end of the day, you don't really understand their family. You've never been to their house. You might have met their wife or husband at an event for three minutes. You sort of know *about it*, but you don't *know* it.'

He says Anthony is very good at building relationships.

'This game is a game of relationships. It works when you've got people who know and trust each other. And he's always been very good at that. He does take it to a human level in a way that many others don't here.'

He believes the qualities he admires in Anthony came at least in part from his mentor, Tom Uren. Before he'd met either of them, Joe had read Tom's memoir, *Straight Left*, which he called 'a magnificent autobiography'.

'He was a man of conviction and firm principles,' Joe says of Tom. 'And he was a patriot despite various moments of opposition to the national policy. No one could doubt Tom Uren's patriotism and loyalty to Australia.'

He says Tom encouraged Anthony's best qualities.

'To be a man of principle. To be honest. Your handshake is your word. And every moment I've ever dealt with Anthony Albanese his word is binding.'

It's high praise for a man whose politics are so different from his own, especially when those views are at the core of the vocation both chose. Indeed, it's almost higher praise than comes from Anthony's own Labor colleagues.

'I like him,' Joe says. 'And he'll always be welcome in my home.'

Asked if Anthony has ever been in his home in the two decades they've known each other, Joe roars with the laughter of someone who's just been busted.

'No,' he admits. And now that he has taken up a new job in Washington DC as Australia's ambassador to the United States, he acknowledges the opportunities will be even fewer.

'I've run out of time,' he says. 'But I'd happily have him in my home.'

CHAPTER 17

Fact and Faction

The early years in Opposition allowed Anthony to pursue some of the issues he cared most about, including some on which the views of MPs and senators crossed party lines and were deeply held and personal.

In late 1996, Victorian Liberal MP Kevin Andrews put forward a private member's bill to overturn laws that had made the Northern Territory the first Australian jurisdiction to allow voluntary euthanasia. With the territories lacking the same constitutional protection as the states when it comes to federal intervention, those in Federal Parliament who for religious or other reasons opposed euthanasia were determined to abolish it.

The Northern Territory law had taken effect in July and on 22 September, a 66-year-old carpenter suffering from prostate cancer, Bob Dent, became the first to use it to end his life with the help of controversial physician, Dr Philip Nitschke.

Two others would follow – 52-year-old Janet Mills, who suffered from a rare form of lymphoma, and a 69-year-old man with cancer, who requested anonymity.

That October, Kevin Andrews' bill was introduced and the parties agreed their members should have a conscience vote, dividing Federal Parliament in other than the usual ideological manner.

'We cannot ignore our emotional experiences, any more than we should ignore the consequences of our decisions for all Australians,' Andrews told Parliament. 'This debate is about passing a bill that protects the vulnerable – or about leaving them exposed to pressure, abuse and a loss of autonomy. It is about having the courage to address an issue of national importance or running away from it.'

Anthony supported voluntary euthanasia and was not in favour of intervening in the NT's legislative business.

'I oppose this bill because I support human dignity,' he told Parliament. 'I oppose this bill because I support freedom of choice. I oppose this bill because I support civil liberties. I oppose this bill because my Christian upbringing taught me that compassion is important. I oppose this bill because modern medical practice should be open and accountable, not covert and dishonest. I oppose this bill because I believe that the national parliament should only intervene against the state or territory legislature when there is overwhelming public support to do so on a national level.'

Conscious of the varying views on the subject in the community, and not wishing to become typecast on such a divisive issue, he did not want to become a frontline campaigner against Andrews' bill. But behind the scenes, he used his organisational skills to help those wanting to vote No.

His former campaign director Tim Gartrell, by then on his parliamentary staff, cites the euthanasia issue as an example of Anthony being willing to step up.

'He's got hold of it and he's organising and he's talking to people,' Tim says. 'And I think that's a good example of what I like about him. He's got a bit of spark. And he'll go, "Right, someone's got to do it and if I don't do it, who's going to do it?"'

Suggesting Andrews' bill discriminated against the NT, veteran Nationals MP Ian Sinclair put forward an amendment, proposing that alternative legislation be introduced for a uniform national approach. He said it would allow people to vote on the substance of the issue and not be caught up in a debate about states' rights.

The Government had restricted debate on the main bill in the House of Representatives to three speakers for and three against, shunting the rest to the parallel Main Committee chamber.

Anthony spoke in favour of Ian's amendment.

'I do not oppose the Andrews bill because of the issue of states' rights,' he said on 9 December, as the parliamentary year neared its close. 'I oppose it because I support voluntary euthanasia and I have got the guts to say it. People should debate the substance of the issue.'

He condemned the use of the parallel chamber that some of its parliamentary critics dubbed 'sideshow alley' and suggested supporters of the main bill were being wilfully inconsistent.

'Let's not have the sort of hypocrisy where people isolate the debate upstairs, in sideshow alley, and say, "We're opposed to voluntary euthanasia because we think people should get proper care," and at the same time put their hands up and vote in the Parliament to cut palliative care funding,' he said. 'It is that sort of hypocrisy which I would like to see exposed by a longer, real, more fair dinkum national debate about national policy.'

He likened voluntary euthanasia to other 'progressive social initiatives' such as environmentalism and feminism, which he said were once radical left-wing issues but were now trumpeted by members of the Coalition Government.

But Anthony also said he respected the right of those opposed to voluntary euthanasia to hold and advocate for their views. Among them were his own friend and colleague, the Member for Melbourne, Lindsay Tanner, who was in the chamber as he spoke.

'There are probably very few people in this House with whom I would have a greater political affinity than the member for Melbourne, who is sitting at the table,' Anthony said. 'I disagree with him on this issue, but I respect his right to be wrong on this occasion.'

The amendment would fail and Kevin Andrews' bill would pass, invalidating the NT law in March 1997.

On issues such as this – and in a sentiment that seemed to contradict his willingness to attack John Howard for being overly Christian – Anthony did not want to disrespect others' religious beliefs.

His own Catholic upbringing and the depth of his mother's faith made him aware that, on what were considered conscience issues, views different to his own were equally deeply held and genuinely founded.

That view would also contribute to him arguing strongly in 2015 against moves to take a party-wide position on same-sex marriage and force all Labor MPs and senators to endorse it. He supported legalising marriage for same-sex couples but believed it should be subject to a free vote.

But it was also about the politics. Having condemned the coalition for binding its members to a policy position against the change, he believed Labor could hardly do effectively the same in reverse.

The day after his euthanasia speech, Anthony raised another issue that would challenge the more conservative views of many of his colleagues. He used the adjournment debate, a nightly opportunity before the House rises for MPs to raise matters of their own choosing, to talk about superannuation.

Anthony argued that same-sex couples should be allowed to access each other's superannuation under the same provisions as those that applied to heterosexual couples in married or de facto relationships.

'I was particularly attracted in part to areas where other people weren't doing work,' he says. 'So the issue of sexuality issues and discrimination against same-sex couples was one that wasn't really on the agenda.'

Under the law, same-sex dependents were not legally entitled to access a partner's super in the event of his or her death. If a legally sanctioned will had been left stipulating that course – and all the forms had been filled out with the super fund – access was possible, but the law considered a same-sex partner to be a non-dependant and therefore subject to tax.

A heterosexual couple in the same circumstance would face no tax bill. Anthony called it 'plainly unfair'. He was under no illusions about rapid redress.

'I daresay, Mr Speaker, that this is not an issue which the Howard Government is likely to embrace in the near future,' he said. 'It is disturbing – but probably not surprising – to see in retrospect that, when John Howard claimed during the election campaign that he stood for all of us, he only meant us as in white, middle-class, Anglo-Saxon, employed members of nuclear families like himself – certainly not gay and lesbian people. The "family values" rhetoric suddenly becomes a bit hollow . . .'

Anthony took the view that in ending discrimination against same-sex couples, there was more than superannuation that needed fixing. But he had to start with something that was easy for the majority to support.

The superannuation change was hard to argue against. It didn't involve any government benefit and it was a logical fairness issue.

'Because that's about people's money that *they* own, essentially,' he says. '[It's] about their asset and why shouldn't they leave it to whoever they want?'

The Howard Government would agree to amend the law, a change Labor would then extend once in office.

From that beginning, Anthony and others pushed their anti-discrimination program along, little by little.

'Once you did that, once you got into the debate and that logic, the principle [that] people should be treated the same was easy to be extended. That led to the debate being broadened into "why shouldn't someone who is sick be able to have their partner visit them in hospital? Why shouldn't they be able to sponsor their partner for migration?"'

Again, he was playing the long game.

Back then, he believes it helped that the MP pressing the case was heterosexual.

'A couple of people said to colleagues, "Oh, I didn't know he was gay,"' he says. 'I think it's important that no one could say I was doing this to gain a personal benefit.'

His Senate colleague, frontbencher Penny Wong, who has two daughters with her partner, Sophie Allouache, credits Anthony with taking the early lead on an issue that's important to her in both policy and deeply personal terms.

'He had the courage to stand up and argue for a position on equality for same-sex couples well before there was any popular support, majority support in the community,' Penny says, 'but also before it was seen as something that politicians should do something about.'

She said the same in the Left caucus meeting at the 2015 ALP national conference, ahead of the vote in which his position favouring a conscience vote on same-sex marriage would win out over hers – and that of deputy Labor leader Tanya Plibersek – which favoured binding Labor MPs to vote for change, in line with its policy platform.

It was one of the few times they had been on opposite sides on that or any issue. Penny found it 'uncomfortable'.

Tanya and Anthony had generally been on the same side in debates historically, too. She was another among the Young Labor Left whose rise into representative politics Anthony encouraged.

When Peter Baldwin announced that he was retiring from politics ahead of the 1998 election having already been preselected, the field of candidates to take over in his seat of Sydney was extensive.

'I had no plan of getting myself elected to Parliament, I just wanted to be active in the Labor Party,' Tanya says. 'And then because Peter Baldwin's retirement was quite unexpected, there wasn't an obvious successor to him. Nobody had been stacking the branches.'

In the end, it came down to a hard-fought contest between two women: Tanya, then aged 28; barrister Chrissa Loukas, 36.

Chrissa had some high-powered backing in the form of endorsements from former Prime Minister Gough Whitlam, former NSW Premier Neville Wran and the first female President of the Australian Council of Trade Unions, Jennie George, who would enter Parliament at the following election in 2001 for the NSW seat of Throsby.

Tanya had worked for Senator Bruce Childs. She ran a strong grassroots doorknocking campaign in the electorate's branches and won solidly.

'I do think I worked harder than any of the other candidates,' she says. 'They all worked hard but I was pretty obsessive about it, and I think people were prepared to take a chance on me, thinking that I'd be there for a long time. They were prepared to believe that I had the capacity of being a Minister one day.'

In the final run-off, she secured 197 votes to Chrissa's 143. Both Tanya and Anthony say he didn't play a big role.

'He actually wasn't very active in my preselection,' Tanya says. '. . . He was always someone that I asked for advice and I talked to him regularly during the preselection.'

She says he was just one of a number of backers.

'He supported me and there was probably about half a dozen votes [from] people that he was quite close to. But I had a lot of different supporters.'

Along with Bruce Childs, she lists Tom Uren, Jeannette McHugh, Ann Symonds, former Hawke Government Minister Robert Tickner and Labor senator Kate Lundy among them.

At the time, Anthony insisted to journalists that he 'did not make a phone call during that preselection', preferring to be described as her 'contemporary' rather than her mentor. Others were convinced the level of support behind the scenes was considerably more extensive and it prompted allegations of patronage. It's an allegation both reject.

Anthony was friends with a number of the candidates, including Leichhardt mayor Kris Cruden – who in 2016 would become his campaign director and was running his electorate office. For that reason, he took the same approach as he'd taken with Damian O'Connor and Luke Foley: he didn't canvass on behalf of any of them.

In more recent years, Anthony and Tanya have been seen as potential future rivals for the Labor leadership.

Their friendship would become further strained after the 2013 Labor leadership ballot between Anthony and the Right's Bill Shorten, when Bill declared he would happily have her as his deputy, should he win.

'I never had any arrangement with Bill,' Tanya says. 'I said that I was interested in being the deputy and that I would stand for deputy . . . He was free to say he was happy to have me as deputy. That was a matter for him.'

It was a position she could potentially find harder to secure if Anthony was leader, given the problem in having both leader and deputy from the Left and from the same state.

As a fellow member of the Left, Tanya voted for Anthony in the 2013 caucus ballot and issued campaign material supporting him. But some of his supporters believe Bill's endorsement of her as a future deputy undermined her factional colleague.

She insists it hasn't affected their professional relationship. But relations have appeared less convivial since. These days, Anthony is closer to Penny Wong.

When Penny was the special guest at a fundraiser for him in Leichhardt in 2015, he called her 'my best friend in the Parliament'.

'I'm very close to Anthony and it was a nice thing to hear,' she says.

Launching his re-election campaign in 2016, Penny returned the sentiment.

'In Albo, I'll say this to you, I think he is the finest and toughest politician of his generation. He's someone who knows how the Parliament works, and he knows how to make the Parliament work for the people he represents. Grayndler needs Albo, the Parliament needs Albo, and I say to you the Labor Party and the Australian people need Albo.'

Penny believes Anthony's campaign for those early changes on superannuation were motivated by a belief in equality.

'It's as simple as that. Equality on the basis of class, equality on the basis of race, equality on the basis of gender, equality on the basis of sexuality. He's been consistent about that.'

Eventually, his was among the advocacy that would lead to policy change within his own party too.

In 2004, John Howard would take the opportunity to entrench the traditional view of marriage and wedge the Labor Party in the lead-up to the federal election, legislating to confirm that legal marriage could only be between a man and a woman.

At the time, aware of the political risks in taking any other position, Labor voted in support. But a year before the 2007 election, the party's national conference would amend its platform to remove discrimination on the basis of sexuality apart from marriage.

When Labor took office, 86 pieces of legislation were amended in a single cognate debate to remove same-sex discrimination across government, leaving marriage the one significant area that remained unchanged. In 2011, the platform was amended in favour of same-sex marriage but with a conscience vote.

Two years later, the ACT Government would legalise same-sex marriage in the capital territory. The law would only operate for five days before the High Court struck it down, invalidating all marriages performed in the period.

In August 2015, a month before Tony Abbott was deposed as Prime Minister, he would announce his intention to hold a national plebiscite on same-sex marriage. It was seen by supporters of legislative change as an attempt to delay and possibly defeat it.

'The problem here isn't that Tony Abbott is stuck in the past,' Anthony declared at the time, during his weekly sparring match with Liberal frontbencher Christopher Pyne on the Nine Network's *Today* show. 'It's that he wants the rest of Australia to go back there and keep him company.'

But Tony Abbott remained firmly opposed and his party maintained its stance against any change. When Malcolm Turnbull took over as Prime Minister, he retained the plebiscite policy despite advocating changing the law. It was a condition of receiving support for his leadership challenge from some of his conservative colleagues.

By 2016, there had been 16 attempts to legislate for same-sex marriage, variously involving MPs and senators from Labor, the Greens, the Liberal Party and the Christian Democrats. All were unsuccessful.

Anthony's outspokenness on policy and politics and his factional influence had raised his profile. After Labor narrowly lost the 1998 election, when the jockeying began for positions in Kim Beazley's shadow ministry, he was one of the backbenchers who decided to nominate for elevation.

Under the factional system, a number of frontbench positions were allocated to the Left and it was up to the faction to decide who filled them. The leader then decided which portfolio went to whom.

In 1998, the divide within the Left was still flourishing and the soft Left, then led by Martin Ferguson, prevailed.

There were to be extra shadow ministerial spots for the Left so, believing there would at least be some representation of their sub-faction in the line-up, a group from the hard Left put themselves forward – Kim Carr, George Campbell, Alan Griffin and Anthony. Kim already had a lesser position as parliamentary secretary and hoped for promotion, while the others took their chances at propulsion straight into the shadow ministry.

None of them were elected.

Among those who voted against them was Julia Gillard, with whom Anthony had clashed in student politics. Years later she would apologise to him, telling him she made the wrong decision.

The soft Left's winner-take-all stance enraged the unsuccessful candidates.

'We didn't exercise power the way that Martin did,' Anthony says.

He decided to employ the same strategy he had used to avenge his loss to Paul O'Grady back in the Young Labor Left ballot all those years before.

Subsequently, when there were preselections for winnable seats where the Left either had the numbers or had negotiated with the Right to select a candidate, he would wheel and deal and 'recruit' branch members to make sure his own part of the faction won out wherever possible. It would take time but it would be effective.

'We got people elected in various places to change the balance in the Left,' he says, matter-of-factly. 'After that there were negotiations across the groups. It was more representative since then. That was the last time there was a brutal exercise with the numbers.'

Before the faction meeting which had sealed their shadow ministerial fate, the hard Left had received word that in recognition of their work and talents and the fact that their own colleagues would not elevate them, Opposition Leader Kim Beazley wanted to offer them one parliamentary secretary's position.

Parliamentary secretaryships were the most junior front-bench jobs, one rung below the outer shadow ministry but off the backbench and on the trajectory to an eventual full portfolio. Kim Beazley regarded them as effectively junior ministries. Doling them out was the leader's prerogative and they weren't subject to factional election.

'I would have been delighted if the Left group had pushed them higher,' Kim says of the four in the hard Left that the soft Left had overlooked for promotion. '. . . Disputes inside factions was always a distraction and the reach of a leader was shallow in handling them. Martin was the bane of their existence but I liked him too.'

By 1998, Kim felt the Left's transition from internal critic to constructively engaged participant was all but complete.

'In Hawke's day they were self-consciously an internal opposition,' he says, naming former Deputy Prime Minister Brian Howe as the exception. 'By 1996 they were committed to winning elections. You wanted to use such commitment.'

The offer of a junior job would go to Anthony. But he decided that, on principle, the hard Left should reject it, to make the point that it wasn't prepared to take appeasement in the face of such a factional affront.

The four had a phone hook-up to discuss the issue and the intended response was outlined. The position would be offered, Anthony would say no. It would then be offered to Alan Griffin, who decided under those circumstances that he would also decline.

The Left faction had its ballot and, having lost as expected, the four joined the rest of the Labor caucus at a traditional post-election dinner at the National Press Club. After dinner, Kim Beazley took Anthony aside and made the offer.

A junior portfolio would give him the scope to get around more of Australia working on both policy and politics. Kim particularly saw the value in that.

'My main concern was to get Albo on the road,' he says. 'He was a tough campaigner and you could see his value in marginal-seat campaigning, and we had lots of marginals to pursue.'

But when the offer was put, Anthony declined as planned, putting a condition on acceptance that he thought couldn't be met.

'I said I wouldn't do it unless Griffo got a spot,' Anthony says.

He then went and told Alan what he'd done.

'I said, "Alright, well, if he makes the offer to me, I'll be rejecting it too,"' Alan recalls.

About 10 minutes later, Kim Beazley approached.

'Alan, got a second?'

He told Alan he wanted him to be a shadow parliamentary secretary.

'And I said, "Listen, mate, I really appreciate the offer and I thank you very much for it,"' Alan recounts. '"But under the circumstances, I feel I need to say no. But thank you very much, I really appreciate it."' And then I turned to go away and he says, "You do realise it's both of you?" And I said, "Sorry?" And he said, "I'm offering you both one."'

This caught Alan somewhat off-guard. They did not have a plan for this scenario.

'Can I get back to you?' he mumbled and headed off to find Anthony. By now, both had had a few drinks with dinner. Anthony was equally flummoxed.

They found the other two and had a quick conference. A few expletives were uttered. Alan thought they should accept.

'That's actually a serious concession and frankly this is dumb,' is how Alan explains his view of their righteous refusal. 'It's a big concession recognising the fact we'd been [done] over and it ought to be recognised as such.'

This didn't please their colleagues. Kim Carr advocated against caving in and so did George Campbell. Neither would benefit from acquiescing; not Kim, who had won a parliamentary secretaryship last time around and was keeping it, nor George, who faced being the only one without one.

Their small meeting dissolved, issue unresolved, and Anthony disappeared. A few minutes later, he reappeared holding his mobile phone.

'It's Carmel,' he said, and then into the phone: 'Talk to Griffo.'

Carmel's view was the same as Alan's. It was a good offer and they should probably get off their high horses and accept. Alan and Anthony decided they should sleep on it and talk the next day.

In the morning when they spoke on the phone, things seemed much clearer. They decided to accept.

When they went to see Kim Beazley soon after, he told them that Alan would be assisting in the health portfolio and Anthony in education and youth. Each flew home, Anthony to Sydney and Alan to Melbourne, pleased that he had new responsibilities.

When the final list of shadow ministers and their parliamentary secretaries was issued later that day, Alan had health, as expected. But Anthony had family and community services.

Sometime between morning and afternoon, the shadow parliamentary secretarial responsibilities for education had returned in their entirety to their previous owner: Kim Carr.

Nevertheless, the fun faction still chalked it up as a win.

Six months before his elevation to the outer reaches of the Labor front bench, Anthony's family home in Marrickville had become a two-politician household. Four years after first considering it, Carmel Tebbutt entered state politics.

Carmel was appointed to fill a casual vacancy created by the retirement of left-winger Ann Symonds from the NSW Parliament's Upper House, the Legislative Council.

The following year, Premier Bob Carr would promote her into the ministry in the tough portfolio of Juvenile Justice, meaning both members of the Albanese-Tebbutt alliance were then frontbenchers, Carmel in government at the state level and Anthony federally, still in opposition.

Anthony was working to Wayne Swan, the shadow Minister for Family Services. Wayne gave him responsibility for housing, which allowed him to do policy work on homelessness and social housing. He was grateful for the trust.

'That's how I really got to develop a relationship with Wayne that was quite close,' Anthony says. 'He was very good to me.'

With Prime Minister John Howard negotiating to introduce the 10 per cent goods and services tax he had proposed ahead of the 1998 election, the detailed impact of the change on some Australians was beginning to emerge.

Permanent residents of caravan parks were angry upon discovering they would pay the GST on their rent, 10 per cent for the first 27 days and five per cent after that.

Anthony took up the issue with zeal, defending the 'battlers' against what he said was the party of privilege. When caravan owners drove their mobile homes to Canberra to protest in March 2000, he addressed their rally and lambasted government MPs for not showing up.

'This is discrimination against the most vulnerable Australians, who can least afford to pay,' he declared. 'It is against all those Australian principles of a fair go.'

He knew what it was like to worry about how to pay the rent.

With both of their careers progressing, Carmel and Anthony had decided they wanted a family. Along with the professional upheaval of those preceding years, Carmel's own family had experienced a crushing tragedy, the death of her younger brother Matthew in a car accident. It made them all focus anew on the importance of those closest to them.

More than a decade after they got together, Carmel and Anthony married in 2000, ahead of their son Nathan's birth late that year. He would be given the middle name Matthew.

Once they had made the decision to formalise their relationship, the couple moved swiftly to organise the wedding.

Anthony's friend Craig Sahlin remembers the phone call telling him they were tying the knot. He was in Hungary, on a long overseas sojourn, and disappointed he wasn't able to rearrange things to get back in time.

The wedding ceremony was at Sydney's Taronga Park Zoo, moved away from the clifftop at Bradley's Head because of high winds on the day, so they sought the relative protection of a pergola instead.

The couple wrote their own vows and exchanged them before celebrant Gordon Sharpe – handily a branch member from Marrickville East – overlooking Sydney Harbour, in the presence of family and a few close friends and colleagues.

One of their readings was 'The Sun Rising', by the English poet John Donne.

> She's all states, and all princes, I;
> Nothing else is.
> Princes do but play us; compared to this,
> All honour's mimic, all wealth alchemy.
> Thou, Sun, art half as happy as we

Maryanne was pretty happy too. She and Carmel's dad, Bede, both gave speeches, as did Anthony, best man Paul Murphy and Carmel's maid of honour and close friend from school days, Shayne Conlon.

Bob Debus was among the guests and, from Anthony's federal circle, Bruce Childs, John Faulkner, George Campbell and Alan Griffin. Jenny Macklin was also invited but couldn't make it.

The reception was at the zoo's nearby function centre, so the guests were treated to a visit from a few small, generally friendly animals as part of the evening's entertainment.

They hired a DJ but Anthony chose the music – a selection of his favourite indie greats.

'People had a good time,' he says.

Despite her afflictions, Maryanne danced all night until the couple left.

'She had a new lease of life,' Anthony says. 'Lots of people who hadn't seen my mum healthy and dancing before – they were pleased for her as well as us.'

The couple would have a one-night honeymoon at the Park Hyatt on Circular Quay, a gift from Anthony's staff. They weren't going to have much of a break.

'I had Monday off and was in Parliament on Tuesday.'

When they arrived to check in, they discovered their room had already been allocated. In a what-are-the-chances episode, it had mistakenly been given to another couple checking in, under the same name.

'There were two Albaneses staying at the Park Hyatt,' Anthony explains.

The other couple, from Bankstown, were soon back at the desk alongside the newlyweds.

Anthony recalls inquiring of the hotel staff: 'This is my wedding night. Are you telling me you don't have a room?'

The problem was swiftly sorted. It was an eventually comical end to a very happy day.

Paul Murphy served as Anthony's best man. Anthony had performed the same duty for him a decade earlier, when he and Nareen had married at Observatory Hill. Like Carmel, Nareen Young is a firm feminist and she and Paul had envisioned a deliberately non-traditional ceremony. She had planned to wear black – until she mentioned as much to Anthony's mum.

'She just said, "That's ridiculous. You can't wear black to your wedding." And I went, "Oh, okay." And changed my mind.'

She wore a dress of her own mother's instead – cream lace and green velvet.

Despite the sartorial acquiescence, Nareen and Carmel held – and still hold – strong views about some of the traditional expectations of women and assumptions about their roles, including in the labour movement.

'I think both she and I shared a view that as feminists we weren't going to rely on our boyfriends,' Nareen says. 'We both have a very strong view that we should achieve without reference to men or relationships that we're in.'

Although Carmel would attract sniping from some within the Left who accused her of succeeding via her partner's status, she forged a strong reputation for being an extremely competent politician.

The former ALP secretary John Della Bosca – Carmel's ministerial colleague – dismisses the historical backbiting as ignorant. He respects her political skills.

'I thought of her as more formidable than Anthony,' John says, laughing. In truth, he rates both as formidable.

'I've been on budget committees with Carmel for years and I've sat next to her in Parliament for God knows how long and I can't recall seeing her lose her cool once. I think that's pretty formidable.'

In 2005, Carmel would switch to the Legislative Assembly by winning the seat of Marrickville in a by-election. She won again in 2007 but after that election, with their young son having just started Year 1, she quit the ministry for the backbench.

'I felt like I had a lot on my plate and it really was crystallised during the election campaign where I just thought, "I just can't keep doing this. It's just too hard."'

With Anthony by then not only in Federal Parliament but a shadow Minister soon to fight a gruelling federal election, Carmel decided for the sake of their son, and having already spent eight years in the ministry herself, that she would step back.

'It was a hard decision,' she says. 'I'm not going to pretend it wasn't a hard decision. It was really hard. And I would have moments where I would feel really like, "God, I've given up a lot." But I knew it was the right choice for me personally and for Nathan.'

Her then leader, Premier Morris Iemma, tried to talk her out of it and then asked Anthony to do it, calling him on election day to see if he'd speak to her about changing her mind.

'I said, "Well, I'm not prepared to speak to her,"' Anthony says. 'She's very definite. She's made this decision.'

Carmel thought she'd see out her time in politics from the backbench. But as one of the Government's best performers, her skills were sorely missed around the Cabinet table. Within two years, her colleagues were urging her to return to the ministry.

'And in the end I did,' she says. 'And I'm glad I did.'

She was back in the ministry, this time as Minister for Climate Change and the Environment and Minister for Commerce. The Left also elected her to take the deputy leader's position, making her Deputy Premier.

Carmel and Anthony had become one of the power couples of Australian politics. With both then serving as senior ministers, they needed a strategy for managing not only the double-craziness impact on their home life, but potential conflicts of interest.

Their respective seniority drove them to set rules to separate their professional and personal lives. The very things that had brought them together – politics and policy – couldn't be discussed at home, at least not fully and freely.

'We couldn't talk about specific policy stuff,' Anthony says. 'But a lot of politics isn't about what's happening in the Cabinet room. And we never did speak about the Cabinet room.'

When they could afford to take holidays together, it was often overseas to escape politics completely.

For much of Carmel's ministerial career, Anthony would be in Opposition. But her return to the frontbench would coincide with Labor's reign in Canberra and they would both need to be conscious of avoiding conflicts of interest. With Carmel as NSW Health Minister during heavy negotiations between the Commonwealth and the states, Anthony would be careful to step out of Cabinet anytime the subject – or anything related – came up.

'I just excluded myself on anything to do with health,' he says. 'It was the right thing to do as a matter of principle. But it was also about having a sensible relationship.'

And whenever ministerial reshuffles saw a reallocation of portfolios, they would ensure their leaders understood what each could and could not do, to avoid crossover.

'We were always very conscious of the fact that we couldn't have . . . portfolios in the same area,' Carmel says. 'And it worked because we had different interests anyway.'

She smiles.

'It was quite useful sometimes.'

It would work that way until Carmel's retirement from politics in 2015.

CHAPTER 18

Cardinal and Myrtle

Catholicism and a love of Labor were only two of the three faiths with which Anthony Albanese was raised. As he frequently and unashamedly declares, his mother instilled in him a third devotion: to the South Sydney Rugby League Football Club.

It had been with him since his boyhood, when mother and son would go to the games and cheer on a team whose supporters were great in both number and passion.

Around Camperdown, everyone supported either Souths, Newtown or Balmain, and in the Ellery-Albanese home, it had always been the Rabbitohs.

The team was named for the cry of the working men of the early 20th century who sold rabbits around the streets of South Sydney on a Saturday morning, shouting, 'Rabbit-oh!'

Some of those morning workers were football players in the afternoon. The story goes that they often wore their jerseys on their rounds, trudging the suburbs with rabbits slung over their shoulders, skinning them as they sold them and turning up at the football match with the team colours smeared in blood and fur. This was the club for ordinary, working people – people who were accustomed to both grit and disappointment.

When Anthony was a boy at St Joseph's Primary, in Camperdown, he and his school friend Lindsay Keevers played in Souths juniors. Their jumpers were black with a white V – and a red bunny.

'All the Souths juniors played with the bunny,' Anthony says, of the emblem that is emblazoned on the club's modern merchandise and the source of its nickname: 'the Bunnies'.

In the higher grades, the teams wore the traditional colours – green jerseys with red hoops. Their description evoked more of a sense of grandeur than the team itself – not just plain old red and green but cardinal and myrtle, the colours of the cardinal waratah, the floral emblem of NSW.

The flower's rich red also happens to be the colour of Vatican clerics' cassocks – completely appropriate given the team's roots are deeply Irish Catholic, deeply working class and deeply local.

Its fans were and are especially devoted. Anthony is a diehard.

'When I was little, Mum used to take me to Redfern Oval,' Anthony recalls. 'And when I was older I used to go with mates . . . and generally have a good time.'

Maryanne wasn't a member of Souths – that cost money she didn't have – but she was as dedicated to supporting them as going to mass or a monthly party meeting.

'We'd sit on the hill,' Anthony says. 'Redfern Oval was mainly a hill – it was just a little grandstand . . . That was a pretty cheap day 'cause you'd go to the footy and it didn't cost that much to get in, in those days.'

In later years, a fellow Souths devotee who would lead the charge to head off the club's demise, broadcaster Andrew Denton, recalls Anthony introducing him to Maryanne.

'I met his mum,' Andrew says. 'When I looked at them . . . they represent every South Sydney family I've ever seen at the football. It is in the blood.'

When they were young, Anthony's cousin Karen Jane Douglas, daughter of his Aunt Lenore, would go with them to the game. Karen Jane lived at Narrabeen on Sydney's northern beaches and was a staunch Manly supporter.

'That was about the only thing we didn't agree on,' she says.

Five years younger than her, Anthony was more like a little brother than a cousin and would regularly go up to Narrabeen for holidays or weekends.

She'd known him since he was born and fussed over him as a baby. She lives with the guilt of almost dropping him on his head.

Before they'd moved to Narrabeen, Karen Jane's family lived at Bondi and on one occasion down on the beach, when a kid running past gave her a fright, she tripped over with the baby in her arms. She managed to land herself between him and the sand, but Maryanne's response almost drowned Anthony's.

'He started screaming and Aunty Mary started screaming,' Karen Jane says. 'I can laugh about it now but at the time it was awful . . . It obviously didn't do him any harm.'

There was no lasting damage to the family ties either.

If Manly played Souths at Redfern, Karen Jane would come along. And if Souths ventured across the harbour to play Manly, Anthony would go over there.

'We'd go to Brookvale Oval with me in my Souths gear and her in her Manly gear,' Anthony says.

Whenever she could, Maryanne would take both kids to the football and if she raised her voice it would be at the field of play.

'She was a fanatical flag waver,' Anthony says. 'She'd cheer and she'd get into it.'

When Souths made the grand final against St George in 1971, Maryanne bought Karen Jane a ticket.

'And I remember thinking, "I don't believe I'm going to the South Sydney grand final,"' Karen Jane says. 'She wanted to deck me out in all this red and green and stuff. That was just typical of Aunty Mary. She would say, "Well, Karen, if you're going to come to the grand final you have to show what team you're supporting."'

Being such a dedicated wearer of the Sea Eagles' maroon and white, the 13-year-old Karen Jane was less than happy about these sartorial arrangements.

'They were obviously so excited about Souths and being in the final and everything else. I couldn't believe I was going to a grand final that Manly wasn't in.'

She agreed to don a single, small piece of Souths merchandise.

'In the end, I had a red-and-green ribbon stuck to my blouse,' she says. 'She wanted to put ribbons in my hair, which I wouldn't cop.'

Anthony was eight. He wore his Souths jumper, onto which his mum had hand-stitched the number one – worn by his favourite player, the legendary Eric Simms.

Indigenous, small and accurate, fullback Eric Simms had played in both the '68 and '70 rugby league World Cups and would become known as one of that century's greatest players and one of the best ever goal-kickers. Anthony was filled with admiration. He tried to copy his kicking style as a schoolkid goal-kicker for St Mary's.

Anthony would snag a precious photo with him and the decorated prop forward and captain, John Sattler, before the 2014 grand final. He still has the autograph book in which he collected his footy heroes' signatures.

Securing a spot on the hill required a very early arrival, so people would be there all day with whole cases of beer and eskies full of more. It made for a fairly convivial atmosphere by the time of the first whistle.

At the '71 grand final, some of the big blokes around them took a shine to the keen little kid with the Souths jumper on who was too short to see above the crowd. They hoisted him up.

'I watched the game on the shoulders of various blokes,' he recalls.

Mostly, they were drunk. Nobody dropped him but Maryanne was beside herself.

'Mum couldn't watch any of the game because she was worried,' Anthony says. 'When Souths would score, they'd throw me in the air – all these big blokes on the hill. And Souths, of course, won.'

The margin was 16–10. Eric Simms scored the only point of the first half with a field goal.

The hero of the day was a young former Mascot wharf labourer, George Piggins. Brought on as hooker to replace season regular Elwyn Walters, George played his heart out.

He would rise to coach the first-grade side in the late '80s and become the club's chairman in the '90s, leading it through the near-death experience of the emergence of Super League and News Ltd's influence – the threatened merger and attempted expulsion that were its darkest days.

The Souths fans were jubilant, claiming their fourth premiership in five years. But after that spectacular season, a whole generation of Bunnies fans would grow up without seeing such a day again for 43 years.

The Super League war had its genesis in the mid-1980s, when the Australian Rugby League, led by chairman Ken Arthurson, and the New South Wales Rugby League hatched a plan to rationalise the existing competition and jettison clubs that weren't seen to be financially viable.

The ARL took over management of the code, and in the early '90s an independent review found that in the long term, the competition should be cut back to 14 teams, including only five from Sydney. That would require others to move home base, merge or be expelled.

The ARL sent invitations to all of the existing clubs to participate in the 1995 season but set criteria for future inclusion based on a minimum home-ground attendance at games. Nine clubs failed to meet the minimum at the end of the season. Souths wasn't among them.

At the same time, a battle was brewing over television rights. Both Kerry Packer's Publishing and Broadcasting Limited and Rupert Murdoch's News Ltd had stakes in rugby league. A News Ltd subsidiary ran the merchandising side and in 1993, PBL had bought the free-to-air broadcasting rights until the year 2000. At that time, because pay TV didn't then exist in Australia, pay TV rights were included for free.

But News Ltd was beginning to build towards a pay TV venture and had begun acquiring the rights to broadcast other sports on a subscription service. News Ltd approached PBL to buy the pay TV rights. But Kerry Packer resisted.

Around the same time, the chief executive of the increasingly successful Brisbane Broncos, John Ribot, wanted the ARL to acknowledge his club's gains and move the 1993 grand final to Brisbane. He also wanted to hold the match at night, to boost both gate takings and TV ratings – in other words, profits.

But the ARL rejected the idea outright.

So Ribot turned his proposal into a vision for a 'super league', with the game expanding nationwide and to Britain and New Zealand and importantly onto pay television, the latter move being a lot less lucrative without the former. To achieve this, the league would have to cut some Sydney teams and generate new teams in other cities.

He began talks with News Ltd.

News was determined to have rugby league on pay TV. It was the perfect showcase game to attract viewers. Unlike Australian Rules football in which the ball is often kicked ahead, in league it is mostly run and only occasionally kicked forward, meaning the action is more contained and easier for a camera to capture close up.

Their first plan was to seek the ARL's cooperation. If that didn't work, they were prepared for an effective hostile takeover of the whole game.

Determined to resist the Super League push, the ARL had clubs sign loyalty agreements and pressed ahead with its own restructure plan.

News wanted a 12-team Super League structure with only four teams based in Sydney.

When its first attempt to pressure the ARL into a joint operation failed, News drafted a new plan which involved running a 10-team parallel competition, first drawing clubs away from the ARL and then enticing individual players by offering to double their pay.

The parallel rebel 10-team Super League went ahead for a single season in 1997, up against the official ARL competition that had 12 remaining teams, eight from Sydney.

The whole thing ended up in the Federal Court. After an initial ARL win, News appealed successfully. Rupert Murdoch and Kerry Packer then held talks and a new company was formed to run the game – the National Rugby League – jointly owned by the ARL and News Ltd.

Before that happened, over at Souths, a group of high-profile businesspeople, politicians and sporting and media personalities had formed a supporters' group aimed at modernising their beloved club to improve its financial position and stave off looming moves to merge or exclude it.

The 'Group 14' prominent supporters included broadcasters Andrew Denton, Ray Martin and Mikey Robbins, former cricketer turned TV personality Mike Whitney, former NSW Premier Nick Greiner, former state and federal Minister Laurie Brereton, his sister and former NSW state MLA Deirdre Grusovin, Botany Mayor Ron Hoenig, and businessmen Martin and Jerry Lissing.

Anthony went to some of their events. He supported their objectives and wanted to help.

With the NRL formation, the group was deeply unhappy with the direction in which News was forcing the league. Andrew Denton told News Ltd executives that they were trying to dismantle history.

'The club does have a very storied history,' Andrew says. 'Amazing players and also a genuine – *the* genuine – working-class club and Indigenous club . . . Sport is about stories and that was always the point I made to News Ltd. This is about *stories* and if you rip out the old stories, you significantly damage the book. You can't just write new chapters without having the chapters that came before them.'

He felt it was somewhat ironic that a company whose business *was* stories didn't seem to understand that.

At around the same time, club chairman George Piggins suggested to Anthony that he join the Souths board.

It was a difficult time for the club. Since the 1970s, its glory days had faded. It was the oldest and biggest club in the league but was seriously struggling, having not won a premiership since that day in 1971.

Its lawyer, Nick Pappas, would make regular presentations to the board outlining what looked to be a bleak future.

'It was a very hard pill for the board to swallow and there were some really dark times,' Nick says.

He appreciated Anthony's input and outlook, inside those meetings and out.

'Anthony was always upbeat. He was never sullen. And that's the other quality – even in hard times when there were some very difficult decisions to be made and some formidable foes, he was always upbeat and he was always encouraging us to march forward.'

By 1999, the NRL was pushing ahead with the plan to cut back the number of clubs. Souths was being urged to merge.

Some senior figures in the club thought they should and a few options were floated. Others, most strenuously George Piggins, resisted. The club refused and was threatened with expulsion.

An unorthodox collection of allies set about running a public campaign against the move. The people's champion, George Piggins, was their figurehead with some of the club's highest-profile defenders backing him, including Andrew Denton and Ray Martin – who had risen to prominence on Kerry Packer's Nine Network – and also broadcaster Alan Jones and TV personality Don Lane.

Anthony played a role in keeping them all together.

'He was a unifying influence,' Nick Pappas says. 'And through his fortitude, gave people a lot of comfort.'

The fight started to gain national attention. On 23 September 1999, the ABC's *Australian Story* ran a program on the campaign to save Souths.

'South Sydney people aren't going to sit on their backsides,' Souths Juniors chairman Henry Morris told the program. 'We get cut on the 15th October – shame. We'll take them to court. If we get beat then – shame. Our legal advice is they've got one heck of a fight on their hands and the people of South Sydney will rally, because we think we're right, we know we're right, we've got right on our side.

'We've got 92 years of serving the game of rugby league in a great manner. We don't deserve to be kicked in the guts like they're trying to kick us and Murdoch – you've got a fight, son.'

He certainly did.

Andrew Denton persuaded media magnate Kerry Stokes to bankroll the fight, which would see the club take on the league all the way to the courts.

A protest march was organised through Souths' heartland and down onto the streets of central Sydney, just five days before the decision was due.

As ever, Anthony loved nothing more than a bruising battle.

'That's Anthony's character,' says Nick Pappas. 'There is a bit of the old street fighter in Anthony. He doesn't shy away from a fight and he sort of bristles at the suggestion that someone is doing something wrong by someone else.'

On Sunday, 10 October 1999, the faithful would gather at Redfern Oval and march to the Town Hall. They told the media they expected at least 30,000 to turn out in support of the league's last remaining foundation team.

When the rally began at 11 am, onlookers counted 6000 to 8000 at most. But as they marched, thousands more joined the cardinal-and-myrtle throng, including people wearing other teams' jumpers, the colours of Parramatta, Wests, Easts, Balmain, Newcastle, Manly, Newtown and even Melbourne. By the time they reached their destination, police estimated there were 50,000.

'They came from pubs and houses and heaven knows where else,' journalist Paul Kent would write in *The Sydney Morning Herald*, the following Monday.

At the Town Hall, Andrew Denton addressed the crowd.

'Ladies and gentlemen, welcome to the first-ever meeting of the major sponsors of the National Rugby League – the fans.'

Ray Martin told them, 'There's something good about protesting when you know you're right.'

There on the steps, speaker after speaker embraced the theme 'how dare they?!'

The biggest cheers went up when the 1971 premiership captain, John Sattler, took the microphone, followed by George Piggins who appeared, as Kent wrote later, 'in his new role as saint'.

Afterwards, the NRL queried the official police estimate on the crowd numbers. The police then revised them down to no more than 30,000.

The organisers thought that was rubbish but it didn't dampen their delight. The public response astonished even them. It seemed people were reacting to the idea that a big consortium was telling them who they could and could not support.

'The business dudes sitting down carving up rugby league didn't understand that this was an attack on people's identity and that they would not just follow another team,' Anthony says. 'People stopped buying the *Telegraph*. It was an enormous response.'

After the march, the *Daily Telegraph* ran only a small item on an inside page.

'That was an absolutely critical mistake that they made,' Anthony says. 'People just went off about it and it became the issue. It highlighted the bias and the power imbalance.'

People began to see it as being not just about football but about power in society in general.

'It was about people saying literally, "These people are taking away my right to follow my local bloody footy club. Get stuffed!"' he says.

The NRL's ruling on the club's future in the competition was due five days after the march, on Friday 15 October. When the decision to exclude Souths was confirmed, the NRL's chairman, Malcolm Noad, did not afford George Piggins the courtesy of a phone call to let him know.

'We haven't got much money compared with them,' George said later. 'But we've got more class.'

After that, like the rest of them, Anthony used every platform he had – including the Parliament – to make his own voice of protest heard. Three days after the decision was announced, he rose in the House of Representatives to warn that it would have consequences. He believed there was more than football at stake.

'The decision by the National Rugby League to exclude South Sydney from the 2000 competition leaves the faceless men who run the game with red-and-green blood on their hands,' he said.

'It is a fatal blow which will be challenged in every arena – in the courts, in the Parliament and in the public arena. The public know that this struggle is not just about South Sydney. It is about community, it is about history, it is about the aspirations of our youth, and it is about whether the dollar can override all human and social relationships.'

He lamented that some clubs had acceded to the merger demands. Balmain and Wests had formed Wests Tigers, Manly and Norths had become the Northern Eagles – only to later de-amalgamate and scrap the Norths element altogether – and St George and Illawarra would turn into the St George Illawarra Dragons.

'Rugby league has lost some of its body parts during this war, but it cannot survive if it has no soul,' Anthony said. 'A scorched earth policy does not make sense.'

And he blasted News Ltd for its role.

'Rugby league's greatest shareholder is not Rupert Murdoch; it is the fans,' he said. 'And that cannot be forgotten.'

Anthony praised George Piggins' 'magnificent leadership' and for having led the way he played: 'with honour, with integrity, with courage, with determination and with principle'.

'The respect he has from his community, who proudly proclaim, "In George we trust," is a commodity which cannot be bought, it can only be earned.'

They took their fight to the Federal Court as promised, claiming the NRL and News Ltd were in breach of the Trade Practices Act, because they were using criteria that were biased towards a pre-determined outcome in deciding which teams were in and which were out.

They lost.

Souths would be out for the 2000 season and by the time an appeal could be mounted and heard, the 2001 season as well. The Souths board had to decide whether to mount a second protest before the appeal was heard. They met at the South Sydney Leagues Club.

'A majority of the board decided that we would roll the dice, have the demo,' Anthony says.

But they had almost no staff to organise it. The club was so broke, it had had to let everyone go except for the woman they all called 'Nanna', the late Eileen McLaughlin, who volunteered to answer the phone with a handful of others.

Anthony rang Frank Sartor, who was then Sydney's independent Lord Mayor – and unbeknownst to most, was about to join the Labor Party – and asked if Souths could book the Town Hall at short notice.

Something else was already scheduled but Anthony explained it was urgent – they needed to move fast, in no more than a week. Frank agreed to shift the other event.

'We didn't have money for advertising or anything, but word got out there,' Anthony says.

There is still debate about how much bigger than the first march the second one was, but reports estimated 80,000 people turned out and some say even more.

'I think they were both pretty bloody big,' Anthony says. 'They were both ginormous. Certainly it was at least as big as the first march and it just showed that people weren't going to give up and go away.'

They passed buckets around, collecting thousands of dollars in donations to help cover the legal fees for the appeal. This time, the demonstration was so big the local News Ltd paper couldn't ignore it.

'They realised,' Anthony says. 'That was the breakthrough when News Ltd realised it was serious.'

The *Daily Telegraph* ran a photograph and story on its front page.

Anthony and his Souths colleagues would celebrate becoming the paper's collective nemesis. But they would not stay enemies forever.

Fifteen years later, the same *Daily Telegraph* would thrust itself into week one of a federal election campaign in which Anthony was facing a threat from the Greens, with a full-page endorsement of him on the front under the screaming headline 'Save Our Albo', with a drawing of his head inside a life-preserver.

It was quite the shift in sentiment. In August 2013, after Anthony was photographed having a beer with his scandal-plagued parliamentary colleague Craig Thomson, the same newspaper had depicted Anthony as Nazi soldier Sergeant Schultz from the 1960s television series *Hogan's Heroes*, famous for the line 'I know nuthink!'

Souths' long-serving chairman, its former lawyer Nick Pappas, says in 2016 that, like Andrew Denton and Ray Martin, Anthony took a big risk with his outspokenness.

'Making an enemy out of an organisation like News Ltd – it's okay to do that when you're a lawyer or a media star,' Nick says. 'But when you're a politician and your fate sort of rests securely in the hands of how you're presented in the media on a day-to-day basis, that requires a lot of fortitude.'

He believes Anthony's strident football-loving parliamentary speeches might have sounded insincere and strange coming from someone else.

'People respect the fact that he's loyal to a football club,' Nick Pappas says. 'In other circumstances it would sound bizarre. If some of our other leading politicians mentioned that as one of the three pillars of their political career, you would say that's ridiculous. But I think it's a function of his integrity and what is ingrained within the Rabbitohs – which is all about loyalty and tenacity.'

Anthony's pro-Souths position won support from others across the Parliament, including Joe Hockey. Joe had been a Norths fan so he'd been through it before.

'I didn't want to see Souths go the way of Norths,' Joe says. 'So I strongly backed the campaign for Souths and did everything I could to support Souths in the NRL.'

Coming from the world of politics, Anthony could say things around the board table that others couldn't as easily. But the reverse was true in the world outside the door. He was certainly outspoken about News Ltd but not quite as much as others.

'It was good for Albo that people like me were there, who were much more outspoken, because it meant he didn't have to be,' Andrew Denton says. 'Which isn't to say he wasn't committed – far from it. But he's a politician. He didn't want to get News offside any more than humanly possible.'

Behind closed doors, though, he said plenty.

After the second demonstration and before the appeal went ahead, Anthony had a meeting in his Parliament House office with News Ltd executive Malcolm Colless. He was looking beyond the case – whatever its result – to the future. He feared the dispute could go on and on in the courts and he wanted to seek a truce.

'You know, if we win this case, we'll just come back [fighting],' he told Malcolm. 'We'll need to stop this.'

They reached an agreement.

'There was an understanding that if we won the court case, it would just stop. The war had to stop. And it was a war.'

The Federal Court's full-bench ruling on the South Sydney Rugby League Football Club's appeal was handed down on Friday, 6 July 2001. It found the original judge had erred and that the respondents had, indeed, breached section 45 of the Trade Practices Act.

Souths fans were delirious.

'It was really seen as this extraordinary victory for the little people,' he says.

Outside the court, Anthony did an interview with 2GB and sang the South Sydney anthem on air. When he rang his mum to tell her about the win, she already knew. She'd heard him singing on the radio.

News Ltd stuck to the deal and the National Rugby League announced the club was back in the competition.

'Everyone welcomed the decision and said, "Souths are back. That's a good thing,"' Anthony recalls.

In capital letters, the poster for Saturday's *Sydney Morning Herald* trumpeted victory for the people's club. Under the footy-shaped logo featuring that bounding bunny, it declared: 'BACK FROM THE DEAD'.

When the euphoria subsided, the Souths board began to survey the damage and look to the future. Some believed resurrection wasn't all that was required. They wanted an internal revolution too.

'There were symptoms of a divergence between perhaps the old guard of the club and a new guard that was seeing that maybe we were victims of our own errors as much as News Ltd,' says Nick Pappas.

Souths had survived the existential threat from outside but it still needed to resolve the rift within. The cost of the fight had been enormous and they had lost players and staff. Some wondered how they would meet the enormous expectations of the jubilant club membership.

George had resisted a nomination for Andrew to join the board – resistance that was overcome – and concerns were being raised about his leadership.

At one board meeting preceding an annual general meeting, there was a discussion about the meeting's rules. George decreed that nobody was going to be allowed to address the meeting until after the vote for directors had been held. The pro-reform board members took issue with that. Anthony challenged George directly.

'Do you know what we call this in the Labor Party, George? We call it a rort,' he told the chairman.

On the board, Andrew Denton and Anthony played good cop, bad cop.

'Because Albo was a federal Member and it was a passion thing for him, not at the core of his political being, he tended to be pretty carefree about what he would say to people like George, which was very healthy,' Andrew says.

He remained respectful but 'called a spade a spade'.

'He's a conviction guy and when he says something, you know he means it.'

Nick Pappas concurs.

'He had an uncanny ability to be forthright, direct, even sometimes rude, but never lose the respect of his opponent.'

A number of directors, including both Andrew Denton and Anthony, believed something had to change to make the club a going concern, both financially and on the field. They believed it was going to require the club's hero, George Piggins, to relinquish control.

'A bunch of us were looking to find a way to ease George out of the club with maximum honour and minimum embarrassment,' Andrew says. 'But he wasn't moving.'

Anthony and fellow directors Deirdre Grusovin and Randwick mayor Dominic Sullivan decided to take a stand and quit the board. On 11 October 2002, they gave George a stinging joint letter of resignation. They complained again about his attitude to Andrew Denton, whose role in securing Kerry Stokes' support had been crucial and who, they said, 'we should be grateful was prepared to serve on our board'.

They said the club owed George a great debt for what he had done to restore Souths to the competition and that the board had been loyal to him. But they had a tough message.

'Real loyalty requires people to tell it like it is and should not be confused with sycophancy,' it said. 'During our fightback we looked to the past to uphold the glories and the magnificent traditions of the club. Now that the fight is over, we look to the future. Now is the time for rebuilding.'

They said that required 'the best and the brightest' and 'a professional approach in the administration as well as the boardroom'.

'While we wish the club every success, we doubt whether this will happen without a fundamental cultural change in the management of the club.'

They noted that George had said he wanted to restore it to where it had been during its 1960s prime.

'Perhaps it is time to realise the game and business of rugby league has moved on,' they wrote, 'that it requires a talented team of professionals and experts to take us forward and that most of us would like to see the club looking 40 years into the future, rather than 40 years into the past.'

The shake-up spurred further action.

'We were a hollow shell actually,' Nick Pappas says. 'That's when Anthony recognised that the club really needed to go through its own internal revolution and reinvent itself and use the opportunity that ground zero gave us to rebuild something better, not fix something that was old and rotten.'

Led by Nick, along with Andrew Denton, the rebels organised a rival board to present to the annual general meeting, to loosen George's grip.

'While George always had the best of intentions and a deep love for the club, he wasn't necessarily the way of the future,' Nick Pappas says. 'So we – with much pain and much internal questioning – decided to challenge him, within a year of being reinstated to the competition.'

Before the meeting, they reached a compromise with George and his supporters. George would step down – but so would Andrew and fellow director and former deputy chairman Mike Whitney.

On 4 April 2003, a few days before the board election, Andrew and George clashed in a heated on-air encounter on radio 2SM's *Saturday Sports Network* program.

George accused Andrew of having supported a merger with Cronulla – something Andrew said was an 'outright lie'.

'I've put my career on the line for two years for this club – not to merge, George Piggins,' Andrew responded angrily. 'You're just telling lies.'

George challenged Andrew to call him a liar to his face, not down the phone on air.

'If you call it, you'll finish on your arse, I'm telling you,' he said.

'If your way of resolving a disagreement is to punch me in the face, well that's fine,' Andrew flung back.

Verbally at least, George kept swinging.

'I'm not going to cop a wimp like you standing over me, I'm tellin' ya. You're a wimp and that's all you'll ever be.'

Andrew accused him of not being able to take criticism.

'I'm not a fighter, George. You could whip me with one hand tied behind your back. And if that's the way you want to do it, George, we'll let that be an example of how Souths is run.'

Andrew phoned George back and apologised. When next they met, they shook hands.

A few days after the stoush, the new board was elected.

Souths had held off the threats of expulsion from the NRL and had begun its internal overhaul, but was still at risk of going under.

In 2006, actor Russell Crowe and businessman Peter Holmes a Court would step forward with a proposal to save it, offering to buy 75 per cent of the club. There was understandable hesitation over the prospect of selling a majority share in the people's club to corporate interests, even if one of them was a Hollywood icon whose commitment to Souths was well known.

But Anthony and others thought it was a proposition worth considering. Russell and Anthony had met in the lead-up to the Super League dramas, when both were concerned about the direction of things.

Russell Crowe saw Anthony as a Souths fan first, a politician second.

'I knew Anthony Albanese as a face in the crowd long before I knew he was a politician,' Russell says. 'As a fellow South Sydney supporter, it always seemed that if there was an important Souths date, Anthony would be there – as passionate in victory as he was in defeat.

'I met him, shook his hand, learned his name and learned about his commitment to the club, to the community and, as the years and his success moved on, ultimately to his country.

'He has been such a positive force at Souths. He's put his hand up and been a great club man, and he has served his country with the same selfless passion.'

Back in 1999, when the NRL merger plans had started sounding the death knell on clubs across Sydney, Souths held a massive fundraiser at the Sydney Convention Centre.

Both Russell and Anthony were among the 2000 or so people who attended the huge shindig, on a Saturday night in late November of that year. Like hundreds of others, both shelled out for auction items, contributing to what became a $300,000 starter for their fighting fund.

On offer were the trophies and keepsakes of Souths' great glories. People handed over whatever they could afford.

Russell dug deepest of all. He paid $10,000 for a framed and autographed copy of a photograph from the club's triumphant 1971 grand-final victory, a shot of Souths legend Ron Coote in his final premiership match before moving to Eastern Suburbs. The photographer's lens had captured him helping St George champion Graeme Langlands up off the ground.

The actor then also bought the most expensive item of the night – the timekeeper's bell used to kick off Souths' match against North Sydney at Birchgrove Oval on Easter Monday, 1908.

It had been the club's first match as part of the fledgling NSW Rugby League's first round. It was also the team's first win, defeating Norths 11–7.

Seven years later, after the club had been through the fire, it was Crowe and his proposed business partner who would emerge as its saviours.

Peter Holmes a Court's pitch was that they would professionalise the club further, leaving behind the embarrassing public controversies involving players and focus on quality – both on and off the field.

'So there wouldn't be players signed because they were someone's mate, or because they needed a [big] break,' Anthony says.

'If that change hadn't happened, we would've had a good team from time to time, but we wouldn't have had a premiership-winning team.'

The board would certainly shake a few things up with a motion to scrap cheerleaders. They debated what the cheerleading culture meant to the club and what it said about attitudes to women. They decided – controversially – to ban it.

'We didn't need cheer girls,' Anthony says simply. He supported the move. What other clubs did was their business but Souths decided it was no longer for them. When the team returned to the competition, they had drummers instead.

'That wasn't popular with all of Souths' supporters, it must be said,' Anthony says, understating things slightly but with no remorse. 'We did stuff. We're a progressive club.'

It was not the last of the changes.

The club's membership would meet to consider the $3 million takeover offer at an extraordinary general meeting at ANZ Stadium on 19 March 2006. Among 75 speakers for and against, Russell Crowe was the final speaker and before him Andrew Denton and Anthony. 'Let's vote yes,' Russell urged them. 'Let's get into bed together. I hope you respect me in the morning.'

Two weeks earlier, the members of the old Group 14 – the pro-change alliance of former directors, disbanded after the board changes – had issued a statement endorsing the takeover proposal.

'The Holmes a Court-Crowe proposal provides the first viable financial plan that can ensure the long-term survival of our great club,' they said in a statement given to the Fairfax Sunday paper, *The Sun-Herald*. 'The proposal is the most positive step forward that the club can take and changes the direction of the club from continued struggle to a realistic opportunity for success.'

But they still had to persuade the members. George Piggins vehemently opposed the buyout.

At the meeting a fortnight later, there was a volatile atmosphere.

'People were booing, there were people angry, people were cheering – it was a full-on meeting,' Anthony recalls.

To be successful, the proposal required 75 per cent support from the 4505 voting members.

Anthony assured the members he'd hesitated about the idea himself at first, but that he now believed it was the way forward. Andrew reinforced that message and Russell sealed the deal.

They voted to accept. The takeover would see the club reach the semi-finals the following year and make a steady climb to eventually win the 2014 premiership – after which Peter Holmes a Court sold his stake to businessman James Packer, son of the late Kerry.

The partial privatisation depoliticised the club, brought stability and enabled it to begin to address past practices that had undermined its professionalism. Failure to enforce a disciplinary code had led to some offensive antics that had embarrassed the club and damaged the brand.

The change professionalised the club's governance, from its hiring practices and training procedures to the way its meetings ran.

'We voted for a non-democratic process essentially – "just get on with being successful",' Anthony says. 'And that has proven to be successful . . . And the proof's in the pudding. The proof's in the premiership.'

For Nick Pappas, who continued as chairman, the proof is also in the pride.

'We have investors of the highest calibre . . . and we have the membership base that's the biggest club in the Rugby League,' Nick says. 'So we're seen now as one of the front-runners in the code, which we're very proud of. But that's very much the product of people like Anthony Albanese who when he was needed on the parliamentary floor he would not hesitate to bring up the Rabbitohs.'

But none of it happened without upheaval.

Understandably, George Piggins was furious. The man who had been the face of the fight, and indeed the club's great defender, was sidelined. He made it clear he felt his commitment was being betrayed and vowed never to attend another Souths match.

'It's unfortunate that someone like George Piggins felt the way that he did about the change,' Anthony says. 'Because without George Piggins' leadership and tenacity, we wouldn't have been in a position to fight back. It was extraordinary, the leadership that he showed. He was one of the mob . . . Everyone had stickers, "In George we trust," and people really did trust him. He was prepared to stand up and fight. He was a fighter. And people liked that.'

But in explaining why he was replaced, Anthony borrows an analogy from modern politics.

'George was a great leader of the opposition of a campaign,' he says. 'But not a great government leader.'

Andrew Denton calls the whole episode 'a brilliant piece of dramatics'.

'No wonder there was so much media coverage because you had a millionaire and a Hollywood movie star coming in and buying the club off the people's champion, George Piggins,' Andrew says. 'I look back on it now and I think of course it was manna from heaven for the tabloid writers.'

And by that, he means even the ones from News Ltd.

'Especially News Ltd,' he says, 'who win even when they lose! God bless 'em.'

George would stay away from Souths games from then on. He would be persuaded to attend the 2014 grand final only after he attached the condition that he'd go along if someone donated $100,000 to charity. Businessman John Singleton and some others stumped up the money and it went to OzHarvest, which collects leftover food from restaurants to distribute to those in need.

George spent the game with his old teammates John Sattler and Bobby McCarthy, his wife, Nolene, and friends Norm Lipson, Jim Lahood and Jim's cousin, Peter.

With them throughout the game to capture the historic moment were a reporter and photographer – from News Ltd's *Daily Telegraph*.

For those at Souths who had taken such a gamble and driven out the man who'd been the face of the club for decades, eight years after they'd done it, that single Sunday was vindication.

But before the hugely anticipated match between Souths and Canterbury, Anthony had one more issue to resolve.

Ahead of the 2013 election, the Labor Government of which he was then a senior member had allocated funding to a number of rugby league clubs for facilities. The two biggest allocations were to upgrade the facilities at both Souths and Manly.

Each had been promised $10 million. At Manly, it was for a facelift for Brookvale Oval. In Souths' case, the funding – with contributions to come from the club itself and the local Randwick Council – was to upgrade Heffron Park at Maroubra with a combination high-performance and community facility to help its community welfare wing, Souths Cares, run an outreach program in schools.

When the Coalition Government took office, the grant for the Manly Sea Eagles, based in Tony Abbott's electorate, proceeded. The Souths grant did not.

When a resurgent Souths fought its way into the 2014 grand final, Anthony saw an opportunity to get the money restored. Both he and his colleague Matt Thistlethwaite – the Labor MP for the seat of Kingsford Smith which includes Heffron Park – raised it with the Government.

Anthony went to see then Prime Minister Abbott and his chief of staff, Peta Credlin.

'I said, "This is just unreasonable and by the way we're about to win the comp and we've got 35,000 members and some pretty high-profile ones. And we're going to run a really big campaign about it because it's outrageous."'

They'd run campaigns before. He knew they could do it. He also spoke to his friend, Joe Hockey.

'When Albo wanted some money for Souths ... he approached Abbo,' Joe says, using the former Prime Minister's nickname. Joe backed him. Tony was persuaded to reverse his decision.

'And I went and found the money and helped make that happen,' Joe says.

Anthony thanked them both and organised a picture opportunity in Canberra involving himself and the Prime Minister with Souths' CEO Shane Richardson and champion player Nathan Merritt, who would announce his retirement before the grand final.

At the game itself, the Prime Minister might have hoped for a little more appreciation from the club's loyal fans. As sometimes happens when politicians turn up at big, tribal sporting events, Tony was booed.

'He said to me afterwards, "Your people weren't very grateful,"' Anthony recalls. 'And I said, "Mate, you should've seen what would've happened if you hadn't given the money."'

On grand final day, the board members and former board members took their families to the game. They were at least as excited as their children. Anthony was especially glad to have his by-then-teenage son, Nathan, beside him, a fourth-generation Bunnies backer.

Five years earlier, after yet another letdown season, Anthony had written a piece for News Ltd about his love of Souths, reflecting on his family's history with the club and full of optimism about the team's prospects in 2010.

'One of my cherished moments was when my son told me that he was a South Sydney supporter,' Anthony wrote, alluding to the general principle that allegiance to a team must also be chosen, not just inherited. 'He has stayed loyal, in spite of disappointment.'

Like his father, Nathan Albanese continued to stay loyal. (What hope did he have, really?)

There was certainly no disappointment at ANZ Stadium in September 2014 when Anthony, Nathan and 83,831 others watched the Bunnies beat Canterbury-Bankstown, 30 points to six. It seemed like there could have been no other result.

'You just knew in your bones,' Anthony says. 'I think Canterbury knew too. They played well.'

Father and son had caught the train out to the game – the 'South Sydney Express' from Redfern station.

'And there was this extraordinary confidence,' Anthony says. 'People were just pumped. It was like we were unbeatable.'

As the game unfolded, it was as emotional on the field as off.

'They scored four tries in the last 20 minutes. And grown blokes – Sam Burgess and Greg Inglis, pretty tough blokes – were on the field crying while the game was still going on. We scored a try after that – they got up and scored another try.'

Before the game, he and Nathan had gone down to 'The Burrow' – the bloc of the most dedicated Bunnies fans that has its own special membership, pre-booked stadium bay and songbook.

'It was amazing to see these people who had waited so long just to be there,' Anthony says.

The Souths' victory song had been written in the 1960s to the rousing tune from the old 'Battle Hymn of the Republic'. On this triumphant night, it rang around the stands:

> Glory, glory to South Sydney!
> South Sydney marches on.

The singing sent them hoarse. Anthony only wished his mother could have been there to see it.

CHAPTER 19

Letting Go

As Anthony's political career had progressed and his public profile increased, Maryanne Albanese was as proud as it was possible for any mother to be.

Like many mums before her and since, she had also made it no secret that she hoped her son and daughter-in-law would have a child of their own some day and she would find herself in the coveted role of grandmother.

Before Anthony and Carmel had married in June of 2000, and before their son Nathan was even an idea, Maryanne had begun planning for the arrival of a grandchild. She bought mail-order children's movies on video, anticipating a little child coming to visit and watching all the classics.

'She had the complete collection of everything that you could imagine from Disney,' Anthony says.

Maryanne kept an eye out for other things a future grandchild would like. She also bought a selection of stories from the Little Golden Books series, ready for a young inquiring mind.

When Nathan was born, she was ecstatic. As the mother of a son, she was extra excited that her son had had a son, too.

'Every time she saw him, she had a present for him – which was regularly,' Anthony says. 'She was just beside herself with joy.'

Before their son was born, Carmel and Anthony had decided to move house. Their place in Marrickville had been built on an old quarry and they didn't think it was the right place for a young child. So they sold it and bought a place in Newtown, with the added benefit that it was also closer to Maryanne's home in Camperdown.

They all looked forward to her being able to spend lots of time with Nathan, and throughout that first year of his life, she did.

'We thought she'd be around for a lot longer than she was.'

Soon after Nathan's birth in December 2000, Anthony went into election mode. They were entering a federal election year and it was just fortunate that the NSW electoral cycle meant Carmel wasn't facing the voters until 2003.

They were already a two-portfolio family – she as NSW Minister for Juvenile Justice and he having had Aboriginal and Torres Strait Islander Affairs and Arts added to Family and Community Services among his federal parliamentary secretary responsibilities. Now they had added an extra member of the family into the mix.

It was to be a tumultuous year nationally and internationally, with an influx of asylum seekers dominating political debate. Anthony felt strongly about the issue, which he believed had taken on an uncomfortable xenophobic tinge since the arrival in Parliament of Queensland conservative ex-Liberal independent Pauline Hanson in 1996.

As election season approached, the Howard Government turned back the Norwegian freighter MV *Tampa* carrying asylum seekers, and Opposition Leader Kim Beazley faced criticism from within his ranks for not taking a firmer stance against the Government.

The September 11 terrorist attacks on the United States followed soon after and Labor's lead in the polls evaporated. The 2001 election went the same way as the previous two: Labor lost.

It was Kim Beazley's second loss as leader and he stepped down, with the Victorian Right's Simon Crean stepping up and the Victorian Left's Jenny Macklin elected as deputy, unopposed.

Simon demanded a front-bench clean-out and told the faction leaders he wanted new faces. The old guard was out and in came a new breed – Kevin Rudd and Craig Emerson from Queensland, Nicola Roxon and Julia Gillard from Victoria, and from NSW, Anthony Albanese.

Five years after his arrival, Anthony had made it onto the front bench proper. Simon gave him the ageing and seniors portfolio. The circumstances of his life over the next six months would make that particular job one he found very hard to do.

On Mothers' Day weekend in 2002, the neighbourhood around the Alexandra Dwellings in Camperdown was preparing for a party. Young Ben Dewstow was turning 18 and his parents, Sherie and Scott, were organising a birthday bash in the hall just across the road from their Lambert Street home.

Sherie and Scott and their three children lived in her parents' old place, over the back fence from Maryanne Albanese. They'd been allowed to take over the lease a few years earlier when her mum and dad, Yvonne and Barry Miller, had decided on a sea change and moved to the south coast.

They and the rest of the family were back in Camperdown for Ben's party and Sherie had decked out the little hall, which the council had built for neighbourhood use at just a few dollars' hire per night.

The Dewstows' closest neighbours were invited, including Beryl and Barrie Anderson from next door and Maryanne, from over the back. But on the night, it was pouring with rain, so when neither Beryl and Barrie nor Maryanne came, Sherie wasn't too surprised.

'The heavens opened,' Sherie recalls of that Saturday, 11 May. 'It was absolutely pelting down that night . . . I didn't worry . . . I didn't think anything of it. It was so wet – I wouldn't expect them to come out in that sort of weather.'

Beryl and Barrie had, indeed, stayed in out of the rain. But Maryanne's absence was due to something else.

The next morning was Mothers' Day and Anthony was flying back from Canberra. He'd been at a two-day national Left faction meeting and was leaving early to take his mum and his Aunty Margaret out to lunch.

Margaret lived at Dundas, over in Sydney's north-west, and she caught the train and then the bus to get to her sister's place, where Anthony was picking them both up. But when she arrived and couldn't get an answer at the door, she enlisted a neighbour's help and they found Maryanne on the bathroom floor.

She'd suffered a stroke, fallen and hit her head.

It was only the ambulance and the commotion that alerted Sherie that something was wrong at Maryanne's place.

'There was all this fuss going on,' Sherie says. 'And then we heard she'd been put into the hospital. She'd had a fall.'

When Anthony landed in Sydney, he received a call from Royal Prince Alfred Hospital. He went straight there. His mum underwent surgery and her condition remained precarious.

In the few days after Maryanne's fall, Sherie and some of the other neighbours went over and scrubbed the bathroom clean for when – they hoped – she would come home.

Anthony's old boss Tom Uren was among those who went to visit Maryanne during those terribly difficult days.

A second, smaller operation was required and twice Anthony received calls from the hospital advising him to come in urgently.

But each time, his mum rallied. She regained consciousness and he was able to talk to her, although she was often confused.

On Saturday morning, 25 May, two weeks after the incident and two weeks before Maryanne's 66th birthday, Sherie's phone rang. It was Anthony.

'What's going on?' she asked, concerned.

'It's Mum,' he said. He was distraught.

'Where are you?'

She remembers the call. 'He said, "I'm at the hospital. She's leaving us. She's leaving us."'

Sherie called out to her husband, 'Scott!'

She told Anthony, 'I'm on my way.'

'And we both went flying up to the hospital.'

RPA is on Missenden Road, a few blocks away across busy Parramatta Road. They ran.

'I went as fast as my legs could carry me,' Sherie says.

Anthony and Carmel were there when they arrived. But his beloved mum was gone.

'He just broke into tears,' Sherie says. 'And we just held each other. I just couldn't contain myself.'

Four days later, on Wednesday the 29th at 1 pm, they and about 200 others gathered at St Joseph's Church, Camperdown, to give thanks for the life of Maryanne Therese Albanese. The church was next door to Anthony's primary school and where his mother and her parents had worshipped for decades. Hundreds of family, friends and Labor colleagues filled the pews.

Sherie and Scott's daughters, Sharnee and Rheannon, served at the altar and their local priest, Father Harry Payne, celebrated the requiem mass. Anthony asked singer Su Cruikshank to lead the hymns and Maryanne's sisters Ronnie and Margaret gave the readings.

On the front of the order of service was a photograph of Maryanne at Anthony and Carmel's wedding almost exactly two years earlier, and on the last page another of her dancing that same night. In both, she was beaming.

Anthony's eulogy for his mother was deeply personal and achingly sad and his composure was tested throughout. Nobody there who knew just how much he loved her expected anything different.

He told those gathered that his last conversation with his mum had been about the grandson she so adored. 'He's a lovely boy' was the last thing she said.

'We must remember my mum for her incredible joy for life,' he said. 'Life is precious and Mum made the most of it under difficult circumstances. The world is a better place for Mum's contribution and heaven is fortunate to have her. Pure, unconditional love is a rare and wonderful thing. My mother gave it to me. Whatever I am is due to her. Whatever I achieve is her achievement. I am forever in her debt and will forever mourn her loss, and love and honour her memory.'

As her coffin was carried from the church and the congregation sang 'Amazing Grace', Anthony broke down and shrieked from the sheer pain of being parted.

As he wept, Carmel steadied him and his cousin, Norm, helped hold him up.

Anthony had made no secret of his closeness to his mum and when he returned to Parliament, many of his colleagues offered their condolences. Among them was a Queenslander who had joined the Labor caucus at the 1998 election, a former diplomat and state government bureaucrat, the Member for Griffith, Kevin Rudd.

Kevin and Anthony had become friends in the Parliament, talking foreign affairs and politics and sharing an occasional drink.

'I found him a very interesting person,' Anthony says.

They discovered they'd both been raised by single mothers and that both women had suffered from debilitating illness.

Kevin's dad had died from complications after a car accident when he was 11. His mother, Margaret, had raised Kevin and his three older siblings in difficult financial circumstances and had been diagnosed in later life with Parkinson's disease. Kevin adored her. When Maryanne Albanese died, Kevin understood better than many how Anthony must be feeling.

'When Mum died, he reached out to me,' Anthony says.

He would return the condolence when Kevin's mum died, two years later. Their family background became one of the things that bound their friendship.

'We were both the product of Catholic working-class mums who took their religion and their responsibilities seriously,' Kevin says in 2016.

They realised quickly that they had quite a lot in common.

'He never had a father growing up – and nor really did I,' Kevin says. 'Without being too melodramatic about it, we grew up poor. He lived in housing commission in Camperdown, and I don't think we had housing commission in Nambour, nor Eumundi. When my father died, I remember being passed from relative to relative. Not terribly dignified.'

In his first speech to Parliament on Remembrance Day, 11 November 1998, Kevin had acknowledged his siblings and both of his parents – mother, Margaret, who was there watching from the gallery and dairy-farmer father, Bert, who had died 30 years before.

'He was the classic Australian, whose response to every question of "How are you, Bert?" was "I've been battling,"' Kevin said.

In this early telling of a personal story that would become better known as his career progressed, Kevin recounted what happened after his father died.

'When my father was accidentally killed and my mother, like thousands of others, was left to rely on the bleak charity of the time to raise a family, it made a young person think. It made me think that a decent social-security system designed to protect the weak was no bad thing. It made me think that the provision of decent public housing to the poor was the right thing to do. When I saw people unnecessarily die in the appallingly underfunded Queensland hospital system of the 1960s and 1970s, it made me think that the provision of a decent universal health system should be one of the first responsibilities of the state.'

As is customary for all new members' first speeches, a number of his colleagues sat listening. Anthony was among them.

'I do not know whether I will be in this place for a short or a long time,' Kevin said in conclusion. 'That is for others to decide. But what I do know is that I have no intention of being here for the sake of just being here. Together with my colleagues it is my intention to make a difference.'

When he finished, Anthony was among those who stepped up to congratulate him and shake his hand.

'He came up and said, "Bloody good speech, mate – and I'm not just bullshitting you,"' Kevin recalls, laughing. 'And I think it was his first opportunity to understand that despite the fact that some people saw me as some sort of shiny-arsed diplomat from central casting, in fact our upbringings had a lot in common.'

They had not known each other before Parliament, though Kevin recalls having seen 'Albo' in action.

'I remember before I entered politics seeing this left-wing Labor firebrand on television always ripping the carotid artery out of the NSW Right at NSW state conferences,' he says. 'And I used to think to myself, "Well, here's a formidable character."'

Eventually, Kevin would hold the NSW Right responsible for his removal as Prime Minister in 2010. As the enemy of those who would become his enemy, Anthony became his friend.

'I think why we, over time, clicked was because we could speak quite naturally and spontaneously about what we believed in and why, because it came directly from experience,' Kevin says.

'That was him having no money as a kid growing up and relying on handouts because life was really tough. And in my case, the really steeling experience of literally, for several years, having no place to call home. And then afterwards as a kid I remember concluding in my own head – not knowing a single thing about politics – that all this was just plain wrong. In fact, it was utterly humiliating, personally degrading, and shouldn't happen to anybody.

'So for those reasons of experience – common experience – when we'd sit down and chat, there was much more in common with each other's upbringing than our pre-politics career paths would suggest.'

In May 2000, journalist Geoffrey Barker interviewed the two of them for inclusion in John Faulkner's 2001 record of the parliamentary Labor Party, *True Believers*.

The joint interview, published under the heading 'I'm Here', canvassed their backgrounds and their perceptions of the Labor caucus. Anthony revealed he expected Labor might soon be out of Opposition – an expectation that would not be realised for another three elections.

'It's become more sub-factionalised than it was prior to 1996,' he said of the caucus at the time. 'There's more a perception that people are fighting over real spoils of power as we come close to government. Some of the tensions become greater and that's probably a natural thing that occurs. It's much more serious now. There's a much greater sense of urgency now.'

He also commented that having more women had 'substantially changed the atmosphere'.

'It's still a macho culture but the networks are broader. If you want to have contact with the whole caucus, you cannot ignore that – and the issues championed by women.'

Kevin observed that Labor MPs had a responsibility to 'get the word out' about the workings of Parliament, because personal contact with people was more effective than 'what they see on TV or read in the paper'.

He also remarked on the social side of being an Opposition MP, describing their Tuesday morning party meetings as 'like the High Church of caucus'.

'Then there's the ongoing caucus beast, which is a cocktail of going out together of a Wednesday night, having a bite in the dining room here, knocking about a bit on caucus committees and conversations in the chamber when what's going on bores you silly,' said the future Prime Minister.

After Maryanne died, Anthony found it hard to face the terrible task of packing up her things. His family kept those children's videos and books for many years. There was also a collection of stuffed toys that Maryanne had bought and not-so-secretly loved.

'They were for her, really.'

Shortly after she died in 2002, Anthony's friend and former adviser Antony Sachs and his partner Carla Stacey had their first baby, Oscar, born in the King George V Hospital right across the road from Royal Prince Alfred. Anthony gave them his mum's teddy, for their brand new little boy. He felt like it was the cycle moving on.

'It was a real thing of death and life,' he says.

After those traumatic final two weeks, Anthony struggled to keep doing his job. It wasn't only the numbness of his grief but the particular challenges of his shadow portfolio that he found difficult to manage under the circumstances.

The portfolio of aged care in which he was serving was a permanent reminder of the saddest dimensions of his mother's life, especially at the end.

He was visiting nursing homes constantly, surrounded by the frail aged. Having spent much of a fortnight by his dying mother's bed in hospital after years of caring for her, it suddenly became too much. He realised he wasn't coping.

'I found it extremely difficult,' he says. 'It wasn't healthy for me to have that job at that time.'

He went to see Simon Crean to ask if he could be considered for a change when next there was a ministerial reshuffle. Simon understood his situation and agreed to accommodate it when the opportunity arose.

Simon was struggling under low poll figures. The previous month, the shadow ministry had gone away on a retreat to the Blue Mountains for a weekend – a 'love-in' as they all dubbed it, aimed at setting a strategic direction.

As future leader Mark Latham would record in what he would later publish as *The Latham Diaries*, deputy leader Jenny Macklin was urging both Mark and Anthony to do more to protect Simon from attacks in the Parliament. Both men had been privately critical of Simon's performance.

In September, when Simon reshuffled his front bench, Anthony was moved into the Education and Training portfolio, in which he would remain until after the 2004 election.

As 2002 gave way to its successor, Anthony was fully engaged in federal politics. But although he had been out of NSW head office for years, he remained deeply involved in state politics too.

Always looking to recruit good people to the Labor Party and preferably his part of the Left, he had persuaded a fellow Labor Party member who had become a close friend, Linda Burney, to seek preselection to run for the NSW Parliament.

Linda had been engaged with Labor since the late 1980s but it was Anthony who coaxed her into formalising that relationship by joining The Warren branch. It was Anthony's practice to identify good potential candidates – especially women – and encourage them into politics, and in that vein he set about convincing Linda she had something to contribute as a representative.

But with Linda, there was an extra dimension to his argument that State Parliament needed her skills. As shadow federal parliamentary secretary for Aboriginal and Torres Strait Islander Affairs, Anthony was conscious of a deficit in Labor's Indigenous representation.

Elected as the Member for Canterbury on 22 March 2003, Linda would become the first Indigenous person to sit in Australia's oldest Parliament.

'I would describe him more as a mentor to me than anything else,' Linda says. '[He's] someone that's completely reliable, someone I can call any time that I want to, someone that I trust and someone that I have an enormous amount of respect for.'

When she gave her first speech in Parliament, speaking first as a Wiradjuri woman in the Indigenous language of the Gadigal people of the Eora nation, Anthony and Carmel – with whom she had become close friends – were among those watching from the gallery.

'Like all first-timers, I am awash with many emotions,' Linda told the chamber. '. . . In debt and empowered by the generosity of people; reinforced and reminded of the importance of loyalty; tremulous about the responsibility of our role as lawmakers and the effects of those laws; humbled to be afforded the task of representing many thousands of people; grateful, wanting desperately to do a good job; and slightly stunned that I am actually in this place.'

She spoke of social justice and of growing up Aboriginal but not knowing her Aboriginal family. She spoke of meeting her father for the first time at the age of 28, when he said to her, 'I hope I don't disappoint you.'

At a reception afterwards when Anthony congratulated her, there were tears running down his face.

Linda becomes emotional as she recounts what a proud and personal moment it was for them both – for the woman who would rise to become the NSW Labor Party's deputy leader and, in 2016, the first Indigenous woman elected to the federal House of Representatives, and for the man who helped put her there.

'He, more than any other man that I can think of, actually shows his emotions in that way,' Linda says. 'And I think that's kind of remarkable when people think, "Oh, he's the head-kicking numbers man, the hard man of the Left." But I think there's an extraordinarily complex, gentle, deep side to Anthony that he keeps for some people.'

For others, he reserved the brute force of his political side. Despite the understanding Simon Crean had shown of Anthony's personal situation the previous year, Anthony had doubts about his leadership. Events in 2003 set back their personal relationship significantly.

Simon's poll ratings had been persistently poor and his popularity remained stubbornly low. As 2003 began, so too did murmurings about who might replace him.

Anthony and his factional colleague George Campbell were in the thick of it. They started canvassing alternatives and speculation grew about a possible return to Kim Beazley.

Over Easter, *The Bulletin* magazine published an interview with Kim under the headline 'If I Were PM'. Unsurprisingly, it was seen as signalling a rekindled ambition to take over. When the talk didn't subside – and attempts to seek assurances from Kim only made things worse – Simon called on a ballot in June.

Despite the unhappiness inside the party about his electoral standing, there was also a strong view that a leader shouldn't be removed without ever having the opportunity to contest an election. Kim Beazley stood against him but Simon was re-elected with a solid margin. Anthony went and saw Simon before the vote and told him he wasn't supporting him. He voted for Kim.

Privately, Mark Latham labelled Anthony a hypocrite for supporting Kim while opposing his refugee policy. And of his own prospects, Mark surmised: 'If Simon loses the election – the Beazley forces won't let him win one – and the party jumps to the next generation, they jump to me.'

Then in late July, Anthony was blindsided by a decision that would see any residual support for Simon evaporate. On Saturday afternoon, 26 July, he was preparing to head out to watch the Wallabies play at ANZ Stadium when one of Simon's advisers rang. It was a courtesy call to let him know that Simon would be announcing the following day that Labor was changing its position on a second Sydney airport. It would no longer support building it at Badgery's Creek.

Concern about the airport plan had been growing in the western suburbs ever since Liberal MP Jackie Kelly had campaigned against it at a by-election after the 1996 election. Western Sydney opponents were using the real-life experience of airport noise in the inner west to oppose having an airport built near them.

Western Sydney MPs, including Laurie Ferguson, were worried. Laurie's brother, Martin, was shadow Transport Minister – both were Anthony's sub-factional opponents.

The Labor policy shift was out of the blue. Shadow Cabinet had not discussed it, the wider caucus certainly hadn't and Anthony hadn't even been warned it was coming. He was stunned.

'Hang on,' he said to the adviser on the phone. 'There's been no process here.'

He pointed out that it was against the party's platform and asked that Simon call him.

Soon after, when Anthony was on the train on his way to the game with Luke Foley, his phone rang again. Simon repeated what his adviser had said earlier.

'You can't do that,' Anthony replied. 'There's got to be a process.'

But Simon told him the decision had been made and dropped – leaked – to the newspapers ahead of an announcement the next day.

'It was done and there was nothing I could do about it,' Anthony says.

The one thing he vowed he would do was hold a news conference opposing it. The next morning, he went to the heart of inner Sydney's airport noise problem, in the suburb of Sydenham, and did exactly that – ahead of Simon's announcement.

'Those members who might have disagreed with the policy weren't consulted and that was a conscious decision by some in the leadership of the party to not consult,' Anthony said.

Simon Crean's policy-change news conference went ahead, he and Martin Ferguson heading out to Laurie's seat of Reid to confirm what by lunchtime was already being well canvassed.

Mark Latham endorsed the change. He'd been made shadow Treasurer in yet another reshuffle after Simon won the ballot. Although he had previously been a Badgery's Creek supporter, Mark's seat of Werriwa was also out west and the west didn't want it.

'We made a unanimous decision of the 15 people on our ALP Western Sydney task force that this was in the public interest, this was the right thing for our region, and that's the basis on which we made the recommendation to Martin Ferguson and Simon Crean,' he declared. 'And in Western Sydney we're delighted.'

The whole episode was a deal-breaker for Anthony. When talk inevitably turned again later in the year to replacing Simon, he felt no loyalty.

'He lost my support over that and I told him really clearly,' Anthony says. 'That's the one time I've really fallen out with a leader.'

His actions matched his words as his colleagues from the Right, Stephen Smith, Wayne Swan and Stephen Conroy – with the support of Anthony and others – set about generating support for Kim Beazley to return.

Two years after running Anthony's successful campaign in Grayndler, Tim Gartrell had gone to work for the ALP's national secretariat. In another two years, he would become assistant national secretary and three years after that, in September 2003, he was elected unopposed as national secretary.

So when Simon Crean's poll ratings were plunging and the talk was turning once again to replacing him, it was Tim who was in possession of the party's confidential data. Given Anthony's likely role if Kim was to try again to make a comeback, Tim was a bit apprehensive. As national secretary, he had to remain neutral. But he and Anthony were mates.

As the figures got worse, access to the research was restricted to Simon, his chief of staff, his confidant Senator John Faulkner and Tim Gartrell.

What would he do if Anthony tried to leverage the relationship? But looking back he says he needn't have worried.

'He never asked me, "Hey, what's the polling say?"' Tim says. 'He never asked for an inappropriate favour in any of those leadership ballots and I had lots of people trying to recruit me one way or the other. And some of those people could never believe that that was the case. They thought I was an agent of his. And if they actually knew the truth – he actually behaved really appropriately during the whole period.'

In late November, the polling Tim delivered to Simon's office was diabolical. With an election due the following year, it showed the party on course to lose between 30 and 45 seats.

Simon ploughed on. But it just wasn't working.

By the end of the year, the pressure became unsustainable and in early December, he agreed to a ballot. This time, after consulting his closest supporters, he decided not to recontest. Determined to keep Kim Beazley out of the job, Simon threw his weight behind the third candidate who had also been positioning himself: Mark Latham.

Mark was already somewhat of a divisive figure in the Labor Party. He was a generator of ideas and good at capturing public attention but he was also aggressive, abrasive and unpredictable.

'He had something about him that got noticed – a larger than life character,' Anthony says. 'But I always thought [the] chip on the shoulder that he had – I didn't find it particularly persuasive and I didn't like his aggression . . . the whole machismo thing that he had going. But you could have a beer with him and I did occasionally.'

On one of those occasions when they'd had a beer – and dinner as well – Anthony had clashed with Mark over immigration policy. He and Mark were out to dinner in Canberra with Mark's wife, Janine Lacy, their fellow MP Joel Fitzgibbon and several journalists – Malcolm Farr from Sydney's *Daily Telegraph*, Matt Price from *The Australian* and Fairfax's Annabel Crabb.

It was soon after the twin events of the Tampa incident and the September 11 terrorist attacks. As the diners talked about the upcoming election, Anthony expressed frustration that Labor hadn't formed a clear and credible argument in favour of 'the principled treatment of asylum seekers'.

Mark responded that asylum seekers weren't 'some innocents who need our help'. As Annabel relays it in her 2005 book *Losing It*, he said, 'They're criminals.'

Mark said working-class people generally – and the people in his electorate in particular – were not interested in trying to help law-breakers. Anthony responded angrily, dismissing Latham's argument as ridiculous.

'Working-class people break the law all the time,' he shot back. 'If you're poor, you have to do it to survive sometimes.'

Mark exploded and the argument descended into an angry slanging match, followed by what Annabel calls an uncomfortable silence. Then Joel spoke.

'Mark – 10 minutes ago I thought you would lead this party one day,' he said. 'Now I'm not so sure.'

The tension eventually subsided and good humour was restored. Anthony instantly dubbed it Mark's 'Osama bin Latham moment' – a jibe that reignited hostilities on the spot.

After the 2004 election, Mark would reflect more favourably on his inner-city colleague.

'I've bagged these inner-city types over the years, but at least they have a sense of the common good in their politics,' he wrote.

But during the election campaign in 2016, Mark would resurrect that original exchange and misquote it with an on-air blast at Anthony.

'I remember, back in the day, having debates with Anthony Albanese where he was screeching at me, "The main problem is the people of Western Sydney are racists,"' Mark told Sky News on 25 May. 'He screeched that at me in front of witnesses one night in Canberra after the Tampa debate and I'm sure that's still his opinion.'

Anthony rejected his comments as 'false and offensive' and a bid to 'get attention'.

'As if I would say that,' he says.

Two years after the original exchange, Mark put his hand up to lead the Labor Party. Anthony did not think he was up to it. Others, including his Left colleague Lindsay Tanner, had also expressed reservations.

Anthony and Stephen Smith were doing numbers for Kim. Over the days between the declaration of the ballot and its execution, they canvassed and counted. But every time they counted, they kept coming up just short.

'I went and saw more than one person and said, "We think there's one vote in this,"' Anthony says. '"Do you really want to make this bloke the leader?" I warned that he just didn't have the character to lead the Labor Party. But they voted for him and he got there.'

He got there by a single vote.

During Mark Latham's time in the leadership, he certainly shook things up.

The issue of where to locate a second Sydney airport remained unresolved but Mark thought he found a solution one day on a road trip from his home in Sydney to Canberra.

Travelling down the Hume Highway, he spotted an area near the Southern Highlands and thought it would make a good site. He rounded up his relevant frontbenchers – including Anthony – along with a member of his senior staff and an adviser from the NSW Transport Minister's office to go and do a site visit. They took one look at the area and determined it wouldn't work.

'There was a school on it,' Anthony says. 'It was undulating. There were power lines. It was just an absurd proposition.'

The group met in a coffee shop at Mittagong to figure out how to deal with it.

'And I said, "Righto, who's going to tell him?"'

The verdict was conveyed and the proposition quietly shelved. At the party's ensuing national conference, the proposed airport's location was left vague in the policy platform.

'It was somewhere in the south-west,' Anthony says.

Despite issues behind the scenes, the Labor Party's decision to elevate someone new saw Labor shoot up in the polls. Prime Minister John Howard was put under pressure as the Latham-led Opposition began to force the Government to make changes.

Early in 2004, Mark announced a new policy to scale back the generous parliamentary superannuation scheme, even vowing to shift onto the new, less generous scheme himself – if he won the election.

Spooked at this sudden turn in political fortunes, John Howard agreed to legislate a more austere version of the parliamentary pension. But to avoid shouts of retrospectivity and a revolt from his own backbench (and some on his frontbench), he applied it only to future, incoming MPs.

All those already in Parliament – himself included – would stay on the old scheme. Some of John Howard's colleagues were dismayed that Mark Latham was being allowed to set the agenda. And some of Mark's colleagues – including both Anthony and Kevin – were dismayed at the agenda he was setting.

'Parliamentary pensions was a completely selfish thing for him to do for a bloke who's now living on one,' Anthony says. 'I opposed that very strongly in the shadow Cabinet.'

Kevin felt the same.

'Both Albo and I could see the impact this would have on the quality of elected representatives over time. In fact, it would increase the opportunities for corruption. You weren't going to provide people with a reasonable long-term income.'

Anthony argues that having a generous super scheme for politicians helps keep the system mostly corruption-free.

'So people don't have to think about what their next job is.'

He also believes having a less generous super scheme makes people less inclined to retire.

'I thought it would make it harder to get people out of Parliament,' he says.

He then hastily clarifies that he's talking about backbench seat-warmers and not people who are progressing and making a national contribution. It has not escaped him, as he is speaking, that he has just clocked up 20 years himself.

Mark Latham had courted controversy from the moment he won the leadership. The Iraq war had begun in 2003 and as 2004 unfolded, Mark declared if he won that year's election, he would have Australian troops out by Christmas.

US President George W. Bush responded that such a move would 'embolden the enemy' and suggest Australia 'doesn't see the hope of a free and democratic society' in Iraq.

At home, Foreign Minister Alexander Downer condemned the policy position – privately the shadow Foreign Minister Kevin Rudd and others in the Labor Party were doing the same.

Alexander also accused Mark of 'taking his cue on every issue' from the American Democratic political strategist, Dick Morris, who had praised Labor's choice of new leader.

Anthony defended Mark in the Parliament, suggesting in return that government ministers were obtaining their advice from 'the shady White House string-puller, Karl Rove'.

He used his speech to deliver a stinging character analysis of both Karl Rove – President Bush's outspoken adviser – and the Howard Government. He laid out what he said were eight examples demonstrating that the Government had drawn tactical inspiration from Karl Rove's playbook – from being photographed with uniformed defence personnel for PR purposes to starting a divisive debate about homosexuality and appointing supporters to the benches and boards of judicial and other institutions.

'While they are busy claiming that Labor have stolen our ideas from Dick Morris, they are busy wrapping themselves in the flag, questioning their opponents' patriotism, destroying reputations, stacking courts, bashing gays and appealing to racial and religious prejudice – all under the inspiration of the darkest, dirtiest political insider of them all, Karl Rove,' he said.

The Republican's name would feature again in Australian politics two years later, when then leader Kim Beazley mistook journalists' questions as being about the US political consultant when they were actually asking about Australian television host Rove McManus – whose popular actress wife had just died after a very public battle with cancer.

It was a stumble that would be used to reinforce criticisms that he was out of touch with ordinary people and would lead to him losing his job.

But before that, Labor faced another election. As the 2004 campaign neared its end, Mark Latham made some stumbles of his own. He pledged that Labor would end logging in old-growth forests and offer an $800 million job-saving package for timber workers.

But he had not consulted some of those whose electorates would be most directly affected. In the middle of an election campaign, Labor's MP for the Tasmanian seat of Lyons, Dick Adams – whose bearded, burly appearance earned him the nickname 'Grizzly' – accused him of selling out regional Australia. He called on Mark to either change the policy or resign.

Anthony supports the intent of the 2004 Labor policy but not the way it was executed. And he emphasises that he was not a part of the decision-making process.

'The problem was how it was responded to and it was so late that the workforce weren't got on board,' he says. 'But if I had been asked – which I wasn't – then I would've supported protecting the Tasmanian old-growth forests.'

It wasn't the only issue that turned sections of the community against Labor as the campaign drew to a close. On 8 October, on the eve of the election itself, the Labor leader and the Prime Minister crossed paths in a Sydney radio studio. As Mark was leaving an interview and John Howard was walking in, what would normally have been a courtesy handshake seemed to symbolise the hesitation some voters had about Mark. The TV cameras showed him almost wrenching his opponent's arm out of its socket.

Labor had begun the campaign hopeful but its prospects had been slipping. Anthony believes that handshake sealed its fate.

'When I saw that I just thought, "Oh,"' he says. '"*Temperament*." And that was problematic. I was never confident going into that election.'

He says he thought voters would have their doubts about Mark Latham.

'And they did.'

After the election, with nobody else willing to contest, the Labor leader was re-elected unopposed.

In his reshuffled shadow ministry, Mark appointed Anthony to the one portfolio he'd always wanted: he became shadow Environment Minister. He insists he didn't ask for it – and that he has never asked to have any portfolio and only the once to be spared from one.

John Faulkner had raised it with him.

'He said, "You want to be the environment shadow, don't you?" and I said, "Yes."'

That was what Mark Latham offered.

'And I accepted it.'

Mark wrote later that he had given Anthony the job because 'he will eventually do to me what he did to Crean'. 'I needed to buy some breathing space for the next six to 12 months.'

While Anthony had the environment job, he loved it. Mark's demise would come within months and it would be all his own work.

After an exhausting election year, everyone in politics was looking forward to a break over summer 2004–05 – hot, lazy days and nothing but cricket on TV.

But the delicious monotony was shattered when the Asian tsunami struck on Boxing Day, causing devastation and horrific loss of life across the region.

As Australia mobilised its practical and financial response, attention shifted to the political response. The Opposition Leader was nowhere to be seen. Mark Latham was on holiday on the NSW Central Coast and believed that the acting leader, his deputy Jenny Macklin, would deal with it.

But his absence rapidly escalated the residual concerns some colleagues had about his judgement. His diaries record a bemused response to requests for him to make public comment.

'Apparently the disaster footage is getting a huge run on TV,' he wrote, in a spectacular understatement. He told his staff to explain to journalists that he'd had a pancreatitis attack – which he had – and was resting.

The same day, Anthony phoned to see if he was alright. He was cynical about the call.

'The only one to call me has been Albo who left a message on my mobile at 9 am yesterday and only wants to find out how sick I am so he can call his mates Smith and Swan,' Mark wrote.

Mark has since said he was already planning to announce he was leaving politics.

When he did so suddenly on 18 January, sporting a shaved head at a chaotic news conference in a Sydney park, Anthony was in Perth. He says what he saw on the news made him concerned.

'When I saw it I was worried about him just as a human being,' he says. 'I was just worried about his health.'

But having called once, he didn't call again.

Asked who should lead the Labor Party, Anthony nominated Kim Beazley. He didn't talk to his friend Kevin Rudd about it. Kevin was on a trip to devastated Aceh in Indonesia, trying to smooth Labor's relationships after what had looked like a lack of concern.

Kevin was furious at what he viewed as a move back to Kim orchestrated by the NSW Right. Anthony saw it as a logical step.

'There needed to be some healing of the party and coming together and I think most of us thought that the person to do that was Kim,' he says. 'I think that overwhelmingly it was recognised that the party made a mistake in not going for Beazley rather than Latham.'

Kim was elected unopposed and Jenny stayed on as deputy.

Anthony retained the environment portfolio and, over the next year, did what he regards as some of his best policy work – designing the party's blueprint on climate change that Kim would deliver in a major speech in March 2006, which would form the backbone of its policy heading into the 2007 election.

It nominated emissions reduction targets and proposed an emissions trading scheme, outlined a plan to protect diversity, make cars and buildings more energy efficient and ratify the Kyoto Protocol.

Anthony employed the House of Representatives standing orders once again to repeat the Question Time stunt he'd used a decade earlier on airport noise, organising to have himself asked a question on climate change.

Mark Latham's *The Latham Diaries* were published in September 2005, full of bitter attacks on Kim Beazley and many others of his colleagues, including Anthony. Many doubted they had been written contemporaneously, figuring they were as much about vengeance as historical record. None of it helped Labor.

By the second half of the year, Kim's poll figures were slipping. Kevin Rudd and Anthony discussed the situation. Anthony acknowledged there was a problem but was loyal to Kim.

Kevin and his supporters began canvassing around the party and Anthony was approached – sounded out – to see if he would be willing to serve as Kevin's deputy in a new leadership team. He declined and told Kevin he intended to stick with Kim.

'The thing about Albo is our conversations were always absolutely straight,' Kevin says. 'I'd tell him what I thought and what I planned to do and that would occur in confidence. And he would tell me the same. It was always straight, clear, transparent. We never bullshitted each other.'

This came, Kevin says, from 'a high degree of trust'.

Anthony's loyalty to Kim extended to warning both him and Jenny Macklin that there was movement.

'I talked to Kim,' Anthony says. 'I thought he was vulnerable and people were organising.'

He didn't just think it. He knew it.

'Albo and I then discussed what was going to happen,' Kevin says. 'I think that's when we got particularly close – long discussions about what was in the best interests of the party. So if we lost again in 2007 and the Liberals engineered, finally, a leadership change to [Treasurer Peter] Costello, we could see ourselves just being out for 23 years – like the whole Whitlam generation.'

Julia Gillard also harboured ambitions to lead the party. Neither Kevin nor Julia had the numbers alone to oust Kim, but they soon worked out that, together, they did.

'I had no desire to see Kim humiliated,' Kevin says. 'What drove me and I think what drove Julia at that stage as well, having been in the Parliament by that stage for eight years, was that we really had no desire to see ourselves in the Parliament . . . in permanent Opposition.'

On Friday morning, 1 December, Kevin went to see Kim and told him he wanted a ballot. Kim acceded to the request. He kept a commitment to attend Labor's national executive meeting that day and also to address the Parliamentary Press Gallery's annual dinner that night.

Anthony and Stephen Smith were doing his numbers. It wasn't looking good. On the morning of the ballot, Monday, 4 December, they went to his office.

'The mood was pretty sombre,' Anthony says. They told Kim they'd done a count.

'And he wasn't going to get there.'

He rejected their suggestion that he consider just standing aside. He wanted to defend his position.

Kevin was victorious, 49 votes to 39. Kim's count was a couple of votes fewer than Anthony had hoped. He says despite the promises people make before a ballot, when it's clear it's going one way there is often slippage.

'People like being on the winning side – with the majority,' he says. 'So if you don't start out with a majority, you're never going to get one.'

When it came to the ballot for deputy, Jenny Macklin decided not to re-contest. Julia Gillard was elected unopposed.

But when she addressed the caucus after the vote, in all the headiness of elevation, Julia neglected to acknowledge

Jenny, who had served as deputy to three leaders over five years. Nobody else had thanked her either. It was an accidental oversight, but Anthony was appalled.

'I thought he was going to put a chair through the window, he was so upset,' one colleague says.

Anthony stood up, acknowledged Jenny's work and thanked her on behalf of the caucus.

'I thought that was something that should've been addressed so I addressed it,' Anthony says. 'Jenny, I think, has been the most significant policy person in the Labor caucus over the last 20 years.'

Both his gesture and his words moved Jenny deeply.

'He got up in the caucus and was incredibly kind and generous to me,' she says.

Jenny and Anthony have a close friendship – a rare commodity in politics.

'He's been enormously supportive of me personally,' she says. 'You know if you want someone to have your back, he is an extraordinary friend.'

After the votes were done, Anthony and other supporters of the vanquished Kim and Jenny walked with the ousted leader back to his office. There, Kim would receive devastating news. A short time earlier, his younger brother David had died of a heart attack in Perth.

Soon after, Kim faced a news conference to concede defeat and urge the party to unite behind its new leadership.

'I had wanted to stay and finish the job but that was not to be,' he said. His composure under the circumstances was extraordinary.

There are moments in politics when humanity pierces the system's veneer and when all the power for which so many fight so hard seems worth nothing at all. This was one of those. As Kim thanked his wife, Susie Annus, he broke down.

'Family is everything,' he said.

In the weeks and months that followed, Anthony would reflect on his own family circumstances and on his personal credo to wring as much out of life as possible.

As he marked a decade in Parliament in March 2006 and then paid his usual visit to Rookwood Cemetery on the fourth anniversary of his mother's death and again on her birthday, his young son Nathan's occasional questions began to resonate.

'Where's *your* daddy, Daddy?'

He decided, after all the years of not knowing, that he needed to try to find out.

CHAPTER 20

At Last

Having decided to try to find his father – or at least find out about him – Anthony didn't really know where to start.

Maryanne had been a huge keeper of memorabilia but beyond what was associated with her trip abroad, there wasn't much with any detail about Carlo.

Anthony knew his name and that his mum had met him on the *Fairsky*. And there was the black-and-white photograph taken in the ship's dining room of Maryanne and her brother Johnny, his mate Mel and Johnny's new acquaintance and eventual wife Joan, with a dark-haired steward standing alongside them all in a crisp white jacket.

He assumed that was Carlo. His Aunt Joan confirmed that it was. But other than that, and Joan's stories from the voyage, there was nothing.

Having kept up the pretence for years that she had been widowed, Maryanne had been careful about who knew the real story. She was close to her neighbour, Yvonne Miller – Sherie's mum, over the back fence – and had told her the truth.

Yvonne says Maryanne didn't talk about Carlo all that much and there was never much detail when she did. But she did reveal that when Anthony was born, she'd tried to contact his father to let him know.

'She said she wrote to him and told him she had Anthony,' Yvonne says. 'Whether she had a letter back from him, I'm not 100 per cent sure. I just know that she didn't have any more contact with him.'

But the depth of her feeling was clear.

Maryanne's experience struck a particular chord with Yvonne.

'My dad was an American sailor,' she says.

Her mother had married him during World War II but he had returned to the United States before Yvonne was born in Paddington, in Sydney, in 1943.

When Yvonne was about four months old, her mother, along with her baby, was among the first war brides to sail to the US to join their American husbands. Three other women her mother knew were also on the ship. All four hoped the love waiting for them would be forever.

'And you know what? Three of them came back.'

Yvonne's mum and her baby daughter were among them. Her marriage had not survived, but her former husband continued to support them and kept in touch.

'I always had birthday cards and Christmas cards,' she says. 'He always sent maintenance for me . . . He had another family and I've been over to America since and I have met them.

'But he died. And I never ever met him before he died.'

So of Maryanne's friends, Yvonne could well understand her sadness and her love. But when Anthony had been told the truth about his father, Maryanne never told Yvonne she'd done it – perhaps to ensure they couldn't swap stories. Anthony has never found any trace of a letter between Maryanne and Carlo – either sent or received.

His mother had rarely spoken about Carlo since that emotional night at the kitchen table when he was a teenager, and he had done his best to put the whole thing out of his mind, away somewhere deep in a locked box where it would not disturb his life. Now, decades later, he was reaching in and hoping he could open it.

Internet searches brought up little. There wasn't any trace of a Carlo Albanese who appeared to fit the demographic.

Aside from his family and closest friends, there weren't many among Anthony's colleagues who knew the full story of his upbringing, let alone that he was beginning this quest.

But as his profile in politics had increased, more and more people had been taking an interest in him and his life story. He talked to Carmel about how hard that was – not being able to speak with any certainty.

'It was very difficult,' Carmel says. 'And I remember having a number of conversations about how this was a challenge for him to explain his background without having much information.'

Having been through his mother's treasured possessions – photographs, letters and postcards – and assembled what little he knew, Anthony spoke to his colleague John Faulkner, who as a Labor historian had some experience with archival searches.

In January 2007, John wrote to the National Archives, seeking advice about searching for the crew of visiting vessels and explaining he was looking for information about a Carlo Albanese, a steward on the *Fairsky*.

The letter he received back in late February contained a copy of the crew list for the *Fairsky*'s voyage to Australia that began in Southampton on 10 September 1962. It listed an assistant steward, Carlo Albanese, aged 30, who had been hired in Naples on 22 April 1961.

The archive's director of access and information services, Anne McLean, had helpfully outlined other options for genealogical searches, including through the National Library of Australia and through archives in Italy.

'You might like to consider engaging a research agent with genealogical expertise to follow through some of these leads as

I suspect the road ahead won't be easy,' she warned, explaining that she had searched for and found some photographs of the *Fairsky* and other information, but nothing else on either Carlo Albanese or M. Ellery, the passenger – Maryanne – about whom John had also inquired.

Anne McLean also said the Australian National Maritime Museum had provided the details of a maritime historian, Rob Henderson, who might be able to help.

John passed all of this on to Anthony, who was grateful for the assistance and advice. The crew list was the first independent evidence he had of his father's name and details. He'd been hoping there might be more clues to Carlo's whereabouts but it was better than nothing.

Anthony wasn't sure where to go next. As 2007 blossomed and federal Labor faced the prospect, according to all the opinion polls, that it would soon finally be in government, he needed to focus on the election campaign ahead. He put his search aside.

After 11 years on the Opposition benches, Anthony was fairly pleased to finally be about to take up a ministerial position on the serious side of the House.

Kevin Rudd's Labor victory at the 24 November election had been comprehensive. Not only had John Howard's coalition Government been swept from office, the Prime Minister had lost his own seat of Bennelong – the first to experience that particular rebuff since Stanley Bruce in 1929. Like everyone else in the shadow ministry, Anthony was waiting to find out what his portfolio would be.

Six days after taking over from Kim Beazley in December 2006, Kevin Rudd had reshuffled his front bench line-up and Anthony had been reassigned to infrastructure and water. His much-loved environment job had gone to someone else: former rock star turned Labor MP, Peter Garrett.

Peter had come into Parliament in 2004 in the Sydney seat of Kingsford Smith, due to the concerted recruiting efforts of a range of people, including John Faulkner who he'd known for some years. He had long been associated with environmental issues through the Australian Conservation Foundation, serving twice as its President, including just before moving full-time into politics.

Anthony had held the shadow portfolio during 2005 and taken to it with enthusiasm, attending international climate-change talks and crafting a policy to challenge Japan's whaling practices in the International Court of Justice. He really wanted to keep the job.

He says he also believed it wasn't a good idea for it to go to Peter – either for Peter or for Labor – because he could find himself subject to unreasonable pressure from the environment movement.

'I think he's a very good person,' Anthony says. 'I thought, though, it was difficult for someone who had been the head of the ACF to manage expectations in the portfolio.'

He put that argument to Peter but Peter didn't agree.

The former Midnight Oil frontman – whose dance style Anthony had emulated at sweaty pub gigs across Sydney years before – had also been receiving a lot of other calls about who should get what job and who was owed what from whom, for reasons dating back way before he was in Parliament.

Non-aligned in a factional sense – a status which had its plusses and minuses – Peter says he was never interested in engaging in the manoeuvrings.

'I just used to bark at people gently and say move on.'

When he took over the portfolio, the policy framework was in place and he credits Anthony for that. He sees his former colleague as a passionate prosecutor of his ideas and a shrewd political operative.

'The thing I like about Albo is that he's got a heart,' he says. 'Like, a real heart. You know he really does feel some things quite deeply. He's had some setbacks along the way and things that he's had to deal with. He's pretty good at brushing controversy and all that sort of stuff off. He's learned to do that well. But he's very hardworking. He's a very capable pollie . . .

'Albo isn't a sinner in my book but you couldn't describe him as a saint.'

Kevin's post-election call about portfolio allocation came in December 2007, the night before the ministry was due to be sworn in. Anthony had retained the infrastructure element and added transport, regional development and local government.

While he hadn't ever asked for any particular portfolio, he had asked on this occasion to stay in the machinery-of-Parliament role he'd had in Opposition. Before the election, Kevin had elevated him from Deputy Manager of Opposition Business to being in charge of Labor's parliamentary operations. It was a tactical job and played to his political strengths.

He approached it as a job of disruption, taking numerous points of order to interrupt ministers' answers in Question Time and moving the occasional dissent motion in the Speaker's ruling.

His opposite number on the government side, in the prestigious Leader of the House position, was Tony Abbott.

'We hardly had any relationship at all,' Anthony says. 'He didn't bother to consult us on anything and I was fine like that.'

Non-consultation cut both ways. The Opposition took the latitude that provided to spring unexpected motions in the House regularly.

'It was like Sussex Street,' Anthony says. 'It wasn't cooperative. It was like Sussex Street in the early years.'

He recalls one Opposition tactics meeting in which some upcoming motion or other was being discussed and Julia Gillard suggested he ring Tony Abbott.

'Have you got his number?' Anthony asked. He'd been in his position for six months and Tony hadn't supplied it.

Anthony took seriously the role of using Parliament to undermine the Government politically. He kept a board in his office that he would mark after every Question Time.

'Who won the day,' he says of the board's purpose, insisting the Opposition was increasingly winning, tactically. Why bother marking it up?

'A discipline thing.'

Heading into Government, Kevin made Anthony Leader of the House and appointed Foreign Minister Stephen Smith his deputy. Kevin took Stephen aside and asked him to help moderate Anthony's instincts.

'When you are in the Parliament your job will be from time to time just to tug on his suit coat and hold him back a bit from completely going over the top,' Stephen recalls Kevin telling him. 'And of course the truth is Albo very comfortably made that transition, without the need for any great help from me.'

Once in government as Leader of the House, Anthony's coalition counterpart was no longer Tony Abbott but Joe Hockey. Joe figured two could play the disruption game.

'He wanted a smooth run in Parliament,' Joe says of Anthony. 'I wanted to create mayhem . . . You always did it in good humour. Sometimes he'd be angry but that's the way it goes. I mean, Cardboard Kev was a great example. They wanted sitting days on Fridays. [Anthony] thought he was being creative.'

Anthony had devised and proposed changes to the parliamentary schedule – he says to consolidate sitting times and save taxpayers money by shifting all private members' business to Fridays, when Parliament normally wouldn't sit.

The argument went that instead of holding private members' business, most of which doesn't involve voting, on a normal sitting day, it should be moved to Fridays when only those involved in the specific items of business would need to attend.

The rest of the sitting week could then be devoted to the actual business of government, resulting in less wasted time in Canberra and fewer sitting weeks being needed overall. Cabinet would also sit on a Friday and, as parliamentary committees often did anyway, members and senators could make a more efficient use of their time by fitting all of those extras in on the one day.

But the coalition Opposition was suspicious that it was designed to draw MPs back to Canberra while the Prime Minister went wandering around their electorates.

Coalition MPs – especially in WA – claimed Kevin was working on Labor's standing in seats it wanted to win back. In protest, WA MP Don Randall brought a life-sized cardboard cutout of the Prime Minister into the chamber to make the point that he wasn't there. The place went into uproar.

'If Parliament was sitting, we wanted a Question Time,' Joe says. 'Kevin wanted to swan around our seats on a Friday whilst we were locked up in Parliament. And we held the great majority of seats in Western Australia and our MPs wanted to get back to their electorates. As soon as Kevin started going to their electorates on Fridays, Don Randall walked in with a cardboard Kev.'

Anthony says that's not what it was for. He says despite that suspicion, he tried to consult the Opposition on important matters.

'I thought it was good for the Parliament to have more co-operation, rather than less.'

If the Government was planning a gag motion to cut short debate, he would let the Opposition know. It didn't mean he would always acquiesce to coalition objections, but at least they knew what was coming. It was in this period and through this kind of cooperation that he developed a relationship with South Australian Liberal frontbencher Christopher Pyne, though Christopher disputes the extent of the alleged cooperation.

'He didn't need me to cooperate with him because he had the numbers and he used them kind of ruthlessly,' Christopher says.

They would work more closely together after 2013 and become a kind of media double-act.

In 2016, when Labor was back in Opposition, Anthony and the Manager of Opposition Business, Tony Burke, would reinforce their point about the consequences of non-cooperation.

He and Tony already knew the plusses there could be in cooperation. Back when Anthony had been in Sussex Street, Tony was the equivalent speaker for the Right and the two would face off in duelling speeches on the floor of the state conference. Factional enemies in public, they would actually sit out of sight and prepare them together to make sure each gave the other the right lead-in to use their best lines.

On this occasion in 2016, the Government wanted to ram non-urgent infrastructure legislation through the House without debate. Tony Burke protested to Leader of the House Christopher Pyne that many Labor members wanted to speak on the bill and could they please be given just five minutes each? When the answer was no, he and Anthony employed time-wasting tactics, forcing 27 unnecessary divisions – votes – and making the Parliament sit until not much before midnight.

'From Opposition you can't stop something from going through, but you can sure as hell make it difficult for them,' Tony says.

Anthony concurs.

'You can always be difficult if you want to be,' he says. 'That was Burkie and myself – two people who knew the standing orders – showing them essentially what the consequences were.'

Taking on the transport portfolio in government put him in the box seat on his pet policy issue – Sydney Airport. Days after the election, Sydney Airport had announced it needed to do major works to the runway safety extension area, and the east–west runway, which the Howard Government had reopened, would be closed for a year – funnelling the air traffic yet again entirely over the inner north.

The works were necessary. But Anthony believed the pre-election secrecy – and lack of mitigation planning – was not.

'The Government had kept it secret and Sydney Airport had kept it secret from people, from the community and from everyone publicly,' he says.

Anthony was irate. He demanded a meeting with the airport's executives. They arrived in Canberra on the morning of the swearing in of Kevin Rudd's new government.

Kevin had phoned him only the night before, confirming that along with infrastructure, he would be responsible for local government and one other key portfolio area. The late notice was standard practice to try to keep line-up details from leaking in advance, and in this case Anthony was extra pleased to have the element of surprise.

Heading up Sydney Airport Corporation was Max Moore-Wilton, former head of John Howard's Prime Minister's Department, who sported an imperious manner and superior outlook.

There was no love lost between Max and Anthony, so much so that when Max announced his retirement in February 2015, Anthony would attract international attention by issuing a media release in response, bearing just one word: 'Good.'

Max could appreciate the joke.

'I thought it was pithy, I thought it was clever,' he says. He laughed when he saw it. 'There's certainly no point in doing anything else.'

Max can also appreciate Anthony's political skills, if not his point of view.

'He is an extremely committed warrior for his cause. I don't agree with him on a number of things. I particularly didn't agree with him on the second Sydney airport.'

He extends his criticism beyond just Anthony to Joe Hockey as well.

'I had spent a great part of my life focusing on good government and proper economic use of public money,' Max says. 'And I thought what he and Joe Hockey had agreed for their own electoral purposes was a clear dereliction of their public duties.'

Max had sent representatives who were waiting in Anthony's office for him to return from the caucus meeting where portfolios were announced, unaware that they were going to be seeing a lot more of him from now on.

'They were waiting there to square off with the Member for Grayndler and in walked the Minister for Transport,' he says, laughing. 'It was great.'

At Kevin Rudd's suggestion, Anthony undertook a full review of aviation, through a white-paper process, with the Sydney Airport issue forming one element of that.

'I revived the second airport, basically, that had been a dormant idea,' he says.

Four years after Labor had sidelined the issue and put the plan for Badgery's Creek on ice, he also established a joint federal-state study of site options. It examined a range of possibilities including Wilton, in the Macarthur region – which had long been nominated as another Western Sydney alternative. But it returned to the original conclusion.

'It was clear that Badgery's Creek was the best site,' Anthony says. 'I thought at that point it would end up somewhere else. We had an objective process that came to the same conclusion that other studies had.'

A white paper in December 2009 had said Sydney needed a second airport. A joint study was commissioned in 2010 and two years later it reported back, leaving open a series of options.

The descent of the global financial crisis and the Government's decision to pump money into smaller-scale infrastructure projects across the country to keep the economy afloat meant there still wasn't the money to advance the airport issue.

Five years on in 2013, with the coalition back in government, the previous government's study became the basis for a decision. Finally, a government would lock in behind it and begin planning the second airport in earnest.

Once he was well settled into his jobs in government, Anthony began thinking again about the personal project that hadn't advanced very far.

Clearly, archival searches were not going to do the trick. He had to think of some other way to unearth more information about Carlo. Some more internet research established that Sitmar Cruises, which had operated the *Fairsky*, had been sold to P&O in the 1980s. The owner of P&O was Carnival Cruise Lines.

When he noticed the chief executive of Carnival Cruise Lines, Ann Sherry, was in Canberra, he sought her out and asked if she could drop in and see him. Anthony knew Ann already and decided he would share his personal story with her and see if she could help.

When she and her colleagues arrived, he asked to see her alone.

I wonder why he wants to see me on my own, she thought. *Is he going to talk to me about something? Is he going to offer me something? Is there a deal to be done?*

She was hoping to talk to him about infrastructure. She had no idea what he was about to ask.

'And I sat down and he said, "I need you to do me a favour,"' Ann recalls. 'And I said, "What would that be?" And then he told me the story. He said, "I'm looking for my father" . . . He said, "Before my mother died, here is the story she told me."'

He told her what he knew. She understood why it was so important to him.

'You need to know who your family are.'

Ann left his office having not discussed her infrastructure issue at all and now having inherited Anthony's predicament. It was a personal, rather than a professional request, but either way she didn't want to let the Minister down.

'Let me see what I can do,' she said.

She realised the import of what he'd told her and what the request meant.

'I left feeling like I'd been burdened by a secret,' Ann says. 'So I came out of there feeling a bit shell-shocked and thinking, "My God, where do I start?"'

Back in Sydney, after giving it some thought, she contacted a maritime historian who was working on the history of P&O in Australia. His name was Rob Henderson – the same Rob Henderson that National Archives director Anne McLean had suggested contacting two years earlier.

'I honestly thought we would not find anything,' Ann Sherry says. 'It was such a long shot.'

When she told him the story, Rob was just as apprehensive. It seemed like the maritime equivalent of a needle-in-a-haystack search.

'I thought, "This is impossible stuff,"' he says.

But Rob has made an art of chasing down impossible details. Through doggedness and absolute blind inexplicable luck, he would defy the odds.

Rob figured he should start where Carlo and Maryanne's romance had started – with Sitmar Cruises. Having worked giving lectures on ships himself and having an incredibly specialised knowledge of the industry, he has a swag of contacts across the world.

'I sent off a message to an office contact for Sitmar in Genoa, I think it was, or maybe it was Monaco,' he says. 'And I never ever got a reply.'

He then tracked down someone he knew who used to work for the Australian office of Sitmar.

'They couldn't help me. They had no record of crew or anything like that. I went to Princess Cruises in Los Angeles, because when P&O took over Sitmar there were a couple of Sitmar ships which went to Princess Cruises in Los Angeles. They couldn't help me.'

Rob was starting to think this really was a hopeless quest.

I'm going to have to turn around and say to Ann that I can't really do anything, he thought. *I'll just think about it for another month or two.*

A few weeks later he went away, again lecturing on a cruise ship. By chance, on board he met a man by the name of Christopher Jolly, who was travelling with his wife. Christopher happened to be an executive in shipbuilding with Carnival Corporation.

Rob didn't think much about that until, back at home, he received a message from Christopher asking for a favour. He was trying to track down details of a ship that had had an accident in Australian waters in the 1880s. Rob agreed to see what he could do.

Christopher thanked him and mentioned he was heading to Genoa, in Italy, the following month to see a new ship they were building. And Rob suddenly thought, *Oh!*

'So I said to him, "While you're in Genoa, is there anything in the old Genoa wharves relating to the old Sitmar company?"'

Christopher had no idea. He figured it would have all been destroyed, but he promised to have a look.

'Then he sent me a message,' Rob says. Christopher had been to Monfalcone, the old shipbuilding town in the Gulf of Trieste, and he'd asked about Sitmar.

'They said, "Oh yes, there's an old shed at the end of wharf number so and so,"' Rob recounts. '"And that used to hold a whole lot of Sitmar records, but nobody's ever looked at them."'

Christopher explained he didn't have time to explore further on that trip as he had to head back to England. But he was returning to the area in a few months and would chase it up then. When months passed and there was no further word, Rob assumed he hadn't found anything. Then, an email arrived.

'All of a sudden I get a message saying, "Are you sitting down?"' Rob recalls, laughing.

Most of the boxes of Sitmar records had been destroyed, but inside the shed at the end of the wharf had been just a few boxes stacked against a wall. Inside one of them, he found a familiar name.

'He said, "I've found this box of cards of stewards and there is a Carlo Albanese and he lives somewhere in the south of Italy."'

The address dated from his time with the cruise line, back in the 1960s.

Apparently determined to see the adventure through, Christopher spoke to a local shipbuilder he knew in Monfalcone and asked how he might go about finding a current address or phone number for this Carlo Albanese.

The local man took up the case. He managed to check a database of seafarers' pensioners. On 5 November 2009, Rob received another message.

'He found Carlo Albanese's name in the social security records,' Rob says. 'He checked the birthdate against the date on the card and he thought, "It's got to be the same man."'

Rob rang Ann. She couldn't believe it.

'Oh my God!' she said.

It was late on a Thursday afternoon. She had Anthony's mobile number and called him straightaway. *This is one of those life-changing moments*, she thought.

'It's Ann,' she said, explaining she had some news. 'I've found him.'

In the moment that followed her words, there was a kind of stunned silence.

'And I could hear him just . . .' She tries to describe it. 'He gulped. He gulped . . . I could almost feel him falling off his chair when I spoke to him.'

'What do you mean?' he asked her. 'How do you *know?*'

She outlined what Rob had told her and detailed what they knew of Carlo – that he had been receiving a seafarer's pension, and once they'd found his old employment record, they'd been able to find him in the Italian pension system and locate an address.

Trying to absorb this information, Anthony explained apologetically that he was about to go to a dinner with state and territory transport ministers ahead of their regular ministerial council meeting the next day, so he wasn't able to talk for long.

'I just thought you'd want to know,' she said. She was right.

'Thanks,' he managed to say. '*Thanks.*'

For such a small conversation it had enormous implications.

'It was so profound,' Ann says. 'Hearing it in his voice – how important it was.'

She thought: *He's a Cabinet Minister. He spent part of his life thinking his father was dead and now there's a live human being on the end of this. What do you do with that?*

When Anthony answered the phone in his Sydney ministerial office at 5.30 pm that Thursday afternoon, the news Ann delivered hit him like a front-row forward.

'She said, "Here's his address in Barletta,"' he says.

'Where's that?' he had asked.

Ann told him what she knew – that it was a town in southern Italy – and he thanked her and hung up.

'And I immediately broke down.'

His office door was closed. Going with him to the dinner starting at 6.30 pm at the Hilton Hotel, members of his senior staff were preparing to leave. But he needed a moment.

'I just sat down and collapsed with emotion,' he says. 'I just broke down. This flood of emotion came over me and I rang Carmel and talked to her.'

Carmel was as astonished as he was.

'I thought it was an almost impossible task and was never terribly hopeful that Anthony would find his father,' Carmel says. 'And so when he did get that information I just was a bit stunned and amazed and also a bit anxious, because I thought, "What are the next steps? What happens now?"'

One of his staff came in and said it was time to go. Anthony asked his advisers to take the Commonwealth car and go on to dinner without him. They were concerned and asked him what was wrong and whether one of them should stay.

'It's okay, you just go ahead,' he told them. 'Something important. I'll be there soon.'

He wanted some time to process what had just happened. For a few minutes, he just sat there. Then he headed out on foot, through Sydney's bustling peak hour, for the Hilton.

'I just walked through the city,' he says.

Wow, he thought as he went. *Wow*.

'It was almost overwhelming.'

He decided he had to set the whole thing aside for the moment. These dinners were where the serious negotiating work was done ahead of the next day's meeting. He had to focus.

Righto, he thought. *I'm going to put that in a box on the shelf and get through the dinner.*

On Friday afternoon, after the meeting had concluded, he rang Ann Sherry back.

'I had a chat with her the next day that was calmer and thanked her,' he says.

Ann is still incredulous that they managed to find Carlo's work record at all.

'So there was a guy in Italy who went hunting and [he] was looking for all the places that records might be stored. There had been fires in offices. There's been everything that would potentially wipe out all this history. But of course in the way things often are in Italy – there's a slight chaotic edge to some of this – you find a few boxes in a warehouse and one of those boxes has got the crew records of the time and in that box is the name.'

Rob Henderson plays down his role – which was, in fact, crucial. Without him, it never would have happened.

'It's just in a day's work for me – these things that I'm asked to find out,' Rob says. 'One of the managers at P&O used to refer to me as a footnote in history.'

But Rob admits that, in this case, he hadn't been terribly hopeful.

'I never thought it would end as successfully as it did, because I knew that so much of Sitmar had been lost.'

The whole thing was a salutary reminder of an important principle.

'It's a question of who you know and never forget a contact. In this case, it just happened to be the right contact. And it was only by chance that I'd met this fellow and his wife on a ship anyway.'

As far as coincidences went, it was just the beginning.

Having made it – miraculously – this far in the search, Anthony now wasn't giving up. The prospect of actually finding Carlo, alive and living in a town in the south of Italy, was real, palpable. The need to pursue this to its end consumed him.

Before this latest development, he had previously confided in the woman who was now Australia's ambassador to Rome, former Liberal senator Amanda Vanstone, and asked for her help.

He knew Amanda from her many years in Parliament and liked her. She was irreverent and plain speaking and he figured she would keep his confidence. He was absolutely correct.

Amanda doesn't recall Anthony specifically asking her not to talk about his search for his father.

'But he wouldn't have needed to.'

Before she left on her posting in mid-2007, he had a meeting with her in Canberra and explained what little information he had and what he was trying to do.

'He basically said he had never met his father,' Amanda says. 'He believed this person was his father and he had decided he would never look to find his father until his mother had passed on, because she'd done such a tremendous job. But she had now passed on and he'd like to see what he could do.'

She agreed to do what she could to help.

Once she was in Rome, Amanda had enlisted – and sworn to secrecy – one of the embassy's very experienced consular officers, who had compiled a list of the Albaneses in southern Italy, around Naples where Carlo had signed up with Sitmar originally. They had eliminated them one by one.

There was one they thought could be him and the consular officer wrote to him.

'We sent the letter off two or three times and didn't get a reply,' Amanda says.

It turned out to be the wrong man.

When Anthony received Ann Sherry's call – and an address – he rang Amanda again. A third person in the embassy also knew about his situation and he rang her too.

In another of the many strange serendipitous twists in his story, one of Amanda's staff at the embassy was Anthony's cousin, once removed. Lisa Golden was the granddaughter of Anthony's aunt and Maryanne's sister Ronnie – the daughter of his cousin Helen.

An accomplished Italian-speaking Australian, Lisa had been living in Italy and had applied for a position as a locally engaged public diplomacy project officer. She was from the Irish side of Anthony's family, with no blood ties to Italy. She just loved the language and she was good at it.

Lisa had worked part-time and then full-time in Anthony's electorate office while attending university in Sydney.

Having won a prestigious scholarship to Italy at the end of high school in Brisbane based on her language competency, and then lived in Italy for more than three years, Lisa returned to Brisbane to complete a degree. She then undertook honours in Italian Studies at Sydney University and won a modern languages prize. Hers was certainly a merit-based appointment.

Amanda Vanstone describes her as 'more than competent, more than qualified'.

When Anthony rang Lisa and told her he'd been given his father's details, she was as gobsmacked as everyone else. He gave her the address and before long she had found a telephone number online.

In a further extraordinary coincidence, as Minister for Transport and Infrastructure, Anthony was due to fly to Italy at the end of that month – and not just Rome, but to Bari in southern Italy, 40 minutes' drive south of Barletta. As a public diplomacy officer, Lisa had been one of those working on plans for the visit.

In Bari, Anthony was meeting the heads of the local construction industry association and touring the local port. The Australian Government was trying to encourage Italian investment in Australian infrastructure. A delegation of Italian companies would later pay a reciprocal visit.

In Rome, he was due to hold talks with European Transport Commissioner Antonio Tajani about the possibility of an air services agreement, which had proven difficult to negotiate. He was then flying on to London to address the International Maritime Organisation on 2 December before heading home.

It was an opportunity he couldn't let slide. But he didn't speak Italian and he couldn't just turn up out of the blue. He needed to try to contact Carlo beforehand and see if he was willing to meet. He asked his Rome-based Italian-speaking cousin Lisa to try to call Carlo's number.

'It was obviously going to be a difficult phone call to even begin to make,' Lisa says. 'I didn't even know that they would pick up the phone.'

She rang and rang. Eventually, someone answered but she couldn't get them to stay on the line long enough to explain fully. When she asked for Carlo she was told he didn't hear very well.

She could understand what seemed like their obfuscation. It was a potentially confusing and alarming thing for any older person to receive a call from strangers out of the blue, and especially in conservative southern Italy where such things were treated with particular suspicion.

'We were worried they thought it would be a shakedown,' Anthony says.

Lisa realised calling wasn't going to work.

'We were able to make absolutely no headway over the phone,' she says.

They were running out of time. The ministerial visit was due in a week. So they decided to try by mail.

Lisa wrote a letter explaining her inquiry was related to an Australian woman, the late Mary Ellery – the name by which Carlo had known Maryanne – whom she understood Carlo Albanese had known.

She outlined that she was writing on behalf of Mary's son, that he was coming to Italy the following week and hoped they might meet. She didn't give any more detail than that – not his name nor his professional status. But she included a copy of the one photograph Anthony had which showed his mother and Carlo in the ship's dining room – to prove their veracity.

'I did a lot of careful drafting of the letter with Italian friends and consulted people,' Lisa says. She especially sought advice from one of her closest friends, who was from southern Italy.

'We only had one shot at it. We needed to make sure that we said what we wanted to say – that we did it respectfully. We wanted to make it clear that we weren't trying to make any fast moves or anything like that – that this is a genuine request.'

She emphasised the very tight timeline, provided her mobile phone number and crossed her fingers.

But as she headed for the post office on 23 November – five days before Anthony was due to arrive – she was plagued by exactly the kinds of concerns she was trying to ease in those at the other end. She didn't know anything about these people.

She was writing in her private capacity, sending the letter registered mail, and she had already included her personal phone number. She wasn't sure she wanted to reveal any more. So she persuaded the man behind the counter to bend the rules and allow her to send the letter without adding her return address.

Four days later, with Anthony already in the air, her phone rang in the late morning but she missed the call. It was an unfamiliar southern Italian number and she tried unsuccessfully to ring it back. She then called Carlo Albanese's number and reached his wife, who said calmly that a family friend of theirs was going to call her.

More calls to the other number went unanswered.

When Lisa's phone rang again it was late Friday afternoon and she and others were rushing to finish binding the booklets containing the schedule for Anthony's ministerial visit beginning the next day.

The woman sounded youngish – in her 30s maybe – and said she was a lawyer from Barletta, and a friend of the Albanese family. It was potentially the breakthrough they were seeking but Lisa was now on the clock, hurrying to get everything ready.

The woman didn't sound hostile. After a brief conversation in Italian, Lisa apologised and arranged to call her back when she was done.

Not finishing work until 8 pm, she phoned as soon as she was out in the street, explaining she couldn't give many more details about her written inquiry until she spoke with the person in question, who was on a plane and arriving from Australia in the morning.

He would be in Bari later that day and also the day after, but was then leaving again, back to Rome and onward. They discussed the possibility of arranging to meet the lawyer in Barletta.

As Lisa was talking and walking along bustling Via Nomentana, a man came off his motor scooter right in front of her.

'Oh my God!' she said suddenly, alarming the woman on the other end of the phone.

'I'm so sorry,' she said to the woman on the phone. 'Can you wait?'

She ran to the man on the ground with the other woman still on the line.

'Are you okay?' she asked in Italian.

'Yeah, I'm okay, I just slipped,' he replied.

'Are you sure you're okay? Do you need me to call an ambulance?'

He assured her he was fine.

Returning to the phone call with another apology, she explained what had happened. They said *ciao* and agreed to talk again the next day.

The lawyer would say later that it was Lisa's willingness to spontaneously help a stranger in the street that convinced her this was a good person whose motives were pure and that she should agree to meet.

Even before Lisa knew that, her head was swimming with the sequence of random events that had led to this moment when – maybe – her cousin Anthony might meet his father.

Her grandmother's closeness to Maryanne, her own decision to learn Italian, working for Anthony, moving to Europe, getting a job at the embassy at just this time – never mind his having unearthed details of Carlo's whereabouts – had all combined to bring this possible reunion about.

How, she asked herself, *did all these apparently unconnected things over such a long period of time come together in such an extraordinary way to enable this weekend to happen at all?*

Nothing could change the exquisiteness of that, no matter how things turned out.

As Anthony flew out for Rome, it wasn't exactly a calm period in politics at home. The Rudd Government had introduced legislation for its proposed Carbon Pollution Reduction Scheme – the bill to set up emissions trading – and was trying to negotiate enough support from other parties to pass it. But there was trouble brewing.

After the Howard Government had lost the election there had already been leadership turmoil on the coalition side. Brendan Nelson had taken over as Liberal leader after the coalition lost government but had only lasted nine months, before Malcolm Turnbull had seized the job.

A previous Environment Minister, Malcolm supported action on climate change, including the introduction of emissions trading. He had agreed to talks on the Government bill, negotiated changes and committed the coalition to supporting it.

Anthony had been among those engaged in the negotiations with Malcolm's office. But the Liberal leader couldn't take enough of his party with him.

Inside the coalition, unhappiness with Malcolm had been growing. Those who were sceptical about the science on climate change, opposed the idea of a new tax – fixed or floating – or were concerned about being seen to collaborate with the Government, were making their views known. They were also making big trouble for their leader.

The day before Anthony flew out, climate sceptic Tony Abbott had quit the Opposition frontbench and written to Liberal Party whip Alex Somlyay, asking for a leadership ballot the following week.

'This isn't all about me,' Tony said. 'The important thing is about getting the policy changed and the party as united as it can be.'

With the Liberals imploding, the last thing Anthony wanted to be doing was leaving the country. Parliament would be sitting on Monday and as Leader of the House, it didn't sit well with him to miss it – never mind the impending Liberal Party leadership showdown.

But the date of the London speech was immovable and given the difficulty there had been with the European air services agreement negotiations – this would be the third ministerial discussion after previous meetings in Leipzig and Brussels – he couldn't defer the meeting on the coming Monday with Minister Tajani either.

When Anthony left Australia, it was unclear what was going to happen with the Liberals and where that would leave the CPRS. As Leader of the House, Anthony had a considerable interest in the outcome. His friend Joe Hockey was emerging as a possible contender, too.

Anthony had with him his ministerial adviser on transport, Mal Larsen, his old friend from Young Labor days. As they arrived in Rome, they were both on the phone frantically trying to find out what had been going on back home while they were incommunicado.

On Monday, 30 November, while Anthony was in Rome, the coalition and Greens would vote down the Government's bill in the Senate. The next day, on 1 December, the Liberals would hold their ballot with Tony Abbott defeating Malcolm Turnbull by a single vote.

It was the beginning of another sequence of events that would have a dramatic and lasting impact on both sides of politics.

The plane from Australia landed at 6.50 am and both Lisa and ambassador Amanda Vanstone were at the airport to meet it.

Anthony, Mal and Lisa were flying straight down to Bari and Amanda was off on a separate trip so wouldn't see the Minister again during his visit. They chatted briefly before going their separate ways.

On the domestic flight, Lisa sat beside Anthony and told him about the phone call. They were to call the lawyer on arrival to see about the prospects of meeting her in Barletta that night. There were hurdles to jump before they could discuss actually meeting Carlo.

Anthony absorbed this update and they chatted for the hour and 10 minutes it took to reach Bari. As he regaled Lisa with parliamentary tales, she thought he seemed in remarkably good form for someone who had just come off a flight from Australia, was facing the prospect of meeting his father for the first time and was already exhausted from all the shenanigans going on back home.

Their meetings in Bari wound up around 4 pm. Lisa had been speaking to their contact and had agreed they would meet at her studio office in Barletta at 7 pm.

They headed out of Bari by road an hour before. Not wanting to be early, they had a quick look around. Barletta was bustling on a Saturday night. The industrial town of about 100,000 people sits atop boot-shaped Italy's heel on the Adriatic Sea, and while its economy relies on cement production, agriculture and fishing, its history dates back before the Roman era.

The lawyer's studio was in the centre of town, upstairs from the street. She welcomed Anthony and Lisa and as they sat down to talk, Anthony deliberately put his folder down on the table so she could see his business card attached to the front. It bore his full name.

Over the next almost two hours they talked, Anthony in English and their lawyer host in Italian with Lisa translating simultaneously. She asked why Anthony wanted to meet Carlo even though he was sure she now knew. She explained Carlo hadn't been well.

He told their host his story – about Carlo and Maryanne.

'I think he's my father,' Anthony said simply. 'I don't want anything else out of him. I'm not after money, I'm not after anything else. I just want to meet him.'

He explained that as a child he'd been led to believe his father had died in a car accident until, in his teenage years, his mother had told him the truth.

Out of loyalty to his mum he had never gone looking, but he said that, in the wake of her death, he'd begun to feel a strong desire – a physical need – to find him.

He talked about his love for Maryanne and his respect and admiration for all she'd done for him, defying the stigma of single motherhood as a young Catholic woman in the 1960s. He explained that she had decided to take Carlo's surname and give it to her son and how they'd made a family of two.

And he told her about his inquiry to P&O, the recent chance discovery of the records and the fact that he was an Australian government Minister who happened to be coming to Italy on business with meetings in Bari and Rome, and that was why his window of opportunity for a meeting existed but was so small.

She listened to all of it and then explained how she'd come to be involved. While chatting to a friend a few days earlier, he had told her about the registered letter his father, Carlo, had just received.

She told him she'd dealt with such things before and offered to help. And she asked him why he'd accepted a registered letter with no return address.

The woman explained to Anthony and Lisa that it was illegal to send something registered mail without a return address. But she also confessed almost apologetically that had the letter *had* an address, she would have responded by mail and not by phone – and the opportunity to meet would have been missed.

She had been moved by Anthony's love for his mother and determination to find and hopefully meet his father. It was an emotional conversation.

When it ended, she said she would talk to Carlo's son and try to convince him to bring his father to her studio tomorrow to meet them. She told them she would do everything she could to make it happen.

In the meantime, she rang a restaurateur friend and booked the pair of visitors a table for dinner where they would be treated as special guests and fed the best regional produce.

When they left the lawyer's office and were safely out in the street, Anthony burst into tears.

At the restaurant, he phoned Carmel to tell her what had happened.

'I remember that being both a really emotional conversation but also really difficult, because it was really noisy and loud and I was back in quiet Marrickville trying to hear,' Carmel says.

Anthony's head was spinning as he tried to describe and just process it all. He had a father *and* a brother and maybe he would meet them.

Wow, he kept thinking. *Wow*.

Next morning, back at the hotel, they met up with Mal again over breakfast. He had been adopted as a child and only met his birth mother 11 years before, so he could understand how Anthony was feeling.

Mal and Anthony were still receiving constant updates on the Liberal leadership. It was Sunday night at home and the vote was Tuesday morning.

But Anthony's primary focus was on what the day would bring here in Italy. He had no meetings scheduled, just the return trip to Rome in the late afternoon.

Their go-between had suggested they come back to Barletta first thing and wait for a call from her to let them know the result of her talk with Carlo's son. Lisa was anxious that it might not work out and that this could be their only chance. But Anthony was more philosophical.

'My attitude was that if it happened, it happened,' he says. 'It couldn't be organised any other way. I had a fixed schedule in Rome and London that couldn't be changed. If it didn't happen, then I'd come back another time.'

It was his way of keeping expectations – and emotions – in check.

They arrived in Barletta and took a look around town. Its most famous landmarks are its castle fortress dating back to the Crusades, and its Colossus, the bronze statue of an eastern Roman emperor standing more than five metres tall.

The locals call the statue Eraclio. Mythology has it that Eraclio was a huge man, who'd saved the city from foreign invaders who were approaching the coast, by waiting on the shore and pretending he was crying.

When the raiders asked why he was so upset, he told them it was because he was Barletta's smallest citizen and the whole town taunted him about his paltry size. The folk story has it that the invaders fled, fearing they could not defeat what was clearly a community of giants.

This was a city built on a tale of quick thinking, courage and trickery – the perfect place for a politician.

Lisa's phone rang and it was good news. The lawyer said her friend would be at her studio at 11 am, with his father Carlo. Waiting for the appointed time, she, Mal and Anthony went for coffee. It finally hit him.

'Then I was really emotional,' he says. 'It was like a flood over me. So I went for a walk just to breathe.'

When he rejoined the others – and just before they left Mal again and headed off to the studio – the trio ducked into a bar. The two blokes had a neat shot of whisky each. Mal wished them well and off they went.

When the lawyer welcomed them back, she was there alone.

After a couple of minutes the buzzer went and in they came – Carlo, his son, and a third person, his daughter. Anthony had two siblings.

Carlo was slight but quite tall, clean-shaven and well dressed. He seemed fit, if a little hard of hearing. *There is some resemblance*, Lisa thought.

He walked in and, without speaking, opened his arms for an embrace.

'I was in tears,' Anthony says. 'I think everyone was a little bit in tears.'

They sat down and began to talk. Carlo still had some English and used a little of it, though he mostly spoke in Italian.

'I said, "You knew my mother,"' Anthony says. 'He acknowledged that straightaway. There was no "Maybe I'm not your father". There was none of that.'

Carlo asked what Anthony calls 'sensible questions' – about Maryanne and what had happened to her.

'He was a gentleman,' Anthony says. 'He was a class act. I liked him. I could certainly see what my mother would have seen in him. He was charming. He was smart. He cared a lot about his family. He was very generous. He was interesting, hardworking.'

Anthony's sister was amazed that he shared their surname.

'She couldn't get her head around it,' he says.

Gradually small fragments of Carlo's life entered the conversation, enough for a blurry picture to emerge. He had been married to his wife – mother of his son and daughter – since 1963, the year Anthony was born in Sydney.

After he left the shipping line, Carlo had worked two jobs – as a school janitor and the maître d' at a local restaurant.

Anthony had no doubt he had found his father at last. But there was one more thing he wanted to do.

Before they took their own photographs together and said farewell, with Anthony vowing to bring his own family back the following year, he pulled out the black-and-white photograph taken on the ship 47 years earlier.

There was his mother and her travelling companions smiling up at them and the suave Italian steward standing beside. He wanted to make absolutely *sure*.

He showed the photo to the Albanese family and they recognised it.

To Carlo, it was especially familiar. For all those years, he had kept a copy of it as well.

CHAPTER 21

Going Back

Anthony had many questions for Carlo but there were some he decided not to ask. In the course of their conversation, his father had said he had heard no news from Maryanne after her return to Australia, suggesting he hadn't known of Anthony's existence.

Anthony's instincts told him his mother would have at least tried to let her baby's father know, and she had told him she did. But if there had been a letter, perhaps it had never reached him – it really wasn't clear.

Anthony decided that having finally found Carlo, there was nothing to be gained from asking directly.

'I didn't want to push it,' he says. 'It was what it was. He remembered my mother but it was a long time ago – almost 50 years by then.'

He could have been forgiven if he'd had some mixed feelings. Carlo's choices – as much as Maryanne's – had contributed to his mother's life's circumstances and also to his own. But any anger Anthony may have felt towards his absent father back in his teens had subsided.

The warmth of his family's acceptance – and especially his father's – ensured none re-emerged. Their meeting was a resolution that healed some hurt.

'Relationships are complex,' he says, simply.

Anthony was pleased to learn at least a little of the life Carlo had led.

'It was a relatively simple existence in the latter part of his life, but in the first half he had been all around the world and he talked about that,' Anthony says. 'He clearly liked travel and it was an exciting life for a young bloke from the south of Italy.'

He was a dignified man.

'In the way that he carried himself.'

As they parted, Carlo embraced him again.

After such an intense experience, Anthony's return to Rome that Sunday afternoon and the scheduled onward journey and important speech meant he had to snap back into work mode. It wasn't easy.

When Lisa arrived at his Rome hotel early on Wednesday morning to take him to the airport for the flight to London, the emotions rose again, and again, he wept.

'It's been so hard,' he said.

She felt honoured to have been able to help.

By the time he returned to Australia, Anthony was more buoyant. The London leg of his trip had been very successful, with Australia elected to the International Maritime Organisation and new rules agreed to introduce stronger protection against maritime accidents.

As Anthony flew in, Kevin Rudd was preparing to fly out for what would prove to be the ill-fated United Nations climate change talks in Copenhagen, Denmark.

With the Senate's failure to pass his legislation to establish an emissions trading scheme, Kevin was placing great store in achieving an international agreement. It would have given him momentum to accuse the Opposition of being obstructionist and possibly to begin positioning for a double-dissolution election on the issue in the new year.

Some of his colleagues were urging him in that direction, regardless. Anthony was among those with whom he discussed the prospects of a negotiated global agreement on emissions reduction in Copenhagen.

As shadow Environment Minister, Anthony had been to two such international meetings – in Nairobi, in Kenya, and Montreal, Canada – and on both occasions 11th-hour agreements had been forged, notably in Montreal where all-night talks preceded the deal.

The experience gave him confidence that the same could happen in Copenhagen and he put this view to Kevin. But the competing interests and issues at these talks were more complex and the outcome was not what they'd hoped.

'I had higher expectations than what came out of it, so I was disappointed,' Anthony says. 'But it didn't mean the issue would go away because climate change wasn't about a political process, it was about the science. And the world will have to respond to the science.'

The failure of nations to reach agreement in Copenhagen – and the doubt cast over proposals for a United States emissions trading scheme – had emboldened the new Opposition Leader, Tony Abbott, and he was campaigning full throttle against emissions trading in Australia, calling the scheme 'a great big new tax on everything'. It was the beginning of an election year and Tony's lines were getting traction.

Anthony says he wasn't part of the discussions which led to the subsequent decision to shelve the emissions trading scheme for at least three years – a move which caused a sharp downturn in Kevin's public-approval rating.

Kevin had declared climate change to be the great moral challenge of modern times, so to set aside the mechanism he'd said was needed to address it caused sudden disillusionment.

'I was opposed to deferring and put that case,' Anthony says. 'Certainly Kevin would have known that was my position.'

Anthony would also be strenuously opposed to the actions of some colleagues that followed that decision, a panic-driven response that would send Labor into a downward spiral and see three changes of leader in as many years.

In 2010, Easter fell in early April and the four-day public holiday provided a chance for Anthony to do what he'd promised his new Italian family five months earlier – bring his partner and son back to Italy to meet them.

He'd brought home photographs and stories of the life-changing encounter but he really wanted Carmel and Nathan to meet his father, brother and sister, and for all of them to meet his siblings' children and his father's wife.

Unsurprisingly, Carlo's wife had not come to the original meeting. But her acceptance in the face of such an unexpected development in her family's life would prove to be the mark of an exceptional woman.

Despite Anthony and Carmel's plans to travel to Italy as a family, politics would conspire to keep Carmel back at home.

The previous few years had been tumultuous in NSW state politics and had seen Carmel's career accelerate. She had switched from the NSW Legislative Council to the Legislative Assembly in 2005, when the unexpected resignation of Premier Bob Carr and two other ministers led to a series of by-elections and opened up an opportunity to move to the more powerful Lower House.

Morris Iemma became Premier and Carmel contested and won the Assembly seat of Marrickville.

She was re-elected at the 2007 state election and opted to return to the backbench to allow her to be more available for son Nathan, as federal Labor's victory in Canberra increased Anthony's responsibilities. But her voluntary retirement from the ministry would only last a year.

In 2008, she was drafted back onto the front bench when her Left faction colleagues elected her to become Deputy Premier. She was sworn in as NSW Minister for Commerce and Minister for Climate Change and the Environment, just as Anthony was being shifted out of the same portfolio federally.

In 2009, when Kristina Keneally took over as Premier, Carmel remained as deputy and took on the important health portfolio. Unfortunately, her family's Easter holiday plans coincided with Prime Minister Kevin Rudd's drive to overhaul funding arrangements for health nationally. The negotiations were intense and controversial and at a crucial stage. Carmel couldn't go.

Anthony and Nathan flew to Rome just ahead of the Easter break. Ambassador Amanda Vanstone and her husband, Tony, had invited them to stay at their official residence and Lisa took them there, introducing Nathan in particular to the Vanstones' beloved dog, a Weimaraner called Gus.

Nathan has inherited his father's adoration of canine creatures and fell in love with the giant Gus, who towered over the nine-year-old. Gus was equally besotted and Amanda enjoyed watching them play. She also observed Anthony's attention and devotion to his son.

'I think he's a good father,' she says.

After a day of sightseeing to shake off the jetlag, Anthony and Nathan picked up a hire car on Good Friday and headed south to Barletta, navigating their way out of Rome in typically crazy traffic.

One lunch stop later – and after the surreptitious purchase of one chocolate rabbit to brighten Nathan's Easter Sunday – they arrived back in the quaint southern Italian town. They were staying at a recommended local establishment: St Patrick's Irish pub.

'The best place to stay in Barletta is an Irish pub,' Anthony says.

On Saturday morning, they were out early, Anthony taking Nathan to the castle fortress and showing him the town. They visited the site of the Disfida di Barletta, a tournament fought in 1503 between French and Italian knights, sparked after a French knight drank too much local wine and badmouthed the Italians.

Back at St Patrick's, Anthony's brother came to collect them, driving with them back through the town to his father's home.

The welcome there was excited and warm. Carlo introduced his wife.

Anthony's sister, his brother's wife and their children were also there. Young Nathan was a bit overwhelmed in the noisy hubbub of greetings and introductions.

They were shown around the flat, which was full of the things Carlo had collected on his travels abroad in his youth. Anthony was amazed to see so many familiar items, the same small souvenirs with which his mother had decorated his own home growing up. *Had they bought them together?* he wondered but did not ask.

There was still a lot to talk about and he wanted some time with his father alone. But it was proving difficult.

In the months since Anthony had met his father and siblings, they had exchanged snippets of personal information and more flowed as they all talked. His sister marvelled at Anthony's constant travel schedule.

The Barletta Albaneses had done some cyber-research on Anthony since his visit and now had a better idea of who he was – and indeed who his partner, Carmel, was – and their standing in politics in Australia. As politicians aren't generally terribly well regarded in the south of Italy, they were more intrigued than awed.

Anthony came armed with Australiana for the whole family – toy koalas and kangaroos, T-shirts and some surf gear for his brother.

The gifts flowed both ways. They gave Anthony a print from a regional artist.

'They bought Nathan a little name bracelet in silver with his name engraved on it,' Anthony says. 'That was a particular tradition.'

Nobody need have worried about a shortage of chocolate. Nathan was also given a large egg, which Italian tradition demanded had to be smashed before eating.

For Easter Sunday lunch, the whole extended family went to a local restaurant, the restaurant where Carlo had been maître d' for years before his retirement. They were treated to an enormous feast, with Carlo insisting on carrying out some of the plates of food himself.

'That was just phenomenal,' Anthony recalls. 'The food just kept coming and coming.'

The lunch stretched through the afternoon and into the early evening, but rather than calling an end to the festivities, the family took them on to the nearby fishing village of Trani, for ice-cream.

'Not that we needed more food.'

Afterwards, they walked around Trani and Anthony had the chance to talk to Carlo again – about the past, his mother and life in general.

Carlo had spoken good English when he was younger but hadn't used it in years, so it was rusty and a bit hesitant. Anthony had no Italian so there were limits to what they could discuss without calling on others to translate.

There were times when the language difficulty covered for what might otherwise have been awkwardness. But Anthony enjoyed the chance to finally be with his father, alone.

'We had some time,' he says. 'We walked a long way.'

The family's joy at having them there was so genuine – unconditional – that it was almost overwhelming.

On his return home, Anthony would reflect on the trip, telling one of the few colleagues with whom he had shared the story of his search, Mark Butler, that it was particularly special to be part of a nuclear family group.

'My sense was there was closure and that was important,' Mark says. 'One of the things he really talked a lot about was just being there with the family – being part of a group.'

He had long been welcomed into Carmel's large and bustling family so it wasn't new in that sense. But it was a different experience, having grown up an only child, to be suddenly surrounded by his own siblings and their families. Anthony wished Carmel could have been there.

'They really wanted to meet Carmel,' he says. 'They were disappointed that she had to pull out. And we promised to come back – which we did the next year.'

Anthony would manage another quick side-trip down to Barletta by train in December 2010, after attending a global transport ministers' conference in Rome, and Carmel would finally meet the Italian family in July 2011.

She, Anthony and Nathan visited Barletta as part of a European holiday that also took in Venice, Paris and London.

If it was possible for the Italian family to be even more welcoming, they were.

'I was amazed by their incredible generosity at welcoming us into their home and their desire to spend time with us when we were there – and look after us so wonderfully,' Carmel says.

The Italian Albaneses had filled their weekend visit with activities, including some beach time to enjoy the heat of the northern summer.

'It was just lovely to be able to connect with that side of Anthony's family,' Carmel says.

She admits to having been a little nervous ahead of the introduction and found the Italians were too, discovering that her inability to join her husband and son the previous year had left them with a certain image of a high-powered politician. Her work was very far from their day-to-day experience.

'So they had this impression that I was going to be this very driven hard-bitten career woman,' Carmel says. 'Because I remember at some stage they expressed some surprise that I was fairly down to earth and normal and natural.'

It didn't take long for any mutual anxiety to dissipate. Anthony's 2010 visit had cemented the Albanese-Tebbutt clan as part of the extended family. On that 2010 trip, after the long and intense Easter Sunday family reunion, Anthony and Nathan had said their goodbyes late in the evening. They were exhausted from two long, emotional days.

On Monday morning, they began the journey back to Rome, but spent a few days exploring Pompeii and the Amalfi Coast. Anthony and Nathan made their way to the capital by road and headed home on Thursday after a packed week.

He had no idea, but Anthony would be flying back into a gathering domestic political storm.

As the weather cooled in autumnal Canberra, there was unrest inside the Labor Government. The months leading into winter are the most colourful and spectacular in the national capital with its European trees sprinkled liberally among the evergreen natives. In 2010, the simmering politics would prove at least as vivid.

Quietly, Kevin Rudd's Cabinet took the decision to defer the proposed emissions trading scheme. As the federal budget loomed on the second Tuesday in May, Kevin was working on a strategy for making the decision public with minimal political damage, when a leak to *The Sydney Morning Herald*'s correspondent Lenore Taylor pre-empted him spectacularly, splashed across the front page on 27 April.

Kevin Rudd has said since that he believed it was a deliberate move on the part of persons unnamed to destabilise his leadership.

The public response was instant and brutal. Kevin's popularity plunged and support for the Labor Party followed. Panic began to set in.

A separate plan to introduce a tax on mining 'super' profits drew hostility from the mining industry, which accused the Government of failing to consult. The industry's concerted effort to roll out a campaign in protest saw criticism rain down from almost every influential advertising outlet available.

The Government changed the policy after just three weeks to redefine a 'super' profit and let the mining companies reap more before the tax cut in, but it wasn't enough.

As Parliament approached its final fortnight in June before rising for the winter break – which along with its equivalent at year's end is known as 'the killing season' for being the period in which struggling leaders are most vulnerable to being replaced – there was dangerous muttering in the Labor ranks.

Anthony picked it up and went to see Kevin at The Lodge.

'I went to basically say to him, "You need to just be aware there's a bit of a drumbeat around." I always thought, though . . . that there wouldn't be a challenge. I didn't see that as a real possibility. I saw it as just chatter.'

He believed it was coming from the corners where the unhappy MPs lived, those who thought their own roles in the government should have been greater. That wasn't unusual.

'Politics in general has people who are disgruntled,' he says.

He picked up idle chatter – the odd throwaway line.

'Some people [were] saying, "We've got to do something,"' he recalls. 'But I didn't think that would galvanise into a challenge. And I remain of the view that a majority of people did not want a challenge to happen. It's just that a majority of people once it was happening viewed that the way to end it was to support the challenger.'

NSW frontbenchers Tony Burke and Mark Arbib had started to think and talk about the possibility of change. Victorians Bill Shorten and David Feeney were part of the conversation, as were South Australian Don Farrell and West Australian Mark Bishop.

With the Newspoll of that week showing Labor ahead 52–48, Anthony thought the reaction of those starting to talk was not real-world.

'It's a reflection of how the bubble in Canberra can distort things,' he says. 'People are away. It can be like a school camp where people don't know what's been going on outside.'

On Monday, 21 June, a colleague raised with him explicitly the possibility of changing leaders.

'I dismissed it as "Don't be ridiculous. What do you do then? How do you defend the Government's record? We've got an election in a few months." And they said, "Yeah, you're right. If anything is happening we'll come back to you."'

Two nights later, he was shocked to see reports on ABC TV's 7 pm news that deputy leader Julia Gillard had gone to see Kevin about the leadership.

As the wider caucus – frontbench and backbench alike – tried to figure out what was going on, a group of former Kim Beazley supporters gathered in Treasurer Wayne Swan's office. Wayne was there, and Anthony's close friend and Left colleague Jenny Macklin, along with Stephen Smith, Chris Bowen and Stephen Conroy.

They watched as news of an imminent leadership challenge was rolling out across the national media like a toxic blanket.

'Originally the feeling was "We've all stuck together, we've got to stick together on this,"' Anthony says. 'People were worried about the government. It was uncharted territory.'

Anthony wanted the Cabinet to resist what was a move brought on by some relative newcomers who weren't senior ministers and, he argued, had never experienced Opposition, and had no appreciation of how hard it was to get in to government, let alone to actually govern.

'If the Cabinet had just said no, it wouldn't have happened,' he maintains.

He said to his colleagues that, once done, this could not be undone.

'If this happens, we will be killing two Labor prime ministers.'

But there were those in the room who took the decision that it had already gone too far to turn back. A number would decide to vote for Julia Gillard. Wayne Swan would become her Deputy Prime Minister.

After maybe an hour of discussing the unfolding drama and watching the awful coverage, Anthony went through to the Prime Minister's office.

Kevin's door was closed and his status was 'do not disturb'. Anthony ignored the protests of staff and burst through the door.

Inside were Kevin, Julia and John Faulkner engaged in this surreal negotiation. They didn't have a television on. They had no idea of the meltdown going on outside.

'He [Anthony] was agitated, personally agitated,' Julia Gillard recalls of his entry into the office where she and Kevin were meeting. 'And because we were in this bubble of stillness not with Sky TV or anything else on – the fact that it was all breaking minute by minute on the news – neither of us knew that. So Albo was personally agitated and the content of what he had to relay . . . was quite startling to us as well.'

Anthony told them that while they were talking, the Labor Government was dying.

'I basically said to them, "The Government's falling out here; you've got to stop talking and make a decision,"' he says in 2016.

'I basically accused the three of them of being irresponsible. The government is melting down and they're in a room . . . It was obvious to me that the longer the discussion went, the harder it was to backtrack from it.'

He left again immediately. Kevin recalls him coming in one more time.

Back in Anthony's own office there was also a gathering. Members of the Left who had been equally blindsided by the events had gone there to try to find out what was going on.

When the meeting between Kevin, Julia and John Faulkner eventually ended and Julia left, Kevin told Anthony that they had reached agreement about a succession and there would be no challenge. So that's what he told others.

'I went and told people, "Well, it's off,"' he says. 'And then it was back on again.'

After Julia had decided to proceed with a challenge and Kevin had held his late-night news conference, Anthony returned to Kevin's office and stayed very late.

'Albo was playing the role of the loyal deputy that Julia Gillard should have been playing,' Kevin says.

As he made calls to gauge colleagues' views, it was becoming clear that there was a growing mood for a change.

He had a difficult conversation with his leader and friend. Anthony told Kevin he still supported him but that the momentum was with Julia and it might be better if she was elected unopposed.

'I was convinced that he couldn't win and I put that to him at night,' he says. 'I was the one who had to tell him. It's a difficult thing to have to say to someone.'

Kevin listened but found it hard to believe. When they parted in the early hours, Anthony wasn't sure what the Prime Minister would decide to do the next day.

In the morning, Anthony received more calls from colleagues who had decided to back the challenger. He went back to Kevin's office early and, again, suggested he consider standing aside – this time for his own sake, as well as for the future of the Labor Government.

As he joined John Faulkner and others walking with Kevin to the caucus room, he still didn't know what the Prime Minister had decided.

'I'd made up my mind by the time I went into the room,' Kevin says.

At that point, as they walked in, Kevin turned to Anthony and said, 'Albo, it'll be alright.'

Once the doors had closed behind them, Kevin told the Labor MPs and senators he would not be contesting the ballot. Julia Gillard was elected unopposed. Wayne Swan was elected deputy, also unopposed.

Anthony maintains it was all utterly unnecessary, a move which would create inter-generational trauma for Labor, made by people who should have held their nerve and had greater respect for the office of Prime Minister.

'They need to not be so concerned about the noise of politics,' he says. 'They need to be more concerned about the *substance* of politics. Was our position on the need to tackle climate change right? Yes, it was. Were there mistakes made? Clearly there were – including the fact that Kevin didn't have enough goodwill from enough caucus members to fall back on. He's got to bear some of the responsibility for that as well.'

Despite his support for the man she'd ousted, Julia Gillard retained Anthony's services as Leader of the House. She was not inclined to give Kevin the job he wanted – Foreign Minister.

Soon after her elevation, during the question-and-answer session following a National Press Club address, the first salvo was fired in what was to become a guerrilla war of leaks undermining her leadership.

Nine Network chief correspondent Laurie Oakes asked her if it was true that in his office that night, she'd given Kevin an undertaking to wait until the end of the year, and he had similarly agreed to stand aside then if things hadn't improved.

'We went into that discussion on the basis that it was a confidential discussion between colleagues, and I intend to respect that confidence for the rest of my life,' she responded.

Three weeks after she seized the leadership, Julia called a federal election for 21 August.

The leaking against her continued, with stories that she had opposed paid parental leave and a proposed pension increase when they were before Cabinet. Kevin denied being the leaker. But some colleagues privately – and eventually publicly – accused him.

'I've always thought it was Kevin Rudd,' Jenny Macklin told ABC journalist Sarah Ferguson in her 2015 series on the Labor leadership woes, *The Killing Season*.

Election night delivered in effect a dead heat. Neither side had achieved a clear majority and negotiations began with the Greens and the newly elected crossbench over which party might be able to form government.

Quickly, Julia signed an agreement with the Greens. Tasmanian independent Andrew Wilkie also gave her his backing, but she still needed support from two more MPs to be able to argue she had more than the coalition – which had only secured support from Queensland maverick independent Bob Katter – and should have the opportunity to form a government.

As Leader of the House, Anthony was engaged in the negotiations. Julia groups their negotiations into categories. First, there was 'How would we work together?' and 'What would we collaborate on?' Julia concentrated on those.

Then there was a third category, particularly engaging crossbench independents Tony Windsor and Rob Oakeshott: 'We should have a better Parliament for everyone'.

'Albo basically took responsibility for that,' Julia says.

Reforming the running of Parliament was one of the conditions the two independents placed on agreeing to support Labor in forming a government. Tony Windsor refers to it by the nickname the talks were instantly given: 'the kum ba yah stuff'.

'I was always a bit cynical about some of that stuff because I'd been through another hung Parliament where you make the changes to the standing orders for the good of the nation forever, and as soon as a majority gets in, they walk away from it anyway,' he says.

After the two independents made their choice and endorsed Labor, the Parliament got underway. In order to try to achieve harmony – or minimise disharmony – Julia gave Kevin what he wanted and made him Foreign Minister.

As Leader of the House, Anthony liaised with Julia several times a day and the crossbench almost as often. The relationships he had built and maintained – including with Bob Katter – became invaluable.

His frontbench colleague Chris Bowen says he 'had a knack of talking to Katter, talking to the independents'.

'He did a lot of work. A lot of work.'

Bob Katter is full of praise.

'Albanese has what used to be called in Australia the common touch. He's comfortable with ordinary people and that is a very rare commodity in Canberra. These people will love the downtrodden or grovel to the rich. Albo treats them all the same . . . I have immense respect for Albanese. You could only describe his performance as brilliant.'

'He was the absolute glue in the machinery,' Tony Windsor says.

'He was possibly the hardest worker Gillard had in trying to make a difficult circumstance work . . . It was more than just doing his job. He was very committed to try and make it work and he was very good to deal with.'

Tony says negotiations – whether with Anthony or Julia – were calm. The independents had made it clear they wouldn't be rushed on legislation. Anthony would run interference between the crossbench and ministers, frustrated that things were moving too slowly.

When Communications Minister Stephen Conroy proposed a controversial set of new controls over the media, Anthony did not advocate for them strongly, according to independent Bob Katter. 'Sensible people like Albanese were desperately looking for a way out and he agreed with Julia that it didn't pass the laugh test,' Bob Katter says.

He says Anthony did not ask him to oppose the legislation. 'Albo in that case maintained a silence and just said, "What are you going to do?"'

Bob told him he couldn't support the move. The bills were withdrawn.

'I had regard for him before it and real respect for him at the end of it,' Tony says. 'To come out the end of it with all the slush and mud that was thrown at everybody [and] have a lasting regard for anybody is a bit of an achievement.'

He has equal regard for Julia Gillard and the other Minister with whom he dealt most constructively, Simon Crean.

In managing the government's legislative agenda in the hung Parliament – which involved constant negotiation – Anthony drew on his experiences back in Sussex Street.

'It was the perfect preparation for being Leader of the House in a minority Parliament, because you had to think in advance what was going to happen.'

There were times when staying in government was a day-to-day and even hour-by-hour proposition.

'There were days when we didn't know whether we'd make it to the other end of the day,' says then government whip, Joel Fitzgibbon. 'There were votes we didn't know whether we'd win, literally when we walked into the chamber or even when we sat in the chamber waiting for the bells to stop ringing and waiting for everyone to come in. So it was an extraordinary effort on his part.'

Anthony recalls his colleague and deputy Leader of the House, Stephen Smith, coming into his office at 7.30 every morning before their tactics meeting, saying, 'We're still here.'

'And he'd do it the next day and the next day. And we passed 595 pieces of legislation.'

At one stage, when a piece of legislation suddenly proceeded to a vote unexpectedly, Anthony discovered the independents were not supporting the Government and the bill was going to fail. If the Government began to lose votes on the floor, it could lead to a vote of no confidence and ultimately the Government could fall.

He enlisted Stephen Smith's help and together they worked on delaying proceedings and engaging in the art of persuasion.

'We didn't have the numbers,' Anthony says. 'We got a message from the crossbenchers. They were going to vote against us.'

Stephen Smith says Anthony had just got to his feet to speak when that message was conveyed.

'Albo just looked at me and said, "I don't care what it takes, just fix it,"' Stephen says.

Anthony then kept on talking while Stephen went to talk to the independents.

'He was on his feet for 15 minutes and during that 15 minutes the only instruction I had from Albo was: "Just fix it."'

He talked them around.

Stephen Smith had first met Anthony in the men's room at a Labor function at Canberra's Lobby Restaurant when he was Assistant General Secretary of the NSW ALP.

'He was smart, he was tough,' Stephen says. 'He would always have a go to try and achieve the position that he wanted. But he was also clearly in my view a decent bloke and someone who you could have a stoush with, but then that night you could have a beer with. And someone who, if over that beer you did a deal, then that deal would stick.'

That characteristic helped in the 43rd Parliament.

Another time, the opposition parties in the Senate attached an appropriation measure – something requiring money – to a bill that wasn't supposed to contain one. There are constitutional rules around how appropriations work and this was not within them.

When the bill came back to the House of Representatives, several of the independents were prepared to join the Opposition in voting for it. But because it hadn't followed proper process, the Governor-General would not have been able to give it the required royal assent.

'It would have led to a crisis,' Anthony says. '. . . You would have had a conflict between the Parliament and the Governor-General and where that led was unknown territory constitutionally.'

Quietly, Anthony set the bill aside while he tried to negotiate a way out.

'We had an issue that went for weeks, I think, without the Opposition knowing precisely how serious all that was. With, I think, only me and Julia and Wayne probably knowing how serious it was.'

It, too, was resolved. He got the numbers to remove the amendment.

During this time, Anthony also developed a good working relationship with his opposite number, Christopher Pyne.

'When I gave Anthony a commitment I never broke it,' Christopher says. 'When he gave me a commitment he never broke it. And there were times when we were asked by both our leaderships to do things and I remember saying, "I can't do that."'

Anthony says occasionally the Liberal leadership would veto an undertaking Christopher had given.

'He has never . . . consciously said he would do something and done the opposite,' Anthony says.

He says Christopher 'enjoys the game' of politics and he factored that into negotiations.

While each of their leaders was trying to persuade Rob Oakeshott and Tony Windsor to help them form government after the 2007 election, Christopher and Anthony worked together in their talks on parliamentary reform to try to minimise promising to introduce procedures that might be unworkable.

For example, Rob Oakeshott wanted ministers to be forced to attend Question Time and answer questions without any notes.

But both Anthony and Christopher thought this would lead to inaccurate answers and accidental misleading of Parliament, which were not in the interest of either side or the public.

'On some of the parliamentary reform stuff, we cooperated to tell the crossbenchers that, no, neither side is going to do that,' Anthony says.

Christopher had noticed Anthony when he had given his inflammatory speech about John Howard, when he'd first arrived.

'I thought, "This is a person I should get to know because he's obviously got a bit of get up and go." And I thought, obviously he's decided that . . . in the jungle in which we live he's going to be one of those catch-and-kill people, as opposed to one of the people who get along by going along and who stay below the radar for potentially 20 years and leave with their pension.'

He thought Anthony seemed interesting, potentially dangerous and should be observed closely. Others were amused at the dynamic.

'He wasn't averse to having a go about Pyne's integrity,' Tony Windsor says of Anthony.

But it was done with good humour, which he also used to defuse difficult situations.

'You could imagine him as a child in kindergarten,' he says. 'He'd have this mischievous half-grin on him whilst he was stealing a pencil from the girl next door.'

Anthony and Christopher have forged an unusual friendship across the divide. They are tough and deliberately provocative but not personally insulting. Christopher notes that when others in the Labor Party were calling him a 'mincing poodle', Anthony never did.

'In Tom Uren's world that would be overstepping the mark and Anthony is a true disciple of Tom Uren,' he says. 'Tom Uren was an old-schooler and Anthony is an old-schooler because of that. I'm an old-schooler and my mentors are people like Steele Hall and Andrew Peacock and Amanda Vanstone and Robert Hill, who also wouldn't do that.'

He hopes he and Anthony can set an example for new MPs that denigrating personal insults are not necessary.

'It's a rare relationship,' Christopher says. 'I have no other friend in the Labor Party.'

Nevertheless he calls Anthony 'an old Marxist' and isn't sure he'd ever be Prime Minister.

'He's an unreconstructed lefty,' Christopher says. 'He has no credibility on the economy and he's too emotional about it. The public would think he's a bit emotional about what he believes in, whereas you have to be a bit dispassionate as the Prime Minister.'

One of Anthony's Labor colleagues uses a similar analogy to Christopher when dissecting how 'Albo' wields his charm with the unsuspecting.

'He seems like a real politician and quite often talks like one,' the colleague says. 'And they're actually not 100 per cent sure if they need to check their pockets after they've shaken hands with him. And those gut reactions are actually probably spot on.'

Julia Gillard expresses it slightly differently.

'Albo is a persuasive person. He's good at talking people into things. He does his own version of soft cop, hard cop – not needing the second police officer, just doing it all himself.'

Soon after the 2010 election, Anthony manoeuvred an arrangement to help Labor maintain its numbers on the floor by breaking with tradition and putting an Opposition member in as Speaker, robbing the coalition of a vote.

The Labor MP in line for the position, Harry Jenkins, was unhappy but as it was about numbers and the Government's survival, the plan went ahead.

Four coalition MPs clandestinely expressed an interest. Anthony will only name two of them. The Government initially offered the job to Alex Somlyay, the coalition's whip. But he came under so much pressure from his Queensland

Liberal National Party that he backed out. Labor's attention then turned to another LNP member who had fallen out with his coalition colleagues, Peter Slipper.

The completion of negotiations to form government then gave Labor enough of a buffer that it did not need to execute its plan immediately. But two years later, in 2012, when Tasmanian independent Andrew Wilkie withdrew his support for the Government, it had to find a way to get an extra vote – or take one from the Opposition. It decided to take action.

Peter Slipper would become a controversial figure for his activities outside the Parliament, becoming embroiled in messy legal proceedings with former staff member James Ashby, who accused him of sexual harassment. The sordid details of the case – including crude text messages that were highly degrading to women – would play themselves out as part of the high-stakes parliamentary contest. The Federal Court found a number of people had used the case as a political weapon.

While he condemns the nature of Peter Slipper's personal behaviour, Anthony reserves greater condemnation for those he believes engaged in a conspiracy to generate the legal case, force him out as Speaker and bring down the government.

'The issue was someone can be engaged in behaviour that people don't approve of, but that isn't grounds to bring down a government,' he says.

The revelations would see Julia Gillard give her now-famous 'misogyny' speech in Parliament, attacking Opposition Leader Tony Abbott as part of the Government's defence of the Speaker, who was allowed to resign rather than suffer the ignominy of being forced out of his chair.

Anthony acknowledges the decision to put Peter Slipper in as Speaker was controversial even within the Government.

'Some people didn't support it,' he says. 'It wasn't unanimous but it was overwhelmingly agreed to.'

But Peter was deemed to have performed well.

'People across the Parliament regarded him as a very good Speaker,' Anthony insists.

But the sustained attacks took their toll. He, Julia Gillard and others in the Government were concerned for Peter Slipper's well-being.

'I think it says a lot about her character that at a time when the government she led was vulnerable, she was concerned about the welfare of this man who she didn't know very well,' he says. 'And she was.'

In the middle of all the white-hot controversy, Liberal MP Alex Somlyay – who had been pressured out of accepting Labor's offer of the speakership in the first place – contacted Anthony.

'While it was all happening, Somlyay offered to become the Speaker,' Anthony says. He says Alex indicated he was willing to take the job, removing one more vote from the coalition on the floor and giving Labor a buffer.

But Peter Slipper had become an independent, so his return to the parliamentary benches was not giving the coalition any particular advantage. Labor didn't need Alex's help.

'I didn't think very much about it,' Anthony says. 'After everything we'd gone through I just dismissed it.'

The Government had also been under fire over the activities of Labor MP Craig Thomson, accused of misappropriating funds belonging to the Health Services Union when he was its secretary, and spending them on, among other things, prostitutes.

The Opposition showed mercy to neither, nor to Julia Gillard, who had already been subjected to a sustained campaign against her from inside and outside the Parliament that had more venom for the fact she was female.

In both cases, Anthony says he was concerned about the men's mental health and well-being.

There had been much greater awareness of the real and direct consequences of pressure on politicians since MPs had lost a Labor colleague, Victorian MP Greg Wilton, to suicide in 2000. Before that, in 1997, another Labor Senate colleague had attempted to take his own life but survived.

'Since Greg Wilton, I made a decision as did other members of Parliament at that time that we would never allow a colleague to be isolated and do nothing about it,' Anthony says.

Christopher Pyne insists the coalition pulled back in both the Slipper and Thomson cases when it was clear people's health was at stake.

'People might not have realised at the time, but we did actually take our foot off the accelerator on both of them,' Christopher says.

Anthony pays tribute to the Nationals' Barnaby Joyce, who would go on to become Deputy Prime Minister, for the sensitivity he showed when some of his colleagues were making political mileage over the fact that Anthony had been seen having a beer with Craig.

'Barnaby Joyce went up in my estimation by understanding that and backing that in the next day.'

Through 2011, Julia Gillard's government was under constant attack, with the coalition and its high-profile supporters among media commentators insisting it was illegitimate and treating it as such.

Opposition Leader Tony Abbott addressed a rally out the front of Parliament House, with protesters waving placards behind him declaring, 'Ditch the witch'.

'I think their behaviour towards Julia as Prime Minister was reprehensible,' Anthony says.

But she had also created some of her own problems. Having promised during the 2010 election campaign not to introduce a carbon tax, she then brought forward legislation to establish what was effectively the same thing – emissions trading, starting with a fixed carbon price.

Unsurprisingly, Tony Abbott opposed it forcefully and constantly.

When the coalition attacked in Parliament, Anthony attacked back. In a debate in November 2011, Anthony quoted the Liberals' hero, Sir Robert Menzies, back at them.

'On far too many questions we find our role to be simply that of the man who says no,' he said.

He accused Tony Abbott of having nodded off in Parliament, late the night before, saying he'd only woken up 'to say no, no, no'.

'This is someone who thinks he will sleepwalk into office,' he said.

He accused the Opposition Leader of being a human vuvuzela – the extremely irritating plastic horn whose loud, monotone blasts featured heavily at the World Cup soccer tournament in South Africa the previous year – and then did an impersonation of it himself. 'Noooo! Nooo! Nooo!'

'He turned the coalition into the No-alition,' he says.

Julia Gillard was managing attacks from outside the Government and from within. Early in 2012, tensions between Kevin Rudd and Julia Gillard had come to a head once again.

With Kevin in Washington DC, embarrassing video of him as Prime Minister swearing in frustration at public servants found its way into the public domain. Enraged at what he saw as deliberate undermining, Kevin resigned from the ministry while still overseas. The incident led to a leadership showdown, with Julia calling on a ballot for 27 February, saying it was time for some 'truth-telling'.

Anthony was dismayed at the parade of press conferences from his frontbench colleagues that followed, condemning Kevin's personal behaviour as Prime Minister, accusing him of being rude, ill-tempered and a poor administrator. They said they'd had trouble working with him before and that he would be a liability if returned.

As he watched one after the other attack their former leader, Anthony was imagining what their political opponents would do with the video clips, come the next election.

On Saturday, 25 February, an emotional Anthony Albanese called a news conference in his Sydney electorate to state his position. He said his mother had taught him to defend his beliefs, no matter what.

'I hope that when I leave politics people will regard me as a straightforward politician who said what he thought, who acted in the interest of the Labor Party – not because that was an end in itself, but because it is only the Australian Labor Party that can advance the long-term national interests of this country.

'Mum raised me with three great faiths: the Catholic Church, the South Sydney football club and Labor. She said to be true to all three. Well, with regard to the Catholic Church, I believe that the social justice values that I was raised with, I have kept. With regard to South Sydney, in spite of 41 years of constant disappointment, I have remained faithful. I have also remained faithful to the Labor Party.'

His emotion overtook him as he declared his loyalties to the party he loved – and ultimately to Kevin Rudd.

'I have devoted my life to advancing the cause of Labor. I have despaired in recent days as I have watched Labor's legacy in government be devalued. We have been a good government since 2007.'

He was turning back the words Julia Gillard had used when she took the leadership – that a 'good government' had lost its way.

He said the Government's difficulties could be traced to the night of Julia's coup in 2010.

'Labor is the party of fairness. It was not fair. It was wrong.'

He said his vote the following Monday would be his way of dissenting from the actions that were taken that June night in 2010. He had offered Julia his resignation but she declined it, saying he still had her confidence.

When a journalist noted his obvious emotion he responded that it was tough – traumatic – to be involved in something that was dividing his party.

'I like fighting Tories – that's what I do,' he said.

As he vowed he would, Anthony voted for Kevin. Julia was re-elected.

Jenny Macklin wasn't surprised by either Anthony's emotional outburst or Julia's response.

'He is Labor first,' Jenny says. 'And she was the Prime Minister. And there was absolutely no doubt that he was the best person to work with the crossbench.'

Anthony praised both Julia Gillard and Kevin Rudd and he still does, calling them both 'good people'.

'The amount of work that I saw both Kevin and Julia do was extraordinary,' he says. 'Both of them worked incredibly hard.'

Before Julia was Prime Minister, Anthony was not especially a fan. They had run up against each other as far back as student politics and she had been in the Ferguson 'soft' Left in Parliament.

'I guess I changed and she changed as well,' he says. 'All of that was totally irrelevant to actually running the government and how the government performed . . . I got to know her quite well and like her and I enjoyed her company. Before that time we hadn't spent too much time together. That's the truth.'

He says he was upfront about his support for Kevin.

'That didn't stop her from trusting me in the day-to-day activities which she did – and it was right to do so.'

Julia also defends her decision to keep him in his senior – and trusted – position.

'I could have taken that resignation but I formed the view for the effectiveness and stability of the government it was important he stay in that job,' she says.

Tony Windsor saw no evidence Anthony was disloyal to Julia – or dishonest.

'Out of all of them, he busted himself for her and she wasn't his natural choice,' Tony says.

Later in 2012, Julia asked Anthony to act as emissary and ask Kevin what he planned to do. Anthony returned to tell her he wasn't going anywhere.

In March 2013, rumours emerged of an imminent challenge. Anthony went to see Kevin.

'What are you doing? What's going on here?' he says he asked the former Prime Minister.

Kevin showed him a message he'd sent frontbencher Simon Crean earlier that morning, urging him not to do anything. Anthony relayed back to Julia and other colleagues that nothing was happening.

Right then, nothing was. But that changed before lunchtime.

Simon suddenly went public calling for a spill of leadership positions. Simon had been talking to those actively involved in plotting Kevin's return and promising he could deliver a swag of votes – a belief which proved unfounded.

Julia Gillard agreed to a ballot, and when the caucus gathered, Kevin did not nominate. He and Anthony left Simon to account for his move.

'We were both utterly stunned by the stupidity of Simon Crean's self-directed suicide mission,' Kevin says. 'Both he and I had concluded by then that a leadership change was simply not going to happen by the time of the next election. And the only reason that a leadership change subsequently occurred was the total outbreak of panic which occurred in June of 2013.'

Simon Crean was sacked from the frontbench and others among Kevin's supporters resigned their frontbench positions in what became the forerunner to an eventual successful challenge three months later.

Anthony was angry at what Simon had done – and especially on that day. Parliament was focused on the Government's apology to child migrants and others who had been forcibly adopted out or put into institutions.

Anthony was finding it especially moving and hard to hear. He reflected on the fact that had his mother succumbed to the pressure on her in hospital after his birth, he might have been in just this situation.

'That's the pressure that was put on my mum,' he says.

By June, Julia Gillard's leadership was under enormous strain. Some of the same people who had been instrumental in installing her had begun to plot her removal. They were planning to replace her with the man they had ousted in the first place – the same man Julia believed was responsible for the destabilisation and leaking which had seen her poll fortunes plummet.

She had scored some own-goals too, not least the 'no carbon tax' promise.

'The great tragedy is I think Julia was an outstanding Prime Minister,' Anthony says. 'Under the circumstances in particular of a minority Parliament, I can't think of anyone who would have handled it as well as she did.'

Nevertheless, in the end, he supported Kevin's return. Victorian MP Alan Griffin – Anthony's 'fun-faction' mate – and NSW MP Chris Bowen were organising Kevin's subterranean re-election bid.

How involved Anthony was in that is a moot point. He insists, not very.

'I just thought it wouldn't happen,' he says, especially after the aborted attempt in March.

'I just said to people at that time, "This is crazy, Kevin doesn't have the numbers. What is the point if you don't have the numbers of just having a negative thing dragging us down further?" And at no stage did I think the numbers were there – I guess until they were. I didn't think they'd get there.'

But others dispute the suggestion that he was not involved. Some in a position to know variously describe his role as ranging from 'pretty ignorant' to 'massive', but never overt. He never attended any of the meetings of those described subsequently as 'the cardinals', but his critics dubbed him the 'silent cardinal', alleging his private advice to Kevin was extremely influential.

There are those in the Labor Party who will never forgive him for favouring – and, they allege, therefore facilitating – Kevin's return. Some did not realise at the time just how close to the former Prime Minister Anthony was and feel like they were betrayed. Some of those who strenuously opposed Kevin's return felt that closeness clouded his judgement.

'I don't think it can be uncontested that he was the guy who always played the pure party role,' one says. 'It's just not so.'

Independent MP Bob Katter takes some personal credit for the return of Kevin Rudd. He called a news conference on the morning of the successful challenge, condemning Julia Gillard's government for damaging the live cattle trade and calling for change.

'Albanese told me that the installing of Rudd the second time, the key role was played by myself,' Bob says. 'I called a press conference in the morning that the government had no one in the driver's seat.'

He insists he told neither Kevin nor Anthony in advance. 'I couldn't ask him or tell him,' Bob says. 'I just had to go straight out there and do it.'

He says he believes the move to help restore Kevin to the prime ministership cost him 8000 votes at the election that followed, but restored the live cattle trade.

He does not believe Anthony betrayed Julia.

'I think Albo was playing a straight bat,' he says.

'We're good friends – Anthony and I . . . I most certainly like Anthony a lot and I regard him as a bloody good friend, and I wouldn't say that of too many people in the federal Parliament, I can tell you.'

He thinks it's time there was another 'ordinary knockabout Australian Prime Minister' and that it's 'inevitable' Anthony will get there one day.

'Since Chifley there's been Bob Hawke and John Howard – that's it out of about 20 prime ministers. It sure would be nice to have another one.'

Anthony's support for and ongoing friendship with Kevin set him at odds with some others among his political friends.

'Obviously we didn't agree about Kevin, so we just agree not to talk about those things,' Jenny says. 'I want to put our friendship first.'

When others among Kevin's supporters approached him to contest a ballot against Julia, Kevin says he said to them, 'What the hell is in this for me?'

'I said, "We can't win the election, I get to improve the result based on what the polling says, which is we'll come home with 50 or 60 seats as opposed to 25 seats . . . Then I get blamed for the result. So what's actually in this for me?"'

But he was persuaded.

When Kevin was re-elected on 26 June 2013, Anthony nominated for the deputy's position and was elected over Simon, who ran against him.

'I rang Carmel and told her I was running,' he says. 'And the next time I spoke to her I rang her to tell her I was Deputy Prime Minister.'

He was overwhelmed.

'To be acting Prime Minister from Marrickville of course on a couple of occasions was an extraordinary honour.'

When his elevation was announced, his mobile phone went into meltdown under the congratulatory messages from friends, family and professional associates.

One text message came from Sherie Dewstow, his old neighbour from over the back fence.

'When's the barbecue at The Lodge?'

Julia Gillard explains her decision to trust Anthony despite his allegiances as a view that he would always put the Labor Government first.

'He would always play that straight in the interests of the Government, even if he was providing aid and comfort to Kevin in the internal processes,' she says.

He insists he never was.

'I was aware of enough information every single day [to do damage],' he says. 'If I was leaking to people who were undermining Julia, then she would've known about it. It would've been all over. That's the truth. She knows that.'

Julia believes Anthony had conflicted loyalties.

'I don't have any sense of umbrage about it,' she says. 'It got to a stage where it was really not possible for him to be completely transparent and truthful with me, as well as playing the role for Kevin that Kevin wanted him to play.'

Some others don't accept Anthony's version of events, believing he was fully engaged with Kevin and fully aware of his plans. He denies that.

'Up until June 2013 I didn't think it was going to happen,' he says. 'I didn't think we'd change and I didn't think we'd win.'

Julia describes his role as being in 'that slightly murky area of human behaviour'.

'Clearly, personally, I didn't view it as unforgiveable or so dishonourable that you would not want to talk or continue to stay in contact.'

Unlike some others who were on the opposite side of the argument from Anthony, she says she continues to hold Anthony in high regard.

'It's not like we spend lots of time talking to each other or anything like that – we don't,' Julia says. 'But if he was in Adelaide or I was in Sydney and had some time, I'd happily catch up for a drink.'

CHAPTER 22

The Day After

The exhilaration of victory was short-lived. The newly elected leadership team had to prepare a budget and then get to an election as quickly as possible. Kevin appointed Chris Bowen as Treasurer and the two of them and Anthony were sworn in immediately.

Although factionally divided to the Left and Right, NSW MPs Anthony and Chris had already worked closely together and Chris – a decade younger – respected Anthony's views.

'When Albo spoke in Cabinet we all listened,' Chris says. 'If he spoke up and expressed concern about something, there was a fair chance he was right. It was certainly worth considering his point of view. I call him a big beast of the Cabinet – one of the more influential ministers.'

Seven frontbenchers who had gone out hard against Kevin in their bid to stop him rising again resigned, leaving the trio operating like a war cabinet for the final day of Parliament, until the weekend and the winter break bought them some breathing space. They had to allow Julia and Wayne Swan time to vacate their offices, so they operated out of Anthony's ministerial digs. When he moved into the deputy prime ministerial suite, Anthony found a generous welcome note from Wayne, wishing him well.

In Question Time, Kevin rattled off a ridiculously long list of portfolios, any questions within which should all be directed to his new deputy.

Some things hadn't changed – like the fact that they still did not command a majority in the Parliament. But other things were about to. Kevin was determined not to replicate Julia's deal with the Greens, a deal which had proven politically damaging.

He and Anthony met with the Greens' leadership in the famously quirkily named Monkey Pod Room in Parliament's ministerial wing.

'They said, "Why should we support you?" Anthony recalls. 'And we said, "You don't have to. You can vote for Tony Abbott if you want." That was really the extent of the negotiations.'

Kevin and Anthony were worried the Opposition might seize the opportunity of the sudden leadership change to test the new Prime Minister's support on the floor of the Parliament.

'What was extraordinary is there was no vote of confidence on the floor of the House,' Anthony says. 'We prepared for it and I had to war-game that night all the potential scenarios, and I did that to make sure we would have won a vote of confidence on the floor. But it was extraordinary that it was never tested.'

The 2013 election was upon them quickly. At Labor's campaign launch, Anthony gave the speech introducing the returned Prime Minister. It was 1 September – Father's Day. His son, Nathan, was with Carmel in the audience and had been warned his father planned to mention him.

'I begin with a big shout out to all the fathers in the audience and at home,' Anthony said. 'And a special shout out to my son and mate, Nathan, and of course his wonderful mum, Carmel, who are here.

'Thank you for your support today and every day. It's certainly a Father's Day to remember.'

What he didn't say was that he was also thinking of his own father. Carlo's health had deteriorated and he was terminally ill.

'My father on the other side of the world who I'd just found and met was dying,' he says. 'And Nathan was there so I acknowledged him. But I was thinking about my father as well as my son.'

Anthony was in a race against the calendar and the clock to get through this election campaign and its aftermath and get back to Italy to say goodbye.

The election result was not unexpected. Tony Abbott's coalition swept Labor from office. Anthony insists it was a lot more respectable than it might have been.

'I think 55 seats meant we were competitive in the future,' Anthony says. 'It didn't knock us out for two terms. Others have put it as saving the furniture and I think it was an outcome where the odds were always stacked against us winning.'

After the election, he faced that same decision again. Was he committed enough to put himself forward at the 2016 election as well and stay on through both terms?

He believed he had achieved a lot, policy-wise, in six years and he was proud of his record. He would, however, receive some blow-back from the incoming government for his insistence that Labor get the credit for infrastructure projects begun on his watch but completed under the auspices of incoming Transport Minister and Nationals Leader, Warren Truss.

In late 2015, the coalition Government would grow tired of Anthony's boasts and push back, just a little. Treasurer Scott Morrison ridiculed the 'boasts of the Member for Grayndler who claims to have laid every single brick in this country over the time they were elected'.

'He was at every concrete pour – so much so that I thought I should go and check on the Sydney Harbour Bridge opening design to see if his name was on it . . . Perhaps he constructed Stonehenge and Macchu Picchu . . . The Member for Grayndler is the great infrastructure builder of the ancient wonders of the world!'

On cue, Christopher Pyne stepped forward in the chamber with a Photoshopped picture of Anthony's head superimposed in place of one of the US presidential visages carved into the rock at Mount Rushmore in the United States.

Christopher insists the now former Deputy Prime Minister, Warren Truss, has delivered more.

'It's Warren Truss that's delivered the second Sydney airport,' he says. 'Anthony could never get that through the Labor Party . . . Every time Warren was taking credit, he'd say, "I did that! Me! I did that!" I'd say, "Oh, you built the bloody Sphinx too, I s'pose?"'

Christopher revels in baiting Anthony because he knows what annoys him. Anthony's approach is much the same.

On their weekly appearance on the Nine Network's *Today Show* in February 2015 – in the midst of the early round of Liberal leadership turmoil – when Anthony quipped, 'See you next week with a new leader,' Christopher responded with the semi-phonetic euphemism for a profanity: 'See you next Tuesday'.

Undeterred, Anthony lists among his achievements in office the creation of Infrastructure Australia – which gives the Government independent advice on what to build – and the Major Cities Unit, reinvigorating urban policy in line with the beliefs of his mentor, Tom Uren.

He points to the completion of the Hume Highway duplication and improvements to the Pacific Highway – especially poignant for him after the death of his namesake cousin decades before – and having reduced the rail freight travel times by rebuilding 4000 kilometres of track.

'We invested more in urban public transport between 2007 and 2013 than all previous government combined from Federation to 2007,' he says. He's especially proud of that.

He streamlined transport regulations, reducing the number of regulators from 23 to three.

He'd been the only Transport Minister invited to roundtable talks in Singapore on the future of global aviation in 2012. His aviation white paper earned him the title of Aviation Minister of the Year in 2010 from the peak global industry group, and two years later he received the equivalent international award in infrastructure.

Qantas Chief Executive Alan Joyce describes Anthony as 'a very good minister who saw infrastructure in terms of the national interest and had a really in-depth knowledge of the portfolio'.

'He understood the way the aviation industry was changing and that came through in the decisions he took as minister, including Australia's first Aviation White Paper,' Alan says. 'He also had a big role in getting reform of the Qantas Sale Act over the line from opposition, which was one of the few pieces of bipartisan legislation in the last parliament. Anthony also played a pivotal role in Qantas securing approval for our major partnership with Emirates. We didn't agree on everything, but he always listened to our point of view and found ways to make sure the industry in Australia was as globally competitive as possible, and personally I found him great company.'

Alan also attended the Singapore leaders' event and recalls Anthony describing it as 'making an ALP conference look meek and orderly'. 'Which I thought was quite something coming from Albo!'

It is a point of pride for Anthony that when he became minister, Australia was ranked 20th in the industrialised world for infrastructure investment, but when he left office it was first. He was so proud of it he put it in almost every press release.

The Labor Government had also overhauled shipping in 2012 – the biggest reform of the industry in a century. He overhauled the grant system to make it less political and more needs-based.

'We did 5500 community projects for the economic stimulus plan without one single complaint or issue by anyone about any of the projects that were funded.'

And Anthony had taken on the cause of local government, creating the Australian Council of Local Government. He advocated for a referendum to include local government in the Constitution – a measure whose explanation got lost in the political dramas, but which was designed to give local government some basis in law.

Anthony argues that has been made more relevant in the wake of arbitrary and unpopular council amalgamations in NSW in 2016.

'The NSW amalgamations are a perfect example of why it actually matters and makes a difference,' he says.

He had attracted national attention when he drew the ire of already angry anti-carbon-price protesters in 2011, who were coming to Canberra in what they called a 'Convoy of No Confidence', demanding a double-dissolution election.

He rubbished their arguments in Parliament, dubbing it the 'Convoy of No Consequence'. His words certainly had consequences – they turned up outside his office in Marrickville.

'They didn't think I'd address them. I told them in advance that I would,' he says. 'I said, "Yep I'll talk to you if you come. But be respectful." And they didn't do that. They had a coffin and they had terrible signs and some of them were quite aggressive and out of control.'

His guiding principle is to 'never duck' an argument.

'I've always been prepared to engage with people who I disagree with,' he says. They include Australia's most outspoken conservative broadcasters, Andrew Bolt and Alan Jones.

'Andrew Bolt, for example, is someone who I have very different views from, but someone who has views and that you can actually have a debate with,' he says. 'It's not so much just talking to them, it's about talking to people who are watching and listening to their programs.'

He likes the intellectual challenge.

'Alan Jones, whatever you might think of him, is a very intelligent, smart man.'

As a person blessed with a steel-trap memory, Anthony has statistics at the ready.

'We built 7500 kilometres of roads,' he says. 'We created Infrastructure Australia. We created a Major Cities Unit to engage with urban policy. The first national urban design protocol. Green buildings standards. The first-ever national cycling strategy. A 10-year national road safety strategy. Ports strategy. Land-freight strategy . . .'

His voice trails off.

'No wonder I was so tired.'

Kevin Rudd says he doesn't recall a single policy disagreement with Albo – not on national security, foreign policy, the economy or anything.

'This is a guy with an economic mind, a pro-business mind and a pro-infrastructure mind,' he says. 'But above all [it's] a mind anchored in the business of nation-building. And as for his commitment to the people with the backside out of their pants, well that goes without saying.'

In the wake of the 2013 election, Anthony came under huge pressure to run for the leadership, mainly – though not only – from the Left. He was interested anyway and believed himself well qualified to lead.

'This was a chance for there to be a leader of the Labor Party who was from the Left,' Anthony says. 'Those chances don't come around every day so I felt a major responsibility. But at the end of the day it was my decision and it wasn't a factional one.'

He decided to contest the ballot. It was a big deal.

'I had to be clear that I wanted to be leader of the Labor Party, that I was prepared to do it, that my family were okay with me doing it.

'I hadn't ever said to anyone on or off the record before September 2013 that I was interested in leading the party. I'd never said it to anybody because I'd never thought about it.'

The Victorian Right's Bill Shorten – former leader of the Australian Workers' Union – had also nominated as a candidate.

Anthony's South Australian friend and fellow left-wing MP Mark Butler acted as his campaign manager. Anthony then ran Mark's campaign to become ALP national President in 2015.

'He does make the point that he managed to win my campaign and I managed not to win his campaign,' Mark says. 'I wouldn't have run without his support so I talked to him deeply about it.'

The US-primary-style process was new for Labor and not entirely comfortable. The two men traversed the country separately and together, addressing large and small gatherings of Labor members.

And throughout, Anthony kept thinking: *What happens if my father dies in the middle of all of this?*

Coming straight after such a bruising defeat, Anthony insists the leadership ballot process was positive – a circuit-breaker that pointed them forwards.

'I think that it enabled a break from the division of the past and it showed that a ballot can be conducted and can be unifying rather than divisive,' he says. 'I think it enabled Labor to talk about the future rather than look back at the past.'

Mark Butler agrees that it energised party members. 'I can say even having run the campaign and lost, it is the best thing I have been involved with in the party by a mile.'

But there were examples of the old tricks being played again. In Auburn in Western Sydney, multiple ballots were found to have been sent to the same addresses and a review found substantial rorting.

Auburn councillor and Labor hopeful Hicham Zreika was held responsible and preselection for the NSW seat of Auburn, which had been earmarked for him, was used to accommodate the incoming state Labor leader – and Anthony's old housemate – Luke Foley instead.

A similar pattern of ballot rorting was uncovered in Victoria.

The new rules gave equal weight to the rank-and-file and parliamentary votes. Anthony won a majority of the rank-and-file members – 59.9 per cent of the 30,000 who voted – while Bill won 40.1 per cent.

But Bill won 64 per cent of the caucus vote to Anthony's 36 – a large enough number to give him a combined total of 52 per cent.

Nine members of Anthony's own faction voted against him. Some are residual members of the Ferguson soft Left and the largest group was loyal to Victorian Senator Kim Carr, who has taken up the mantle of opposition to Anthony.

'I don't think he realised the number of left-wingers who weren't voting for him in the caucus,' says frontbench colleague Chris Bowen, whose office in Opposition is next door to Anthony's. 'It became real for him. He got a taste for it.'

For a man who prides himself on knowing a result before it happens – and who insists he knew this one, albeit a couple of votes out – Anthony was a bit taken aback.

'He's understandably disappointed with the leadership ballot,' says the man who defeated him, now Opposition leader Bill Shorten. 'But to his credit, I think he just got on with it. He's been on top of his portfolio – no one can doubt that. And he's got a good sense of the parliamentary mood. I value his advice.'

Although others – who refuse to put their names to their criticisms – are less charitable, Mark Butler believes Anthony managed his disappointment well.

'It was such an act of treachery that did him in,' Mark says. 'You can imagine a whole lot of people getting very bitter and he didn't. I mean he's not happy but he didn't let that bitterness cloud what had been a great process. There's a lot of anger around the country at what happened. All those Left activists – they did their bit . . . And then they saw a handful of malcontents – in their view – do over the first genuine candidate from the organisational Left to lead the party in 130 years or whatever. They were very cross.'

But he says that anger wasn't directed at Bill Shorten.

'I think Bill played a fair game and . . . however members voted, there was a lot of respect for how both of them conducted themselves in the campaign.'

There would be a glimpse of some of his disappointment at discovering several colleagues did not do what they promised, during his 20th-anniversary dinner speech in 2016. He would reflect on what he said was his habit of being open with people.

'I'm sometimes a bit too trusting,' he said. 'I can honestly say, in 20 years, I've never told anyone I was voting for them unless I was.'

Former Labor MP Stephen Smith says that is his experience in dealing with Anthony, but that he has earned himself some enemies over the years.

'There are plenty of people, particularly in the Left, who over the years Albo has done over,' Stephen says. 'And he's done them over because he's got his position up over their position and that tends to make people unhappy. In my experience in the ALP, a person who has done things, achieved things, gone places, is generally most unpopular in those areas where he's been most effective. So you'll find Albo's greatest critics among those people of the Left – particularly of the NSW Left – who he has effectively beaten over the years. And he's beaten them on the argument. He's beaten them on the numbers.'

On this occasion, his critics certainly beat him on the numbers. Despite that disappointment, Anthony used his concession speech in the caucus to help along a mate who was also hoping for advancement.

Tony Burke, with whom he had artificially sparred back in NSW Labor and who he knew had a good grip on the way Parliament ran, had long aspired to be Leader of the House in Government and Manager of Opposition Business out of it.

When Anthony had won the role in Opposition, he had proposed to leader Kevin Rudd that Tony be his deputy, but Kevin had proposed Stephen Smith and Anthony readily agreed.

Ahead of the leadership ballot, Tony applied the same principle that Anthony generally followed: he told Anthony upfront that he wasn't voting for him. He was voting for Bill Shorten.

Conceding defeat in front of his colleagues, Anthony confirmed that he wouldn't be seeking to be Manager of Opposition Business and seized the moment to say he believed it should go to Tony Burke.

'He just announced it to the caucus, straight after I'd voted against him,' Tony says. 'When people are upfront and say what they're going to do – that's how he's operated. That's why people who might not have liked the conclusions he's reached haven't lost any respect for him. And he treats people on the cxact same rules.'

Anthony lodged no formal protest about the rorting, which favoured his opponent, though some Left colleagues thought he should have. He believes to do so would damage Labor, its leader and its new unity.

'That's indulgent,' he says.

In the early part of the parliamentary term, some of Anthony's friends sensed a bit of drift, like he wasn't certain of his role in the new regime. He wasn't included in Bill's inner circle, nor in the party's tactics group.

Anthony's class of '96 colleague Joel Fitzgibbon says they missed his expertise.

'That was an error,' Joel says. 'You have to have someone with his experience and talent. You should have him at the centre of tactical decision making all the time.'

In early 2016, he was restored to that group.

'I came to the realisation that I just need to have the best people doing the best jobs they can do,' Bill says. 'And he's one of the best people. Either you focus on Turnbull and having a positive agenda or you worry about people.'

Over summer leading into 2016, muttering had begun about Bill Shorten's leadership in the wake of a leadership change in the Opposition from Tony Abbott to Malcolm Turnbull.

The new Prime Minister's approval rating was stratospheric and his Labor opponent's – while never especially strong – looked a lot worse in comparison. Some in the NSW Right were warning they would try to move against Bill by February if things didn't improve. They wanted Anthony to replace him.

Anthony insists nobody attempted to draft him. But NSW Right veteran Graham Richardson says Anthony knew what was being discussed.

'I don't care if he doesn't like that, I think Albo's aware of what's going on,' Graham said in December 2015. 'But there's been no decision made to do it.'

He said that in NSW, hard-headed comparisons were being made between Anthony and Bill Shorten.

'The question is out of the two of them, who would get us closer? And I think more and more people are coming down to saying Albo would.'

Before the 2016 federal election, former Speaker and Anthony's foe turned friend Leo McLeay endorsed the credentials of his successor in Grayndler.

'I think if Anthony had won the leadership last time, we would be in a lot better position than we are now,' Leo said. 'And I think if he won the leadership after the next election [referring to 2016], he would be better placed I think to put the party back together than any of the other contenders.'

After Labor's unexpectedly good result in 2016, Leo said, 'Well, you can't be right all the time. Bill had a great election and deserved another go.'

But he continues to praise Anthony's credentials.

'He tends to think through what he's going to do,' Leo says. 'He tends to have his facts right and he can prosecute an argument very, very well. Ultimately if a person is going to be the leader, the ability to sell the argument and to have people believe in what you're saying is the real important characteristic they need.'

Bill Shorten called returning and likely new Labor MPs to Canberra six days after the cliffhanger 2016 election – and before conceding defeat – to have his leadership re-endorsed in the caucus. Some in the NSW Right who would prefer Anthony as leader had again been talking up the prospect of him mounting a challenge and intended to support him if he did. He insists he was not involved.

'On the morning after the election, I went to watch my son play football,' Anthony says. 'If you're running for the leadership you'd be on the phone, not on the sideline. You can't half-run, you've got to go full pelt.'

Some believed his public comments after the election failed to explicitly rule it out. He dismisses such suggestions.

In the party room, after negotiations over the wording and insistence that the rules be followed properly, Anthony moved a motion thanking the party's volunteers, congratulating Shorten on the election's 'outstanding' outcome and authorising him to negotiate with the parliamentary crossbench – pointedly within the caucus rules.

Bill Shorten dismisses the talk of any threat before the election.

'There wasn't a big queue of people to sit out the Turnbull wave of popularity except for me. That was fine. I just got down to business.'

Graham thinks Anthony's time may come.

'I think Albo will be terrific,' he says. 'I think he'll get there too.'

But his endorsement comes with a qualification.

'I always would prefer to see a good right-winger lead the Labor Party.'

In an observation that won't please others with long-term ambitions to lead, he nominates a future prospect from the generation coming behind: Victorian MP Richard Marles.

'I think there is a good right-winger who will lead the Labor Party down the track and that's Richard Marles.'

He warns that anyone wanting the Labor Party leadership has to seize it.

'My view is if you want to be a leader, you've got to have balls,' Graham says. 'You've got to have courage. And when the leadership comes up, you don't duck it. If you want it and someone says here it is, you can't say, "Oh, I'd prefer it in two years' time, thank you." To me that says you're piss weak if you do that – and you don't deserve it. You don't get given the Labor leadership as some sort of free gift at Christmas. You earn it.'

Leo McLeay agrees. 'As everyone finds out, to become leader you've usually got to kill the king.'

Once the ballot was finalised, Anthony got on a plane to Italy. He was missing some of Parliament but he needed to go. He flew to Rome and headed straight to Barletta.

Anthony wanted to make the trip to prove to his father and his family that having them in his life was important to him.

'It was very emotional,' he says.

He spent the day at Carlo's flat. By now largely bedridden, Carlo got up and ate with the family. Anthony left Carlo and his wife to themselves that night and returned to the house the following day.

'The day I was leaving, I went to see him and both of us knew we were saying goodbye.'

Anthony had already said most of what he needed to say.

'I just said I was very pleased I got to meet him,' he says, as his eyes fill with tears. 'He said the same. He said he was proud of me.'

Anthony returned home knowing the next time he heard from Barletta it would be bad news – and it was.

Carlo Albanese died on 17 January 2014, just over four years after he and his son, Anthony, had been reunited. In his grief, Anthony felt resolved.

'It was a sense of gratitude for what we had, not loss of what we hadn't,' he says, glad that all of those many serendipitous things had come together when they did and not five years later.

'I could have very easily found him now – gone.'

It was the end of an incredible journey.

The man who had beaten him to the Labor leadership just weeks before his personal loss says he now feels he understands Anthony and what has contributed to his emotional side better than he used to.

'I think he's quite an emotional person,' Bill Shorten says. 'He doesn't talk a lot about it. Reconnecting with his father, then losing his father, is a big thing. I suppose with the passing of my own mum, I guess that sensitised me a lot more. But also, a lot of what people are in politics is based on their childhood and their relationship with their parents – good, bad, present or absent.'

After the years of emotional and political upheaval culminating in several kinds of loss, his mate Paul Murphy recalls just how tired he actually was.

'He was exhausted. I think more than anything else the overwhelming sense was just a sense of exhaustion.'

A year out from the 2016 election, the Labor Party held its national conference in Melbourne to set its policy platform.

The issue of asylum seekers attracted considerable controversy and set sections of the Left against the dominant Right on whether to support the coalition-initiated policy of turning boats back when it was safe to do so. Opposition Leader Bill Shorten backed the policy but members of the Left did not, putting forward a motion to oppose boat turn-backs.

Former Immigration Minister Tony Burke, from the NSW Right, gave an emotional speech in favour of turning boats back. He told how after a boat sank and a baby was among those who drowned, he asked his department for the child's name – not to release publicly, just for his own knowledge.

'He was 10 weeks old,' Tony said. 'He died on my watch. I just want to know his name. His name was Abdul Jafari.'

Shadow Immigration Minister Richard Marles backed him. 'A future Labor government must have at its disposal the full suite of measures to keep this journey shut,' he said.

Anthony voted for the motion and against the policy. His colleagues Tanya Plibersek and Penny Wong – both members of the leadership group – did not attend the vote, allowing proxies to support the motion on their behalf. The vote was lost and the policy stayed.

Also ahead of the election, Anthony began working on broadening his image. While colleagues and friends engaged in some eye-rolling about what seemed like an indulgence, he pursued extracurricular appearances with a very clear strategy in mind.

With the help of some young and savvy staff, he ramped up his social media presence, shamelessly kicking along Twitter exchanges featuring his 1980s 'Hot Albo' photo.

He parlayed his well-known interest in music into a new persona – 'DJ Albo' – first doing guest spots at Labor fundraisers but eventually appearing at local and interstate events, unashamedly exploiting the novelty factor of a 50-something politician from the vinyl era sporting a leather jacket and spinning a few tunes. He also played in Reclink Community Cup AFL games at Henson Park in his electorate.

It wasn't for no reason. A redistribution had made his seat greener than ever. He needed to boost his appeal to the lefty youth in Green-leaning suburbs like Balmain. And his electorate has the highest concentration of practitioners of the arts of any in the country.

But Anthony is also genuinely interested in the arts, beyond his love of indie music. He and Carmel occasionally go to the opera.

'The talent of opera singers I find quite extraordinary,' he says. He likes the theatrics and the drama of opera and of live theatre and music generally.

'It's entertainment that gives pleasure,' he says. 'But it is also, I think, very healthy for your mental health in terms of just closing off outside influences for a while. When you're at the opera or the theatre, which I very much enjoy going to, you don't think about the mundane. And good theatre I find intellectually stimulating as well.'

Anthony argues the arts are also about 'providing a critique of the sort of society that we're in'. And in that respect, they intersect neatly with politics – especially in his own seat.

He had contemplated switching seats to neighbouring Barton – which was safer for Labor than Grayndler – and left his decision as late as possible.

In mid-January 2016, with a lot to consider, he took a few days off and flew to Italy to visit the Italian family. It was the second anniversary of his father's death and he wanted them to know he remained committed to the family relationship.

The long flight gave him time to think. While he was in the air, the Australian Electoral Commission's final redistribution maps were produced, which confirmed that his electorate office remained in Grayndler but showed his home now in Barton. He decided to run for Grayndler and announced it on his return as the parliamentary year was beginning.

And in another recruitment coup, he and Bill Shorten revealed Labor's candidate for Barton: NSW deputy Labor leader Linda Burney. Anthony had persuaded Linda to go federal and break new ground, aiming to become the first Indigenous woman in the House of Representatives.

The change in electoral boundaries had made Liberal-held Barton more winnable for Labor but Grayndler harder to retain. Anthony would seek to use his name recognition to try to add to Labor's total, hoping between them he and Linda could win both – something they would indeed go on to do.

As election year, 2016, began, Anthony was marking a milestone. On 2 March – also his birthday – he clocked up 20 years in Parliament. Just ahead of the anniversary, he held a celebratory fundraising dinner at the Canterbury Hurlstone RSL Club, taking the stage to a blast from The Killers' hit song 'Mr Brightside'.

He praised those closest and dearest to him – his son, Nathan, and wife and partner, Carmel. Nathan, he noted, had lived his whole life in 'this strange world' around politics and was 'a remarkable young man who we are both very proud of'.

'He would have had every excuse to be not sane at all,' Anthony said. 'It's a difficult life. It's a *difficult* life and Nathan makes us proud, and he is growing into a very fine young man with some very good friends.'

His composure wavered as he mentioned his life partner.

'Carmel is, of course, my confidante – the love of my life and the rock that I rely on,' he said. 'And I thank you.'

Of course, he also thanked his late mother, Maryanne, and her 'three great faiths'.

'In terms of the values that I hold, it's the product of the upbringing that I got in my two-person family,' he said. 'I think part of what made me is that background, that understanding. She used to say to me, "Never forget where you came from."'

Former Prime Minister Bob Hawke was the guest speaker. Anthony called him 'the father of modern Labor'.

'It's Bob Hawke who taught us that it's actually possible – and indeed necessary – to have long-term Labor governments,' he said. 'You need long-term Labor governments to make sure that reforms are entrenched, that they are made permanent, that they change the nature of Australia.'

Bob Hawke praises Anthony's loyalty and dedication to the cause.

'We're all shaped via history and I think Albo particularly,' the former Prime Minister says. 'His mother must have been a remarkable woman and he's been absolutely true to the fundamental principles and beliefs of the Labor Party. He's never wavered.'

Anthony remains extremely proud of his background.

'Growing up where I did, I had a much better chance of going to jail than going to federal Parliament,' he told the dinner crowd in February.

Kevin Rudd describes Anthony as the 'Mick Young' of his generation, demonstrating ahead of Labor's return to government in 2007 that he shared the late former Hawke government Minister's capacity to employ the vernacular in firing humorous, brutal salvos at his opponents in Parliament.

'By the time the government changed it was very difficult to find anyone from the conservative Opposition who'd want to sit there and have the blowtorch put on them by Albo,' Kevin says. 'He was effective because he employed the full skills of the larrikin at play but with a deep sense of political strategy as well.'

Tony Burke singles out what he says is Anthony's political courage.

'I think one of the qualities that often gets underestimated is whether or not someone is fearless,' he says. 'Lots of people can be smooth on a good day and all of that. But it's when you're under pressure – whether you'll be fearless and stand your ground.'

He says Anthony always knows what he is fighting for because before Labor won government in 2007, he had spent so long on a losing side.

'[From] the moment he left Young Labor, he was never at a major vote again where he was on the winning side,' Tony says. '... So he'd had that long experience of a period where everything was stacked against [his side], and what mattered was how you stood your ground and how you explained to people why what was about to happen was wrong.'

Former Prime Minister Paul Keating added his voice in support ahead of the 2016 election, officially launching Anthony's campaign. 'I wanted to come and say how much I admire Anthony. He has always put his hand up for the important social changes.'

As Anthony faced his eighth election, the man who ran his first reflects on the politician and friend.

'He's a complex character but he's pretty unique in today's buttoned-up, professionalised political world,' Tim Gartrell says. 'There's not too many other pollies like him – not too many in the Parliament who have come from where he has – and done it without a chip on his shoulder. He's not your soulless factional leader that's become cold-blooded and too cynical. There's still a warm, good human being there.

'He's capable of pretty ruthless stuff – and he's earned some lifelong enemies. But the cynicism hasn't consumed him. You see a lot of hardened factional warlords – across all sides of politics – and you wonder if much of a heart is left. I think he's still got one – it's a bit scarred but it's still there.'

It's what they call conviction politics and voters respond well to it. Although his enemies don't agree, Anthony's ability to relate easily to people regardless of their circumstances would attest to his authenticity.

'He passes the authenticity test in spades,' says Kevin Rudd of his chosen deputy. 'With Albo, it's the real thing ... In politics, it ain't all that complicated in the end. The punters want to know two things: that you know what you're talking about and that you believe in what you're saying. Surprisingly, very few politicians pass that test. I hope I did. I believe I did. I know Albo does.'

Bob Hawke also referred to it in his speech for Anthony's parliamentary anniversary.

'Right from the very beginning . . . those remarkable intellectual qualities he's got, the personality he possesses, were all harnessed in the interests of those people of his electorate,' he said.

'He wanted to see them enjoy the opportunities of a better, more prosperous, more equitable Australia. It's not often enough realised the significant contribution he made with the relatively limited ministerial opportunities he had. But he was, without a doubt, one of the most outstanding infrastructure ministers we've had. He tackled these issues with a sense of cooperation. He didn't try and stand over [people] and say, "This is what it's going to be." And there are lasting monuments, Albo, to pay tribute to the imagination and the dedication which you brought to that job.'

There are literally monuments – or at least one. The former Minister for Infrastructure can claim his own footbridge, at Western River Cove on Kangaroo Island in South Australia. Opened in 2011, Albo's Bridge was so named in tribute to his work on infrastructure in government. With its own plaque, the footbridge is in a municipality in the traditionally blue-ribbon Liberal seat of Mayo wrested by the Nick Xenophon Team in 2016.

'It's been ignored because it's in Mayo,' he says. '. . . So no-one had ever done anything for it.'

He's had a beer named after him, too. Willie the Boatman, a brewery in his electorate, has had huge success with Albo Corn Ale.

'It's on tap in 14 pubs and bars around here,' Anthony says. 'That's called good politics.'

And if imitation is indeed a form of flattery, Anthony has both impressed and diversified. He's received letters and photographs to let him know there is an Albo the dog, which lives in Camden outside Sydney, and an Albo the cat, an inner-city feline living in Redfern. There was even an Albo the chicken – though he admits that Albo belonged to one of his staff.

'Albo the chicken got eaten by a fox,' he says, straight-faced.

Albo the man isn't sure about the future.

More than one of his present and former colleagues are prepared to say he may yet be leader one day.

'I think Albo has the capacity to be Prime Minister,' former minister Stephen Smith says. 'To date, the party hasn't afforded him that opportunity, and that opportunity may never come for him.'

Julia Gillard says she hopes that, whenever the transition out of politics comes for the man who's given his life to Labor, he's ready for what's next.

'I think however long the political journey lasts, there's always the day after, and what I fear for Albo is that he might find – even though he's got a wonderful family and loves his son so much – it quite difficult to conceptualise what that day should look like. I hope for him that he works that out.'

In 2016, Anthony Albanese's thoughts are not turning in that direction just yet. He feels he has more to do and doesn't rule out being a leadership candidate in future.

'Obviously, anyone who has put their hand up for leadership, as I did, can't pretend that hasn't happened,' he says. 'And you do wonder about what might have happened, but you can't change history, you get on with life. I have always been loyal to the Labor cause and believe that as MPs we have a responsibility to do the job we have got at any time to the best of our ability, rather than worry about the job we don't have.'

Perhaps the best clue was in his speech at his own 20th-anniversary dinner.

'I'm patient,' he told his applauding audience. 'I'm patient – I'm a Souths fan.'

CHAPTER 23

Never Say Never

The 2016 election would set the course for the next chapter of Anthony's political career. The campaign was to become a much more home-based battle for the Member for Grayndler than campaigns past had been.

Normally, the solid margin in such a safe seat would allow Anthony to roam widely, supporting Labor candidates in harder-to-win seats across Australia and concentrating on the broader objective of toppling the government.

After just three years in office, that government was surprisingly wobbly. Under Malcolm Turnbull, its second leader in its first term, the coalition's vulnerability was strangely familiar. But as election year began, Anthony was contemplating a situation in his own seat that would require him to stay, in the beginning at least, a little closer to home. The Australian Electoral Commission had undertaken one of its regular redistributions to account for population growth, rearranging the electoral boundaries in areas with significant shifts, so all electorates still had roughly the same number of voters.

In 2016, electorates in Sydney's inner west had been affected, including Grayndler. Whenever there is a redistribution, political parties make submissions on where the new boundaries should go, armed with the booth-by-booth results from previous elections that reveal which suburbs and parts of suburbs tend to vote which way. Unsurprisingly, their ambit claims generally include as many favourable booths as possible, to maximise their own chances of winning next time. The electoral commission seeks a compromise.

In the 2016 NSW redistribution, it had issued a draft set of boundaries for Grayndler. On previous voting, the Liberals were likely to run second to Labor on primary votes in Grayndler and the Greens third. That meant the Greens' preferences would be distributed first. As more Greens' voters usually give second preferences to Labor than to the Liberals, Labor would likely have finished in front.

Among the slabs of Anthony's electorate that were to be redistributed, the draft boundaries placed his family home and electorate office within Barton, instead of in Grayndler. He had to decide whether to stay and contest the new hybrid electorate – but live in another one – or follow those excised parts of it and contest Barton instead.

Naturally, Anthony wanted to run where he could win. He also wanted Labor to recapture seats it had lost. Barton had fallen to the Liberals in 2013, but on the draft boundaries it had become much more winnable for Labor, especially if it had a high-profile, well-known candidate.

Anthony had a decision to make. His staff had begun preparing for a shift. But when the final boundaries were issued after a round of feedback on the draft, things had changed.

The potential Labor boost under the draft boundaries in Grayndler had been more than reversed. Grayndler had kept Green-heavy areas including Balmain. Anthony's home street in Marrickville would still fall within Barton but his electorate office had stayed in Grayndler.

On paper at least, his seat had become harder for Labor to hold and much more favourable to the Greens. The Greens held two seats in the State Parliament and under the redrawn federal boundaries, Grayndler took in half of one of those seats and almost three-quarters of the other.

'If they could've done the redistribution, that is the seat that they would've drawn,' Anthony says of the Greens' good fortune. 'It was drawn perfectly for them.'

The booths with the highest Labor vote previously had been shifted into the increasingly-Labor-inclined seat of Barton or into Watson, held by fellow frontbencher Tony Burke. Grayndler had long been the Greens' best hope after Melbourne – their only seat in the House of Representatives.

In Labor's factional carve-up of winnable seats, preselection for Barton normally went to a candidate from the Right. Anthony's standing in the party meant if he wanted to switch to the safer seat, the Right would not have stood in his way. But then, who would hold off the Greens in Grayndler? And how would he feel if the seat was lost?

'I thought about election night and being on Channel Nine,' Anthony says in 2017, 'and them saying, "Oh and you've won the seat of Barton, congratulations," on 60 per cent of the vote or what have you. "And now we cross to the Greens victory party in Grayndler."'

He couldn't escape the conclusion it would seem like he'd abandoned the good ship Grayndler and left it to sink. He didn't want that to be his legacy after 20 years' incumbency, redrawn boundaries or not. He decided to stay and fight.

That left the question of who should contest Barton against the Liberal incumbent, Nikolas Varvaris. There was another possible high-profile candidate who would be a virtual sure bet to secure Barton for Labor if she could be persuaded to run. She happened to be in the Left and if she successfully contested Barton and Anthony stayed in Grayndler and won again, that meant an extra seat both for Labor and the faction of which he is king.

So, Anthony approached then deputy NSW Labor leader, long-time friend and political protégé Linda Burney, to see if she could be convinced. He argued it was a logical opportunity for someone who had long been interested in national affairs. Barton also overlapped the state electorate of Canterbury she had held for 13 years. Linda agreed to move to federal politics, putting Barton likely back in the Labor column.

Anthony would recontest Grayndler where his profile and his history made him the best candidate to combat the more difficult demographics and try to turn one Labor seat back into two. Double success would also boost the Left's numbers in caucus. In the factional battleground of Labor politics, personal survival and party advancement are not the only considerations.

Because there was so much of the newly drawn seat that he'd never represented before – particularly parts of that highly gentrified former working-class suburb – he had a lot of work to do.

He and colleague Tanya Plibersek from the neighbouring seat of Sydney organised a 'handover' event at the Sackville Hotel in Rozelle which had been shifted from her electorate to his. Tanya wrote to constituents in the migrating suburbs thanking them for past support and inviting them to the pub to mark their transition to the other seat. They had to turn people away, an encouraging sign for them both.

As the election campaign got off the ground in earnest, Anthony needed to follow the first rule of safety in flight: be sure you can save yourself before trying to save others. He and his campaign team doorknocked every house in the newly included bits of Grayndler. It was old-fashioned marginal-seat-style electioneering and Anthony followed his own standard advice for anyone who wanted to get themselves elected: you have to ask people to vote for you.

Team Albo ditched its usual campaign colour – orange – and used red instead, matching with Labor's brand identification nationwide. They organised what they called the 'New Grayndler Federation Establishment Tour' – a gussied-up pub crawl – with Anthony and his supporters rolling down Balmain's hotel-heavy Darling Street and surrounds, collecting party members and other cheerful drinkers along the way, like the Pied Piper of the pint. When he appeared in a double-page spread in the local paper, News Corp's *Inner Western Suburbs Courier*, pulling an Albo Ale at the Unity Hall, he knew he was doing okay.

On election day, he would do a stint as guest DJ at the Annandale Public School fete in his electorate, which like most schools was doubling as a polling booth, at the invitation of Peter Oxley, former bass player for 1980s pop-rock band the Sunnyboys and a parent at the school. Once again, it got him on the news, television pictures showing kids dancing around him and radio bulletins blasting out their voices, singing along to Taylor Swift's 'Shake It Off'.

Some of Anthony's critics – including inside the Labor Party – deride the shamelessly populist way he sometimes plays his politics. He doesn't care. It's seen as genuine, not bunged on, and that's why it works.

As the campaign progressed and Anthony became more confident of victory, he had increased his travels around Australia to help other Labor candidates striving for victory in tough seats.

Those Labor colleagues in danger of defeat were mostly battling challengers from the right. But in Grayndler, in Tanya Plibersek's seat of Sydney and the inner-Melbourne seats of Wills and Batman, the attack was from the left. Although the Greens were the challengers – even confidently eyeing the Victorian Labor seat of Melbourne Ports and blue-ribbon Liberal seat of Higgins, Richmond in NSW and Fremantle in WA – Liberal preferences would be crucial.

The Greens had seized on the possibility of victory in the inner-city Labor-held seats and had crafted a campaign to target them. Anthony and Grayndler topped their list.

Targeting Lower House seats aggressively, parliamentary Greens leader Senator Richard di Natale had kicked off his party's campaign on 9 May in Petersham, on Anthony's turf. 'I share my predecessor Bob Brown's views that we're not just there to keep the bastards honest,' Richard told ABC TV's *7.30*. 'We're there to get rid of them.'

Appearing with Greens candidate Jim Casey, a firefighter and secretary of the NSW Fire Brigades Employees' Union, Richard declared that although Anthony was 'a decent person', he believed Jim would be a more consistent progressive representative.

'We will be taking the fight right up to Anthony Albanese in the seat of Grayndler and I am really confident that we will give this seat an almighty shake,' Richard told journalists.

The Greens leader had telegraphed his plan when the election was called the previous day and Anthony was straight onto the airwaves in the morning with a pre-emptive strike.

'It says a lot about Richard di Natale that his priority today on day one of the election campaign . . . is removing me from the Federal Parliament,' Anthony told ABC Radio National's Fran Kelly. 'If you think that Parliament will be a more progressive place without me in it, without me in the Labor Party and within the Parliament, then by all means.'

A fortnight before Prime Minister Malcolm Turnbull had fired the starter's gun for a marathon eight-week campaign and a rare double-dissolution election, Anthony had commissioned polling in his seat – the only polling he would conduct for the duration. It tested issues including Labor's negative-gearing policy – which attracted support – and approval ratings for Anthony and his main rival, Jim Casey.

On approval, 72 per cent rated Anthony positively and 13 per cent negatively, with 15 per cent unsure. Jim Casey rated 18 per cent positively and nine per cent negatively. Another 59 per cent said they didn't know who he was and 14 per cent weren't sure what they thought.

'People wanted us to win but they weren't necessarily voting for us,' Anthony says. 'So we needed to get out there and do it.'

The result convinced him that voters in his seat didn't know his Trotskyist, anti-capitalist opponent well at all. He set about shaping their views. Anthony and his team designed a campaign slogan to emphasise three things: his own politics, his membership of a party of government and his long standing in the electorate and sense of connection voters felt with him, as detected in the poll. 'Progressive. Effective. Ours.'

Ahead of the campaign proper, the team had discovered a two-year-old video online of Jim Casey declaring he'd rather have the coalition in office than Labor if it allowed more left-wing protest movements to flourish.

'I would prefer to see Tony Abbott returned as Prime Minister with a labour movement that was growing, with an anti-war movement that was disrupting things in the streets, with a strong and vital women's movement, indigenous movement and a climate change movement that was actually starting to disrupt the production of coal,' Jim said in the video, with NSW Greens Senator Lee Rhiannon and MP Adam Bandt watching. 'I would prefer to see Abbott as Prime Minister in that environment than Bill Shorten as Prime Minister without it.'

He also described how the union movement had the power to 'hurt people financially in the way that most of our social movements don't'.

Anthony's campaign staff wanted to draw attention to it immediately, suggesting he backed protest over policy change. 'Patience, patience,' he told them.

He was waiting for the right time to roll out what he would later describe as a 'shock and awe' campaign to introduce Jim Casey to the electorate at full volume. The time came just three days after the election was called.

On 11 May, Sydney's *Daily Telegraph* took the extraordinary step of advising its readers in Grayndler that they should vote for a member of Labor's left faction and return the bloke who had already represented them for 20 years, Anthony Albanese.

The News Corp tabloid editorialised in his favour and against the Greens, plastering a caricature of Anthony's head inside a life-preserver across the front page, with a double-page spread inside. The screaming headline, which coincidentally echoed the sentiment detected in Anthony's opinion polling and indeed his own campaign slogan, was 'Save our Albo'. The Nine Network, where he appeared every Friday morning with Liberal minister Christopher Pyne, would join the campaign, donning t-shirts bearing the same line.

Greens leader Richard di Natale was interviewed on ABC TV's *Lateline* the night the front-page endorsement appeared.

'What you're seeing in politics at the moment is the Coles and Woolworths of politics – Labor and Liberal getting together, trying to shut out the Greens, keeping out a bit of competition,' he said. 'And the corporate media is piling in, the big end of town who make those huge donations to both sides of politics . . . They want to protect their people.'

Anthony denies colluding with the *Daily Telegraph*. He insists that while he knew the newspaper was planning to editorialise in his favour, he didn't know about the giant drawing or front-page treatment until it appeared on social media the night before publication.

He certainly knew enough to mobilise all his firepower to follow up the remarkable corporate endorsement with a public-relations blitz against Jim Casey.

'I'm in politics to make a difference . . . to make things work, not just to protest,' he says in 2017. 'I want to be around the Cabinet table making decisions, not protesting after decisions have been made.'

Jim Casey defended his Tony Abbott comments as 'a figure of speech' and explained he had 'very little confidence' that a government led by Bill Shorten would take the necessary steps to improve society without social movements forcing it to do so.

Anthony was pleased with the free publicity from one of the nation's highest-selling newspapers. He had been lampooned by the *Tele* in 2013 as *Hogan Heroes* character Sergeant 'I know nuthink' Schultz, but in 2016 the newspaper was on Anthony's team and attacked Jim Casey over a 2011 tweet he had issued advocating the overthrow of capitalism.

Anthony told *New Matilda* online magazine at the time that the paper was 'simply expressing their view' that they would prefer him to the candidate for the 'Greens political party', a deliberate descriptor he always used lest anyone mistake the Greens for mere conservationists.

His opponent's spokeswoman, Julie Macken, told *New Matilda* that the *Daily Telegraph* had supported the incumbent because he 'clearly reflects their values'.

'He is entrenched power,' Julie was quoted as saying. 'Certainly, he describes himself as a progressive politician but I don't know any progressive politician who votes to imprison children, to gag doctors and nurses, to support metadata surveillance, to oppose a national ICAC. So, whatever he says, in fact, how he votes represents a very conservative politician.'

Anthony was determined to suggest it was the Greens who had links to the conservatives and laid the groundwork in advance. He had first raised the issue on ABC radio two months before the election was called.

After the Jim Casey video emerged, Anthony also attacked what he said was a preferences deal between the Greens and the Liberals to try to defeat Labor MPs in target seats. He said the Liberals planned to recommend that their supporters put the Greens ahead of Labor in seats the Greens were trying to win – such as Grayndler.

In return, in some Victorian Labor-held seats the Liberals fancied, he accused the Greens of planning to issue open tickets – double-sided how-to-vote cards recommending the Liberals ahead of Labor on one side and vice versa on the other.

The idea was that by the Greens not actively advocating for second preferences to go to Labor, more of their voters than usual were likely to preference the Liberals – boosting their chances. The Greens strenuously denied any 'deal'.

'There is no preference deal with the Liberal Party,' they said in a statement on their website. 'It is disappointing that the

Labor Party and the Murdoch media are spreading lies to scare progressive voters.'

The Liberal Party also issued a statement denying any deal.

'Preferences are allocated consistent with the electoral interests of the party, our values, principles and priorities, and the best interests of the Australian people in having an effective national government,' the then federal director Tony Nutt said. 'Decisions are made by the party organisation on a collaborative basis, coordinated Australia-wide by the national campaign director.'

Malcolm Turnbull was not keen to have his government linked with the Greens. In mid-June, a month into the campaign, he announced that Liberal how-to-vote cards across Australia would recommend putting the Greens below Labor. It was a slap-down of Victorian Liberal Party president Michael Kroger who had said the Greens had changed and Liberals should not always put Labor ahead of them.

Anthony took every opportunity to attack the Greens over the failed arrangement, accusing them of being willing to horse-trade with the conservative side of politics.

'I stand on my record,' he said. 'What you see is what you get with me. I'm prepared to stand up for my values in a consistent way. I've been doing it for years and that's why I will be returned as the Member for Grayndler.'

He was right. He was returned. Jim Casey finished third behind the Liberals' David van Gogh.

Unsurprisingly, Linda Burney also won in Barton. Becoming the first indigenous woman to hold a seat in the House of Representatives, she joined the Liberals' re-elected Member for the West Australian seat of Hasluck, Ken Wyatt, as one of only two Aboriginal members of the Lower House. Along with Labor senators Patrick Dodson and Malarndirri McCarthy, who replaced the retiring Northern Territorian Nova Peris to become only the second indigenous woman in the Senate, Linda formed part of the largest indigenous federal parliamentary intake ever.

Standing beside Linda announcing her candidacy two months earlier, Bill Shorten had been flanked by Anthony and deputy leader Tanya Plibersek. He declared it proof that Labor was a real chance to snatch victory.

'The fact that she's willing to step back from a career in state politics, and the relative sort of security of that, is because Linda believes, like my team here and all of the Federal Labor Party, that at the next election Labor's very competitive,' Bill told journalists.

That belief turned out to be well held. Malcolm Turnbull's coalition government lost 14 seats and Labor did better at the 2016 election than even the most battle-hardened officials thought it could. After the rout of three years earlier, to come within a single seat of victory was almost miraculous.

Bill Shorten was credited with having comprehensively out-campaigned the Prime Minister. Months of quietly travelling around the country fielding questions at local town-hall-style meetings had served him well in the confidence stakes. So had the personal trainer he hired to encourage him to walk and run regularly around Canberra's Lake Burley Griffin to shed extra kilos and boost his physical fitness.

Labor's highly contested suggestion that the Government was planning to sell off the public health-care provider, Medicare, resonated with voters in the home stretch, despite howls of protest that it was mischievous and based on nothing at all. Furious members of the coalition dubbed it 'Mediscare' and called it a blatant lie. Some journalists supported that view. But it worked for Labor when it counted.

From outside the Labor caucus, the success of the Labor campaign made it particularly curious that speculation emerged before the count had even concluded about Anthony preparing to put his hand up for the leadership.

Privately, when colleagues had pressed him before the election, Anthony had not ruled out running afterwards, indicating it would depend on how things turned out. That guaranteed speculation emerged immediately election day had passed.

Certainly, the new Kevin-Rudd-initiated rule that the leadership was declared open after an election meant it was one of the now-few opportunities for a contender to put himself or herself forward.

The Albanese v Shorten rumour received widespread coverage, fuelled by those who preferred Anthony to Bill, regardless of the result. But those who entertained the prospect of an Albanese challenge failed to ask themselves one important question: how would he justify seeking to challenge for the leadership when the incumbent had almost snatched victory after a single term in Opposition and was being hailed by many as a Labor hero?

'I wasn't running,' Anthony says in 2017. 'I knew that from the result.'

Before the caucus had even met to begin the process of re-endorsing him, Bill Shorten hit the road on a jubilant tour, the closest thing to a victory lap that a losing side could stage. Putting him in contact with party members around the country, it looked like a pre-emptive strike against any possible challenge.

Much as the leadership remains unfinished business for a bloke who does not like to lose – and much as the pair of them are not exactly friends – Anthony was not going to try to unseat a successful leader straight after his near-victory.

On the Monday night after the 2 July election, before Labor's parliamentary caucus was scheduled to meet to open the process to determine its leadership going forward, Anthony appeared on ABC TV's *7.30* to rule himself out. At the time, he argued that, with some seats still too close to call, neither side had yet formed a government.

'This is like a footy game that's gone into extra time,' he said. 'Now you don't even consider changing who the captain is in extra time.'

He insisted the Labor Party was 'very united' and that he wanted to use his own 'great deal of experience' to help Bill and others with parliamentary tactics and strategy. He had not put himself on Labor's tactics committee and Bill had not sought to include him until late in the previous parliamentary term.

'I've always been a team player,' Anthony told Leigh Sales. 'I've always put the party first, before my own interests, and I certainly will be continuing to do that, as I always have.'

Some colleagues continue to question where the party's interests end and his own begin.

In his weekly Friday-morning appearance on the Nine Network's *Today* show the next morning, Anthony confirmed Bill would be re-elected unopposed at the meeting later that day. 'There will only be one candidate,' he said. 'That candidate will be Bill Shorten.'

To reinforce his point, when the Labor caucus met to begin a week-long process of formally selecting its leader, it was Anthony who moved the motion of congratulations to – and confidence in – Bill and the leadership team. The move headed off a rumoured plan to seek to adjust the rules again, to have Bill endorsed on the spot, without the required week-long waiting period for other nominations.

There was a reason Bill Shorten was concerned about a last-minute contest. The numbers in the caucus had not only increased, the factional breakdown had changed too.

After the 2013 election, there had been 47 in the Right, 36 in the Left and three non-aligned. With Kevin Rudd not recontesting the post-election leadership, Bill won the ballot against Anthony, 55 votes to 31.

The nine members of the Left who voted for Bill and against Anthony were a mixture of the so-called Ferguson Left and members of the Victorian Socialist Left who were aligned with Senator Kim Carr, Anthony's other nemesis.

After the 2016 election, only three of the four members of the Ferguson group remained and none of them were Fergusons – Victoria's Brendan O'Connor, Warren Snowdon from the Northern Territory and Julie Owens from NSW. Two others – Martin Ferguson's older brother, Laurie, and ACT former senator Kate Lundy – had retired from politics.

Kate had been among the nine who had voted against Anthony, despite assuring him initially she was voting for him. After that, rank-and-file left-wing Labor members in the ACT let her know they were unimpressed with her decision to vote against their candidate.

Her faction also overlooked her for a shadow ministerial position after the 2013 election. It was clear she was not going to progress further. In late 2014 after 18 years in Parliament, Kate had announced her intention to retire at the 2016 election. She left the Senate early, in March 2015, making way for former ACT Chief Minister Katy Gallagher – a member of Anthony's part of the Left. The voters returned Katy to the Senate in 2016 along with her Lower House ACT colleagues Gai Brodtmann, from the Right, and Andrew Leigh, who was non-aligned.

After the 2016 election, Andrew was the only non-aligned member of caucus. The Right's numbers had increased by three to 50 and the Left's by seven to 44. Factional proportions dictate the shape of Labor's front bench, with positions allocated according to numbers. Because of its increase, the Left was entitled to an extra frontbench position.

When he was Labor leader, Kevin Rudd had claimed the right to bypass the factions and name his own frontbench. But after he left, they took it back, drafting their own list of nominees to present to the leader, who only determined portfolios, not who was in the line-up.

When the Left met to decide its frontbench candidates, there were a range of considerations, including seniority and geographical representation. In Tasmania, the Labor Party had swept almost all before it among the Lower House seats, ousting the three sitting Liberal MPs. Their Labor replacements were all from the Left and the collective success earned them a frontbench spot between them. They nominated longstanding Senator Carol Brown to fill it.

The rest of the Left's list was to be compiled by old-fashioned popular support. With the accomplished Linda Burney now among them, there were hard decisions to be made. When they were, former frontbencher Kim Carr was out and Linda in. A subsequent newspaper report suggesting it was because she was indigenous enraged many of her factional colleagues.

Kim and Anthony are not friends. With Anthony commanding a significantly larger bloc of Left support than his rival, the faction voted to promote Linda and let Kim know that, as far as they were concerned, his ministerial days were done.

'The group wanted renewal,' Anthony says in 2017. 'He didn't have the support of the group.'

But Kim is a Bill backer, one of those in the Left who had voted for him over Anthony – choosing Right over Left – in the 2013 leadership ballot. Not willing to go without a fight, Kim split formally from the Left to form his own sub-faction and took his three supporters with him. Fellow Victorians Gavin Marshall, Maria Vamvakinou and Lisa Chesters then elected him as *their* nominee for the front bench.

Kim and his group were important future numerical insurance for Bill in caucus. He created an extra spot to facilitate Kim's inclusion. The move came at a cost. In the monetary sense, it was borne by others.

Parliamentary rules stipulate that only 30 people may collect a frontbencher's salary. Not wishing to sack anyone, Bill expanded his frontbench to 32 – except two of them were to be paid as backbenchers.

Influential NSW Labor Senator Sam Dastyari was elevated to the shadow ministry with the implied promise of future promotion, but remained on a backbencher's salary. Non-factionally-aligned Andrew Leigh, an accomplished former economics professor at the Australian National University, kept his place on the front bench.

But without anyone to fight for him, he had his salary downgraded to a backbencher's pay, a cut of $40,000 a year.

Despite the security of his position, Bill Shorten continued to look over his shoulder. In the otherwise celebratory post-election atmosphere – which was about as euphoric as losing could get – one other move would cost him the respect of some of his colleagues and, in some cases, their outright support.

Just three months after the election, he lost the most important member of his Praetorian Guard, with the sudden retirement of fellow Victorian right-wing powerbroker Stephen Conroy from the Senate.

On the night of Thursday 15 September, as the Senate prepared to adjourn for a month, Stephen stood up in the chamber and asked to incorporate a 20-minute speech in Hansard instead of delivering it in person. Later, the content was revealed: after 20 years and five months in Parliament, Stephen was retiring from politics without warning the leadership. His decision stunned his colleagues.

Anthony was a member of Labor's national executive which was meeting the following day. He had scheduled a news conference and when a morning news report appeared, suggesting Stephen Conroy had flagged his political departure, Anthony rang him.

'Mate,' he said. 'There's this story you've resigned.'

'I have,' Stephen told him.

But others were caught unawares. With Bill away, Tanya Plibersek was acting leader. The news blindsided her at a press conference and she was unable to confirm it. Stephen should have called her, but hadn't.

Then, with the long-serving senator leaving in a fortnight, there was a scramble to fill his spot. Bill Shorten defied the advice of colleagues – including Stephen – and insisted on the election of a controversial figure in Victorian Labor, his long-time friend and fellow former union official Kimberley Kitching. It put him at odds not only with the retiring senator but with others among his Victorian protectors still in Parliament, including frontbench colleagues Richard Marles, Mark Dreyfus and David Feeney.

Kimberley was a controversial figure. She had tried unsuccessfully, previously, to secure preselection in several Victorian seats. A former general manager of the Health Services Union – the same union that delivered disgraced former officials Craig Thomson, also a former MP, and Kathy Jackson – she had been called to give evidence before the trade union royal commission amid allegations of improper behaviour.

In its interim report, the royal commission had found Kimberley had taken right-of-entry permit tests on behalf of other people. It said prosecution should be considered. 'Ms Kitching's conduct in sitting the relevant right-of-entry tests may have involved the aiding and abetting of offences. The Fair Work Commission had found subsequently that Kimberley's evidence before it was also not either 'truthful or reliable'.

In Victorian Labor and further afield, there was concern that Kimberley would be an easy target and make Labor one too. The coalition had already demonstrated how much mud it was willing to throw in its attacks on then Prime Minister Julia Gillard over the questionable historical activities of her one-time boyfriend, union leader Bruce Wilson. In response to Labor goading him over his wealth, Malcolm Turnbull would respond with attacks on Bill Shorten over his past links to both the unions and big business.

Bill's colleagues warned him if he forced a reluctant Labor Party to choose Kimberley, she would be unavoidably his: a useful extra vote for him inside the caucus, for sure, but a potential political albatross everywhere else.

She was preselected and took her seat in the Senate. It was viewed as a captain's pick that would come at a price and entrenched some existing concerns about values, judgement and non-consultation.

In the Senate, the Government passed a motion, backed by the Greens, designed to cause maximum embarrassment to both Kimberley and Bill. The Government taunted Labor over the choice.

'One of the reasons Mr Shorten is supporting her for the Senate is because she would be a vote for him in the party room,' Cabinet Secretary Arthur Sinodinos said in October 2016. 'Mr Shorten knows that the longer the Coalition stays in power, the more tenuous his position is and that is another indication that he wants [an extra] vote in the party room to buttress him against the claims of [potential leadership rival] Mr Albanese.'

A year after the election, Anthony maintained a public disinterest in challenging for the leadership – a take-it-or-leave-it attitude, which neither persuaded nor appeased his rivals.

Although they maintain a functional working relationship, he and Bill Shorten weren't friends. Bill remained suspicious of his former rival, who continued to be one of Labor's most popular figures. Anthony was civil if not always silent.

The relationship was not improved when Bill appeared in a Labor Party advertisement promising a Labor government would 'employ Australians first' and featuring a group of workers without a non-white face among them. The ad, produced to be screened in Queensland ahead of the state election but not cleared more widely in the party, attracted immediate criticism from some quarters of the Labor Party. They thought it deliberately dog-whistled at xenophobia.

Anthony was disgusted. Living up to his plain-speaking reputation, he said so. 'I think the ad's a shocker,' he told reporters in May 2017. 'It should never have been produced and it should never be shown.'

Shadow Treasurer Chris Bowen called it 'inappropriate'.

Asked about the advertisement, Bill Shorten had initially defended the party's policy and said he thought diversity should be encouraged, that the ad should have 'more diversity in it', and he would speak to the Labor Party about it. Later, he toughened his language.

'Some people have pointed out the lack of diversity in the ALP's video about local jobs,' he followed up in a tweet. 'Fair cop. A bad oversight that won't happen again.'

But as is standard procedure for a political ad featuring a party leader, Bill's office saw the ad before it screened. Again, it raised murmurings about values and judgement.

The government's Minister for Social Services and Multicultural Affairs, Zed Seselja, was quick to capitalise on both the ad and Anthony's response. Talking to Sky News, Zed suggested it was 'harking back to the ALP's White Australia policy of many decades ago'. 'I was surprised at how hard [Anthony] went publicly in expressing those sentiments towards the ad,' Zed said. 'I expected that he might have had a quiet word to Bill Shorten and said, "Get it off the air."' But he's decided to give him a public whack. I think Anthony Albanese is suggesting that there should be some standards, there should be some places that you wouldn't stoop in order to get some cheap votes. And I think he's right.'

In mid-2017, a commonly held view in Labor was that should the leadership be in contention again before the next election, Anthony was unlikely to be the only aspirant. Tanya Plibersek and Chris Bowen would also likely contemplate a tilt.

Senior Labor figures said that without significant unforeseen developments in federal politics – like a coalition upturn or change of leadership, some dramatic downturn in Labor fortunes or Bill Shorten being hit by the proverbial bus – Anthony was unlikely to make another run.

That was the reluctant view of NSW Labor Right powerbroker and former factional opponent, Graham Richardson. 'He's not a wrecker,' Graham said of Anthony in 2017. 'I have a high regard for him. I think he's put the baton very firmly in the knapsack.'

Graham predicted Labor would win the next election with Bill Shorten as leader. He credited Bill with 'doing pretty well' and reiterated that, in the end, it's all about the numbers. 'As long as Labor's got 50 per cent of the two-party preferred vote, no-one's going to have a go at him. The likelihood therefore is that Anthony won't make it, which I think is a shame.'

Asked around the same time if he would ever challenge for the leadership, Anthony would say neither yes nor no. 'I think politics remains a noble profession where you can make a difference to individuals' lives and where you can make a difference to the nation's future,' he said. 'I am happy with the job that I have.'

For all those in the Labor Party lamenting that Bill Shorten should not devote quite so much energy to looking over his shoulder, there is one truism worth remembering. As Joseph Heller famously wrote in his novel *Catch 22*: 'Just because you're paranoid doesn't mean they aren't after you.'

If the last decade in politics has delivered any lessons to practitioners and observers alike, it is that change can come quickly, often outrunning predictions and defying expectations. On that basis, until any former incumbent or previous aspirant walks out of that parliamentary chamber for the last time, you never say never.